The Power of Images in Paul

# The Power of Images in Paul

*Raymond F. Collins*

A Michael Glazier Book

**LITURGICAL PRESS**

Collegeville, Minnesota

www.litpress.org

A Michael Glazier Book published by Liturgical Press.

Cover design by David Manahan, OSB. Painting by Vignon, Claude the Elder, 1593–1670, Saint Paul, Galleria Sabauda, Turin, Italy. Photo credit: Alinari/Art Resource.

1    2    3    4    5    6    7    8    9

**Library of Congress Cataloging-in-Publication Data**

Collins, Raymond F., 1935–
    The power of images in Paul / Raymond F. Collins.
        p.   cm.
    Includes bibliographical references and index.
    ISBN 978-0-8146-5963-2
    1. Bible. N.T. Epistles of Paul—Criticism, interpretation, etc.   2. Metaphor in the Bible.   I. Title.

BS2655.M47C65  2008
227'.066—dc22

                                            2008005837

# CONTENTS

# Preface

For the past twenty-five years a major part of my life has been devoted to the study of the letters in the New Testament that bear the name of Paul. Those studies have led to the publication of two major commentaries, *First Corinthians* (SP 7; Collegeville, MN: Liturgical Press, 1999) and *1 and 2 Timothy and Titus* (NTL; Louisville, KY: Westminster/John Knox, 2002), and a comprehensive study of Paul's first letter, 1 Thessalonians, the very first item in the Christian bibliography, *The Birth of the New Testament: The Origin and Development of the First Christian Generation* (New York: Crossroad, 1993).

Increasingly I have come to realize that Paul's letters are the product of his inspired religious genius and his biblical background, and that they were formed within the cultural world of Hellenism, whose customs and manner of communication had their influence upon Paul. He had to speak and write persuasively in the language of Hellenists if he was to convince his Greek-speaking audiences of the truth of the gospel that he had been called to proclaim.

The great theorists in the art of effective communication of the Hellenistic world, Aristotle, Cicero, and Quintilian, highlighted the importance of metaphor in ordinary human speech. They drew particular attention, however, to the important role that metaphor plays in compositions that were designed to persuade their audience.

Paul's letters were written in order to persuade his audience of the truth of the gospel in various sets of circumstances and in its many ramifications. An attentive reader of his letters cannot help but be aware that the apostle used figurative speech throughout his letters, sometimes on a grand scale, sometimes with a clever turn of phrase, and sometimes by the use of a single word that paints a bright picture.

My study was born of my desire to clarify for a contemporary readership the verbal pictures that Paul had painted for his audiences of long ago. I shared my vision with Mark Twomey of Liturgical Press who encouraged me to undertake the endeavor. I owe a debt of gratitude to him for his support.

When my work began in earnest five years ago, only one major study on Paul's use of metaphor was in print. That was David J. Williams's *Paul's Metaphors: Their Context and Character* (Peabody, MA: Hendrickson, 1999). With its reference-book format, that was and remains a useful volume. My purpose was, however, somewhat different. I wanted to study how Paul used metaphors in each of his letters in order to clarify the gospel for a particular audience and persuade the various churches to whom he wrote his letters of the truth of his message.

Since I began the project a number of significant monographs have appeared on the topic. I would like to acknowledge them, all the while confessing that their work has not been fully integrated within my own study. For my debt to them, I would like to mention the names of Reider Aasgaard, whose initial research I heard presented at an SBL meeting some few years back, Mary Kate Berge, a former student of mine, Trevor Burke, Stephen Finlan, Jung Hoon Kim, and Sam Tsang. The titles of their respective studies appear in the general bibliography.

I must also express my gratitude to those without whose effort and support this study would not have seen the light of day. Kelly Iverson and Juraj Fenik served as my research assistants in the initial stages of this project. They tracked down bibliographic references and drew my attention to typos, especially in the scriptural references. I would also say a word of thanks to Hans Christoffersen, editorial director of Liturgical Press, who saw the work through to its final publication.

Throughout the time of this research, I have thought ever so often about the title of Martin Buber's important little book, *I and Thou*. The title reminds me that human love is a living metaphor of the love that Christ has for his church and that God has for all his people. This book is a work of human love. May it help those who read it to appreciate more fully the love of God and his Christ.

Raymond F. Collins

# Note on References

Biblical references are given according to the New Revised Standard Version. Where the LXX numbering of some passages in the Old Testament is different and it seems appropriate to call attention to this, the LXX reference is given in brackets [LXX . . .] following the primary reference.

The English translation of the Septuagint is that of Lancelot C. L. Brenton, *The Septuagint with Apocrypha: Greek and English* (London: Bagster, 1851; reprint, Peabody, MA: Hendrickson, 1986). References to Pseudepigrapha of the Old Testament are given according to the collection edited by James H. Charlesworth, *The Old Testament Pseudepigrapha*, 2 vols (Garden City, NY: Doubleday, 1983, 1985). References to Qumran material (though not necessarily the translation) follow the edition of Florentino García Martínez, *The Dead Sea Scrolls Translated* (Leiden: Brill, 1994), except that in the case of the Thanksgiving Psalms (1QH) the more traditional column numbering has been retained.

References to classical authors are given according to the editions and translations published in the Loeb Classical Library (Harvard University Press).

# Abbreviations

Versions of the Bible

| | |
|---|---|
| CEV | Contemporary English Version |
| JB | Jerusalem Bible |
| KJB | King James Bible (Authorized Version) |
| NAB | New American Bible |
| NIV | New International Version |
| NJB | New Jerusalem Bible |
| NJPS | New Jewish Publication Society Translation |
| NRSV | New Revised Standard Version |
| RSV | Revised Standard Version |
| RevNAB | New American Bible, Revised New Testament |
| REB | Revised English Bible |

Qumran Literature

| | |
|---|---|
| 1QH | Thanksgiving Psalms (*Hodayot*) |
| 1QM | War Scroll (*Milhamah*) |
| 1QpHab | Pesher Habakkuk |
| 1QS | Rule of the Community (*Serek Hayahad*) |
| 4QpNah | Pesher Nahum |
| CD | Cairo copy of the *Damascus Document* |

Church Fathers

| | |
|---|---|
| Ign. *Magn.* | Ignatius, *Letter to the Magnesians* |
| Ign. *Pol.* | Ignatius, *Letter to Polycarp* |
| Ign. *Eph.* | Ignatius, *Letter to the Ephesians* |
| Ign. *Rom.* | Ignatius, *Letter to the Romans* |
| Ign. *Trall.* | Ignatius, *Letter to the Trallians* |

Papyri

| | |
|---|---|
| P.Fayum | Fayûm Papyrus |
| P.Grenf | Grenfell Papyrus |
| P.Oxy | Oxyrhynchus Papyri |

Other Important Abbreviations

| | |
|---|---|
| *b.* | Babylonian Talmud |
| *G. Thom.* | *Gospel of Thomas* |
| LXX | Septuagint (The Greek Bible) |
| *m.* | Mishnah |
| *T.* | *Testament* |
| TM | Massoretic Text (The Hebrew Bible) |

Journals, Periodicals, Major Reference Works, and Series

| | |
|---|---|
| AASF | Annales Academiae Scientiarum Fennicae |
| AB | Anchor Bible |
| *ABD* | *Anchor Bible Dictionary* |
| ABRL | Anchor Bible Reference Library |
| AGJU | Arbeiten zur Geschichte des Spätjudentums und Urchristentums |
| ASCS | American School of Classic Studies |
| BAGD | Bauer, W., W. F. Arndt, F. W. Gingrich, and F. W. Danker. *Greek-English Lexicon of the New Testament and Other Early Christian Literature.* 2nd ed. Chicago, 1979 |
| *BBR* | *Bulletin for Biblical Research* |
| BDF | Blass, F., A. Debrunner, and R. W. Funk. *A Greek Grammar of the New Testament and Other Early Christian Literature.* Chicago, 1961 |
| BETL | Bibliotheca ephemeridum theologicarum lovaniensium |
| *Bib* | *Biblica* |
| *BJRL* | *Bulletin of the John Rylands University Library of Manchester* |
| BNTC | Black's New Testament Commentaries |
| BTN | Bibliotheca theologica norvegica |
| CBET | Contributions to Biblical Exegesis and Theology |
| *CBQ* | *Catholic Biblical Quarterly* |
| CC | Continental Commentaries |
| CNT | Commentaire du Nouveau Testament |
| ConBNT | Coniectanea biblica: New Testament Series |
| *CurTM* | *Currents in Theology and Mission* |

| | |
|---|---|
| *DBI* | Ryken, L., et al. *Dictionary of Biblical Imagery: An Encyclopedic Exploration of the Images, Symbols, Motifs, Metaphors, Figures of Speech and Literary Patterns of the Bible.* Downers Grove, IL, 1998 |
| *EBib* | *Etudes bibliques* |
| *EDNT* | *Exegetical Dictionary of the New Testament* |
| EKKNT | Evangelisch-katholischer Kommentar zum Neuen Testament |
| *EncJud* | *Encyclopedia Judaica* |
| *ER* | *Encyclopedia of Religion* |
| ESEC | Emory Studies in Early Christianity |
| *EstBib* | *Estudios bíblicos* |
| *ETL* | *Ephemerides theologicarum lovaniensium* |
| *ExpTim* | *Expository Times* |
| FRLANT | Forschungen zur Religion und Literatur des Alten und Neuen Testaments |
| GNS | Good News Studies |
| *GNT*[4] | *Greek New Testament*, 4th. rev. ed., Stuttgart, 2001 |
| HTKNT | Herders theologischer Kommentar zum Neuen Testament |
| *HTR* | *Harvard Theological Review* |
| IBC | Interpretation: A Bible Commentary for Teaching and Preaching |
| ICC | International Critical Commentary |
| *IDB* | *The Interpreter's Dictionary of the Bible.* Edited by G. A. Buttrick. 4 vols. Nashville, 1962 |
| *IEJ* | *Israel Exploration Journal* |
| *IG* | *Inscriptiones graecae.* Editio minor. Berlin, 1924– |
| *Int* | *Interpretation* |
| *JBC* | *Jerome Biblical Commentary.* Edited by R. E. Brown et al. Englewood Cliffs, 1968 |
| *JBL* | *Journal of Biblical Literature* |
| *JPT* | *Journal of Pentecostal Theology* |
| *JSNT* | *Journal for the Study of the New Testament* |
| JSNTSup | Journal for the Study of the New Testament: Supplement Series |
| JSOT | Journal for the Study of the Old Testament |
| *JTS* | *Journal of Theological Studies* |
| KEK | Kritisch-exegetischer Kommentar über das Neue Testament (Meyer-Kommentar) |

| | |
|---|---|
| *Laur* | *Laurentianum* |
| LCL | Loeb Classical Library |
| *LS* | *Louvain Studies* |
| LSJ | Liddell, H. G., R. Scott, H. S. Jones, *A Greek-English Lexicon.* 9th ed. with revised supplement. Oxford, 1996 |
| LTPM | Louvain Theological and Pastoral Monographs |
| LUÅ | Lunds universitets årsskrift |
| MM | Moulton, J. H. and G. Milligan. *The Vocabulary of the Greek Testament.* London, 1930. Reprint, Peabody, MA, 1997 |
| MTS | Marburger theologische Studien |
| N-A²⁷ | Nestle, E., *Novum Testamentum Graece.* 27th. rev. ed. by B. Aland et al. Suttgart, 1993 |
| NClB | New Clarendon Bible |
| *Neot* | *Neotestamentica* |
| NIGTC | New International Greek Testament Commentary |
| *NJBC* | *The New Jerome Biblical Commentary.* Edited by R. E. Brown et al. Englewood Cliffs, 1990 |
| *NovT* | *Novum Testamentum* |
| NTAbh | Neutestamentliche Abhandlungen |
| NTD | Das Neue Testament Deutsch |
| *NTL* | *New Testament Library* |
| NTS | New Testament Studies |
| *OCD* | *Oxford Classical Dictionary.* Edited by S. Hornblower and A. Spawforth. 3rd ed. Oxford, 1996 |
| OTL | Old Testament Library |
| PG | Patrologia graeca. Edited by J.-P. Migne. 162 vols. Paris, 1857–1886 |
| *PiNTC* | *Pillar New Testament Commentary* |
| *RB* | *Revue biblique* |
| *RevExp* | *Review and Expositor* |
| *RivB* | *Rivista biblica italiana* |
| *RSPT* | *Revue des sciences philosophiques et théologiques* |
| SBL | Society of Biblical Literature |
| SBLAB | Society of Biblical Literature Academia Biblica |
| SBLDS | Society of Biblical Literature Dissertation Series |
| SBLit | Studies in Biblical Literature |
| SBLSBS | Society of Biblical Literature Sources for Biblical Study |
| SBS | Stuttgarter Bibelstudien |
| SBT | Studies in Biblical Theology |
| *SESJ* | *Suomen Eksegeettisen Seuran Julkaisuja* |

| SIG | *Sylloge inscriptionum graecarum*. Edited by W. Dittenberger. 4 vols. 3d ed. Leipzig, 1915–1924 |
| SMBen | Série monographique de Benedictina: Section paulinienne |
| SNT | Studien zum Neuen Testament |
| SNTSMS | Society for New Testament Studies Monograph Series |
| SP | Sacra Pagina |
| *STDJ* | *Studies on the Texts of the Desert of Judah* |
| Str-B | Strack, H. L., and P. Billerbeck. *Kommentar zum Neuen Testament aus Talmund und Midrasch*. 6 vols. Munich, 1922–1961 |
| TBINTC | Trinity Press International New Testament Commentary |
| *TDNT* | *Theological Dictionary of the New Testament* |
| THKNT | Theologische Handkommentar zum Neuen Testament |
| *TLNT* | *Theological Lexicon of the New Testament* |
| *TTZ* | *Trier theologische Zeitschrift* |
| *TynBul* | *Tyndale Bulletin* |
| *TZ* | *Theologische Zeitschrift* |
| WBC | Word Biblical Commentary |
| *WDNT* | Aune, D. E. *The Westminster Dictionary of New Testament and Early Christian Literature and Rhetoric*. Louisville, 2003 |
| *WTJ* | *Westminster Theological Journal* |
| *ZNW* | *Zeitschrift für die neutestamentliche Wissenschaft und die Kunde der älteren Kirche* |

# 1

## The Role of Metaphor in Hellenistic Rhetoric

Toward the end of the first century CE, an anonymous author wrote:

> Paul, a servant of God and an apostle of Jesus Christ, for the sake of the faith of God's elect and the knowledge of the truth that is in accordance with godliness, in the hope of eternal life that God, who never lies, promised before the ages began—in due time he revealed his word through the proclamation with which I have been entrusted by the command of God our Savior. (Titus 1:1-3)

This comprehensive portrait sets the apostle Paul squarely between "before the ages began" and life eternal. A fuller expansion of time is beyond the abilities of the human mind to conceive.

The author of Titus uses language that reflects both Paul's religious heritage and his Hellenistic world. Readers of the Hebrew Bible in its Greek translation, the Septuagint, surely recognize the rich resonances of expressions, such as "servant of God," "God's elect," "he revealed his word," and "the proclamation." Hellenists would recognize other expressions in the author's description of Paul, expressions such as "knowledge of the truth," "godliness," "who never lies,"[1] and "our Savior." Thus,

---

[1] In his Greek, the author used the abstract adjective *apseusdēs*, literally, "without falsehood." The use of such abstracts is characteristic of Hellenistic philosophy and

Paul stood not only at the intersection of time but at the intersection of cultures as well: Semitic culture with its Hebrew Bible and a Hellenistic culture with its philosophical traditions.

Paul's time was the time of salvation history. Rooted in a vision of God who had created all things, salvation history began with the promise to Abraham and reached its fulfillment in his offspring, the Christ (Gal 3:16). Raised from the dead and constituted Lord (Rom 1:5), Jesus the Christ instituted the eschatological era which culminates in the parousia when the Lord Jesus hands all things over to the Father who created them (1 Cor 15:24). Those who believe in Jesus Christ the Lord look backward to the fulfillment of the promise made to Abraham; they look forward to the parousia when the reign of the Lord will be complete. Despite himself, Paul was caught up in that moment of temporal transition from expectation to anticipation (Gal 1:13-17). He was the reluctant prophet who was to announce the coming of the Lord Jesus Christ.

Deeply immersed in the faith of his Semitic forebears, he was, in his own words, "zealous for the traditions of [his] ancestors" (Gal 1:14). He spoke the Hebrew language (Acts 22:2) and studied the Hebrew Bible (Acts 22:3). Regularly he returned to his people's holy city, Jerusalem (Rom 15:25; 1 Cor 16:3-4; Gal 1:18; 2:1), in whose temple he worshiped (Acts 22:17). He was "a member of the people of Israel, of the tribe of Benjamin, a Hebrew born of Hebrews; as to the law, a Pharisee" (Phil 3:5). Yet, Paul lived in the Hellenistic world of the Greco-Roman Empire. He was born in the city of Tarsus, in Cilicia, a region in the Roman province of Asia. He was a Roman citizen who had his brushes with imperial authorities. He was familiar with the athletic contests of the Greeks (1 Cor 9:24-25) and the spectacles of their amphitheaters (1 Cor 15:32; 2 Cor 12:14). And, before he was born, he was chosen by God to preach the gospel to the Gentiles (Gal 1:15-16; 2:2). Hence, the need for Paul to employ language that would convince his Greek-speaking audiences.

## Aristotle

Faithful to the Law as he was, it is not likely that Paul attended a rhetorical school or studied the works of Aristotle. As a man of Hellenistic culture, he learned both the art of public speaking and the art of letter

---

contrasts sharply with the dynamic and concrete descriptions of God's fidelity, his truth, found in the Hebrew Bible.

writing through cultural immersion. His writings are evidence of the rhetorical traditions of the Hellenistic world in which he lived.

One of the oldest surviving manuals of Hellenistic tradition is Aristotle's *Art of Rhetoric*.[2] Aristotle taught that metaphor, the application of a word that belongs to another thing,[3] is important in both prose and poetry but is especially important in prose, since the writer of prose has fewer resources than the poet. "We must," says Aristotle, "make use of metaphors and epithets that are appropriate."[4] He notes, however, that the art of metaphor cannot be learned from anyone else.[5] It is, he implies, an innate skill. If so, those who read Paul's letters must consider that Paul was innately endowed, so well did he exercise the art of metaphor.

Metaphor provides perspicuity, pleasure, and a foreign air to what a person writes.[6] The perspicuity (*to saphes*) of which Aristotle speaks is clarity and accuracy in speech. One of the principal functions of metaphor, even in poetry, was to clarify, usually by appeal to familiar experience.[7]

Writing about the pleasurable quality of metaphor (*to hēdu*), Aristotle effectively states that metaphor appeals to the human senses, indeed, the entire range of human emotions. Writing about the appropriate use of metaphor in *Rhetoric* 3.2.13, Aristotle mentions the beauty of metaphor's sound, its sight, or "some other sense" (*ē allē tini aisthēnei*). He elaborates in particular on the use of metaphor as an appeal to the sense of sight,[8] explaining what he means when he says that a metaphor sets something "before the eyes" (*pro ommatōn*).[9]

---

[2] The *Rhetoric to Alexander (Rhetorica ad Alexandrum)*, another early manual often attributed to Aristotle, was written by Anaximenes of Lampsacus (380–320 BCE). Principally devoted to forensic rhetoric, this work does not contain a study of metaphor.

[3] *Poetics* 21 [1457b].

[4] *Rhetoric* 3.2.9 [1405a].

[5] Ibid., 3.2.8 [1405a].

[6] Ibid.

[7] See Michael S. Silk, "Metaphor and Simile," *OCD* 966–68, 967. Silk lists this function as the first of "the main poetic functions of metaphor and simile."

[8] *Rhetoric* 3.11.2–4.

[9] He also uses the expression in *Rhetoric* 3.2.13 [1405b] and 3.10.7 [1141a], "before the eyes" (*pro ommatōn*). Quintilian employs a comparable phrase, *sub oculos* (*Training* 8.6.19). Similarly, the unknown author of *Rhetorica ad Herennium* wrote that metaphor is used "for the sake of creating a mental image" (*rea ante oculos ponendae cause*, literally, "for the sake of putting something before the eyes" (*Rhetorica ad Herennium* 4.34.45).

The immediacy that results from an orator's or poet's use of metaphors that appeal to the human senses is, however, "less a matter of making clear than of making alien ('defamiliarizing,' in modern theoretical terminology) and thereby making listener or reader experience anew."[10]

Finally, Aristotle speaks of a foreign air (*to xenikon*) as one of the qualities of metaphor. In and of itself, "foreignness," in Greek as in English, connotes an alien land and a different culture. In a derived sense the terminology connotes strangeness or novelty, something that is unusual or out of the ordinary. Especially in poetry, the use of metaphor can exploit the associations beyond any limited point or basis of comparison, even to evoke a contrary association.[11]

Aristotle, however, offers a caveat, noting that only appropriate metaphors should be used in prose. According to Aristotle, the skillful use of metaphor imparts a foreignness to one's speech along with clarity of meaning.[12] In this combination of alienness with clarity, says Aristotle, lies the chief merit (*aretē*) of rhetorical language.[13]

Aristotle distinguished four kinds of metaphor. "A metaphor," he wrote, "is the application of a word that belongs to another thing, either from genus to species, species to genus, species to species, or by analogy."[14] Metaphors based on proportion (*kat'analogian*) are those that enjoy the greatest popularity.[15]

It cannot be said that Aristotle established rules on the use of appropriate metaphors, but several of his observations are worth noting. For example, when one uses a metaphor to embellish, one should employ the better species under the same genus. On the other hand, if a metaphor is used to depreciate, then a worse species under the genus should be employed.[16]

Metaphors should not be "far-fetched" (*ou porrōthen*), Aristotle says.[17] He further remarks that one metaphor is better than another because it creates a better likeness and is therefore "better suited to putting the matter before the eyes."[18] Finally, he notes that metaphors should be

[10] Silk, "Metaphor and Simile," 967.
[11] Ibid.
[12] *Rhetoric* 3.2.6 [1404b].
[13] Ibid.
[14] *Poetics* 21 [1457b].
[15] *Rhetoric* 3.10.7 [1410b].
[16] Ibid., 3.2.10 [1405a].
[17] Ibid., 3.2.12 [1404a].
[18] Ibid., 3.2.13 [1405b].

derived "from what is beautiful either in sound, or in signification, or to sight, or to some other sense."[19]

Aristotle's understanding of metaphor is not limited to some narrow or overly precise definition of this important rhetorical tool. To metaphor in the strict sense Aristotle would add the simile, the proverb, and hyperbole. "Similes are always in a manner approved metaphors," he writes.[20] He argues that similes always consist of two terms and that similes "are excellent when there is a proportional metaphor."[21] Continuing his exposition of the fuller understanding of metaphor, Aristotle adds, "Proverbs also are metaphors from species to species," and "[a]pproved hyperboles are also metaphors."[22]

## Cicero

Marcus Tullius Cicero (106–43 BCE) was probably the greatest orator of his day. He gained his reputation from his success in the courtroom and in the political arena. To a large extent Cicero's observations on rhetoric followed the conventions of Greek rhetoric, which Cicero supplemented with his vast knowledge of culture, literature, and philosophy.

Cicero repeatedly notes that three rules should be followed in one's choice of language:[23] (1) use metaphorical words frequently, but not too often;[24] (2) use new coinages occasionally;[25] and (3) use archaic words but rarely. Cicero considers that metaphor enjoyed a wide breadth of applicability.[26] He once observed that there is nothing in the world whose name cannot be used in connection with other things.[27] Elsewhere, Cicero states that there is no mode of speech more effective in the use of a single word than metaphor.[28] He also notes that poets use metaphors more frequently and with greater boldness than do writers of prose.[29]

---

[19] Ibid.

[20] Ibid., 3.11.11, 13 [1412b–1413a].

[21] Ibid., 3.11.13 [1413a].

[22] Ibid., 3.11.14–15 [1413a].

[23] *De oratore* 3.152, 201; cf. 3.170; *Orator ad Brutum* 201.

[24] "Not too often" was a note that Cicero added in the *Orator* (*Orator ad Brutum* 82).

[25] Cf. Aristotle, *Poetics* 21 [1457b].

[26] *De oratore* 3.155.

[27] Ibid., 3.161.

[28] Ibid., 3.166.

[29] *Orator ad Brutum* 202.

Cicero says that metaphor was born of necessity because of the limitations of language; it became popular because of its agreeable and entertaining quality.[30] When recognized, metaphor gives pleasure.[31] "Everyone," he writes, "derives more pleasure from words used metaphorically . . . than from the proper names belonging to objects."[32] Even when there are more than enough words available to designate an object properly, "metaphorical terms give people much more pleasure."[33]

Cicero offers several reasons why this is so: the ability of metaphor to demonstrate the cleverness of the speaker, to allow the listener to think of something else without losing the train of thought,[34] to capture something within a single gestalt, or to appeal directly to the senses. It is the latter about which he writes most extensively:

> Every metaphor, provided it be a good one, has a direct appeal to the senses, especially the sense of sight, which is the keenest: for while the rest of the senses supply such metaphors as "the fragrance of good manners," "the softness of a humane spirit," "the roar of the waves," "a sweet style of speaking," the metaphors drawn from the sense of sight are much more vivid, virtually placing within the range of our mental vision objects not actually visible to the sight. (*De oratore* 3.160–161)

Speaking about the delectability of the metaphor, Cicero emphasizes much more than Aristotle the impact of metaphor on those to whom it is addressed. As such, the use of metaphor is an important component of what rhetoricians would call the argument from *pathos*. This rhetorical argument is an appeal to the audience. In deliberative rhetoric, the argument from *pathos* often takes the form of an appeal to the advantage that would accrue to the hearer(s) if they followed the orator's advice or, conversely, to their disadvantage if they did not heed the orator's plea. The use of metaphor is a more subtle form of the argument from *pathos*. It appeals not to the intellect with its ability to calculate advantage and

---

[30] Cicero writes of its *delectatio iucunditasque* (*De oratore* 3.155), its ability to give pleasure and to entertain, and again, of its *frequentata delectationis* (ibid.), its frequent use for the sake of giving pleasure.

[31] "*Si agnoscitur, delectat*," *De oratore* 3.157. See also *Orator ad Brutum* 92.

[32] *De oratore* 3.159. "Words used metaphorically" translates Cicero's *translatis verbis*; metaphors are *translata verba*. Writing about Aristotle's classification of "metaphor," Cicero uses the word *tralatio* (*Orator ad Brutum* 94).

[33] Ibid.

[34] This, says Cicero, "is a very great pleasure" (*De oratore* 3.160).

disadvantage for the future but rather to the sensate person, endowed with emotion and with sight, hearing, touch, taste, and smell.

Although Cicero stresses metaphor's ability to appeal to the senses and give pleasure, he is just as emphatic in teaching that only those metaphors should be used that either make the meaning clearer or convey better the whole meaning of the matter, adding that metaphors are occasionally used for the sake of brevity.[35] He later observes that when something does not have a proper name, a metaphor is used "in order to make the meaning clear"[36] and notes that in the use of metaphor care must be taken to avoid obscurity.[37]

Cicero lays down several rules for a good and appropriate use of metaphor but, like Aristotle, he does not use the term "rule" to describe the several bits of advice that he offers in this regard. In instances where there is no real semblance, metaphors are to be avoided.[38] Second, the resemblance must not be too far-fetched.[39] Third, all unseemliness in the thing to which the use of metaphor leads the hearer's mind is to be avoided[40]—a rule that reiterates the notion that a metaphor should give pleasure. Fourth, metaphors are to be avoided that are on too large a scale,[41] too small a scale, or too narrow in focus, a rule that echoes Aristotle's importance of proportion in the use of metaphor. Finally, if metaphors appear too harsh they should be softened by an introductory word or qualifying phrase.[42]

As the Greek-speaking Aristotle before him and Quintilian after him, Cicero is aware of the similarity between simile and metaphor. "Metaphor," Cicero writes, "is a short form of simile, contracted into one word."[43] Quintilian says much the same: "On the whole metaphor is a

---

[35] *De oratore* 3.157–158.

[36] *Orator ad Brutum* 82; cf. Aristotle, *Rhetoric* 3.2.12 [1405a]; Quintilian, *Training* 8.6.5.

[37] *De oratore* 3.167.

[38] Ibid., 3.162. In similar fashion, the author of *Rhetorica ad Herennium* wrote: "They say that a metaphor ought to be restrained, so as to be a transition with good reason to a kindred thing" (*Rhet. Her.* 4.34.45).

[39] *De oratore* 3.163; cf. *Orator ad Brutum* 83; Aristotle, *Rhetoric* 3.2.12 [1405a]; Quintilian, *Training* 8.6.17.

[40] *De oratore* 3.163–64.

[41] Similarly, Aristotle (*Rhetoric* 3.2.10 [1405a]) writes that metaphors that exceed the dignity of the subject are inappropriate.

[42] *De oratore* 3.165.

[43] Ibid., 3.157.

shorter form of simile."[44] He notes, however, that there is a further difference insofar as in the case of simile, objects are compared with each other, whereas in the case of metaphor, they are substituted one for the other.[45]

Aristotle takes another tack in describing the relationship between metaphor and simile. For him, the simile is a metaphor;[46] or again, similes are "always in a manner approved metaphors."[47] The difference, he says, is to be found in the fact that a simile is not as simple as the metaphor.[48] According to Aristotle, there is "little difference" between the simile and the metaphor;[49] the difference lies in the fact that a simile is a metaphor without the detail.[50]

Both rhetoricians noted the close relationship between metaphor and simile; the rhetoricians differed from one another not in the way they understood the difference between metaphor and simile but in the point of departure from which they explained the difference.

## Quintilian

Cicero was one of the rhetorical masters of Marcus Fabius Quintilianus (ca. 34–100 CE). Born about eighty years after the death of Cicero, Quintilian composed his magnum opus, the *Institutio oratoria*, "Training in Oratory," more than four centuries after the death of Aristotle. Many of his ideas on metaphor are, nonetheless, similar to those of the rhetorical masters who preceded him. Defining a trope[51] as "the artistic alteration of a word or phrase from its proper meaning to another,"[52] he discusses what he calls "by far the most beautiful of tropes, namely, *metaphora*, the Greek term for our *translatio*."[53]

---

[44] Quintilian, *Training* 8.6.8.

[45] *Training* 8.6.9.

[46] *Rhetoric* 3.3.1 [1406b]; see also, again, similes are "metaphors of a kind" (*Rhetoric* 3.11.13 [1413a].

[47] Ibid., 3.11.11 [1412b].

[48] Ibid., 3.11.11 [1413a].

[49] Ibid., 3.4.1 [1406b].

[50] Ibid., 3.4.3 [1407a].

[51] In Latin a trope is called *tropus* or *modus*. See Quintilian, *Training* 8.5.35.

[52] *Training* 8.6.1.

[53] Ibid., 8.6.4. In his writing, Quintilian sometimes used a transliteration of the Greek *metaphora* (e.g., *Training* 8.6.18); sometimes he used the Latin *translatio* (e.g.,

Like Aristotle, Quintilian teaches that metaphor is "so natural a turn of speech that it is often employed unconsciously or by uneducated persons."[54] Thus everyone, from the best educated to the least educated, uses metaphors in conversation and does so in order to persuade, which is why Paul the Apostle so frequently employs metaphors. He uses ordinary language to persuade his audience about the truth of the gospel that he proclaimed.

Quintilian considers that a well-used and appropriate metaphor cannot possibly be commonplace, mean, or unpleasing.[55] In addition, metaphor "succeeds in accomplishing the supremely difficult task of providing a name for everything."[56] This is similar to Aristotle who writes: "We must give names to things that have none by deriving the metaphor from that which is akin and of the same kind, so that, as soon as it is uttered, it is clearly seen to be akin."[57] Metaphor's ability to name the unnamed makes metaphor particularly helpful for Paul as he writes about the Transcendent God.

Quintilian echoes Aristotle when he describes metaphor as "designed to move the feelings, give special distinction to things, and place them before the eye"[58] (Aristotle's "pleasure"). Similarly, Quintilian says that metaphor is used for the enhancement of meaning (*significandi gratia*,[59] Aristotle's "perspicuity"). Quintilian, nonetheless, speaks about a purely ornamental metaphor,[60] all the while noting that a too frequent use of metaphor only serves to obscure language and weary the audience.[61]

Like Aristotle, Quintilian identifies four categories of metaphor, but they do not entirely correspond to Aristotle's categories. Quintilian's categories substitute a living thing for another: (1) an inanimate thing for another inanimate thing; (2) an inanimate thing for an animate thing; (3) an animate thing for another animate thing; and (4) an animate thing for an inanimate thing. The most vivid metaphor occurs when an inanimate

---

*Training* 8.6.19). One of Quintilian's motivating forces was his desire to show that Latin authors were on a par with the Greeks.

[54] Ibid. Cf. Aristotle, *Rhetoric* 3.2.6 [1404b]; Cicero, *De oratore* 3.155; *Orator ad Brutum* 81.

[55] *Training* 8.6.5; cf. Aristotle, *Rhetoric* 3.2.13 [1405b], in the passage quoted above.

[56] Ibid.

[57] Aristotle, *Rhetoric* 3.2.12 [1405a].

[58] *Training* 8.6.19.

[59] Ibid., 8.6.7.

[60] Ibid.

[61] Ibid., 8.6.14.

thing is given life.[62] Similarly, Aristotle, drawing on Homer, notes that when metaphor is used to speak of inanimate things as if they were animate, such usage provides "actuality" (*energeia*) to one's speech.[63]

Aristotle wrote at length about the appropriate use of metaphor, Quintilian less so, but he stresses many of the same points as did the Greek philosopher when he wrote about the temperate and timely use of metaphor. Referencing Cicero, Quintilian observes: "He [Cicero] also points out that a metaphor must not be too great for its subject or, as is more frequently the case, too little, and that it must not be inappropriate."[64] Quintilian urges that metaphors not fail from meanness or coarseness.[65] Likewise, following Cicero,[66] Quintilian teaches that it is important to avoid grossness[67] and that it is excessive to use metaphors that are harsh or far-fetched.[68] For Quintilian, however, the greatest misuse of metaphor is attempting to use in prose metaphors that are appropriate only in poetry, a topic to which he devotes considerable attention in *Training* 8.6.17–20.

Paul did not read the writings of Quintilian, whose magnum opus was composed after Paul wrote his letters to the churches. Neither had he read Aristotle or Cicero. He was, nonetheless, a citizen of the Hellenistic world whose rhetorical contours were limned by that trio of rhetoricians. They wrote about metaphor as a technique to be employed by an orator or writer who wanted to persuade. Paul spoke and wrote in order to convince his audience of the truth of the gospel. Metaphor was one of the techniques that he employed.

---

[62] This is what Aristotle called "the appearance of actuality," giving several examples from Homer. See *Rhetoric* 3.11.2–3 [1411b–12a].

[63] Ibid., 3.11.3 [1411b].

[64] *Training* 8.6.16.

[65] Quintilian (*Training* 8.6.14) uses the adjectives *humiles* and *sordidae* to speak of such inappropriate metaphors.

[66] *De oratore* 3.164–65. Quintilian cites many of the same examples given by Cicero.

[67] Quintilian's adjective is *deformis* (*Training* 8.6.15).

[68] *Training* 8.6.17. Cf. Aristotle, *Rhetoric* 3.2.12 [1004a].

# 2

# The First Letter to the Thessalonians

The First Letter to the Thessalonians is the oldest of the extant letters written by Paul. Dictated about the year 50, it has all the characteristics of the friendly letter illustrated by Pseudo-Demetrius in his list of epistolary types.[1] Personal transparency was an important trait of this kind of letter whose raison d'être was *philophronēsis*,[2] the expression of friendship and warm affection.

In 1 Thessalonians Paul truly bares his soul. He writes about his memories (1:2-3), his prayer (1:2; 2:13; 3:9-13; 5:23-24) and his need for prayers (5:25), his suffering (2:2), his integrity (2:3-7, 10), his desire to share himself (2:7-8), his parental love (2:7-8, 11-12), the pain of separation from the Thessalonians (2:17; 3:1, 5), his desire to see them again (2:17-18; 3:5, 6, 10), and what the Thessalonians mean to him (3:7-9). Paul's affection for them is apparent in the way he repeatedly calls them *adelphoi*, siblings.[3]

---

[1] See Abraham J. Malherbe, *Ancient Epistolary Theorists*, SBLSBS 19 (Atlanta: Scholars, 1988), 32–33.

[2] See Heikki Koskenniemi, *Studien zur Idee und Phraseologie des griechische Briefes bis 400 n. Chr.* (Helsinki: Suomalaisen tiedeakatemian toimatuksin, 1956).

[3] See 1:4; 2:1, 9, 14, 17; 3:7; 4:1, 10, 13; 5:1, 4, 12, 14, 25; cf. 3:2; 4:6, 10; 5:26, 27. The Greek *adelphoi* is a masculine plural whose ordinary meaning is "brothers." Centuries before Paul orators used the vocative form as a formula of direct address when speaking to public assemblies. Hence, the translation "brothers and sisters" appears to be the appropriate translation in a letter addressed to a community of men and women.

## Siblings

First Thessalonians begins with a long thanksgiving in which Paul reminisces about his recent visit, addressing the Thessalonians as "brothers and sisters" (*adelphoi*, 1 Thess 1:4).[4] None of the Thessalonians were Paul's immediate blood relatives. He hailed from Tarsus in Asia Minor (Acts 21:39; 22:3); they were residents of the capital of the Roman province of Achaia. He was of Hebrew ancestry (2 Cor 11:22; Phil 3:5); they were Gentiles. He knew the living and true God; they had been devoted to idols (1 Thess 1:9).

In such circumstances and in the context of Paul's reminiscence and God's singular love for them, the vocative *adelphoi*, "brothers and sisters," is a powerful metaphor evoking the bonds of affection that Paul and his companions had for the Thessalonians and the ties that linked the members of the community to one another.[5] Togetherness, interdependence, goodwill, affection, friendship, protection, glory, and honor are among the values that come to mind when people talk about family relationships.[6]

Paul commends the Thessalonians for the quality of their sibling love (*philadelphia*), urging them to continue to love one another as they had been doing (1 Thess 4:9-10). Paul's exhortation enables us to appreciate more fully the nature of the "labor of love" (1:3) that he remembers so fondly. The sibling quality of their love enabled it to be expressed in action, even when it was difficult to do so.

The second section of 1 Thessalonians' opening thanksgiving rehearses what the Thessalonians experienced because of his visit to them (2:1, 5, 9, 11). Paul again addresses his audience as "siblings" (*adelphoi*, 2:1, 9). The formula of direct address[7] evokes the depth and breadth of the Thessalonians' relationship with one another. The ties that bound them together were as tight as the bonds of family relationship. The bonds that linked them to one another were such that they made a sexual offense against a member of the community all the more egregious. Encouraging

---

[4] On the "usage, characteristics and function of the term" *adelphoi*, see Trevor J. Burke, *Family Matters: A Socio-historical Study of Fictive Kinship Metaphors in 1 Thessalonians*, JSNTSup 247 (London and New York: T&T Clark, 2003), 165–75.

[5] On the significance of the metaphor, see especially Reidar Aasgaard, *"My Beloved Brothers and Sisters!" Christian Siblingship in Paul*, Early Christianity in Context; JSNTSup 265 (London and New York: T&T Clark, 2004).

[6] Philip A. Harland, "Familial Dimensions of Group Identity: 'Brothers' (*ADELPHOI*) in Associations of the Greek East" *JBL* (2005): 491–513, 513.

[7] Cf. 1:4; 4:9-10.

the community to avoid sexual immorality, he urges them not to wrong or exploit a brother (*adelphon*, 4:6)[8] in this matter. Taking sexual advantage of a brother's wife is tantamount to incest.

Other passages in the letter suggest that Paul also used kinship language to evoke the bonds that linked him and his fellow missionaries to the Thessalonians. In 1 Thessalonians 2:17-19, perhaps the most self-revelatory passage in all his correspondence, Paul speaks from the depth of his heart. For the first time in the letter, he uses the first person singular (2:18).[9] Even more than his companions, he experiences the pain of being separated from the Thessalonians. He pines for them; he longs to see them. Begrudgingly he admits that the separation has been only for a short time (2:17) but the bonds of kinship (*adelphoi*, 2:17) intensify the pain of Paul's suffering as he writes with *pathos* about his desire to visit the Thessalonians.

In the immediately preceding passage, Paul writes: "For you, brothers and sisters . . . suffered the same things from your own compatriots as they [the Judean churches] did from the Jews, who killed the Lord Jesus and the prophets, and drove us out; they displease God and oppose everyone by hindering us from speaking to the Gentiles so that they may be saved" (1 Thess 2:14-16a). Paul speaks to the Thessalonians as an elder brother who, like them, has been miserably ill-treated by his own people. In effect, he is saying to them, "What you are going through is similar to what I had to go through." The Thessalonians are expected to take courage from the example of their elder brother. Such is the rhetorical force of *adelphoi* in this problematic passage.[10]

Paul uses the language of the family to evoke the close relationship that exists among himself, his companions, and the Thessalonians when he describes his reaction to Timothy's return to Athens with good news about the faith and hope of the Thessalonians: "For this reason, brothers and sisters [*adelphoi*], during all our distress and persecution we have been encouraged about you through your faith. . . . How can we thank God enough for you in return for all the joy that we feel before our God

---

[8] On my interpretation of the text, the *adelphon* of 4:6 must be translated "brother" rather than "brother or sister" [NRSV].

[9] An emphatic *ēgo* appears in 2:18. The NRSV captures the intensity of Paul's expression with the translation "certainly I, Paul."

[10] Some authors have called into question the authenticity of all or part of the passage. See Raymond F. Collins, "Apropos the Integrity of 1 Thess," *ETL* 65 (1979): 67–106, esp. pp. 68–76, 95–99; reprinted in *Studies on the First Letter to the Thessalonians*, BETL 66 (Leuven: University Press–Peeters, 1984), 96–135, pp. 97–105, 124–28.

because of you?" (1 Thess 3:7-9). The vocative *adelphoi* speaks volumes. The bonds of family relationships had been strained by Paul's separation from the Thessalonians; now Paul affirms that the assurance of his fictive family's love for him sustains him in the midst of the difficulties that he has been encountering.

As Paul brings his letter to a close, he pronounces a blessing upon the Thessalonians (5:23-24), following the blessing with a request that the Thessalonians pray for him and his companions: "[Brothers and sisters (*adelphoi*)],[11] pray for us" (5:25). Paul's request is predicated upon the relationship that Paul and his companions have with the Thessalonians, their own siblings.

Having asked for the Thessalonians' prayers, Paul asks that his greetings be extended to all: "Greet all the brothers and sisters with a holy kiss" (5:26). This greeting makes all the more sense when it is understood to mean "greet all my kin with a holy kiss." Finally, Paul formally directs the Thessalonians to make sure that his letter is read to all the brothers and sisters (5:27).[12] Paul desires that none of his kin be without the expression of affection, encouragement, and instruction that his letter contains.

Paul's repetitive use of sibling language in the epistolary closing of his missive confirms the personal character of this letter. First Thessalonians is unique among Paul's extant letters in its lack of titles (*intitulationes*) attached to the names of the senders of letters. Paul, Silvanus, and Timothy present themselves simply as having a strong affective relationship with the Thessalonians, one that is appropriately expressed in the language of kinship. Paul's use of the vocative *adelphoi* contributes substantially to the *ēthos* and *pathos* nature of his argument. He builds up his stature in their eyes by asking them to remember that he is their brother; he appeals to their affection by calling upon them as his kin.

This relationship has an important function in the hortatory sections of 1 Thessalonians. Using *adelphoi* as a formula of direct address in each unit of paraenesis, Paul appeals to the Thessalonians as members of his own family. He begins with a pair of verses (4:1-2) that commend and encourage his "brothers and sisters" (4:1).

The introduction leads directly to the first parenetic unit, an exhortation on holiness (4:3-8). In the course of his argument, Paul evokes the respect that the Thessalonians should have for their brothers (4:6). Paul's

---

[11] For stylistic reasons the NRSV renders Paul's *adelphoi* (5:25) as "beloved."

[12] "All of them" is the NRSV's stylistic paraphrase.

second exhortation is on sibling love. Paul again uses *adelphoi* as a formula of direct address, reminding the Thessalonians that the object of their love is their very own brothers and sisters:

> Now concerning love of the brothers and sisters [*philadelphias*], you do not need to have anyone write to you, for you yourselves have been taught by God to love one another; and indeed you do love all the brothers and sisters throughout Macedonia. But we urge you, [brothers and sisters],[13] to do so more and more, to aspire to live quietly, to mind your own affairs, and to work with your hands, as we directed you, so that you may behave properly towards outsiders and be dependent on no one. (1 Thess 4:9-12)

Paul's words indicate that the kinship relationship among the Thessalonian believers also existed at the level of an extended family. They lived in the capital city of the Roman province of Macedonia. Movement to and from the capital to towns in the province was part of daily life. In fact, Paul evangelized the Roman colony at Philippi, a hundred miles away, just prior to his visit to the Thessalonians (Acts 16:12-40; 1 Thess 2:2). Philippian Christians supported Paul's Thessalonian mission (Phil 4:15-16); they are to be counted among those whom the Thessalonians loved. Thessalonian and Philippian believers and other Christians throughout the province constituted a single extended fictive family.

After the exhortations of 4:1-12, Paul turns to the matter that concerned him most, the gap in their faith. This lack was one of the reasons why he had so much wanted to visit them (3:10). The issue was that some of the Thessalonians died before the parousia occurred. Unable to visit in person, Paul wrote a letter to assuage their grief and complement what was lacking in their faith. He spoke about the parousia and the resurrection from the dead (4:13-18), beginning his reflections by appealing to the sibling relationship that he enjoyed with them (4:13). Paul adds to this *ēthos* factor the *logos* argument of their shared belief that Jesus had been raised (4:14), God himself being the agent of Jesus' resurrection.

If the future and resurrection from the dead are in the hands of God, the present is in the hands of human beings. So, having encouraged the Thessalonians to entrust the future to God in the first apocalyptic disclosure (4:13-18), Paul emphasizes the Thessalonians' ethical responsibility in a second apocalyptic period (5:1-11). The two apocalyptic sections

---

[13] To render *adelphoi* the NRSV uses the paraphrase "beloved."

of Paul's letter should be read together. They are, as it were, two sides of the same coin.

As was the case with the first apocalyptic unit, Paul begins the second exhortation with a rhetorical preterition that enhances his *pathos* argument: "Concerning the times and the seasons, brothers and sisters, you do not need to have anything written to you" (5:1). Before concluding the exhortation, Paul again appeals to them as his brothers and sisters: "But you, [brothers and sisters][14] are not in darkness, for that day to surprise you like a thief; for you are all children of light and children of the day" (5:4-5).

Paul's final exhortation (5:12-22) is an olio of individual hortatory remarks. He twice uses his favorite formula of direct address in appealing to the Thessalonians: "But we appeal to you, brothers and sisters, to respect those who labor among you, and have charge of you in the Lord and admonish you" (5:12) and, again, "We urge you, [brothers and sisters (*adelphoi*)],[15] to admonish the idlers" (5:14). This familiar formula continues to appear in the short exhortations that follow Paul's final blessing. Paul asks the Thessalonians to pray for him and to greet one another because they are members of a single family (5:25, 27).

The sibling language that peppers Paul's first letter substantially contributes to it being what it is: an expression of friendship, a kind of fraternal presence, and a message that the older brother wants his siblings to hear and heed. First Thessalonians was not, however, the only form of Paul's extended fraternal presence among them. Before sending the letter, Paul had sent an emissary, Timothy, "our brother [*ton adelphon hēmōn*] and coworker for God [*synergon tou theou*]" (1 Thess 3:2). The second epithet identifies Timothy as Paul's fellow evangelist, the first identifies him as someone with whom Paul has a family relationship. Paul sent to the Thessalonians his own brother, and theirs.

### Other Kinship Language

The use of kinship language in 1 Thessalonians is not restricted to a horizontal relationship among siblings. Paul writes about fathers and mothers, children and orphans, employing these metaphors taken from the familial constellation to speak about the relationship that exists between himself and the Thessalonians.[16] His crossing of kinship lines

---

[14] Again, the NRSV translates Paul's *adelphoi* as "beloved."

[15] Again, the NRSV translates Paul's *adelphoi* as "beloved."

[16] See further, Burke, *Family Matters*, 130–60.

shows that he was not disinclined to mix his metaphors when doing so served his rhetorical purpose.

Paul describes himself as being like a mother and a father to the Thessalonians: "like a nurse tenderly caring for her own children" (2:7) . . . "like a father with his children" (2:11). The phrases are parallel in form and in function. They both begin with the comparative particle "like" (*hōs*), followed by a mention of the image (*trophos, patēr*), a mention of children (*tekna*), and the use of a reflexive pronoun (*heautēs, heautou*). The similes serve to dispel any idea that Paul and his companions might burden the Thessalonians (2:7a, 9b). Far from it! Like a mother they shared not only their message but also their very selves; like a father they worked night and day so as not to be burdensome. Paul and his companions are like parents to the Thessalonians; the Thessalonians like children to them.

Paul expands on his idea of what it means to be a father to the Thessalonians, writing: "As you know, we dealt with each one of you like a father with his children, urging and encouraging you and pleading that you lead a life worthy of God, who calls you into his own kingdom and glory" (2:11-12). Paul's "as you know" appeals directly to their experience of Paul, their father. They know that he fulfilled his parental responsibilities, encouraging them and challenging them as occasion demanded.

Paul's maternal imagery is richly evocative. Like a mother, Paul spent himself on behalf of his children. To speak of a mother's endearment for her children, he uses the term "nurse" (*trophos*), a wet nurse or nursing mother. The term identifies a woman who gives life-sustaining milk from her breasts to children, who may not be her own but in this case they are. The image[17] evokes tender care and life-sustaining closeness.[18] Writing about the maternal care that he provides, Paul speaks about "caring tenderly" (*thalpē*). Used as a metaphor, the verb evokes affection, tender attachment.[19] Literally, it means to heat or keep warm, like a bird who sits on its eggs until they hatch. Only in 1 Thessalonians does Paul use the images of the nursing mother and nature's tender care to speak of his affection for and attachment to those whom he evangelized.

---

[17] The image is found only here in Paul's extant correspondence.

[18] See Beverly Roberts Gaventa, "Apostles as Babes and Nurses in 1 Thessalonians 2:7," in *Faith and History: Essays in Honor of Paul W. Meyer*, eds. John T. Carroll, Charles H. Cosgrove, and E. Elizabeth Johnson, 193–207 (Atlanta: Scholars, 1990).

[19] See *TLNT* 2:184–85.

The picture evoked by this striking imagery becomes complicated as Paul once again mixes his metaphors. He describes himself and his companions as infants (*nēpioi*, 2:7).[20] Most modern translations take an easy way out of a textual problem, translating as "gentle" the Greek term *ēpioi* found in most of the ancient manuscripts. Text critics, however, generally agree that *nēpioi*, the reading that appears in the writings of the fathers of the church[21] and that is properly translated "infants," is the preferable reading.[22] So, in the same passage where he describes himself as father and mother, he now characterizes himself as an infant.

In 1 Thessalonians 2:17-18, Paul again has recourse to kinship language as he poignantly writes about the pain of his separation from the Thessalonians. Again he mixes his metaphors and the family relationships. Having addressed the Thessalonians as siblings, intimating that they are his brothers and sisters (2:17), he writes, "we were made orphans [*aporphanisthentes*] by being separated from you" (2:17). An active form of Paul's verb—from whose root the word "orphan" is derived—means "to bereave." The passive form used by Paul means "to be made an orphan."[23] Paul hailed from Tarsus, not Thessalonica; the Thessalonians were not his parents. In the strict sense he was not an orphan; "being orphaned" is a powerful image of the pain of his loss.

Many modern translations, including the RSV and the NAB,[24] fail to capture the poignancy of Paul's language, but the NRSV is attentive to the etymology of Paul's use of language, translating Paul's verb "we were made orphans."[25] Chrysostom may have best understood the meaning of Paul's language, commenting:

---

[20] Accepting *nēpioi* as the correct reading, Crawford has argued that the word is a vocative, an appeal to the Thessalonians. See Charles Crawford, "The 'Tiny' Problem of 1 Thessalonians 2,7: The Case of the Curious Vocative," *Bib* 54 (1973): 69–72.

[21] See Jean Gribomont, "Facti sumus parvuli: La charge apostolique (1 Thess 2,1-12)," in *Paul de Tarse*, ed. Lorenzo de Lorenzi, SMBen 1, 311–338 (Rome: Benedictina, 1979).

[22] The *nēpioi* reading appears in NA²⁷, *GNT*⁴. See the discussion in Bruce Metzger, *A Textual Commentary on the Greek New Testament*, 2nd ed. (Stuttgart: Deutsche Bibelgesellschaft, 1994), 561–62. Critics who opt for *nēpioi* as the preferable reading consider that *ēpioi*, "gentle," represents a scribal accommodation to the text.

[23] See Aeschylus, *Libation-Bearers*, 249.

[24] These versions translate the participle as "we were bereft of you."

[25] The NRSV adds as an explanatory comment "by being separated," words not found in the Greek text.

He has not said "separated" but what was much more . . . Because he
has said above, "as a father his children," "as a nurse," here he uses
another expression, "being made orphans," which is said of children
who have lost their fathers. . . . For if any one should examine our
longing, even as little children without a protector, having sustained
an untimely bereavement, long for their parents, not only from the
feelings of nature itself, but also on account of their deserted state, so
truly do we feel. ("Homilies on Thessalonians," ch. 2, homily 3)[26]

Chrysostom grasped the pathos of Paul's metaphor in a way that few
moderns do.[27] To capture the intensity of his feelings of having been
separated from the Thessalonians because of a superhuman force—note
the reference to Satan in verse 18—Paul evoked the experience of children
who have lost their parents in death. A more powerful image of loneliness and separation is difficult to imagine.

Paul's use of kinship language was undoubtedly facilitated by the fact
that the church to which he was writing was a group of people that
gathered in someone's home, where kinship language properly belongs.
Kinship language allows him to speak of the bonds that unite the members of the small community of believers and provides him with a way
of speaking about the relationship between himself and those whom he
had recently evangelized. He uses this language to encourage the Thessalonians to pursue a directed course of action and complement their
faith with an element of hope. Mixing metaphors, Paul employs the
images of mother and father to speak of the loving care and paternal
responsibility that he and his companions had for the Thessalonians,
children to their fictive parents. On the other hand, the parents were as
orphans when they confronted their own loneliness and the pain of
separation. At times they were no more than mere infants.

## A Crown of Boasting

Shifting the field of his images, Paul writes excitedly about the expectation of the Lord's parousia, "What is our hope or joy or crown of boasting [*stephanos kauchēseōs*] before our Lord Jesus at his coming [*parousia*]?"
(2:19). A "crown" is anything that encircles, specifically something that

---

[26] PG 62.407.
[27] An exception would be Reidar Aasgaard, "Paul as Child: Children and Childhood in the Letters of the Apostle," *JBL* 126 (2007): 129–59, 142–43.

encircles the human head. Typically a crown was awarded to victorious athletes or was worn as a badge of office by the emperor or one of his subordinates. Hellenists used the image of the crown as a metaphor. They spoke about a crown of honor and glory[28] and the crown of freedom.[29] Devotees of the mystery religions had a particular use for a crown. During the initiation rites a mystagogue, experiencing the nearness of a god while participating in the rites, placed a wreath upon his own head in anticipation of death.[30]

What was Paul's crown of boasting, something of which he could be proud, something about which he could boast? Hope, joy, and a crown of victory[31] evoke the parousia, the coming of the Lord. In the presence of the Lord, the source of Paul's joy and the realization of his hope, the "trophy" in which he will take pride, is none other than the Thessalonian community itself. They are his crown of boasting, the crown in which he can take pride.

## Walking through Life

Having rehearsed various aspects of his relationship with the Thessalonians in the first part of his letter, Paul changes his epistolary style with an apostrophic "finally, brothers and sisters" in 4:1. Offering advice and providing information, Paul begins by writing about sanctification and sibling love. He addresses these themes as he writes about walking through life in 1 Thessalonians 4:1-12.

The verb "walk" (*peripateō*) creates a ring construction that identifies and isolates the hortatory unit, setting it apart from the preceding and following parts of his letter. The fact that the NRSV has translated the verb *peripateō* as "live" (4:1), "do" (4:1), and "behave" (4:12) but not as "walk" is proof positive that Paul's use of the verb is metaphorical. In ancient literature the verb rarely has any meaning other than its usual sense, "walk." Aristotle's disciples were known as the peripatetic school of philosophy because he walked with his disciples as he taught them.

One exception to the normal use of the verb is found in the writings of Philodemus, a first century BCE philosopher and poet. In his essay "On Speaking Frankly," Philodemus used the verb with the metaphorical

---

[28] Thus, Sophocles, the fifth-century BCE tragedian (*Ajax* 465).

[29] Thus, the fifth-century lyricist, Simonides (Simon. 50).

[30] See Heinrich Kraft, "*Stephanos, stephanoō*," *EDNT* 2:273–74, 274.

[31] Cf. 1 Cor 9:25.

sense of "live."[32] Paul employs the verb in a figurative sense, not only in the letter to the Thessalonians but also in each one of his extant letters, save the short note to Philemon.[33] He never uses the verb to speak about movement by foot from one place to another. The way in which Paul uses "walk" in 1 Thessalonians 4:1, 12 shows that the applied meaning of the verb is "behave" or "act" not simply "live" or "exist," as it was used metaphorically by Philodemus. This is also the meaning of Paul's first use of the verb. Recalling how he had acted as a father toward the Thessalonians, Paul writes about his "urging and encouraging you and pleading that you should lead a life [*peripatein*] worthy of God, who calls you into his own kingdom and glory" (2:12).

Because a metaphorical sense of "walk" is rarely attested in Greek literature, the reader must look at Paul's Jewish background to discover the source of his metaphor. The Hebrew Bible frequently uses the verb "walk" (*halak*)[34] in a metaphorical sense. The sage speaks of walking "in the way of righteousness" (Prov 8:20) while the psalmist's praise of the Law speaks of those who walk "in liberty" because they seek the precepts of the Law (Ps 119:45). On the other hand, the psalmist proclaimed as blessed those "who do not follow [*halak*, meaning walk according to] the advice of the wicked" (Ps 1:1) while the prophet spoke of those "who walk in pride" (Dan 4:37). In later generations the body of rules of conduct derived from the Torah eventually came to be known as *halakah*, its several precepts as the *halakoth*.

The kind of "walking" that Paul has in mind is consistent with a faithful response to the reign of God. It is a way of life that is pleasing to God. Paul was successful in urging the Thessalonians to live that way. In 4:1 he introduces his hortatory remarks by reminding the Thessalonians that they had learned to live (*peripatein*) like that and were continuing to do so (*peripateite*). In his later letters Paul describes this kind of behavior as walking in newness of life (Rom 6:4), by the light of day (Rom 13:13), in

---

[32] See Alessandro Olivieri, *Philodemi Peri parrēsias libellus*, Bibliotheca Scriptorum Graecorum et Romanorum Teubneriana (Leipzig: Teubner, 1914), 12. Philodemus's writings were well known and were referenced by several ancient authors, but those works have not yet been published in a single critical edition.

[33] See Rom 6:4; 8:4; 13:13; 14:15; 1 Cor 3:3; 7:17; 2 Cor 4:2; 5:7; 10:2, 3; 12:18; Gal 5:16; Phil 3:17, 18. In Rom 6:4; 8:4; 14:15; and 2 Cor 5:7 the NRSV translates *peripateō* as "walk," but the meaning is clearly metaphorical.

[34] See "Walk, Walking," in *DBI* 922–23; Robert Banks, "Walking as a Metaphor of the Christian Life," in *Perspectives on Language and Text*, eds. Edgar W. Conrad and Edward G. Newing, 303–13 (Winona Lake, IN: Eisenbrauns, 1987).

love (Rom 14:15), by faith (2 Cor 5:7) or by the Spirit (2 Cor 12:18; Gal 5:16). It is leading the life that God has assigned (1 Cor 7:17) or conducting one's life following the example given by Paul (Phil 3:17).

There are other ways of living one's life and Paul was well aware of them. He will contrast the way of life that he is promoting with life according to the flesh (Rom 8:4; 2 Cor 10:2, 3) and with behavior like that of ordinary folks (1 Cor 3:3). The kind of life that believers should shun is described as walking "with cunning" (2 Cor 4:2) or "walking" as enemies of the cross of Christ (Phil 3:18).

### Buying a Dish

Paul introduces his moral exhortation by saying, "we ask and urge you in the Lord Jesus" (4:1). The words have a certain solemnity and even the tone of authority. "Urge" (*parakaloumen*) is an epistolary formula, often used in diplomatic correspondence as a tactful reminder that the person writing the letter is the representative of some higher authority. In ordinary parlance, the "Lord" (*kyriō*) is not only someone who commands respect but also someone whose directives and commands must be heeded. Notwithstanding the formality of his language, Paul's approach to moral exhortation is paternal and pastoral. He commends the Thessalonians for following the way that he has pointed out to them and encourages them to continue in this way of life. After his pastoral introduction (4:1-2), Paul turns his attention to "God's will," but his real subject is sanctification. The words "God" (*theou, theon*), "you" (*hymōn, hymas*), and "holy" (*hagiasmos, hagion*)[35] encompass the passage, establishing it as a discreet literary unit (4:3-8) in the letter. Within the pericope, the holiness motif occurs again in verses 4 and 7. Holiness is God's will and God's call. God calls his people, the church of the Thessalonians, to live as if they belonged to him, for that is what holiness really means. They are to lead a life worthy of God (2:12), not like Gentiles who do not know God (4:5).

---

[35] Some words derived from the root *hagi-* are translated as "holy," "holiness," and "make holy," reflecting the Anglo-Saxon heritage of the English language. Other translators use "saintly, "sanctification," and "sanctify," reflecting the Romance heritage of the English language. The NRSV renders the Greek *hagiasmos* as "sanctification" in verse 1 but renders the same noun as "holiness" in verses 4 and 7. The translation differences are stylistic; there is no semantic difference between "sanctification" and "holiness."

God's holy people, the Jews, had long considered that one aspect of life that distinguished them from those who were not God's very own people was their sexual ethos.[36] Reminding the Thessalonians of the reality of their sanctification, their being co-opted into God's people accomplished through the gift of God's Holy Spirit to them, Paul tells them that holiness entails the avoidance of *porneia*, sexual immorality in all its forms. Explaining what this means, Paul tells them that each one should *"heautou skeuos ktasthai"* (4:4), literally, "acquire a vessel for himself," "get a dish." The phrase is translated in the NRSV as "control your own body."

The Greek Bible used *skeuos* to speak of the sacred vessels used in temple; the evangelists used the word in reference to ordinary household utensils.[37] Paul uses the term to talk about pottery (Rom 9:21). What does he mean when he says that "acquiring a vessel" is the way to avoid sexual immorality (4:4)? Paul is not telling the Thessalonians that the acquisition of a dish or some other household utensil is the best way to deal with inordinate sexual desire. What is the meaning of his metaphor? Was *skeuos* intended to evoke the human being who must get himself or herself under control? Were Paul's words directed to men, urging them to keep their penises under control? Or did Paul intend to evoke the image of a wife, with whom a man might consummate his sexual desire?

Arguments can be advanced in favor of each of these possibilities. Does *skeuos* mean the human person? Paul uses the term in a metaphorical sense to designate the human person (Rom 9:22-23; 2 Cor 4:7).[38] Does *skeuos* signify the male sexual organ? Hellenistic authors such as the first-century CE epigrammatist Antistitius and the early third-century writer Aelian, used the term to designate the private parts of a man or woman.[39] Does *skeuos* evoke the idea of a woman, a wife? The author of 1 Peter, whose work was influenced by Paul, advised husbands to show

---

[36] See especially Lev 18 and 20.

[37] See Matt 12:29; Mark 3:27; 11:16; Luke 8:16; 17:31; John 19:29. Mark 11:16 uses *skeuos* to refer to vessels used in the temple, Acts to describe a container of pure and impure foods (Acts 10:11, 16; 11:5) or a piece of nautical equipment (Acts 27:17).

[38] See also 2 Tim 2:20-21 and Acts 9:15, where Luke designates Paul as "an instrument whom I have chosen" (*skeuos eklogēs*).

[39] See Antistitius, in Hubo Stadtmüller, *Anthologia graecarum epigrammatum cum Planudea* (Leipzig: Teubner, 1894–1906), 4.243; Aelian, *De Natura Animalium* ("Nature of Animals"), 17.11. Jay E. Smith argues that in 4Q416 2ii.21 the word *kly* is a euphemism for the sexual organs and that *skeuos* should be so construed in 1 Thess 4:4. See J. E. Smith, "Another Look at 4Q416 2ii.21, a Critical Parallel to First Thessalonians

consideration for their "wives . . . paying honor to the woman as the weaker sex" (*hōs asthenesterō skeuei*,[40] 1 Pet 3:7).

On the other hand, there are arguments against each of the three possibilities. Were Paul's skeuos in 1 Thessalonians 4:4 to designate the human person, the reflexive pronoun *heautou* and the infinitive *ktasthai* become problematic. How does one acquire one's own self? A person is born as one's own self. Some commentators translate *skeuos* as "body," suggesting that Paul is urging the Thessalonians to get control of their bodies,[41] as if the body were the instrument of the soul.[42] This kind of anthropology is rooted in Hellenistic dualism which considers that the human person is a composite of spiritual and corporeal elements. Paul's anthropology is, however, holistic and is rooted in the Semitic and biblical traditions. When Paul uses terms such as body, flesh, spirit, and soul, these terms do not designate parts of the human person, as they do in the Hellenistic world; rather, in Semitic fashion, they designate the whole human person under one or another aspect.

Were Paul's *skeuos* to have been a metaphor for the male penis, a euphemism for the male sexual organ, the verb *ktasthai* would have to mean something like "gain control of."[43] Boys are born with a penis; they don't acquire them at some later time in life. The difficulty with this interpretation is that the verb *ktasthai* means "get," "acquire," "obtain," "buy."[44] No other meaning of the verb is attested in ancient literature.

Fewer difficulties seem to be attendant upon the interpretation of the passage as "acquire a wife for oneself."[45] The Greek text of Sirach 36:29 (= Sir 36:34 [LXX]) uses the phrase *ktasthai gynaika* in the aphorism, "He who acquires a wife gets his best possession."[46] The expression is used in much the same way by Xenophon (*Symposium* 2.10). Rabbis used

---

4:4," *CBQ* 63 (2001): 499–504; "1 Thessalonians 4:4: Breaking the Impasse," *BBR* 11 (2001): 65–105.

[40] Rendered literally, the Greek means "to the feminine as the weaker vessel."

[41] The meaning "gradually obtain the complete mastery of the body" is probably to be preferred in 1 Thess 4:4," says MM 2932, s.v. *ktaomai*. See also J. E. Smith, "1 Thessalonians 4:4."

[42] See, for example, LSJ s.v. *skeuos*.

[43] See the discussion of *membrum virile s. v. skeuos* in BDAG 754.

[44] See the range of meanings of the verb in LSJ, s. v. *ktaomai*.

[45] See *EDNT* 2:324, s. v. *ktaomai*.

[46] More than one term in the Hebrew text of Sir 36:29 refers to the Genesis story of the creation of woman. See Patrick W. Skehan and Alexander A. Di Lella, *The Wisdom of Ben Sira*, AB 39 (New York: Doubleday, 1987), 427.

"acquiring a wife" as a way of speaking about marriage.[47] As for the possibility of *skeuos* serving as a metaphor for a woman, there is the usage of 1 Peter 3:7. Moreover, both later rabbinic usage[48] and early Akkadian usage[49] employ terms that mean "vessel" in their respective languages as metaphors for a woman.

If Paul were encouraging the Thessalonians to marry, thus satisfying their sexual needs and avoiding sexual immorality, his advice would be substantially the same as that which he later gave in 1 Corinthians: "Each man should have his own wife[50] and each woman her own husband" (1 Cor 7:2).

## Wronging a Brother

Continuing his discussion of sanctification and the avoidance of sexual immorality, Paul writes that "no one wrongs or exploits a brother or sister in this matter" (1 Thess 4:6). The verbal couplet, "wrongs or exploits" (*hyperbainein kai pleonektein*), is a hendiadys which means "wrong, by exploiting." In its literal and usual meaning, the *hyperbainein* means "to step over" as a threshold, or "go beyond" as a river overflows its banks. Paul, however, uses the term in a metaphorical sense to mean "transgress"[51] or sin as did Homer (*Iliad* 2.4) and Plato (*Republic* 366a) in previous centuries.

The second verb *pleonektein* normally means to "have a larger share than others"; the related noun, *pleonexia*, means "avarice" or "greed." A later, extended sense of the verb was "take advantage of" or "defraud." Since Paul urges the Thessalonians not to wrong or exploit a brother in this matter, that is, in regard to sexual immorality, it would appear that he did not want any of them to deprive another member of their community of what was rightfully theirs. In Paul's patriarchal society, a wife rightfully belonged to the husband who had acquired her.[52]

---

[47] See *m. Qiddušin* 1:1.

[48] See Str-B, 3.632–633; Christian Maurer, "*Skeuos*," *TDNT* 7:358–67, 360–61.

[49] See BDAG *s. v. skeuos*, citing only a communication from Ludwig Koehler as evidence.

[50] The Greek text reads *hekastos tēn heautou gynaika* (1 Cor 7:2). In 1 Thess 4:4 Paul writes *hekaston hymōn to heautou skeuos*.

[51] Sometimes Greek authors used the verb as a transitive verb. Thus, Heraclitus wrote about "transgressing the laws" (*Allegoriae* 94).

[52] The Mishnah (*m. Qiddušin* 1:1) teaches that a woman was acquired in one of three ways: by money, by writ, or by sexual intercourse.

With regard to sexual matters, a man would be taking advantage of another man if he had sexual intercourse with the latter's wife. From this perspective it would appear that Paul's second bit of advice with regard to sexual immorality is that members of the community should not commit adultery. This would imply that *adelphon*, the third metaphor in 4:6, is not to be taken as "brother or sister." The "brother" is the man, the aggrieved husband, who would be wronged were a member of the community to commit adultery with his wife. That the husband who is wronged is the adulterer's sibling makes the affair all the more egregious.

## The Great Parade

Having used evocative images to remind the Thessalonians how they should live as God's holy people and as members of a real family, Paul turns his attention to the principal topic of his letter. Like Paul, the Thessalonians had expected an imminent parousia, an early appearance of the Lord Jesus Christ. Some of their number had died, perhaps as a result of mistreatment at the hands of their fellow citizens (1:6; 2:14; 3:2-4; cf. Acts 17:5-8),[53] and the parousia had not yet taken place. This was a source of concern for them, which was the occasion for Paul's pastoral concern. Paul was concerned lest these neophyte believers "grieve as others do who have no hope" (4:13).

Something was lacking in their faith (3:10). What appears to have been missing was the eschatological dimension of faith, an aspect of faith that Paul identifies as hope.[54] Paul added hope[55] to the basic dyad of faith and love that is characteristic of the life of believers in 1:3;[56] he does so again in 5:8.

To speak about the future is to speak about the unknown, a reality about which a person might have some certainty, yet a reality that has not yet been experienced. For about two centuries, the first centuries BCE and CE, the period in which Paul lived, Jews wrote about the future

---

[53] With regard to the persecution of the Thessalonian believers, see Karl P. Donfried, *Paul, Thessalonica, and Early Christianity* (Grand Rapids, MI: Eerdmans, 2002), 119–34.

[54] See Raymond F. Collins, *The Birth of the New Testament: The Origin and Development of the First Christian Generation* (New York: Crossroad, 1993), 150–56.

[55] Cf. 1:10.

[56] See Gal 5:6.

in a way that would sustain them as they experienced oppression coming from different quarters. That genre of literature is known as apocalyptic. Apocalyptic literature is the product of an active religious imagination that weaves together experiences and images from the past in order to create an image of the future. Christians are familiar with this type of writing from the New Testament's book of Revelation, but there are other instances of apocalyptic writing in the New Testament[57] and a great many more in the Jewish literature of that period.[58]

The result of religious imagination, the language of apocalyptic literature is necessarily metaphorical. Hellenistic rhetoricians recognized that one of the values of metaphor is that it enables a person to name the unnamable. Properly speaking, one cannot name any of the realities of the future, apart from God himself, but one can use metaphor to speak about that future. Paul does this in an attempt to assuage the grief of the Thessalonians.

He begins with a disclosure formula, clearly stating the reason for his concern and the reason why he is writing to them: "We do not want you to be uninformed, brothers and sisters, about those who have died, so that you may not grieve as others do who have no hope" (4:13). The rhetorical understatement (litotes) and Paul's apostrophic appeal to the Thessalonians as his brothers and sisters underscore his desire to make his appeal as forcefully as he can.

The opening statement contains two images: Paul writes to the Thessalonians as members of his family and writes to them about "those who have fallen asleep" (*tōn koimōmenōn*), that is, those who have died. Images of sleep and rising from sleep are part of the technical language used by early Greek-speaking Christians to talk about the Resurrection. The verb that Paul ordinarily uses to speak about the Resurrection, *egeirō* (1 Thess 1:10),[59] was commonly used in reference to waking someone up from sleep. The other verb used in the New Testament to speak about the Resurrection, the verb *anistēmi* (4:14, 16),[60] used intransitively, often

---

[57] See especially Mark 13 and 2 Thessalonians 2.

[58] For an English translation of nineteen of these works, see Charlesworth, *The Old Testament Pseudepigrapha*, 1: *Apocalyptic Literature and Testaments*. This collection does not include the apocalyptic literature from Qumran, of which the most widely known example is the *War Scroll* (1QM). See Martínez-Tigchelaar, *The Dead Sea Scrolls*, 1: 1Q1–4Q273, 112–45.

[59] Cf. Rom 4:24, 25; 6:4, 9; 7:4; 8:11 [2x], 34; 10:9; 13:11; 1 Cor 6:14; 15:4, 12, 13, 14, 15 [2x], 16 [2x], 17, 20, 29, 32, 35, 42, 43 [2x], 44, 52; 2 Cor 1:9; 4:14; 5:15; Gal 1:1.

[60] Cf. Eph 5:14.

meant rise from bed, rise from sleep. These verbs appear in early Christian credal formulae[61] and predate Paul's use of them.

Even without the resurrection-oriented nuance of Paul's use of "sleep," the metaphorical meaning of "sleep" would have been understood by the Thessalonians. Greek authors such as Homer, Sophocles, and Callimachus used the metaphor to speak about those who had died.[62] The metaphor appeared in funerary inscriptions and has been preserved on at least one papyrus.[63] "Falling asleep" is also used in the Septuagint[64] and in the New Testament[65] in reference to those who were dying or who had already died. The widely used euphemism avoided the brutal reality and offensiveness inherent in the word "death."[66] What Paul is really saying in 4:13 is that he was going to write about Thessalonian believers who had died. His Hellenistic audience would have understood what he meant.

To sustain their faith and build up their hope Paul paints a picture of the eschatological future to provide them with some perspective on what is to come. The image is that of a great procession, a parade, some of whose elements might be particularly striking for any contemporary American who has watched a Veterans Day or Fourth of July parade.

Paul's language is simple enough; he writes about the "coming [*parousian*] of the Lord"[67] and "meeting with the Lord" (*apantēsin*). The basic meaning of *parousia* is "presence."[68] Derivatively and contrasted with previous absence, the term means "coming" or "arrival." Paul uses the term to speak about Titus and Stephanas visiting him (1 Cor 16:17; 2 Cor 7:6, 7; cf. Phil 1:26; 2:12). The term *apantēsis*, hapax in Paul's writings,

---

[61] The verb *egeirō* in 1:10; 1 Cor 15:4; cf. 2 Tim 2:8; the verb *anistēmi* in 4:14.

[62] See Homer, *Iliad* 11.241; Sophocles, *Elektra* 509; Callimachus, *Epigrams* 11.2.

[63] See *IG* 14.929, 1683; *P.Fayûm* 22.28.

[64] See 3 Kgdms 2:10; Matt 27:52; Acts 7:60; 13:36; 2 Pet 3:4. Cf. 1 Cor 7:39; 11:30; 15:6, 18, 20, 51.

[65] See the footnote in the NRSV and the translations found in the KJV, RSV, NIV, and NJB. The NEB and REB offer an interpretive expansion of Paul's words: "those who sleep in death."

[66] Cf. Piotr J. Maysz, "Paul's Use of the Imagery of Sleep and His Understanding of the Christian Life: A Study in the Thessalonian Correspondence," *CTQ* 67 (2003): 65–78, 73.

[67] See also 2:19; 3:13; 5:23; 1 Cor 15:23; and Matt [24:3] Matt 24:27, 37, 39; Jas 5:7, 8; 2 Pet 1:16; 3:4, 12. The eschatological context of all these passages makes it clear that the term *parousia* is being used in a technical, eschatological sense.

[68] See 2 Cor 10:10.

was a word that Hellenists used to describe all sorts of meetings, from a happenstance bumping into a friend on the street to a strategic meeting of an enemy in battle. Paul's use of "Lord" offers some hint as to how Paul is thinking about this meeting.

The epithet conjures up the image of a powerful lord, whose every command was to be obeyed. No lord was more powerful than the emperor himself. The lord's arrival in a town, with military escort, was announced by a herald. A blast from a trumpet would announce the impending arrival. Perforce the inhabitants of the city would go out to meet the lord. More often than not the lord would arrive as a "Savior" bestowing various benefactions on the citizens. Similarly impressive was the arrival of a victorious general, whose victory march would be greeted with appropriate fanfare by the citizenry. They could hope for the distribution of some of the booty of war.

Paul evokes the scene[69] to create an impressive image of the coming of the Lord. The Lord himself will give the command to start the parade. The beginning of the parade will be announced with the archangel's cry and a blast of God's trumpet, effectively the "forward march" of the adjutant and the blast of the herald's trumpet. The Lord will be accompanied by "all the saints," the heavenly hosts. The arrival of the Lord descending from heaven and accompanied by hosts of angels[70] will be an impressive sight.

Denizens of the earth will go out to meet the arriving Lord. The first contingent will consist of those who died in Christ. God himself will raise these up from the dead, just as he had raised Jesus (4:14, 16). These will be followed by those who are still alive. Paul considers that he and his companions will be alive at the time of the parousia (4:15, 17). They too will go out to meet the Lord, rapt[71] into the air, transported on the clouds.

Final salvation will be achieved because those who belonged to Christ will finally be "with him" (4:14, 17; 5:10), Paul's capsule formulation for

---

[69] Erik Petersen developed the classic exposition of this approach to Paul's understanding of the parousia. See "Die Einholung des Kyrios," *ZST* 7 (1930): 682–702 and "*Apantēsis*," *TDNT* 1:380–81.

[70] See, among others, Earl J. Richard, *First and Second Thessalonians*, SP 11 (Collegeville, MN: Liturgical Press, 1995), 167, 177–178.

[71] John Gillman draws attention to the importance of Paul's use of the passive voice in 1 Thess 4:17: "rapture" is the result of God's action. See John Gillman, "Signals of Transformation in 1 Thessalonians 4:13-18," *CBQ* 47 (1985): 263–81, 276.

what theologians call "eternal salvation." Ultimate salvation is other than an earthly experience; it is being with the risen Jesus. Everything has its place in this scenario. Joining the parade are the various "units" that come from the earth, first those who have died in Christ, then the living.[72]

Paul repaints the scene in 1 Corinthians 15 when he reprises the motif of the parousia to respond to the denial of the resurrection of the dead[73] by some members of the Corinthian church (1 Cor 15:12, 35). Everything has its place in his scenario: "Each in its own order," writes Paul, "Christ the first fruits, then at his coming those who belong to Christ. Then comes the end, when he hands over the kingdom to God the Father, after he has destroyed every ruler and every authority and power" (1 Cor 15:23-24). The resurrection of the dead occurs at the blast of the final trumpet (1 Cor 15:52).

The resurrection of the dead is indescribable. In Thessalonians 4:13-18 and 1 Corinthians 15 Paul grounds Christian hope on belief in the resurrection of Jesus from the dead. Traditional credal formulae (4:14; 1 Cor 15:3-4) express this belief that Jesus has been raised from the dead.[74] Paul supplements this belief with images that offer some suggestion as to how the dead might participate in the resurrection, taking stock motifs from Jewish apocalyptic to portray an eschatological scenario. The presence of the archangel, the sounds from/in heaven, a blaring trumpet, and clouds that serve as a vehicle for heavenly transport are classic.[75] A periodic view of history in which everything has its place in a scenario arranged by a sovereign God is likewise classic Jewish apocalyptic.[76]

---

[72] Paul has developed the scene to respond to the Thessalonians' concern about those of their number who have died. His response is issue-specific. He has nothing to say, either positively or negatively, about the fate of those who did not die "in Christ" nor about the living who are not believers.

[73] He speaks about the resurrection of the dead as their being made alive in Christ (1 Cor 15:22).

[74] Matthew's earthquake motif (Matt 28:2-4), an apocalyptic motif, categorizes the resurrection of Jesus as an eschatological event.

[75] See Joseph Plevnik, "The Parousia as Implication of Christ's Resurrection (An Exegesis of 1 Thess 4, 13-18)," in *Word and Spirit: Essays in Honor of David Michael Stanley on his 60th Birthday*, ed. Joseph Plevnik, 199–277 (Toronto: Regis College, 1975), 233–72; Joseph Plevnik, *Paul and the Parousia: An Exegetical and Theological Investigation* (Peabody, Mass: Hendrickson, 1997), 84–90.

[76] See, among others, D. S. Russell, *The Method and Message of Jewish Apocalyptic*, NTL (London: SCM, 1964), 224–34.

Paul Hellenizes the scenario with images of a great parade. The scenario evokes in his audience the experience of the "Joyful Entry"[77] of a visiting emperor or triumphant general. Paul Christianizes the scenario with references to Christ in terms that are carefully chosen.

"Jesus" is the name of the human being whom God raised from the dead. The use of Jesus' personal name—the name of the human being—is very important in Paul's argument: If God has raised one human being from the dead, namely, Jesus, then God can and will raise other humans from the dead (4:14; 1 Cor 15:23).[78] The apostle writes about those who have died in "Christ" (4:16). He customarily uses this title to evoke the memory of the death of Jesus.[79] Finally, Paul writes about the coming of the "Lord" and believers joining the "Lord." This title evokes the power and majesty of the parousiac Lord, reigning over all.[80] Paul's message of hope, intended to assuage the grief of mourning Thessalonians, is that those who have died in Christ will be raised as Jesus was raised and they will be with him, the Lord, forever. This powerful message is expressed through the imagery of an ultimate victory parade.

## Until Then

Ultimate salvation is a matter of God's action and God's timing. The parousia will happen suddenly. It surely will happen but no one knows when. Everything depends on God. What is the believer to do while awaiting the parousia? Those considerations and the answer to this question are the matters that Paul takes up in the other wing of his apocalyptic diptych, 5:1-11.

To speak of the suddenness and the inevitability of the Day of the Lord, Paul uses two powerful metaphors, the thief in the night and the woman in labor (5:2-3). As he did in 2:7-12, Paul juxtaposes a male and a female metaphor to underscore two aspects of a single reality. Each of the images enjoys a singular poignancy. The thief in the night evokes

---

[77] The French "joyeuses entrées" beautifully captures the scene.

[78] An alternate reading of 1 Thess 4:14, found in the Codex Vaticanus and a few medieval Greek manuscripts states clearly that "God will *also* bring with him those who have died. Paul's description of the risen Christ as the "first fruits" in 1 Cor 15:23 (*aparchē*) suggests that "other fruits" will come along in due time.

[79] See Hans Conzelmann, *An Outline of the Theology of the New Testament*, NTL (London: SCM, 1969), 73.

[80] See ibid., 82–84.

surprise and fear; the woman in labor evokes pain and joy. Paul's masculine image expresses the suddenness of the Day of the Lord; his feminine image verbalizes the experience of pain before the inevitable birth and suggests the joy of the experience of new life.

The image of labor pains seems to have been influenced by Paul's Jewish tradition.[81] The Scriptures used the image of the pain of a woman about to give birth to represent the persecution of Israel.[82] The image is found in the Targumim, Aramaic paraphrases of the Scriptures,[83] at Qumran,[84] and in Jewish apocalyptic literature.[85] The image of a woman in pain before the delivery of her child relates well to the situation of the Thessalonians, who experienced the pain of oppression (1:6; 2:14; 3:3-4) and the loss of some of their number. The image evokes danger, pain, inevitability, suddenness, and hope. Paul's use of the traditional image[86] speaks volumes about his perception of the pain that the Thessalonians were experiencing and of the joy that would be theirs at the moment of the parousia.[87]

The image of the thief evokes surprise, danger, and fear. These elements are all the more present insofar as the night is a period of darkness and of slumber. Nighttime brings the quiet peace of sleep; darkness hides the approach of a stealthy thief. Paul uses the image to rouse the Thessalonians from any lethargy or false security into which they might lapse.

"Peace and Security" was a slogan that captured the mood of those living in one of the Roman Empire's free cities.[88] A contemporary describes the atmosphere in these words:

---

[81] See Conrad Gempf, "The Imagery of Birth-Pangs in the New Testament," *TynBul* 45 (1994): 119–135, 122, 124–25, 127–28, 131.

[82] Isa 13:8; 26:17-18 [LXX]; 66:7-9; Jer 6:24; 13:21; 22:23; 30:6; Mic 4:9-10; 5:3; Ps 48:6; cf. Hos 13:13. The Scriptures and subsequent Jewish tradition also used the image to describe the "birth pangs" of the Messiah, the Messianic woes. Any specifically messianic reference is absent from the metaphor of 5:3.

[83] *Tg. Isa* 26:18; 66:7.

[84] 1QH 4:7–10; 5:30–31.

[85] Thus, *1 Enoch* 62:4; 4 Ezra 4:40, 42; 9:38–10:57.

[86] Homer uses the image of the pregnant woman about to give birth in the *Iliad* 11.265–71.

[87] See Wolfgang Harnisch, *Eschatologische Existenz: Ein exegetische Beitrag zum Sachanliegen von 1. Thessalonicher 4,13–5,11*, FRLANT 110 (Göttingen: Vandenhoeck & Ruprecht, 1973), 60–77.

[88] See Holland Lee Hendrix, "Archaeology and Eschatology at Thessalonica" in *The Future of Early Christianity: Essays in Honor of Helmut Koester*, ed. Birger A. Pearson 107–18 (Minneapolis: Fortress, 1991).

On that day there sprang up once more in parents the assurance of safety for their children, in husbands for the sanctity of marriage, in owners for the safety of their property, and in all men the assurance of safety, order, peace, and tranquility. (Velleius Paterculus, *Compendium of Roman History* 2.103.5)

Paul wants to dispel false complacency because the Day of the Lord was at hand. To do so, he employs the image of the thief (in the night), a well-known New Testament figure whose use hearkens back to Jesus himself.[89] The saying about the thief existed as an independent logion in early Christianity. Matthew incorporates the saying from the Q source (Matt 24:43) into his eschatological discourse (Matt 23–24), where it is appended to other sayings on vigilance (Matt 24:37-42). Luke juxtaposes the logion with another exhortation to be ready when the sure but unexpected moment arrives (Luke 12:35-38). The image of the thief was so popular in early Christianity that it recurs in eschatological contexts in two of the late books of the New Testament, Revelation (Rev 3:3;[90] 16:15) and 2 Peter (2 Pet 3:10) and is found in the *Gospel of Thomas* (*G. Thom.* 21).

The woman in labor and the thief in the night are striking images, but the Day of the Lord is also a metaphor, albeit a familiar one in the Bible's prophetic literature, especially Isaiah, Joel, and Zephaniah.[91] The prophets and those who followed in their tradition were not talking about a twenty-four-hour-day that went from sunset to sundown, nor were they talking about a period of daylight, from dawn to dusk. Rather, they were writing about the time of YHWH's manifestation as Lord. That "day" is

---

[89] Scandinavian authors, in particular, have noted the similarity between the imagery of 5:1-7 and Luke 21:34-36. See Lars Hartman, *Prophecy Interpreted: The Formation of Some Jewish Apocalyptic Texts and the Eschatological Discourse Mark 13 Par*, ConBNT 1 (Lund: Gleerup, 1966), 192; Lars Aejmelaeus, *Wachen vor dem Ende: Die traditionsgeschichtlichen Wurzeln von 1 Thess 5:1-11 und Luk 21:34-36*, SESJ 44 (Helsinki: Finnische Exegetische Gesellschaft, 1985). See also Claus-Peter März, "Das Gleichnis vom Dieb: Überlegungen zur Verbindung von Lk 12,39 par Mt 24,43 und 1 Thess 5,2.4," in Ferdnand van Segbroeck et al., eds., *The Four Gospels: Festschrift for Franz Neirynck* BETL 100A (Leuven: University Press–Peeters, 1992), 635–48. März speaks of a connection between Paul and the pre-synoptic tradition.

[90] Rev 3:2, 3 and Matt 24:43 urge that their readers be awake (*grēgoreo*), as does Paul in 5:6-10.

[91] See also Amos 5:18, 20; Lam 2:22. In various forms, the expression "the day of the Lord" occurs almost two hundred times in the Bible. See Richard H. Hiers, "Day of the Lord," *ABD* 2:82–83, 82.

especially a day of judgment,[92] of judgment on the nations and judgment on Israel.

That day will also be a day of deliverance and blessing for God's people. Almost one-third of the biblical texts that mention the Day of the Lord highlight its salvific nature, especially for Israel but also for the nations.[93] Paul presumably mentioned this powerful symbol when he was with the Thessalonians,[94] but how much these Gentiles actually knew about the Day of the Lord is impossible to tell.

With the Day of the Lord about to come, as suddenly as the appearance of a thief in the night[95] and as inevitably as the labor pains of a woman about to give birth, what were believers to do? Simply stated, they were to be different (see 4:5, 13). Urging them to be ready for the coming of the Day of the Lord, Paul employs a powerful series of rhetorical contrasts that image their situation as different from that of other people. The mention of the Day of the Lord and the thief in the night foreshadows a contrast between day and night which leads to a contrast between light and darkness. Believers are children of light and children of the day; they are not, says Paul, children of the night and of darkness (5:5). The chiastic construction and the twofold contrast highlight the point that Paul is making.

Describing the Thessalonian believers as "children of the day," a newly minted expression,[96] Paul employs another pair of contrasting expressions to emphasize the kind of conduct that is appropriate to their new situation. The antithesis between sleeping and being awake and between drunkenness and sobriety interlock with Paul's situational contrasts. Sleeping and being awake are modes of behavior that are consistent with the coming of night and the arrival of day. Nighttime is the time of peaceful slumber, the time of complacency for one rapt in the arms of Morpheus, giving the intrusive thief his opportunity. The day is the time when a person is alert, ready for any eventuality that may come along. Daytime

---

[92] See, for example, Isa 2:12-20; Jer 46:10; Ezek 30:2-3; Amos 5:18-20; Zeph 1:14-18.

[93] Thus, Isa 2:2-4; 11:10; 19:18-25; 25:6-9; Mic 4:1-3; Zech 2:11.

[94] Thus, Beverly Roberts Gaventa, *First and Second Thessalonians*, IBC (Louisville: John Knox, 1998), 69–70.

[95] Among the several uses of the image of the thief in the New Testament only 5:2 specifies the thief's nocturnal appearance.

[96] See Camille Focant, "Les fils du Jour (1 Thes 5,5)," in *The Thessalonian Correspondence*, ed. Raymond F. Collins, 348–355, BETL 87 (Louvain: University Press, 1990), 348, 354.

existence—the Thessalonians are children of the day!—means that one can hear the exhortation to be vigilant and respond accordingly. Paul's neologism, "children of the day," implies that the Thessalonian believers' existence is characterized by its daytime quality (5:8). They exist in the light of the Day of the Lord. Given their eschatological existence,[97] they are not to be caught unawares, as they might be if they lived in the night and were surprised by a thief who operates under the cover of darkness. Believers are daytime people, "eschatological persons;"[98] they are to live accordingly.

Paul urges the Thessalonians to "be awake" lest the Day of the Lord catch them unprepared. The verb *grēgoreō*[99] is sometimes translated "be vigilant" when it appears in hortatory and eschatological contexts but it really means "be awake,"[100] that is, be fully awake, be watchful, be vigilant. How often teachers tell students to "wake up!" when they really mean "pay attention!" Coaches tell players to "wake up!" when they really mean "don't get caught off guard." Paul's wake-up call is an exhortation to vigilance.[101]

Paul complements the exhortation to vigilance with the metaphor "sober" (5:6, 8), which he contrasts with drunkenness (5:7). Paul does not otherwise use the language of sobriety and drunkenness, let alone use it in a metaphorical sense. For Paul drunkenness is a nighttime state; sobriety is appropriate for the day. Philo provides a clue as to the meaning of the antithetical metaphors in his treatises on Noah, *On Drunkenness* and *On Sobriety*.[102] Strong drink is presented as a symbol of "foolish talking and raving, complete insensibility, and insatiable and

---

[97] See Focant, "Les fils du Jour," 355, and especially note 27, with its references to studies by Schlier, Harnisch, Fuchs, and the commentary of Traugott Holtz. See also Plevnik, *Paul and the Parousia*, 109–10.

[98] See Harnisch, *Eschatologische Existenz*, 121, 129.

[99] See 1 Cor 16:13; cf. Matt 24:42, 43; 25:13; 26:38, 40, 41; Mark 13:34, 35, 37; 14:34, 37, 38; Luke 12:37, 39 (some Greek manuscripts); Acts 20:31; Col 4:2; 1 Pet 5:8; Rev 3:2, 3; 16:15.

[100] The English word "wake" is derived from an Old English verb, wacan, "to awaken." The Old English term is related to another verb, wœccan, which means "to watch."

[101] See Evald Lövestam, "1 Thessalonians 5:1-11," in *Spiritual Wakefulness in the New Testament*, LUÅ 1.55.3 (Lund: Gleerup, 1963), 45–58.

[102] In Greek the names of the respective treatises are *Peri Methēs*, "On Sobriety," and *Peri hōn ho Nōe euchetai kata kataratai*, "On the Prayers and Curses Uttered by Noah when he Became Sober."

ever-discontented greediness" (*Drunkenness* 4). Sobriety is clear vision, accompanied by thoughts that lead to good actions.[103]

## *The* Agon *Motif*

Paul also explains what it means to be sober. Daytime people that they are, believers are to "be sober and put on[104] the breastplate of faith and love, and for a helmet the hope of salvation" (5:8). The Thessalonians are to be ready for action, ready for battle. Paul encourages them to don the armor of faith, love, and hope. The imagery of being girded for warfare was easily understood by Paul's audience. Philosophic moralists of his day often used the agon motif, whose images are drawn from the spheres of athletic competition and military activity, to speak about the struggle, the "contest" (*agōn*) for truth and virtue.

Earlier in the letter, Paul employs the agon motif[105] to speak about his preaching. He told the Thessalonians that after he had been shamefully treated in the nearby city of Philippi, he and his companions "had courage [*eparrēsiasmametha*] in our God to declare to you the gospel of God in spite of great opposition" (2:2). Paul may have considered that the courage with which he preached was similar to the courage of the biblical prophets,[106] but his words would have led his Greek-speaking audience to think about the kind of freedom of speech demonstrated by Demosthenes and other political orators. In this context, the phrase "in spite of great opposition" (*en pollō agōni*) is a metaphor[107] that evokes the

---

[103] See *Sobriety* 1–5. Striking because of its similarity with Paul is this affirmation: "If the mind be safe and unimpaired, free from the oppression of the iniquities or passions which produce the frenzy of drunkenness, it will renounce the slumber which makes us forget and shrink from the call of duty and welcoming wakefulness will gaze clear-eyed on all that is worthy of contemplation" (Philo, *Sobriety* 5).

[104] The NRSV renders Paul's *endysamenoi* as "put on" as if it were a verb coordinate with the subjective verb "be sober." In fact, *endysamenoi* is a participle qualifying the emphatic *hēmeis*, "we ourselves," the subject of Paul's hortatory subjunctive verb.

[105] See Victor C. Pfitzner, *Paul and the Agon Motif*, NovTSup 16 (Leiden: Brill, 1967); Martin Brändl, *Der Agon bei Paulus: Herkunft und Profil paulinischer Agon metaphorik*, WUNT 2/222 (Tübingen: Mohr Siebeck, 2006).

[106] On Paul's use of biblical motifs describing the prophets to describe himself, see Raymond F. Collins, *Studies on the First Letter to the Thessalonians*, BETL 66 (Leuven: University Press–Peeters, 1984), 189–91.

[107] On the significance of interpreting the phrase as a metaphor, see Otto Merk, "1 Thessalonians 2:1-12: An Exegetical-Theological Study," in *The Thessalonians Debate: Methodological Discord or Methodological Synthesis?* eds. Karl P. Donfried and Johannes

apostle's struggle on behalf of the truth of the gospel. The apostle uses the very word (*agōn*) with which students of rhetoric identified the rhetorical topos.

The topos was well known in the Hellenistic world. Properly speaking, the "struggle" (*agōn*) is a military battle or an athletic contest. Greek- and Latin-speaking Stoics used the term in a metaphorical sense. Plato uses the image to describe the struggle to live an ethical life.[108] Stoics used the term in their diatribes to describe the discipline required for a virtuous life. Images of the wrestler, the boxer, the gladiator, and the runner were used to illustrate the struggle against the passions. Thus Seneca exhorts Lucilius: "Strive toward a sound mind at top speed and with your whole strength" (*Epistle* 109.6).

Epictetus, Paul's contemporary, writes: "The man who exercises himself against such external impression is the true athlete in training. . . . Great is the struggle [*megas ho agōn estin*], divine the task; the prize is a kingdom, freedom, serenity, peace" (*Discourses* 2.18.27-28). Epictetus stressed the fact that this struggle entailed considerable effort and sometimes provoked opposition, often from the most unlikely of sources: "You must keep vigils, work hard, overcome certain desires, abandon your own people, be despised by a paltry slave, be laughed to scorn by those who meet you, in everything get the worst of it, in office, in honor, in court" (*Discourses* 3.15.11).

The agon motif was appropriated by Greek-speaking Jews who exploited the metaphor to speak of the struggle against Satan (*T. Ash.* 6:2) and the struggle against the evil impulse with which a person was born: the Sovereign Lord said, "This is the meaning of the contest which every man who is born on earth shall wage, that if he is defeated he shall suffer what you have said, but if he is victorious he shall receive what I have said" (4 Ezra 7:127).

The Fourth Book of Maccabees speaks about suffering endured for the sake of the Law: "Do not leave your post in my struggle [*ton mou agōna*] or renounce our courageous brotherhood. Fight the sacred and noble battle [*strateian*] for religion" (4 Macc 9:23-24). The struggle entails suffering. Describing Eleazar, the author of 4 Maccabees writes: "Like a noble athlete [*gennaios athlētēs*] the old man, while being beaten, was victorious over his torturers" (4 Macc 6:10). To the one who was victorious

---

Beutler, 89–113 (Grand Rapids, MI: Eerdmans, 2000), 100. See also, Collins, *Studies*, 185–87.

[108] See *Gorgias* 526d-e; *Phaedo* 247b.

in the struggle belonged the crown: "Reverence for God was victor and gave the crown to its own athletes [*tous heautēs athlētas stephanousa*]. Who did not admire the athletes of the divine legislation?" (4 Macc 17:15-16).

Philo used the topos to speak about living according to the Law, mentioning the Olympic Games as he did so: "Yield to others," he wrote, "the prizes in these unholy contests [*agōnōn*], but bind upon your own head the wreaths won in the holy ones" (*Husbandry* 113). For Philo, only the Olympic contest (*olympiakos agōn*) could properly be called sacred, "not the one which the inhabitants of Elis hold, but the contest for the winning of the virtues which are divine and really Olympian" (*Husbandry* 119).

The Thessalonians would have understood Paul's use of the topos, but he would have seen much more in the image of the warrior's armor than the Thessalonians did. The panoply in 5:8 alludes to the imagery of the biblical motif of the Divine Warrior: "He put on righteousness like a breastplate, and a helmet of salvation on his head" (Isa 59:17). For a Jew familiar with the Scriptures, "righteousness" was the epitome of correct relationships with God and one's neighbor. For Paul, a Jew addressing a Hellenistic audience, correct relationships with God and one's fictive kin can be summed up in the dyad "faith and love." For believers facing the impending eschaton, faith and love must be complemented by hope, the attitude that faith takes in the face of the future.[109]

### Finally, "Do Not Quench the Spirit"

Before ending the letter with a number of closing conventions (5:23-28), Paul fires a series of exhortations at the Thessalonians in rapid order (5:12-22). Apart from the first, each of these exhortations is short and sweet, characterized by the terseness of its formulation. Among them is the exhortation, "Do not quench the Spirit" (5:19).

Writing about the Spirit as if it were a fire, Paul uses a metaphor that he does not otherwise employ. The verb *sbennymi* usually meant "put out" a fire.[110] This is what the verb means in other New Testament passages where reference is made to the extinguishing of various kinds of fire from that of the smoldering wick (Matt 12:20, citing Isa 42:3) to a raging fire (Heb 11:34), including the flame of a lamp that is about to die

---

[109] Cf. 1:3, 10; 3:10; 4:13-18; 5:2, 9.

[110] The verb was also used of the evaporation of liquids.

out (Matt 25:8), a flaming arrow (Eph 6:16), and the fires of Gehenna that cannot be extinguished (Mark 9:48).

A metaphorical use of "quench" was, however, common among Hellenists who employed it as a metaphor meaning quell or check. This metaphorical use dates back at least to the fifth century BCE. The poet Simonides used it to describe a person's ability to keep pride in check (Simon. 132). Euripides, the tragedian, used the image to talk about drowning out a sound by means of a louder sound (*Madness of Hercules* 40). Hellenistic Jewish literature employed the metaphor to speak about the quenching of emotions (4 Macc 16:4) and the drowning of sorrow (Josephus, *Ant.* 11.40). Writing about a prophetic priestess who had stopped giving oracles, Plutarch portrays an interlocutor saying that perhaps "the spirit has been completely quenched [*apesbesmenou*] and her powers have forsaken her" ("Oracles at Delphi" 17 [*Moralia* 402C]). Paul's metaphorical "Do not quench the Spirit" has a meaning analogous to that found in Plutarch, his philosophic contemporary.

Paired with the exhortation, "Do not despise the words of prophets" (5:20), Paul's "Do not quench the Spirit"[111] means "Do not attempt to check the manifestation of the Spirit," especially in reference to prophetic utterances. Contemporary readers of Paul's letters, perhaps more familiar with the great books of the New Testament than they might be with Paul's short letters, might appreciate the intertextuality between Paul's use of a fiery metaphor and Luke's description of the manifestation of the Spirit who came in "tongues, as of fire" (Acts 2:3).

The final metaphor of 1 Thessalonians is the repeated "brothers and sisters" of 5:26-27. Paul asks that the Thessalonians greet one another with a holy kiss and that his letter be read to all of them. This kinship metaphor would prove to be one of Paul's favorites. Its social setting is the home in which believers gathered to hear the reading of Paul's letters. Those who listened heard a proclamation of the gospel that teemed with imaginative language. Some of its figures were familiar to the Hellenistic audience; others were striking images whose source was the apostle's Bible, a book with which the audience was largely unfamiliar.

---

[111] The parallelism between 5:19 (*to pneuma mē sbennyte*) and 5:20 (*prophēteias mē exoutheneite*) is more readily apparent in the Greek text than it is in English. The sentences are comparable with respect to their terseness, the sequence of their wording, and the initial *p* of the objects of the verb. This use of *p* is a feature of the alliteration that unites the terse exhortations in 5:16-22.

# 3

# The Letter to the Philippians

Paul wrote the Letter to the Philippians while he was in prison (Phil 1:13, 17; cf. 4:22). Although imprisoned, Paul received companionship and support from Timothy, his regular companion, and from Epaphroditus whom the Philippians had sent to assist the prisoner. Paul intended to send Timothy to the Philippians, hoping that his envoy would return with an encouraging report about the situation of the believers in the Roman colony (2:19-20). Every bit as urgent on Paul's agenda was his wish to send Epaphroditus back to the community (2:25-30). During his time with Paul, Epaphroditus had become gravely ill. Paul was anxious that he return home in relatively good health.

## Paul's Affection for the Philippians

Paul's desire to send these men to Philippi was evidence of the quality of the relationship that Paul and the Philippians had with one another. Not only did the Philippians send Epaphroditus to Paul in the hour of his need (2:25), they had also sent material help to Paul when he was in Thessalonica, not once but twice (4:16). That Paul would accept this help was unusual for a man who valued his independence and his ability to provide for himself as he proclaimed the gospel of God. That Paul did so in the case of the Philippians was a sign of the closeness of the relationship between them.[1] Six times Paul addresses these friends as his

---

[1] Paul enjoyed the hospitality of both Lydia (Acts 16:15) and an unnamed jailer (Acts 16:33-34) during his second missionary voyage.

"brothers and sisters" (*adelphoi*, 1:12; 3:1, 13, 17; 4:1, 8; cf. 4:21). Toward the end of the letter, Paul calls them "my brothers and sisters, whom I love and long for" (4:1), reinforcing the expression of his affection for the Philippians by repeating "my beloved" at the end of this short sentence. The hendiadys, "love and long for," bespeaks the intensity of Paul's love for the Philippians. Missing them and longing for them[2] with tender affection:[3] longing for them, Paul loves them.

Other expressions of mutual affection permeate the letter. None is more striking than the expression of mutual affection imbedded in the opening thanksgiving: "It is right for me to think this way about all of you, because you hold me in your heart, for all of you share in God's grace with me, both in my imprisonment and in the defense and confirmation of the gospel. For God is my witness, how I long for all of you with the compassion of Christ Jesus" (Phil 1:7-8). Such an expression of mutual fondness is out of the ordinary for Paul. The personal tone of his words is accentuated by his threefold "all of you." "All" bespeaks the universalism of Paul's love for them. None of the holy ones at Philippi lie beyond the pale of Paul's affection. He loves each and every one of them.

Paul's Semitic anthropology provides the background for his use of bodily metaphors to express the intensity of their mutual love. He writes about them holding him in their heart.[4] The language is similar to language that we continue to use today but merits further exploration since "heart" is one of Paul's favorite anthropological terms, albeit never used in its biological sense.

For Paul and his Semitic forebears the heart is much more than the biological organ that pumps blood throughout the body; it is much more than the seat of feeling. For Semites the heart (*lēb*) is the very core of a human being, there where the human being encounters God, either positively or negatively. The heart is the seat of understanding, knowledge,

---

[2] 4:1 is the only instance of the verbal adjective *epipothētoi* in the New Testament. Among New Testament authors it is principally Paul who employs the verb and its cognates, the verb in Rom 1:11; 2 Cor 5:2; 9:14; Phil 1:8; 2:26; 4:1; 1 Thess 3:6; the noun "longing" (*epipothēsis*) in 2 Cor 7:7, 11; the noun "desire" (*epipothia*) in Rom 15:23.

[3] See Spicq, "*Epipotheō*," *TLNT* 2:58–60, 60.

[4] 2 Cor 6:11-13; 7:2-4 is the only other passage in which this expression occurs. In other passages of the New Testament "in the heart" connotes concealment (Matt 24:48; Luke 12:45; Rom 10:6; Rev 18:7).

and will.[5] The center and source of one's entire life, "the heart" can be used metonymically to designate a human being to the very depths of his or her being.

Although Paul's notion of the heart is basically Semitic, his Hellenistic audience would have caught something of what he meant.[6] For Hellenists the heart was the source of mental and spiritual feeling.[7] In 1:7 Paul is saying much more than that the Philippians hold him in warm positive regard or that they have positive thoughts and feelings about him. The Philippians holding Paul in their heart relates to the grace of God in which the Philippians and Paul share. The expression "For all of you share in God's grace with me" indicates that the Philippians' very being has been so transformed by the grace of God that they experience a heartfelt affective unity with Paul. Their love was manifest in their support for him while he was in prison and in the support that they rendered to him as he evangelized, preaching the gospel and defending it.

"To hold in the heart" is a beautiful metaphor used to signify truly personal and profound affection. There is, however, a discussion among exegetes as to the subject of the love about which Paul writes in 1:7: Is he writing about his love for the Philippians or their love for him? The NRSV's translation of *to echein me en tē kardia hymas* suggests that the phrase describes the Philippians' love for Paul, but a footnote indicates that an alternative translation is possible, namely, "because I hold you in my heart," a translation that applies the metaphor to Paul's love for the Philippians. This alternative understanding is found in the RSV, the NRSV's predecessor, and in the AV, JB, NIV, REB,[8] RevNAB, the Dutch-language Willibord translation, and the German *Einheitsübersetzung*, the standard German-language ecumenical translation.

The ambiguity arises because Paul uses the metaphor in an infinitive clause. In Greek, both the subject and the object of an infinitive are in the accusative case. Hence, the question arises, is "me" or "you" the subject of the phrase? Those who hold that "you" is the subject argue that this interpretation is supported by the word order of Paul's Greek,[9]

---

[5] Similarly, Peter T. O'Brien, *Commentary on Philippians*, NIGTC (Grand Rapids, MI: Eerdmans, 1991), 68.

[6] See Robert Jewett, *Paul's Anthropological Terms: A Study of Their Use in Conflict Settings*, AGJU 10 (Leiden: Brill, 1971), 323.

[7] See, for example, Ovid, *Tristia* 5.4.23–24.

[8] The REB's predecessor, the NEB, read "because you hold me in such affection," a translation similar to that of the NRSV.

[9] That is, "I/me in the heart you," *me en tē kardia hymas*.

the parallelism between verses 7 and 8, and the fact that Paul's epistolary thanksgivings generally focus on his experience of the addressees.

Those who argue that "me" is the subject of the problematic phrase note that a heartfelt feeling of affection demands reciprocity.[10] The Philippians' manifold and unwavering support of Paul was a clear sign of their affection for him. Would he not then have at least mentioned that affection in his thanksgiving to God?

Despite the NRSV's translation of 1:7,[11] commentators generally take Paul's words to be an expression of what Lohmeyer describes as Paul's "heartfelt unity with and affective feeling" for the Philippians.[12] O'Brien speaks of Paul's "deep personal affection for the Philippians."[13]

In verse 8 Paul complements his expression of affection for the Philippians with an oath, "For God is my witness."[14] The oath confirms the truthfulness of Paul's claim, adding intensity to Paul's emotional expression of his love for the Philippians. Along with his oath Paul adds a theological reflection on the nature of his love for the Philippians: He longs for[15] the Philippians "with the compassion [*en splanchnois*] of Christ Jesus."

Like "heart" (*kardia*), "compassion" (*splanchna*) is a biological term. In its proper sense the term designates the internal organs, the viscera of animals, including human beings. Philo describes these internal organs in this way: "The inward parts, 'called entrails' [*splanchna*], are stomach, heart, lung, spleen, liver, two kidneys" (*Creation* 118).[16] Hebrew terms designating these organs were used to identify the deepest and inmost parts of the human being; as such, the innards were considered to be the seat and source of a person's emotions. Emotions arise from deep within

---

[10] See 2 Cor 6:11-13; 7:2-4.

[11] Hawthorne, for example, reads "because you hold me in such affection." See Gerald F. Hawthorne, *Philippians*, WBC 43 (Waco, TX: Word, 1983), 23.

[12] Ernst Lohmeyer, *Die Briefe an die Philipper, Kolosser und an Philemon*, KEK 9 (Göttingen: Vandenhoeck & Ruprecht, 1964), 22.

[13] See O'Brien, *Philippians*, 68; see also Joachim Gnilka, *Der Philipperbrief*, HTKNT 10/3 (Freiburg: Herder, 1976), 47.

[14] Cf. Rom 1:9; 2 Cor 1:23; 1 Thess 2:5, 10.

[15] See also 4:1.

[16] The list is repeated in *Allegorical Interpretation* 1.12, where Philo identifies the seven divisions of the body as the head, neck, breast, hands, belly, abdomen, feet. Cf. *Drunkenness* 106; *Special Laws* 1.62. In *Creation* 118, Philo specifies that there are seven internal organs just as there are seven visible parts of the body: the head, breast, belly, two hands, and two feet.

the human being; they come from what is most hidden and intimate in the human person.

With regard to the ambivalent use of biological terms, Philo writes: "While the bodily eyes see only the outward surface, the eye of the mind penetrates within, and going deep gets a clear view of all that is hidden up in the very heart [*ta en autois splanchnois*]."[17] The use of "entrails" (*splanchna*) to evoke the notion of human emotions arising from deep within a person abounds in Hellenistic and intertestamental literature. Aristophanes, reflecting older Greek usage in which the entrails were viewed as the source of violent and aggressive emotion, warns, "Do not overheat your entrails with anger" (*Frogs* 244). Ben Sira says that if a man spoils his son, his entrails will be shaken (*tarachthēsetai*[18] *splanchna autou*) (Sir 30:7). Describing the young Egyptian maiden falling in love with Joseph at first sight, *Joseph and Aseneth* says that when the Aseneth fell in love with Joseph "her entrails were crushed" (*Joseph and Aseneth* 6:1). Evoking a contrary emotion, the *Testament of Abraham* describes Isaac clinging to his father, fearing that he would die. Reacting to his son's emotion, "Abraham's heart [*splanchna*] was moved, and he too cried with him in a loud voice" (*T. Ab.* 5:10). Philo describes despair and sore distress arising from the entrails (*Rewards* 151).

In biblical, intertestamental, and New Testament literature pity or compassion is especially associated with the entrails.[19] Evoking pity and compassion, the entrails serve as a metaphor for the mercy of God in the *Testament of the Twelve Patriarchs*. The *Testament of Zebulon*, for example, says, "To the extent that a man has compassion on his neighbor, to that extent the Lord has mercy [*splanchna*] on him" (*T. Zeb* 8:2).[20]

Lest the contemporary reader wonder at the naiveté of ancient authors who described human emotions in terms of biological organs, he or she should not overlook the reality that a similar understanding of human emotions is reflected in contemporary colloquial language. We continue to speak of a "gut feeling" and of courageous persons "having guts." We speak of people "giving their heart away" when they fall in love and of "losing heart" when they fail in courage. In addition, any number of physiological and psychological studies attest to the physical effects of

---

[17] Philo, *Posterity* 118. The passage uses the same phrase as is found in 1:8.

[18] In its physiological sense, the verb and its cognates often described a disturbance of the bowels. See, for example, Hippocrates, *Praenotitiones coacae* 205.

[19] Thus, Gen 43:30; Prov 12:10; Matt 9:36; Mark 1:41; Luke 7:13; 15:20; etc.

[20] Cf. *T. Levi* 4:4; *T. Naphtali* 4:5.

intense emotion. While these studies point to the effect of the emotions on the body and its organs, the ancients saw the organs as the source of emotions. Though disagreeing with one another in their "scientific analysis," ancient and moderns are as one in affirming the profound link between human emotions and human physiology.

As the seat and source of human emotions, Paul's *splanchna*[21] is equivalent to "the heart."[22] As the heart, the "entrails" are the source of warm, positive affection.[23] Accordingly, the metaphor of 1:8[24] is rendered in terms of various positive emotions in contemporary versions of the New Testament: affection (RSV, NIV, RevNAB), deep yearning (NEB, REB), warm longing (NJB), and love (JB).

Attentive to the connotations of the word in the Greek biblical tradition, the NRSV renders Paul's biological metaphor as "the compassion of Christ Jesus" (1:8). One must question, however, whether the specification of this emotion as compassion is truly justified.[25] Nothing that Paul writes suggests that the Philippians were suffering from any kind of pain or tremendous difficulty that would lead Paul to pity them with the very pity of Christ Jesus. Moreover, would Paul whose letters give so few hints of familiarity with the Jesus tradition have known the various stories about Jesus' compassion for the sick and hungry that would later be incorporated into the Synoptic Gospels? Does not the parallelism between verses 7 and 8 suggest that "the compassion of Christ Jesus" is somehow parallel with "God's grace with me"?

Paul was aware that Christ acted in and through him to such an extent that he could say, "to me, living is Christ" (1:21) and that "Christ Jesus has made me his own" (3:12). Paul was so transformed by his relationship with Christ that he would write to the Galatians: "It is no longer I who live, but it is Christ who lives in me" (Gal 2:20). What Paul is affirming in 1:8 is that his yearning for the Philippians, his longing to be with them was an expression not only of his profound and heartfelt love for them but also an expression of the love of Christ expressed in the

---

[21] See also 2 Cor 6:12; 7:15; Phil 2:1; Phlm 7, 12, 20. The NRSV generally renders Paul's *splanchna* with "heart."

[22] In Phlm 12 *splanchna* is translated "heart" by the NJB, REB, and RevNAB.

[23] See Spicq, "*Splachna, splanchnizomai*," *TLNT* 273–75, 275.

[24] The King James Version renders the expression literally "the bowels of Christ Jesus." See also Phlm 12 (KJB).

[25] See Nikolaus Walter, "*Splanchnon*," *EDNT* 3:265–66, 266, who writes, "The meaning pity, compassion occurs in the NT (apart from 1 John 3:17) only in combination with synonyms."

love of Paul for the Philippians. "It is, as it were," writes Nicolaus Walter, "the *heart* of the Kyrios himself that 'speaks' in Paul's heart and yearns for fellowship with his brethren; that is how Paul describes the depth of his yearning."[26]

## Paul's Hope

As is often the case, Paul's epistolary thanksgiving ends on an eschatological note in the form of a prayer report which is actually a prayer because Paul's language is performative throughout the thanksgiving period:

> And this is my prayer, that your love may overflow more and more with knowledge and full insight to help you to determine what is best, so that on the day of Christ you may be pure and blameless, having produced the harvest of righteousness that comes through Jesus Christ for the glory and praise of God. (Phil 1:9-11)

Paul prays that the love that the Philippians have for him may continue to abound so that they be found blameless on "the day of Christ," the Day of the Lord. His prayer is similar to one offered on behalf of the Thessalonians (1 Thess 3:11-13).

A distinguishing feature of the Philippians' prayer is the appearance of an agricultural metaphor, the harvest.[27] The metaphor is all the more striking in that Paul's images normally derive from life in the city rather than from life in the country. "To produce a harvest" is "to bring the fruit to completion," "to produce a full complement of fruit" (*peplēromenoi karpon*).[28]

Paul specifies that the "fruits" produced in full measure are "fruits of righteousness" (*karpon dikaiosynēs*). In the Greek Bible, "fruits of righteousness" reflects Semitic idiom and occurs in Amos 6:12 and Proverbs 11:30.[29] The Hebrew sage proclaims, "The fruit of the righteous is a tree

---

[26] Walter, "*Splanchnon*," 266.

[27] Every trace of the image has been removed from the translation found in JB, "perfect goodness which Jesus Christ produces in us."

[28] Thus, F. W. Beare, *The Epistle to the Philippians*, BNTC, 2nd ed. (London: Adam & Charles Black, 1969), 55. The NRSV, NEB, REB and Beare read the participle *peplērōmenoi* as a participle in the middle voice.

[29] See also Prov 13:2 where the Greek text reads: "Good persons shall eat of the fruits of righteousness," the Hebrew, "from the fruits of their own words good persons eat good things."

of life" (Prov 11:30).[30] This biblical expression was not without parallel in Hellenistic culture. An epigram attributed to Epicurus uses the expression: "The fruit of righteousness is abundant calm."[31]

In Amos, the expression "fruit of righteousness" occurs in an oracle about the coming of the Day of the Lord where fruits of righteousness are paralleled with "justice" and opposed to wormwood. The prophet reproves those who have turned the fruit of justice into wormwood, a bitter plant which symbolizes oppression of the poor.[32]

In the biblical texts the "fruit of righteousness" indicates correct behavior, behavior that results from a correct relationship with God and one's neighbor. When the expression appears in New Testament texts it is generally linked with peace, but that is not the case with Paul's use of the metaphor in 1:11. The apostle prays that the Philippians will produce a full measure of the fruits of righteousness. What is the meaning of Paul's metaphor? Some suggest that the fruit of righteousness consists in a person being found pure and blameless at the parousia. Others consider that "righteousness" is a genitive of definition, meaning that the "fruit" is righteousness itself.

Paul writes about fruit in four of his extant letters, in this letter and in letters to the Romans, the Corinthians (1 Cor), and the Galatians. Apart from 1 Corinthians 9:7 where Paul cites the example of the viticulturist who deserves to eat some of the fruit that he has grown, the apostle uses the term "fruit" in a metaphorical sense, often to describe something that human beings can produce (Rom 1:13; 6:21; 15:28; Phil 1:22; 4:17) but sometimes to describe something that only God can produce (Rom 6:22; Gal 5:22).

In 1:22 Paul speaks about fruit to describe his own apostolic activity: "If I am to live in the flesh, that means fruitful labor for me." The biblical expression "fruitful labor" is found in the books of Isaiah (Isa 3:10) and Jeremiah (Jer 17:10; 32:19), both of which had significant influence upon Paul's understanding of his own ministry.

---

[30] This translation appears in both the NRSV and the NJPS. Scott draws attention to a text-critical issue, translating the Hebrew as "right conduct." See B. B. Y. Scott, *Proverbs. Ecclesiastes*, AB 18 (Garden City, NY: Doubleday, 1965), 87.

[31] Epicurus, Fragment 519. The epigram also appears in the writings of Clement of Alexandria, *Miscellanies* 6.2.

[32] See Francis I. Andersen and David Noel Freedman, *Amos*, AB 26A (New York: Doubleday, 1989), 578–79, 601–4.

A third metaphorical use of the word "fruit" in Philippians occurs in 4:17: "Not that I seek the gift, but I seek the profit [*ton karpon*] that accumulates to your account." Paul's metaphor operates on two levels. Associated with language that comes from the world of business and commerce,[33] "fruit" suggests the profit that comes from a business transaction.[34] On another level, however, Paul's agricultural metaphor evokes the "heavenly interest"[35] that is constantly accruing to the advantage of the Philippians. Paul tells the Philippians that he is not concerned with accumulating some material or financial gain for himself; rather, he is interested in the spiritual advantage that will accrue to them for having generously supported him in his imprisonment and his missionary endeavors.

In an aside, Paul uses commercial language to affirm that the Philippians have given him all that he needs, and even more. "I have been paid in full," he writes, "and have more than enough" (4:18). "Paid in full" (*apechō de panta*) is a technical formula. Hellenistic papyri and ostraca provide ample evidence of the formula being used on receipts[36] much in the same way that a clerk stamps "paid in full" on a bill. A dynamic translation of Paul's words might read, "Here's my receipt."[37]

The profit that will accrue to the Philippians is eschatological salvation on the Day of the Lord: "My God will fully satisfy every need of yours according to his riches in glory in Christ Jesus" (4:19). Again, Paul uses the language of finance to make his point. "Riches" (*to ploutos*) is a common term for wealth in the form of precious metal or abundant produce. God's riches are experienced in the abundance of his many gifts. Life with Christ in the eschaton is the fullest manifestation of God's gifts, but one must not restrict the "profit" [= fruit] of "I seek the profit that accumulates to your account" (4:17) to a final, eschatological reward. God's

---

[33] Baldanza suggests that 4:10-20, a very personal pericope, must be read in the light of the financial support that Paul received from the Philippians and refused to accept from others. See Giuseppe Baldanza,"La portata teologica di *osmē euōdias* in Fil 4,18," *Laur* 47 (2006): 161–85.

[34] Thus, C. H. Dodd, "The Mind of Paul," *BJRL* 17 (1933): 91–105, 95–96, reprinted in *New Testament Studies* (Manchester: University Press, 1953), 67–82, 71–72; Beare, *Philippians*, 155; Gnilka, *Philipperbrief*, 179; O'Brien, *Philippians*, 126–27.

[35] So, O'Brien, *Philippians*, 534.

[36] See MM 568.

[37] Thus, for example, "Here, then, is my receipt for everything" (GNB) and the NAB's "Herewith is my receipt, which says that I have been fully paid and more." The CEV renders the phrase "I have been paid back everything and with interest."

glory is even now a present reality. From the abundance of God's riches, the Philippians will receive material and spiritual gifts, now and in the life to come.

"Accumulates" suggests that the profit accruing to the Philippians continues to amass; the fruit that accrues to the Philippians is similar to perpetual compound interest eventually reaching its fulfillment in the eschaton, as a gift from God, analogous to the gift that the Philippians had given to Paul (4:18).

The Philippians will be filled with "the fruit of righteousness," says Gnilka with reminiscence of 1:11.[38] In both 1:11 and 4:17 Paul's "fruit" suggests an eschatological reward. The similarity between the two verses suggests that perhaps 1:11 should be construed to mean "filled with the fruits of righteousness"[39] rather than "having produced the harvest of righteousness." In which case, "fruit" is the result of the righteousness that comes from Jesus Christ unto the glory and praise of God.[40]

### Profit and Loss as a Journey Begins

Paul delved into the semantic domain of the world of commerce to mediate the meaning of "fruit" in 4:17. Philippians 4:17 is not, however, the only place in the letter in which Paul derives theological advantage from the economic sphere. Describing a personal dilemma, Paul has recourse to the world of economics as he writes: "For to me, living is Christ and dying is gain [*kerdos*]. . . . I am hard pressed between the two" (1:21, 23). In the business world, as the Hellenistic papyri[41] and various New Testament texts[42] indicate, *kerdō / kerdainō* and *zēmia / zēmioō* were the common terms for profit and loss.

Writing from the heart, Paul uses the language of profit and loss as he writes about his personal dilemma in 3:7-8:

---

[38] See Gnilka, *Philipperbrief*, 179.

[39] The AV, RSV, NIV, NJB, and RevNAB, along with many commentators (e.g., Lohmeyer, *Die Briefe*, 30; O'Brien, *Philippians*, 79–80), take the participle in 1:11 as a genuine passive, rather than the middle voice suggested by the NRSV translation. If the participle is truly passive, Paul's words should be rendered, "filled with the fruits of righteousness."

[40] Thus, O'Brien, *Philippians*, 80–81.

[41] See MM 2209, 2210, 2770, 2771.

[42] Matt 25:16, 17, 20, 22; Titus 1:11; Jas 4:13.

> Yet whatever gains [*kerdē*] I had, these I have come to regard as loss [*zēmian*] because of Christ. More than that, I regard everything as loss [*zēmian*] because of the surpassing value of knowing [*gnōsis*] Christ Jesus my Lord. For his sake I have suffered the loss [*exēmiōthēn*] of all things, and I regard them as rubbish, in order that I may gain [*kerdēsō*] Christ.

Prior to this moving attestation of the value of his experience[43] of Christ, Paul spelled out six qualities which counted to his advantage as a Jew: born a member of the people of Israel, belonging to the house of Benjamin, circumcised according to the Law, a Pharisee, a zealous persecutor of the church, and blameless and righteous with regard to the Law. All of these were nothing—indeed, less than nothing—in comparison with his personal experience of Jesus Christ as Lord.[44] Paul is referring to his experience on the road to Damascus, for it was then that he had a personal experience of Jesus Christ as his Lord. In comparison with that unique experience, the very qualities that Paul had previously counted among his assets he now counts among his losses. "These profits," Pierre Bonnard comments, "were not just wiped out; they became losses; their mathematical sign changed from plus to minus."[45] Paul's profit was not simply wiped out; it was reduced to a loss.

Paul knew that his language properly belonged in the world of finance. In 1 Corinthians 3:15 he uses the verb *zēmioō*, "loss," to describe the penalty imposed on a builder whose work was not up to standard. His Hellenistic contemporaries used the term and its antonym to describe financial liabilities and assets. Rabbis used the corresponding Hebrew terms.[46]

---

[43] Notwithstanding the mid-twentieth-century debate between Bultmann and Dupont over the precise meaning of "knowledge" (*gnōseōs*) in the phrase "knowing Christ Jesus my Lord," the term should be understood within the parameters of its Hebrew counterpart where it has experience as its primary connotation. Cf. Rudolf Bultmann, "*Ginōskō, gnōsis, ktl.*," *TDNT* 1:689–719; Jacques Dupont, *Gnōsis: La connaissance religieuse dans les épîtres de saint Paul* (Bruges and Paris: Desclée de Brouwer, 1949) 415; Bultmann, review of Dupont in *JTS* 3 (1952): 10–26.

[44] That Paul's experience of Christ was very personal is underscored by his reference to "Christ Jesus *my* Lord."

[45] Pierre Bonnard, *L'Épître de saint Paul aux Philippiens*, CNT 10 (Neuchâtel and Paris: Delachaux & Niestlé, 1950), 63.

[46] See Str-B 1:749; Jean-François Collange, *The Epistle of Saint Paul to the Philippians* (London: Epworth, 1979), 128.

Outside of the commercial world, the antonyms profit and loss were often used to denote gain and loss, reward and penalty. Rabbi Judah says: "Be heedful of a light precept as of a weighty one, for thou knowest not the recompense of reward of each precept; and reckon the loss through [the fulfilling of] a precept against its reward, and the reward [that comes] from transgression against its loss."[47] In the Hellenistic world, Epictetus asks, "Was it not, then, a great gain [*kerdos mega*] to lose a frail and adulterous wife?" (*Discourses 3.22.38*).[48]

Aristotle draws attention to the metaphorical nature of such language:

> The terms "loss" and "gain" in these cases are borrowed from the language of voluntary exchange. There, to have more than one's own is called gaining [*kerdainein*], and to have less than one had at the outset is called losing [*zēmiousthai*], as for instance in buying and selling, and all other transactions sanctioned by law." (*Nichomachaean Ethics* 5.4.13 [1132b])

Since the economic antithesis was commonplace among both Jews and Greek speakers and since Paul himself often used the terms in a wider sense (*kerdainō*, "gain," in 1 Cor 9:19, 20, 21, 22, *zēmioō*, "harm," in 2 Cor 7:9), it is not necessary to hold that the language of 1:21, 23 and 3:7-8 hearkens back to the Jesus logion, "For what will it profit them to gain [*kerdēsai*] the whole world and forfeit [*zēmiōthēnai*] their life?" (Mark 8:36; Matt 16:26).[49] Paul's use of the widely used economic metaphor also makes it unnecessary to postulate that he suffered some sort of material loss as a result of his embrace of Christ Jesus as Lord.[50] Metaphor allows the apostle to avoid the use of pejorative language to describe his experience as a Jew. Throughout his life he remained a Jew, holding Israel in high regard (Rom 9:4-5).

The way that Paul speaks about gaining Christ suggests a future experience of Christ. For Jan Lambrecht, this would be the experience of

---

[47] *m. ʿAbot* 2:1.

[48] The reference is to Menelaus's loss of Helen of Troy. See Epictetus's use of similar language in *Discourses* 1.28.13.

[49] O'Brien (*Philippians*, 390–91) notes the similarity between Paul's autobiographical statement and the saying of Jesus insofar as both make use of the antithetical language and Paul's "everything" (*panta*) and "all things" (*ta panta*) is comparable to the saying "the whole world." Despite the striking similarities, there is little evidence that Paul was familiar with the tradition of the sayings of Jesus.

[50] Beare (*Philippians*, 115) intimates that such a loss might have occurred.

"Christ's resurrectional power" operative in Paul's own future resurrection.[51] O'Brien says, "[T]he apostle is looking forward to the day of Christ. His ambition is to gain Christ perfectly—the same Christ Jesus who is Paul's Lord—and this goal will be fully realized on the last day."[52] One expectation does not exclude the other. Paul's desire to experience Christ includes both a desire to experience the resurrectional power of Christ in his own resurrection and the desire to experience the fullness of Christ as Lord at the parousia, for it is then that Christ Jesus will be fully present as Lord and Savior.

In the three passages of Philippians in which Paul uses the language of accounting, the horizon is that of the Day of the Lord. For Paul to die is already profit (1:21), for then he will be with Christ (1:23). He wants to gain Christ, to experience Christ, and to be found in him (3:7-9). He seeks the gain that will accrue to the Philippians because of their supportive participation in his missionary work. The language of economics enables Paul to speak about the as yet indescribable parousia of the Lord.

As Paul weighs the pros and cons of his personal dilemma (1:23a), he realizes that he must die in order to be with Christ: "my desire is to depart [*analysai*] and be with Christ" (1:23b). The language is pictorial. "Depart" [*analyō*], hapax in the Pauline corpus, is a nautical term; it means to be freed from the moorings, weigh anchor, and set sail. Greek-speaking Hellenists often used the word to mean "leave" or "depart,"[53] but it was sometimes used to speak metaphorically of death, as it was used in the second century CE by Diogenes of Oenoanda in a description of the basic tenets of Epicureanism.[54]

The image of cutting loose from the moorings and setting sail is not the only nautical metaphor in the pericope. The passage begins with Paul proclaiming: "Yes, and I will continue to rejoice, for I know that through your prayers and the help of the Spirit of Jesus Christ this will turn out [*apobēsetai*] for my deliverance" (1:18-19). The verb *apobainō*

---

[51] See Jan Lambrecht, "Our Commonwealth is in Heaven," *LS* 10 (1984–85): 199–205, 202; reprinted in *Pauline Studies*, BETL 115 (Leuven: University Press–Peeters, 1994), 309–15, 312.

[52] O'Brien, *Philippians*, 391.

[53] See Polybius, *Histories* 3.69.14; Babrius, *Fables* 42.8.

[54] See Joannes William, *Diogenis Oenoandensis Fragmenta*, Bibliotheca Scriptorum Graecorum et Romanorum Teubneriana (Leipzig: Teubner, 1907), 2. Another inscription, attributed to Macestus and using the same image, can be found in Georg Kaibel, *Epigrammata Graeca ex lapidibus conlecta* (Berlin: Reimer, 1878), 340.7.

essentially means "disembark from a boat." By extension the word came to mean "depart" or "succeed." Paul uses the term to speak about the result of the Spirit's action on his behalf as the Spirit responds to the prayers of the Philippians. Facing the possibility of death (1:20-23), Paul is confident that his experience will result in his final salvation through the working of the Holy Spirit.[55]

Paul's words about the Philippians' prayer alludes to a prayer of Job (Job 13:16).[56] Job prayed to be saved from physical ills; Paul hoped that his present experience would result in his salvation. The apostle's reliance on Job for the nautical metaphor of 1:19 would mitigate the impact of the nautical image were it not for the fact that the recently evangelized Philippians would not recognize the allusion to the story of Job. In fact, Paul's letters rarely allude to the book of Job, a sign that the book was not an important element in the early Christian catechesis of Gentiles.

Although the apostle was quite familiar with sea-faring,[57] nautical images do not play a significant role in his argumentation. The nautical images of 1:18-26 suggest, however, that death is a passage, the beginning of a journey. For Paul the end of the journey means that he will be with Christ.[58]

## Living as a Citizen Should Live

Ceslas Spicq states that civic language is apropos to the Christian vision of the cosmos and life within it.

> The "urban" or "civic" metaphors for the Christian life in the New Testament, and especially in St. Paul, are quite coherent. Heaven is like a city (*polis*); Christ is its sovereign (*Kyrios*), and it has its own laws and constitution (*politeia*), namely, the gospel. Christians are its citizens (*politai* . . .) and are not treated as foreigners or sojourners

---

[55] Thus, Gnilka, *Philipperbrief*, 66. Similarly, G. B. Caird, *Paul's Letters from Prison*, New Clarendon Bible (Oxford: Oxford University Press), 112; O'Brien, *Philippians*, 109–10.

[56] See Marvin H. Pope, *Job*, AB 15 (Garden City, NY: Doubleday, 1965), 96.

[57] See Rom 15:28; 1 Cor 16:6; 2 Cor 11:25-26; as well as the many passages in Acts in which Luke employs the motif of a sea voyage in his narrative of Paul's missionary activity.

[58] Paul's use of "with" (*syn*) as a preposition with an object or as the prefix of a compound verb often has soteriological significance. See, for example, 1 Thess 4:14, 17; Rom 6:5-8.

there; they have the rights of citizenship (*politeuma*) and are fellow-citizens of the saints (*sympolitai*). Such a citizenship carries with it rights and privileges but also obligations and responsibilities. Each one is then required to "live as a citizen" (*polieuomai*).[59]

Paul employs this kind of imagery in Philippians. He urges his audience to "live your life in a manner worthy of the gospel of Christ" (1:27). "Live your life" is a very weak translation of *politeuesthe*, etymologically linked to the noun *polis*, meaning "city." Apart from its usage in Christian and Hellenistic-Jewish texts, extant Greek texts contain only one instance of the verb in which it means "live one's life." Typically the verb means "live as a citizen," "be a citizen."[60]

Philippians is a letter in which political considerations are important. Paul used the time of his imprisonment to evangelize the imperial guard (1:12-14) and sends greetings from members of the emperor's household (4:22). The formal name of the Philippians' city was *Colonia Augusta Iulia Philippensis*. The name was a reminder of the number of military retirees who lived there and also of the great Roman emperors, Augustus and Julius Caesar. Enjoying the *ius Italicum*, the inhabitants of Philippi were considered to be living on Roman soil, somewhat in the way that modern embassies are considered to be extraterritorial.

The circumstances of Paul's imprisonment and the city[61] to whose inhabitants he was writing must be taken into full account in the interpretation of the letter. Only in Philippians does Paul use the verb *politeuō* and the related noun *politeuma*, "citizenship" (3:20). In ordinary conversation these words have political connotations. The antonym of *politeuō* was *idiōteuō*, "live as a private individual," devoid of social responsibility and neglecting to fulfill the laws of society. To live as a citizen, remarks Spicq, is "to consider oneself in all one's actions as a member of a social body, and accordingly to say nothing and do nothing that is not appropriate for a citizen."[62] To live as a citizen is to live with a sense of social responsibility.

[59] See Spicq, "*Politeia, ktl,*" *TLNT* 3:124–33, 124.

[60] See the etymological argument and the survey of usage of the verb in Hermann Strathmann, "*Polis, ktl.,*" *TDNT* 6:516–35, 517–18.

[61] See Mikael Tellbe, *Paul Between Synagogue and State: Christians, Jews, and Civic Authorities in 1 Thessalonians, Romans, and Philippians*, ConBNT 34 (Stockholm, Almqvist & Wiksell, 2001), 212–20.

[62] Spicq, "*Politeia, ktl.,*" 132–33.

Is Paul then exhorting Philippian Christians to fulfill their obligations as citizens of the Roman colony?[63] The answer is to be found in 3:20 where Paul states, "Our citizenship is in heaven." Philippians 3:20-21 speaks of the eschatological future of Christians; its language uses the idiom of the christological hymn in 2:6-11.[64] Although most English translations and various studies of 3:20-21 render the noun *politeuma* as "citizenship," this is not the most common meaning of the term. The term ordinarily meant "commonwealth"[65] or "state." This being the case, the term *politeuma* may well represent another of the apostle's attempts to render Semitic idioms in terms that Hellenists would easily understand. Paul may have considered the term *politeuma* to be the Hellenistic equivalent of the Semitic "kingdom of God," a reality whose fullness will be attained in the eschaton.

On the other hand, "citizenship" may well impart the meaning of the term as Paul used it in 3:20. In Paul's usage *politeuma* has the connotation of belonging to a social body that exists in time and space with pertinent rights and responsibilities.[66] With a large number of Roman citizens among its inhabitants, Paul's addressees in Philippi would have understood what citizenship meant. Just as Roman citizenship entailed responsibilities as well as rights, so heavenly citizenship brought with it not only privileges but also responsibilities.

Writing about citizenship, Paul urges the Philippians not to live as enemies of the cross, like people whose god is their belly and destruction their end (3:18-19). Heavenly citizenship stands in sharp contrast with these folks' focus on earthly things. More important than the Philippians' loyalty to the successors of Julius Caesar and Augustus is their allegiance to Christ Jesus, the Lord (3:20). Heavenly citizenship provides the Philippians with the hope that their bodies will be transformed (3:21). Their citizenship should move them to act in such a way that they manifest their allegiance to Christ and responsibility for one another, "to live [*politeuesthe*] in a manner worthy of the gospel of Christ," as Paul wrote

---

[63] Raymond R. Brewer ("The Meaning of *Politeuesthe* in Philippians 1:27," *JBL* 73 [1954]: 76–83) argues that the question deserves an affirmative reply.

[64] See Lambrecht, "Commonwealth," 205. Reumann opines that the brace of verses may contain a non-Pauline hymn but argues against those who consider these verses to have belonged to the hymn cited by Paul in Philippians 2. See John Reumann, "Philippians 3.20-21—A Hymnic Fragment?" *NTS* 30 (1984): 593–609.

[65] This translation appears in the RSV at 3:20.

[66] Cf. Spicq, "*Politeia, ktl.*," 131.

in 1:27. That is, to live, as Lambrecht notes, "as citizens whose constitution is the gospel."[67]

Striving to live as citizens of heaven, the Philippians will be helped by a gift of God, the very peace of God. As his letter comes to its end, Paul expresses his conviction that "[t]he peace of God, which surpasses all understanding, will guard [*phrourēsei*] your hearts and your minds in Christ Jesus" (4:7). The verb often describes an exercise of the state's police power as it does in 2 Corinthians 11:32. Applied to the personified "peace of God" in 4:7, the verb serves as a metaphor[68] that speaks of the protection with which the God of peace provides the Philippians as they live as citizens of heaven with the gospel of Christ Jesus as their constitution.

*Teammates*

Paul mixes his metaphors in the pericope in which he urges the Philippians to be socially responsible. Having appealed to the Philippians' sense of civic pride in their heavenly citizenship, Paul turns his attention to the athletic arena. Confidently he says that he hopes to learn:

> that you are standing firm in one spirit, striving side by side [*synathlountes*] with one mind for the faith of the gospel, and are in no way intimidated by your opponents [*tōn antikeimenōn*] . . . you are having the same struggle [*ton auton agōna*] that you saw I had and now hear that I still have." (Phil 1:27-28, 30)

The language is that of the athletic event (*agōna*) in which athletes vie together (*synathlountes*) against the opposition, their common opponent (*tōn antikeimenōn*). Even those who are not versed in Greek can recognize the root of the words "athlete" and "athletics" in Paul's participle. The compound verb form is a composite of syn ("with," "together") and *athleō* ("take part in an athletic contest," "be an athlete"), whose root was employed by Simonides and is found on an inscription discovered at Aphrodisias.[69]

---

[67] Lambrecht, "Commonwealth," 199.

[68] Cf. LSJ, 1958, *s.v.*; Tellbe, *Between Synagogue and State*, 249–50. Paul also uses the verb metaphorically in Gal 3:23 in reference to the Law.

[69] Simon. 148, 155, 166; for the inscription see August Böckh, *Corpus Inscriptionum Graecarum* (Berlin: Officina Academica, 1877; repr.: Hildesheim: Olms, 1977), 2.810b.

Paul has a predilection for compound verbs with the prefix *syn*, many of them of his own coinage. He typically makes use of such words to emphasize the believer's union with Christ, but in 1:27 he has a different emphasis. The rare compound "strive side by side"[70] points to the fact that believers at Philippi are not a bunch of individuals in their striving to lead the Christian life in the face of adversity. Rather, they stand together in this struggle; indeed, they participate in the same "contest" as Paul. In this sense, they are teammates[71] with one another and with Paul in the struggle on behalf of the Christian life.

Urging Euodia and Syntyche to be of one mind in the Lord, Paul again uses the image of teammates:

> I urge Euodia and I urge Syntyche to be of the same mind in the Lord. Yes, and I ask you also, my loyal companion, help these women, for they have struggled beside me [*synēthlēsan moi*] in the work of the gospel, together with Clement and the rest of my co-workers, whose names are in the book of life. (Phil 4:2-3)

Apparently the two women had been spatting with one another. Paul's appeal urges them[72] to be united in the Lord and asks an unnamed woman in the congregation to facilitate the reconciliation between the two other women. The reason: both women, together with Paul, Clement, and unnamed other coworkers, had been teammates in the work of the gospel.

For Paul the great struggle to be waged was the common struggle of believers on behalf of the gospel, to preach it and to live it. The proclamation of the gospel provoked opposition and led to persecution. For believers it was truly a struggle, requiring a common effort, mutual support, steadfast endurance, and a willingness to suffer.[73]

Paul's use of the agon motif was influenced by his Hellenistic Jewish heritage and the Philippians' familiarity with the language of the Stoics,

---

[70] The synonym *synagōnizomai* appears far more often in ancient sources. Cf. Rom 15:30.

[71] I owe this translation to one of my former students, Kathleen McGlynn, a star in women's volleyball and basketball during her years at The Catholic University of America.

[72] He repeats the verb *parakalō*, "I urge," so that there is a direct appeal to each of the women.

[73] Influenced by Paul, Clement of Rome wrote about the martyrs who "were persecuted and contended even unto death" (*1 Clement* 5:2).

but it was facilitated by events that took place in the local amphitheater.[74] There, athletic contests regularly took place in honor of various local deities. There, too, the popular imperial games were held, especially gladiatorial contests in honor of the emperor.[75]

## *An Imaginative Exhortation*

Athletic imagery recurs in an exhortation that is enriched by two other and very powerful metaphors:

> Do all things without murmuring[76] and arguing, so that you may be blameless and innocent, children of God without blemish in the midst of a crooked and perverse generation, in which you shine like stars in the world [*phainesthe hōs phōstēres en kosmō*]. It is by your holding fast to the word of life that I can boast on the day of Christ that I did not run [*edramon*] in vain or labor in vain. But even if I am being poured out as a libation over the sacrifice and the offering [*spendomai epi tē thusia kai leitourgia*] of your faith, I am glad and rejoice with all of you—and in the same way you also must be glad and rejoice with me. (Phil 2:14-18)

As important as is Paul's use of one of his favorite images, that of the runner[77] (1 Cor 9:24-26; Gal 2:2;[78] 5:7; Rom 9:16), it is not the athletic imagery of 2:14-18 that is particularly striking. What strikes the reader is Paul's recourse to powerful images drawn respectively from astronomy and worship. A traveler like Paul could not help but notice the stars shining in the sky. Their presence enabled the skippers of the ships in which Paul sailed to find their bearings by night. Shining stars provided a shipwrecked voyager with some hope and consolation as he drifted at sea during the dark of night (2 Cor 11:25). The brightness of the starlit

---

[74] Archeological excavations have revealed a compact amphitheater built during the reign of Antonius Pius (128–61 CE). This second-century amphitheater probably replaced an earlier construction.

[75] See Paul Collart, *Philippes, ville de Macédoine depuis ses origines jusqu'à la fin de l'époque romaine*, École française d'Athènes: Travaux et Mémoires 5 (Paris: E. de Boccard, 1937), 380–87.

[76] "Murmuring" is the onomatopoeic *gongusmōn*.

[77] Since running is hard work, O'Brien (*Philippians*, 303) sees in Paul's "labor in vain" (2:16) another athletic metaphor. In my judgment Paul's repeated "in vain" and his general use of "labor" (*kopiaō*) argue against the claim that Paul has used a second athletic metaphor in 2:17.

[78] Gal 2:2 uses the phraseology of 2:14.

sky enabled Paul to prolong an occasional day's journey as he moved from town to town.

Paul distinguishes stars from the sun and the moon in 1 Corinthians 15:41, a verse in which "star" (*astēr*) occurs three times. In the simile of 2:15, however, Paul does not use the ordinary word for star; rather he uses *phōstēres*, literally, something that gives light. Hapax in Paul, the term essentially evokes a vision of stars shining brightly in the sky. The Greek Bible used this term exclusively for the great lights of heaven, the sun and the moon (Gen 1:14, 16; Wis 13:2; Sir 43:7 [LXX]).

The *kosmos*, the world ordered and created by God, is Paul's horizon. Within this orderly universe there exists the darkness of a crooked and perverse generation, but the Philippians shine like bright stars. From them comes the light of the gospel[79] to which the Philippians remained faithful despite the crookedness and perversity of those around them.

Paul's horizon shifts from the universe to the sanctuary as his train of thought becomes autobiographical: "I am being poured out as a libation over the sacrifice and the offering of your faith." The language is the language of worship: the pouring of a libation (*spendomai*), sacrifice (*thysia*), and offering (*leitourgia*) belong to the realm of cult.[80] Paul compares himself to a drink offering poured on the Philippians' sacrifice. Dating to the Bronze Age, the pouring of a liquid offering as a gift to the deity is one of the oldest religious rituals known to humankind. Practiced almost universally in the ancient world, even in the worship of Israel,[81] libations were sometimes poured over sacrificial offerings. These liquid offerings generally consisted of wine, water, honey, or oil, but they sometimes included the pouring of the blood of a sacrificial animal.[82] As such, libations were a natural symbol for death, especially the death of someone whose life was one of service to God. The libation symbolized the martyr's death which Paul thought to be possibly at hand.[83]

---

[79] So Spicq, "*Phōs, ktl.*," *TLNT* 3:470–491, 487–88.

[80] A somewhat dated overview of these and other cultic metaphors can be found in Albert-Marie Denis, "La fonction apostolique et la liturgie nouvelle en esprit. Étude thématique des métaphores pauliniennes du culte nouveau," *RSPT* 42 (1958): 401–36, 617–56.

[81] See, for example, Lev 23:37, "sacrifices and drink offerings." Phil 2:17 similarly juxtaposes drink offerings and sacrifice.

[82] See Dennis J. McCarthy, "The Symbolism of Blood and Sacrifice," *JBL* 88 (1969): 166–76; "Further Notes on the Symbolism of Blood and Sacrifice," *JBL* 92 (1973): 205–10.

[83] Lohmeyer, Gnilka, Balz, and Tellbe consider the drink offering to be a reference to Paul's possible martyrdom. Balz comments: "Paul wants to accept his approaching

Paul alludes to the ritual as he describes himself as being poured out over the "sacrifice and the offering of your faith" (2:17). Is "sacrifice and offering" a hendiadys to be understood as a single expression, "a sacrificial offering"? Since both sacrifice and offering are part of a priestly function, is Paul to be considered a priestly figure making an offering of the Philippians' faith?[84] Should "your faith" be understood as a subjective genitive, suggesting that the offering proceeds from the faith of the Philippians?[85] In which case, is their offering their own virtuous life[86] or the assistance that they gave to Paul?[87] Or does the offering consist of their faith, with the genitive *tēs pisteōs* taken as a genitive of explanation, so that faith is the offering itself?[88] These few questions are indicative of the complexity of the attempt to comprehend adequately what it was that Paul was saying in 2:17.

Liturgical language recurs in 4:18, whose vocabulary suggests that the "sacrifice and offering" of 2:17 at the very least alludes to the gifts that Paul received: "I have received from Epaphroditus the gifts you sent, a fragrant offering, a sacrifice acceptable and pleasing to God." Given Paul's predilection for triads, the absence of any conjunction in Greek, and the rhythm of the phrase, the sacrificial language of 2:17 should be taken as a triad of reciprocally interpreting expressions: "a fragrant offering, an acceptable sacrifice, and pleasing to God."

---

martyrdom joyfully as a 'drink offering,'" but Gnilka correctly observes that Paul's martyrdom would hardly be a source of joy for the Philippians. See Horst Balz, "*Leitourgia, ktl.*," *EDNT* 2:347–49, 348; Lohmeyer, *Die Briefe*, 113; Gnilka, *Philipperbrief*, 155; Tellbe, *Between Synagogue and State*, 226. Focusing on joy, Collange holds that the libation refers only to Paul's apostolic activity. See Collange, *Philippians*, 113, with reference to Denis, "La fonction," 630–45.

[84] Thus, Beare, who translates *leitourgia* as "priestly service" (*Philippians*, 94). Similarly, Lohmeyer, *Die Briefe*, 113; Gerhard Friedrich, "Der Brief an die Philipper" in Jürgen Becker et al., *Die Briefe an die Galater, Epheser, Philipper, Kolosser, Thessalonicher und Philemon*, NTD 8, 14th ed. (Göttingen: Vandenhoeck und Ruprecht, 1976), 125–75, 156; and Gnilka, *Philipperbrief*, 155.

[85] Thus, Caird, *Letters from Prison*, 127.

[86] So ibid.; Beare, *Philippians*, 94.

[87] Scholars who take this route generally make reference to the presence of *leitourgia* in 2:30. Beare, who opts for the Christian life as the basic connotation of *leitourgia* in 2:17, adds that there might be a "specific reference" to the material supplies provided by the Philippians.

[88] So J. L. Houlden, *Paul's Letters from Prison: Philippians, Colossians, Philemon and Ephesians*, PNTC (Harmondsworth, GB: Penguin, 1970), 88; similarly, Gnilka, *Philipperbrief*, 155, and Spicq, "*Leitourgia, ktl.*," *TLNT* 2:378–86, 383.

The biblical term "fragrant offering" (*osmēn euōdias*), often used in reference to Levitical offerings (Lev 1:9, 13, 17, etc.),[89] described the pleasantly odiferous sacrifices offered to God since the time of Noah (Gen 8:21). The expression evokes the picturesque image of God enjoying the smell of the sacrifices that are offered. To this evocative description of the Philippians' gifts, Paul adds another: "an acceptable sacrifice." The word "sacrifice" (*thysia*), occurring hundreds of times in the Greek Bible, was used for all kinds of sacrifice, both animal and cereal. The equivalent Hebrew term was later used of spiritual sacrifices, like the prayer and praise of the Qumran community (1QS 8:7-9; 9:3-5; 10:6). The sacrifice of the Philippians is not only acceptable; it is also pleasing to God (*euareston tō theō*). As far as God is concerned, the gifts given to Paul are like the sweet-smelling, acceptable, and pleasing offerings of God's people of old. Paul's cultic language underscores the religious value of the support that the Philippians gave to the apostle in his hour of need.

Interpreting the liturgical language of 2:17, Joachim Gnilka understands "faith" to be the equivalent of "offering."[90] For him, "faith" refers to the entire life of faith. The Philippians' sacrificial offering includes their prayer, their preaching of the gospel, and their support of Paul. The emphasis lies on the Philippians' life of faith, the source of Paul's joy. The apostle desires that the Philippians likewise rejoice in their life of faith. Paul is willing to add[91] his own martyrdom, should it occur, to their life of faith, an offering to God and a witness to the gospel.

## Paul's Companions

Before urging the Philippians, his "brothers and sisters," to rejoice (3:1a), Paul speaks about Timothy and Epaphroditus, whom he intended to send to the Philippians. He hoped that Timothy would return from Philippi with good news about the community of believers, news that would cheer Paul up.[92] Timothy is to Paul "like a son with a father" (*hōs patri teknon*, 2:22). Ostensibly this is because Timothy worked with Paul

---

[89] See Baldanza, "La portata teologica."

[90] The grammatical form would be a genitive of explanation. See Gnilka, *Philipperbrief*, 154–55.

[91] O'Brien (*Philippians*, 307) takes the preposition *epi*, "over" (NRSV) as "in addition to."

[92] Cf. 1 Thess 3:1-10.

in proclaiming the gospel.[93] Yet, there is more in Paul's use of the simile than the mere fact that Timothy was one of Paul's coworkers.

For the rabbis, it was a father's duty to teach the Torah to his sons (*b. Qidd.* 22a). When a man taught the Torah to someone who was not his own son, his instruction was considered comparable to having begotten the child (*b. Sanh.* 19b). The young man became like a son to his teacher. Paul shares this point of view, substituting, as a Christian, the gospel for the Torah. Those to whom Paul preached the gospel, those evangelized by the apostle, were his children (1 Cor 4:15; Phlm 10). Notwithstanding Acts 16:1-3, Timothy seems to have been introduced to the Christian tradition by Paul and was therefore to be considered as Paul's son.[94]

An old Jewish proverb proclaimed the wisdom of a father teaching his son his own trade because of his love for the child.[95] As a loyal child, Timothy worked with Paul in the proclamation of the gospel (2:22; 1 Cor 16:10). No wonder Paul could say that Timothy was like a son to him. Timothy even shared Paul's sentiments;[96] no one was as genuinely concerned for the Philippians' well-being as was Timothy (2:20).

Paul considers Timothy to be like a son; he considers Epaphroditus to be like a brother. Multiplying epithets to describe the gift-bearing envoy who had become gravely ill while at Paul's side, Paul praises Epaphroditus, "my brother and co-worker and fellow soldier, your messenger and minister to my need" (2:25). The kinship language evokes the affection that linked Paul and his caretaker. Sent by the Philippians to care for Paul, Epaphroditus was their messenger, a minister[97] to the imprisoned Paul.

As one who worked with Paul in preaching the gospel, Epaphroditus is described as Paul's coworker and fellow soldier (*synergon kai systratiōtēn*). Military officers, including Julius Caesar,[98] sometimes em-

---

[93] In 1 Thess 2:11 Paul used paternal language to speak about both himself and Timothy. See Pedro Gutierrez, *La Paternité spirituelle selon saint Paul*, EBib. (Paris: Gabalda, 1968), 87–117.

[94] Cf. 1 Cor 4:17; 1 Tim 1:2; 2 Tim 1:2.

[95] See John 5:19-20.

[96] The word *isopsychon* means "of like mind," a kindred spirit."

[97] The Greek word is *leitourgon*, akin to the *leitourgia* of 2:17. There is no need to speak of a cultic metaphor; etymologically the terms suggest "the work of the people." The term *leitourgos* was often used to describe someone who rendered service to another, as it does in 2:25.

[98] Caesar addressed his troops as *commilitiones* (Suetonius, *Julius* 67). Before the battle of Philippi in 42 BCE, Brutus is said to have addressed his troops as "O, fellow

ployed "fellow soldier" as a title of honor to praise their troops. Since neither Paul nor Epaphroditus were soldiers in the Roman army, the military language[99] is metaphorical, an example of the agon motif.[100] The image of Paul and Epaphroditus as comrades in arms evokes the idea of the common struggle[101] involved in the preaching of the gospel. The preacher encounters difficulties, opposition, and even persecution. Like Paul, Epaphroditus endured a lot for the sake of the gospel of Christ. Paul's metaphor points to their camaraderie, their struggle, and the adversity that they faced together.

Paul's military imagery is particularly apropos, not only because of the presence of the military during Paul's imprisonment (1:13; 4:22), but also because Philippi was a military town. The city was settled by veterans of the Roman armies, including the troops of Octavian and Marc Anthony, victors in the battle of Philippi (42 BCE) and members of the praetorian guard (cf. Phil 1:13) who settled in Philippi after Anthony's defeat by Octavian (Augustus).

## A Pack of Animals

Having urged the Philippians to rejoice (3:1a), Paul's tone changes dramatically. He exhorts the Philippians to "beware of the dogs, beware of evil workers, beware of those who mutilate the flesh!" (3:2). The dramatic change of tone leads many scholars to consider that canonical Philippians is a composite of fragments of two letters.[102] A study of Paul's use of metaphor does not require extensive consideration of the issue of the integrity of the letter, but it is noteworthy that the images of the so-called Letter B (Phil 3:1b–4:1, 8-9) are very earthy. Were they not found

---

soldiers (*ō systratiōtai*)." See Appian, *Civil Wars* 4.117; cf. Polyaenus, *Strategemata* 8.23.22.

[99] See Tellbe, *Between Synagogue and State*, 247–48.

[100] Military imagery was also used by Philo who, however, did not use the compound "fellow soldier." See Philo, *Allegorical Interpretation* 3.14; *Drunkenness* 75–76.

[101] The prefix *syn*, "co-," "fellow," highlights the common activity of Paul and Epaphroditus.

[102] Among them are Gnilka (*Philipperbrief*, 5–11), Joseph Fitzmyer ("The Letter to the Philippians," *JBC* 247–53, 248), and Brendan Byrne ("The Letter to the Philippians," *NJBC* 791–97, 791–92). Beare (*Philippians*, 1–5) and a few other authors consider the canonical text to be a composite of three epistolary fragments. See the discussions of the integrity of the letter by John T. Fitzgerald, "Philippians, Epistle to," *ABD* 5:318–26, 320–22; and O'Brien, *Philippians*, 10–18.

in the canonical Scriptures, ecclesiastical censors might find them offensive to pious ears.

Paul begins by labeling the opponents a pack of "dogs" (*kynas*), his only use of such language. In the biblical tradition dogs, hyenas, vultures, and pigs were considered to be despicable animals. Prowling around as they do, they eat whatever is thrown out as garbage. Attacking the weak and defenseless, they were thought to be dangerous.[103] The idea that dogs are dangerous and base animals appears in Josephus and the tale of *Joseph and Aseneth*.[104] A saying attributed to Jesus in the *Gospel of Thomas* illustrates people's opinion of dogs: "Do not give what is holy to dogs, lest they throw it on the dung-heap" (*G. Thom.* 93).

Warning the Philippians to beware of the dogs, Paul speaks in derogatory terms about the opponents of the gospel. To complement his picture, Paul adds the demeaning epithets "evil-doers" and "mutilators." The multiplication of these mutually interpreting terms serves Paul's rhetoric well. The opponents of the gospel are simply no good.

Although the NRSV translates the third of Paul's passionate warnings as "beware of those who mutilate the flesh," his Greek really means "beware of mutilation" (*blepete tēn katatomēn*). The image is a good example of Paul's ability to play on words. He uses the rhetorical technique of paronomsia, a play on words that sound alike. "Mutilation" (*katatomē*), hapax in the New Testament, contrasts with "circumcision" (*peritomē*) in which Paul and other Jews take pride (3:3). Paul's pun (3:2-3) and his rehearsal of the sources of his Jewish pride (3:3-6) suggest that those of whom the Philippians should be wary are "Judaizers" who want Gentile Christians in Philippi to be circumcised.[105]

Having derided those who opposed his gospel, Paul listed the claims to privilege that he had as a Jew. As he considers the value of his claims to fame and privilege, his language becomes calculating and scatological. Using street language Paul says, "I regard them as rubbish, in order that I may gain Christ" (3:8). "Rubbish" (*skybala*), a word that is not otherwise used in the New Testament, means scraps, rubbish, or refuse.[106] The term

---

[103] See Exod 22:31; 1 Sam 17:43; 2 Kgs 8:13; Ps 22:17, 21; Isa 56:11; etc.

[104] See Josephus, *Jewish Antiquities* 15.289; *Jewish War* 4.324; *Joseph and Aseneth* 10:13; 11:1; 13:8. Cf. Rev 22:15.

[105] Paul deals with the Judaizers in the churches of Galatia in much the same fashion. See Gal 5:12.

[106] Spicq notes that the word was also used of a rotting human corpse. See Spicq, "*Skybalon*," *TLNT* 3:263–65, 263.

was commonly used to describe dung[107] or excrement. Pleading for a more faithful translation of the New Testament, Émile Osty attempted to convey the earthiness of Paul's language, saying, "It's crap."[108]

Continuing his personal reflection (3:12-16), Paul returns to the stadium: "straining forward [*epekteinomenos*] to what lies ahead, I press on toward the goal for the prize [*brabeion*] of the heavenly call of God in Christ Jesus" (3:13-14). Paul previously compared himself to a runner (2:16). With a similar eschatological horizon, he anticipates the prize that will be his on that day. His prize (*brabeion*[109]) will be the victor's laurel. The language comes from the sports arena where such prizes were given to those who won the races. With this as a clue, one can see in Paul's "straining forward"—*epekteinomenos*, a participial form of a verb meaning "stretch" or "extend"—the image of the runner lunging forward as he crosses the finish line.

Throughout Philippians Paul ponders the possibility of his imminent death. The athletic imagery of 3:13-14 suggests that Paul's race is coming to an end, all the while proclaiming his conviction that he will have run a successful race.

The next pericope (3:17–4:1) contains a mixed bag of metaphors. Paul introduces his plea that the Philippians imitate him by appealing to the sibship that they enjoy, calling them his "brothers and sisters." He uses the verb "walk" to speak both of the lifestyle of the Philippians (3:17) and of the way that the enemies of the cross were living their lives (3:18).

Writing about the enemies of the cross, Paul uses language that is as graphic as it is demeaning: "Their god is the belly" (*hōn ho theos hē koilia*, 3:19).[110] What is the meaning of this striking image? Since those about whom Paul had previously used derogatory language were most likely Judaizers (3:2), some commentators hold that Paul is writing about Judaizers who maintain that the observation of dietary laws is an expression of fidelity to God.[111] On the other hand, Philo considers the belly to be the seat of passion: "To the lustful portion of the soul they assign the

---

[107] In the KJV "dung" is used as the translation of *skybala*.

[108] See Émile Osty, "Pour une traduction plus fidèle du N.T.," in [Institut catholique de Paris], *Mémorial du Cinquantenaire 1914–1964*, Travaux de l'Institut catholique de Paris 10 (Paris: Bloud & Gay, 1964), 81–96, 82.

[109] In the NT the term appears only in 3:14 and 1 Cor 9:24.

[110] Cf. Rom 16:18.

[111] See, for example, Johannes Behm, "*Koilia*," TDNT 3:786–89, 788.

quarter about the abdomen and the belly, for there it is that lust, irrational craving, has its abode" (*Allegorical Interpretation* 3.115).[112] From this perspective, Paul's "belly" might be a metonym for the satisfaction of passion and physical desire.[113] That Paul uses "belly" in Romans 16:18 in this metonymic sense and that his usage is somewhat similar to that of 3:19[114] suggest that "belly" may refer to the satisfaction of passions.

Friedrich,[115] however, noting that the Bible sometimes uses "belly" as a synecdochic epithet for the human person, opines that Paul's metaphor describes those who live in that self-centered fashion which Paul usually describes as living in the flesh (Gal 5:19-21, for example). Since Paul does not rail against the human passions as did some of his disciples, and since his anthropology draws heavily on the Bible, it is probably along these lines that Paul's metaphor is to be understood. "Their god is their belly" is a graphically demeaning synecdochic expression for those who live "in the flesh," people concerned only with themselves, folks whose lives are not touched by the gospel and the Spirit. In contrast with those who are so earthly, whom Paul can describe in such earthy language, are the Philippians whose citizenship is in heaven (3:20).

Should the canonical Letter to the Philippians be a two-part composite text, its second fragment most likely concludes with the peroration found in 4:1, 8-9. Paul again addresses the Philippians as his siblings (4:1; cf. Phil 3:13, 17), expressing his love and desire for them, calling them his joy and his crown (*stephanos mou*). The image recalls the victor's crown at the end of a race.

Many commentators opine that the crown to which Paul is referring is the crown that will be his on the Day of the Lord.[116] It is, however, not certain that Paul's perspective is the eschaton.[117] Paul appears to consider

---

[112] Similarly, *Allegorical Interpretation* 3.116. The *Letter of Aristeas* (140) contrasts the "men of God" with "those who are concerned with meat and drink and clothes, their whole attitude (to life) being concentrated on these concerns."

[113] Thus, Caird, *Letters from Prison*, 136; Beare, *Philippians*, 136.

[114] In Rom 16:18 Paul contrasts serving the Lord Christ with serving one's "belly," while Phil 3:18 invites a comparison between god and the belly. Paul's only other uses of the word *koilia* are in 1 Cor 6:13 and Gal 1:15, where the word is used in a physical sense, in 1 Cor 6:13 to refer to the stomach, in Gal 1:15 to the womb.

[115] Friedrich, "Brief an die Philipper," 165; similarly, Lohmeyer, *Die Briefe*, 155; Gnilka, *Philipperbrief*, 105–6.

[116] Thus, for example, Lohmeyer, *Die Briefe*, 164; Friedrich, "Brief an die Philipper," 167; Gnilka, *Philipperbrief*, 220.

[117] Cf. 1 Thess 2:19.

the Philippians to be his joy and crown even as he writes. His death may be at hand, but he presently considers the Philippians to be his joy and his crown. Perhaps there is some analogy with the mystagogues' practice of placing a laurel upon their head in anticipation of their death during the ritual of initiation into the mysteries.[118]

## Summing Up

The gifts that the Philippians sent to Paul via Epaphroditus helped Paul and warmed his heart (4:10). Their concern for Paul was like a fresh flowering of their faith. Like a new bloom (*anethalete*, 4:10), their concern for him revived. This analogy comes from agriculture. The metaphor is unusual in this letter insofar as its metaphors were generally drawn from the sociopolitical environment in which his addressees lived. He used political metaphors that would make a powerful impact among the citizens of an extraterritorial Roman colony.[119] He used the military metaphors that would be meaningful in a city populated by old soldiers. He used the image of the athletic arena for people who reveled in the imperial games. He used the language of worship and the language of the street. And for the inhabitants of a city that was so strikingly Roman, he used the idiom of the Stoics whose philosophy and language was that of the empire itself.[120]

---

[118] See Heinrich Kraft, "*Stephanos, ktl.*," *EDNT* 3:273–74, 274.

[119] Cf. Tellbe, *Between Synagogue and State*, 243.

[120] Ibid., 249.

# 4

# The Letter to Philemon

The Letter to Philemon appears in the canonical New Testament after the letters to Timothy and Titus. The compilers of the New Testament apparently considered this missive to have been a personal letter from Paul to his friend Philemon. In fact, the letter has many of the characteristics of a personal letter, but it is not a letter addressed to one person. Like the letters to the Corinthians, Galatians, and Thessalonians, Philemon is ultimately addressed to a church, the one that met in Philemon's house.

The letter belongs to what Pseudo-Demetrius calls the supplicatory form of letter, the *typos axiomatikos* (*Epistolary Types* 12). It was not written to say "Hello. How are you?" It was written because Paul had a serious request to make. Paul wanted to plead the case of Philemon's slave, Onesimus, who was then with the imprisoned Paul. Onesimus seems to have taken advantage of a provision of Roman law that allowed an aggrieved slave to appeal to one of the master's friends, the *amicus domini*, asking that he intercede with the master on the slave's behalf.[1]

Paul's letter asks that Philemon accept Onesimus back into his household—perhaps the reason why the letter was addressed to the church

---

[1] See the discussion in Gerhard Friedrich, "Der Brief an Philemon," in Jürgen Becker et al., *Die Briefe an die Galater, Epheser, Philipper, Kolosser, Thessalonicher und Philemon*, 277–86, 284–85, and in Joseph A. Fitzmyer, *The Letter to Philemon*, AB 34C (New York: Doubleday, 2000), 20–23. These authors refer to correspondence from Pliny the Younger to Sabinianus. Fitzmyer also mentions an incident in the life of Caesar Augustus as evidence of the practice.

which gathered in Philemon's house[2]—no longer as an ordinary slave but as a fellow believer, because Onesimus had become a Christian in the course of his visit with Paul.

A remarkable feature of this short letter is the way in which Paul uses kinship metaphors to make his plea. Without these metaphors, Paul's argument would have been far less convincing than it was. Putting oneself into Philemon's sandals, the reader must, with Philemon, begin at the beginning of the letter.

## The Salutation

Including the church in Philemon's house, there are six literary characters in the letter's first few verses: "Paul, a prisoner of Christ Jesus, and Timothy our brother, To Philemon our dear friend and co-worker, to Apphia our sister, to Archippus our fellow soldier, and to the church in your house" (Phlm 1-2). The titles given to each of the named individuals are striking, as is the designation of the locale of the gathering. The *intitulationes* of ancient letters were neither merely descriptive nor identifying; they were intended to establish the letter writer's authority vis-à-vis those to whom he was writing. Thus, the titles of Philemon 1-2 become a powerful instrument in the rhetoric of Paul's appeal.

The apostle's description of himself as a prisoner of Christ Jesus, imprisoned because of his fidelity to Christ Jesus, was designed to win the sympathy of his addressees. It would be difficult for them to say no to a request from an acquaintance who was in prison, especially when he had been imprisoned not because he was the perpetrator of some crime but because he was faithful to Christ Jesus.

Paul creates a family atmosphere as the setting for his request by describing Timothy, his companion, as "our[3] brother." Having thus identified Timothy, Paul identifies those to whom he is writing. Apphia is identified as a member of the family. Since patristic times it has been argued that Apphia was probably the wife of Philemon.[4] That may be

---

[2] Unlike the English language that distinguishes "house," a building, from "household," the inhabitants of that building, the Greek words *oikos* (Phlm 2) and *oikia* have a gamut of meanings ranging from structures to those who dwell in them.

[3] The pronominal adjective "our" (*hēmōn*) appears four times in the NRSV translation of Phlm 1–2. In the Greek text, the pronoun appears only twice, qualifying "coworker" and "fellow soldier" but not "brother" or "sister."

[4] See especially the writings of Chrysostom and Theodoret. Among recent commentators, see Eduard Lohse, *Colossians and Philemon*, Hermeneia (Philadelphia:

so, but Paul does not identify her as Philemon's wife; he identifies her[5] as a believer, "our sister," a member of the same fictive family as himself and Timothy. Belonging to the same family, Paul, Timothy, and Apphia were at home in Philemon's house.

Philemon is described as Paul's friend, someone who was loved (*tō agapētō*) by the imprisoned Paul. Philemon is also portrayed as having worked with Paul in the task of evangelization. He is "our co-worker" (*synergō hēmōn*), an epithet that Paul uses to describe other promoters of the gospel, such as Timothy (1 Thess 3:2; Rom 16:21), Titus (2 Cor 8:23), Prisca and Aquila (Rom 16:3), Urbanus (Rom 16:9), Epaphroditus (Phil 2:25), and Clement (Phil 4:3). Presumably, Philemon labored on behalf of the gospel in the area of Asia Minor where he and his household dwelt, perhaps in and around the city of Colossae.

Employing the agon motif, Paul describes the otherwise unknown Archippus as "our fellow soldier." Imprisoned, Paul was certainly not on active duty when he was writing this letter. Moreover, as a Jew, he would have been exempt from service in the Roman army. Only in a metaphorical sense can he describe Archippus as a fellow soldier.[6]

The epithets that appear in these first verses set a dramatic rhetorical setting for his appeal on behalf of Onesimus. Having described his own situation as a prisoner for the sake of Christ, thereby assuring that his audience would listen to the reading of the letter with ears and hearts at the ready (see Phlm 9), Paul writes about the family, friendship, the common task of evangelization, and a common struggle to ensure a favorable response to his plea for Onesimus. The powerful metaphors of family and of the agon were very much a part of the setting.

### Mutual Love

Paul heard about Philemon's love for all the saints (Phlm 5). To a large extent his appeal is based on Philemon's renowned love.[7] "I would rather

---

Fortress, 1971), 190; Joachim Gnilka, *Der Philemonbrief*, HKKNT 10/4 (Freiburg: Herder, 1982), 16; O'Brien, *Colossians, Philemon*, 273; James D. G. Dunn, *The Epistles to the Colossians and to Philemon*, NIGTC (Grand Rapids, MI: Eerdmans and Carlisle, UK: Paternoster, 1996), 312.

[5] See Florence Morgan Gillman, "Apphia," *ABD* 1:317–18; *Women Who Knew Paul*, Zacchaeus Studies: New Testament (Wilmington, DE: Glazier, 1992), 76–78.

[6] Cf. Phil 2:25.

[7] Friedrich observes, "The working out of love in the Christian life is one of the important themes of the Letter to Philemon (vv. 5, 7, 9, 16)" ("Der Brief an Philemon," 280). See also Lohse, *Colossians and Philemon*, 195; Dunn, *Epistles*, 321. Commenting

appeal to you," he writes, "on the basis of love" (Phlm 9). He was encouraged by Philemon's expression of love since "the hearts [*ta splanchna*] of the saints" (Phlm 7) were refreshed because of Philemon. To be refreshed (*anapepautai*) is to rest; used of persons, the verb means not only to rest but also to regain one's strength. Paul is not thinking about the physical strength of God's holy ones; he is thinking about their inner renewal.

To speak about these people at the core of their very being, Paul employs a metaphor used in Philippians. He says that their very innards (*ta splanchna*) have been renewed. They have been renewed to the depths of their very being as a result of Philemon's love. "The word [*splanchna*]," writes Helmut Koester, "is used . . . for the whole person which in the depths of its emotional life has experienced refreshment through consolation and love."[8]

The innards and all that this metaphor evokes are an important part of the rhetoric of this short letter. The metaphor appears more often in this brief note than in the longer letters in which the figure appears (Phil 1:8; 2:1; 2 Cor 6:12; 7:15). Paul uses the image to speak about his own heart: "I am sending him [Onesimus], that is, my own heart[9] [*tout'estin ta ema splanchna*], back to you" (Phlm 12). Such is the depth of Paul's relationship with Onesimus that he can speak of Onesimus as a profound part of his very being, his innards,[10] almost his very self (Phlm 17). F. Forrester Church comments, "He [Paul] doesn't substitute himself for Onesimus: He embodies himself in him."[11] Toward the end of the letter, Paul makes one last appeal to Philemon, writing, "Yes, brother, let me have this benefit from you in the Lord! Refresh my heart [*anapauson mou ta splanchna*] in Christ" (Phlm 20).

Paul's plea is based on his fictive sibling relationship with Philemon (Phlm 7). It employs the fraternal formula of direct address that Paul employed in verse 7 to describe the effects of Philemon's renowned love for all the saints. If Philemon had such a love for all the saints that they

on verse 9, Caird somewhat simplistically writes: "Philemon is to be guided in doing the right thing by *love* alone" (*Letters from Prison*, 221, his emphasis!).

[8] See Helmut Koester, "*Splanchnon, ktl.,*" *TDNT* 7:548–59, 555.

[9] "Bowels" is the translation of Paul's *splanchna* in the KJV and the RSV.

[10] According to Eusebius, Dionysius the Great, bishop of Alexandria (d. ca. 264 CE), used similar language to describe the faithful of Alexandria: "I have great need to send epistolary addresses to those who are as my own bowels [*splanchna*], my associates and dearest brethren and members of the same church" (Eusebius, *Ecclesiastical History* 7.21.3).

[11] F. Forrester Church, "Rhetorical Structure and Design in Paul's Letter to Philemon," *HTR* 71 (1978): 17–33, 27.

were inwardly renewed by various expressions of Philemon's generosity, could Paul expect anything less from his friend, fellow evangelist, partner (Phlm 17), and brother (Phlm 7, 20)? A modern commentator might quip that Paul has made a really gutsy appeal to Philemon.

## A Family Matter

The crux of Paul's appeal to Philemon is that he is writing about a family matter. Philemon is not only Paul's friend and fellow evangelist, but he is also Paul's brother (Phlm 7, 20). Apphia is Paul's sister (Phlm 2). The group to whom the missive is addressed gathers in Philemon's home. The unusual mention of Apphia in the list of addressees and the epithet "sister" that is used of her may suggest that as the "lady of the house"[12] she would have had a particular responsibility with regard to household matters, including the supervision of slaves.

The crux of Paul's plea appears in the middle of the letter:

> I am appealing to you for my child, Onesimus, whose father I have become during my imprisonment . . . so that you might have him back forever, no longer as a slave but as more than a slave, a beloved brother—especially to me but how much more to you, both in the flesh and in the Lord. (Phlm 10, 15b-16)

The Onesimus who is about to be sent back to the slaveholder is not the same Onesimus who came to request help from Paul, his master's friend. Paul evangelized Onesimus; doing so, he became his father. Paul acknowledges Onesimus's new state by calling him "my child" (*tou emou teknou*, Phlm 10), "whose father I have become during my imprisonment." Literally translated, the phrase (*hon egennēsa en tois desmois*) reads: "whom I have begotten while in chains." Onesimus is Paul's love child, his very heart (*ta ema splanchna*, Phlm 12).

The image of father and son provides Paul's letter with powerful rhetorical force. The apostle appeals to the members of his fictive family on behalf of the child whom he has begotten while in prison. What family member could resist such a plea, a heartfelt request to accept a newborn child into their home?

Paul uses the figure of a father to describe the relationship that had developed between himself and Onesimus because he had evangelized

---

[12] So, Lohse, *Colossians and Philemon*, 190.

the slave. Among Jews it was considered a father's responsibility to teach the Torah to his sons. When another person assumed that role, that other person was considered to have been as a father to the young man, the child a son to him. The Talmud attests to various rabbinic dicta confirming this idea.[13] A convert to Judaism newly introduced into the Torah and the lore of Judaism was like a "child just born" (*b. Yebam.* 22a). Qumran's Teacher of Righteousness proclaims in praise of God: "Thou hast made me a father unto sons of kindness and a nursing-father to men of wonder and they have opened (their) mouths as suckl[ings of the breasts of his mother and] as the play of a child in the bosom of his nursing fathers" (1QH 7:20-22).[14]

Paul uses a paternal image in the letter to the Thessalonians, encouraging them like a father to lead their lives in a manner that was worthy of God (1 Thess 2:9-12). In Philippians 2:22 he describes Timothy as being to him like a son with his father. He commends Timothy as a beloved and faithful child (1 Cor 4:17). He portrays the Galatians as his children (Gal 4:19). Now he says that Onesimus is his newborn son. Little wonder then that the letter can describe Onesimus as Paul's innards. In his biblical tradition children are often described as being in the loins of their father or ancestor. Since Onesimus is a member of the family, Paul pleads with Philemon to accept him into the household "no longer as a slave but more than a slave, a beloved brother,"[15] a beloved member of the family.

For an appreciation of the full effect of Paul's family language, the letter must be read in Greek. Paul uses sibship language to speak of Timothy, Apphia, and Philemon before he mentions Onesimus. He makes an appeal on the basis of love, still without mentioning Onesimus. He pleads on behalf of the child whom he has begotten while he languished as a prisoner in chains. Only then does he name the child whom he had begotten. Onesimus[16] is the last word in the Greek text of verse 10.

---

[13] See Str-B 3:339.

[14] The translation is that of Menahem Mansoor, *The Thanksgiving Hymns*, STDJ 3 (Leiden: Brill, 1961), 150–51. Cf. CD 13:9. Philo describes an unruly Gaius taunting his mentor Marco. Gaius suggests that Marco boasted, "It is I Marco who made Gaius, I am his begetter (*gegennēka*) more or not less than his parents" (*Embassy* 8, par. 58).

[15] Cicero (*Epistulae ad familiares* 16.16.1) says that he freed Tiro, the literate and competent slave to whom he dictated many letters and to whom he addressed twenty-one of his letters, so that he would be "our friend instead of our slave."

[16] Cf. Col 4:9. The word *onēsimos* was a common adjective meaning "useful." The root *onēsi-* suggests use or advantage. Paul creates a pun on Onesimus's name by

## Debts to Be Paid?

Before bringing his short note to a close, Paul discusses the financial issues that might arise upon Onesimus's return. A financial issue might have been the source of the difficulty between Philemon and Onesimus. Perhaps Onesimus had not wisely administered some funds; perhaps he had stolen some money or other property. In any event, Paul uses the language of accounting as he considers the matter. A conditional clause shows that a financial obligation on Onesimus's part is only a possibility:

> If he has wronged [*ēdikēsen*] you in any way, or owes [*opheilei*] you anything, charge that to my account [*touto emoi elloga*]. I, Paul, am writing this with my own hand: I will repay it [*apotisō*]. I say nothing about your owing me [*moi prosopheileis*] even your own self. Yes, brother, let me have this benefit [*onaimēn*] from you in the Lord! (Phlm 18-20a)

The financial language[17] is not common in the New Testament. "Charge to an account" (*elloga*), "repay" (*apotisō*, normally meaning "pay in full"), and "benefit" (*onaimēn*) do not appear elsewhere in the New Testament.

The hypothetical situation[18] is that Onesimus has wronged Philemon. "Wronged" (*ēdikēsen*) can be used to describe just about any kind of harmful behavior,[19] but the verb was often used to describe theft or shoddy work. "Owes" was commonly used as a metaphor to mean "be indebted to,"[20] but its proper sense is "have to pay (money)" as rent or in repayment of a loan.[21] "Charge it to my account" (*touto emoi elloga*) is

---

means of the antithesis between *euchrēstos* and *achrēstos*. *Euchrēstos* is a synonym of *onēsimos*.

[17] Dunn (*Epistles*, 336) characterizes the entire passage as "a sustained commercial metaphor. . . . This is no doubt in large part because slavery was itself a commercial transaction."

[18] There is no reason to suppose that Onesimus had stolen something from his master, as older commentators were to assume. See, for example, H. A. W. Meyer, *The Epistle to the Ephesians and Philemon* (Edinburgh: T&T Clark, 1880), 378; Caird, *Letters from Prison*, 222–23. It is more likely that Paul is using the rhetorical device of anticipation (cf. *Rhetoric to Alexander*, 36), setting aside any objection that Philemon might have to accepting Onesimus back into his household.

[19] Thus, Lohmeyer (*Die Briefe*, 190), holding the traditional opinion that Onesimus was a runaway slave, considers Onesimus's flight to have been the injustice inflicted upon Philemon.

[20] A metaphor in English as well.

[21] See MM 3784.

clearly the language of someone who assumes a financial responsibility on behalf of someone else just as it is in the language that we use today.

Despite Paul's uncertainty about the circumstances, he underscores the seriousness of the responsibility that he has undertaken by means of a hand-written IOU, "I am writing this with my own hand: I will repay it." He promises to make proper compensation to Philemon for whatever debts Onesimus may have incurred. The IOU supports the promise that Paul makes in verse 18.

Did Paul, writing from prison, have the possibility to pay back to Philemon anything that Onesimus might have owed? Since slaves were not always without some financial resources in the ancient world, did Paul also expect Onesimus to contribute to the compensation to be rendered?

These questions are almost impossible to answer for many reasons, not the least of which is that immediately after writing about a debt that might need to be repaid Paul begins to use financial language in a figurative sense. Paul is willing to incur a debt on behalf of Onesimus, but Philemon owes a spiritual debt to Paul.[22] Paul's rhetorical preterition emphasizes the debt: "I say nothing about your owing [*prosopheilas*] me even your own self" (Phlm 19b). The compound verb (*pros-opheilas*)[23] adds additional emphasis, implying either that Philemon's debt to Paul was long overdue or perhaps that Philemon himself was responsible for Onesimus's debt. Philemon," writes Eduard Lohse, "will understand that within this relationship one can no longer balance debt against debt."[24]

Within this perspective, Paul asks that he may receive some profit (*onaimēn*, Phlm 20),[25] that is, some benefit from Philemon. The benefit that he wants to receive is a positive response to his plea, namely, that Philemon accept Onesimus, the slave, back into his household, now as a member of the family—certainly without any financial obligation on the part of Onesimus, perhaps none on the part of Paul as well.

---

[22] In an essay titled "The Rhetorical Function of Commercial Language in Paul's Letter to Philemon (Verse 18)," Clarice J. Martin describes Philemon as a "metaphorical debtor." See Duane F. Watson, ed., *Persuasive Artistry: Studies in New Testament Rhetoric in Honor of George A. Kennedy*, JSNTSup 50 (Sheffield, UK: JSOT, 1991), 321–37, 337.

[23] The verb is an emphatic form of the verb used in verse 8 to speak about the debt that Onesimus might have incurred.

[24] Lohse, *Colossians and Philemon*, 205.

[25] Both *prosopheilō*, "owe," and *onaimamai*, "have benefit," are hapax in the New Testament.

The short note is a letter in which the image of the family plays a powerful role. Were it not for the Letter to the Galatians, one might say that in no other text of the New Testament does kinship language have such importance as it does in the Letter to Philemon and the church in his house.

# 5

# The Letter to the Galatians

T he apostle's first letter is a warm document. His affection for the Thessalonians is evident at every turn. Rather than chiding them, he gently helps them to overcome the lacuna in their faith (1 Thess 4:13-18). In contrast, Paul's Letter to the Galatians is a stern document. Paul's passion, if not his anger, is apparent. He shows himself to be not above name-calling and confrontation (1:20; 2:6, 11, 14; 3:1, 3-4; 4:20; 5:10, 12). There is hardly a soothing word in the entire letter. Instead, Paul affirms his authority from the get go (1:1-2). He omits the words of thanksgiving that customarily follow the opening salutation. Instead of expressing gratitude, Paul begins the body of his letter by writing, "I am astonished that you are so quickly deserting the one who called you" (1:6).

Paul was irritated because some "Judaizers" had come from Jerusalem, teaching that even Gentile Christians had to be circumcised if they were to be saved. This went contrary to the gospel that Paul preached. He had proclaimed that we are justified by faith in Christ (2:16). Any further requirements placed on the Galatian believers would make both Paul's preaching and their faith in vain.

## The Courtroom

To make this point Paul has recourse to judicial imagery, the language of the courtroom. Paul writes, "[N]o one is justified before God by the law" (3:11a). As a warrant for this affirmation, Paul cites the Scripture: "The one who is righteous [*ho dikaios*] will live by faith" (Hab 2:4; Gal 3:11b; cf. Rom 1:17). Using the fact that Abraham "believed God and it was reckoned to him as righteousness [*dikaiosynēn*]"[1] as his premise, Paul argues that "God would justify the Gentiles by faith" (3:6, 8).

Properly speaking, the verb "justify" (*dikaioō*) and its cognates belong to the realm of legal and juridical terminology. To justify is to find that someone is righteous or declare that someone is righteous, to find that a person is just, that is, has acted in accordance with standards of justice. The role properly belongs to a judge. Typically, the standard by which a judge renders judgment is the law. But that is not the standard by which God judges: "No one is justified before God by the law" (3:11).

What, then, is the standard of righteousness? Faith, for "[a] person is justified not by the works of the law but through faith in Jesus Christ" (2:16a; cf. 2:16d; 3:21). Believers await a declaration of righteousness: "Through the Spirit, by faith, we eagerly wait for the hope of righteousness" (5:5). On the other hand, the desire to be declared righteous on the basis of the law makes the death of Christ superfluous (2:21) and cuts the sinner off from Christ (5:4).

Images drawn from the courtroom, from the sphere of the judiciary, are a key element in the rhetoric of Galatians. Vocabulary pertinent to declaring a person righteous appears throughout the letter. With various terms derived from the root *dikaio-*,[2] Paul writes about "righteousness" (*dikaosynē*) and the "righteous" (*dikaios*) and uses the verb "justify" (*dikaioō*).[3]

### Family Language

Despite its harsh tone and the judicial images, the letter employs the familiar *adelphoi* as a form of direct address some nine times.[4] The editors

---

[1] Gen 15:6, cited in Rom 4:3, 9. Cf. Gen 12:3, cited in Gal 3:8.

[2] As is the case with the translation of terms derived from the root *hagi-*, some translations of the root *diakaio-* make use of the Anglo-Saxon heritage of the English language, whereas other translations make use of its Romance language background. From the Romance tradition we have "justification," "just," and "justify" as renderings of *dikaiosynē, dikaios,* and *dikaioō,* respectively. These same words are translated as "righteousness," "righteous," and "make [declare] righteous," when recourse is had to our Anglo-Saxon tradition.

[3] "Righteousness," *dikaosynē,* in 2:21; 3:6, 21; 5:5; "righteous," *dikaios,* in 3:11; "justify," *dikaioō,* in 2:16 [3x], 17; 3:8, 11, 24; 5:4.

[4] 1:11; 3:15; 4:12, 28, 31; 5:11, 13; 6:1, 18.

of the NRSV render *adelphoi* more often as "friends" (4:12, 28, 31; 5:11; 6:1) than as "brothers and sisters" (1:11; 3:15; 5:13; 6:18). The editors' translation option seemingly indicates a desire to take into account the fact that Paul's tone is less friendly and the bonds of affection far less intense than they were in the Letter to the Thessalonians. On the other hand, there are "brothers and sisters" and there are "brothers and sisters." All of us feel more closely connected with some of our siblings than we do with other members of our family.

The most striking feature of Paul's use of sibling language in the Letter to the Galatians might well be that the letter opens and closes on the theme of sibship. Within Paul's correspondence Galatians is unique in that its greetings come not only from Paul but also from "all the [brothers and sisters] who are with me."[5] Typically Paul names his companions as he begins his letters and identifies two of them, Timothy (2 Cor 1:1; Phlm 1) and Sosthenes (1 Cor 1:1), as brothers, but Galatians stands alone in saying that "all the [brothers and sisters] who are with me" send greetings. Presumably this was a fairly large group, if indeed the letter was written from Ephesus as is quite likely the case.

"May the grace of our Lord Jesus Christ be with your spirit, brothers and sisters" (6:18) is the final salutation of Galatians. In many respects this salutation is typical of the final greetings of Paul's letters. Galatians is, however, unique insofar as this is the only letter in which Paul directly calls upon his addressees as "brothers and sisters" as he brings the letter to a close. Paul's insistence on sibship is all the more noteworthy insofar as it has been penned by Paul himself (6:11), virtually his last word to the Galatians.

With respect to texts circumscribed by literary inclusion (1:2; 6:1), commentators frequently observe that the construction identifies the composition as a literary unit and sets a tone or creates a theme for the composition. From this perspective it can be said that the Letter to the Galatians has been written from the perspective of sibship.

Paul's final *adelphoi* (6:18) is a reminder that he wants the Galatians to act as if they were members of the same family.[6] Confirming the plea, he adds an "Amen"—the only time in the extant correspondence that he

---

[5] The NRSV renders Paul's initial *adelphoi* as "all the members of God's family." This "translation" confirms the age-old adage that every translation is an interpretation.

[6] In a remark that is apropos of Paul's letters in general but is particularly pertinent to Galatians, Horrell notes: "Paul on a number of occasions stresses repeatedly the believers' identity as *adelphoi* in order to appeal for a degree of solidarity and mutual

does so. Paul's use of this formula of affirmation is his final plea. When the Hebrew *'āmen* appears in the Scriptures, the Greek translators usually render the term as *genoito*, "so be it." In effect, Paul is saying to the Galatians, "Please, please, act like brothers and sisters to one another." Thus, when *adelphoi* occurs as a formula of direct address in Galatians, it should always be translated according to its usual meaning of "brothers and sisters." Only in this way can the formula retain its rhetorical force.[7]

That Paul's use of the formula of direct address should be taken as an appeal to the Galatians' sense of what it means to belong to a family is confirmed by Paul's use of family language throughout the letter. "*Hyios*," meaning "son" or "child," appears thirteen times in the letter, twice as often as "brothers and sisters."[8]

In 1:16; 2:20; 4:4 and 6 *hyios* identifies Christ as the Son of God. In 4:6-7 *hyios* identifies each Christian in the Galatian region as a child of God: "Because you are children [*hyioi*], God has sent the Spirit of his Son [*hyiou*] into our hearts, crying 'Abba! Father!' So you are no longer a slave but a child [*hyios*], and if a child [*hyios*] then also an heir, through God." In 3:26, Paul generalizes the expression to speak of all the Galatians as children of God (*hyioi theou*) in Christ Jesus through faith. The link between Christ as "son" (*hyios*) and believers as "sons"[9] (*hyioi*) is established insofar as the latter have been adopted (*hyiosthesia*, 4:5). Their prayer invoking God as "Abba! Father!" confirms their sonship. The paternal metaphor used of God in Aramaic and in Greek prayer is a powerful affirmation that Jewish and Gentile Christians are "sons" of the divine Father.

Paul also uses the singular *hyios* to speak of Isaac or Ishmael, the sons of Abraham, in 4:30 [3x] and the plural *hyious* to speak about the two sons in 4:22. In 3:7, Paul generalizes the expression to speak about the Galatians as sons (*hyioi*) of Abraham. Since many, if not most, of the

---

care that is currently lacking." See David G. Horrell, "From *adelphoi* to *oikos theou*: Social Transformation in Pauline Christianity," *JBL* 120 (2001): 293–311, 309.

[7] The circumlocution used by the NRSV in 4:12, 28, 31; 5:11; 6:1 weakens Paul's rhetorical argument.

[8] *Adelphoi* appears in the singular form *adelphon*, "brother," in 1:19. *Hyios* appears in the singular in 1:16; 2:20; 4:4, 6, 7 [2x], 30 [3x]; in the plural in 3:7, 26; 4:6, 22.

[9] Hopefully the reader will tolerate my use of gender-exclusive language in the ensuing discussion. Use of such language is not only predicated on the status of sons in the Jewish and Greco-Roman worlds, but it is also required in order that the reader capture the subtleties of Paul's rhetoric, as he carefully distinguishes between the "child" (*teknon*) and the "son" (*hyios*) and then uses the root *hyio-*, "son," to press his theological argument.

Galatian Christians are Gentiles, Paul uses "sons of Abraham" in a metaphorical sense, but he would have his audience understand that the metaphor was not a mere comparison; rather, it was the bearer of profound theological meaning.

The key to understanding Paul's metaphor is Christ, whom Paul describes as *the* descendant of Abraham: "The promises were made to Abraham and to his offspring [*spermati*]; it does not say, 'And to offsprings [*spermasin*],' as of many; but it says, 'And to your offspring [*spermati*],' that is, to one person, who is Christ" (3:16). Paul's midrashic explanation of the phrase "to his offspring" (Gen 13:15; 17:8) capitalizes on the biblical text's use of a singular form of the word. Paul is working with the hermeneutical principle of exclusion, popularized by the school of Akiva, the legendary second-century Jewish rabbi. Using this principle, Paul is able to argue that the text was speaking about a singular descendant of Abraham and that Christ was that one descendant. Accordingly, it was to Christ that the covenantal promise was directed.

The biblical expression *sperma Abraam*[10] means "seed of Abraham." Paul adopts the biblical expression to speak about all those whose ancestry could be traced back to Abraham.[11] He counted himself as one who belonged to the seed of Abraham (Rom 11:1; 2 Cor 11:22), but in Galatians his line of reasoning takes another tack. In this letter, he argues that it is Christ who is *the* descendant of Abraham.

Why does Paul employ his exegetical skills to conclude that Christ is *the* descendant of Abraham? The answer is simple: So that he can argue that each member of the churches of Galatia can be counted among the descendants of Abraham. Incorporated through baptism into Christ, *the* descendant of Abraham, Galatian Christians are the offspring, the descendants, the seed of Abraham: "There is no longer Jew or Greek, there is no longer slave or free, there is no longer male and female; for all of you are one in Christ Jesus. And if you belong to Christ, then you are Abraham's offspring [*ara tou Abraam sperma este*], heirs according to the promise" (Gal 3:28-29). The conclusion that Paul drew as he unfolded the meaning of "seed of Abraham" was an important element in his argument against the Judaizers.[12] If Gentile Christians are descendants

---

[10] See 2 Chr 20:7; cf. Gen 15:5; 21:12.

[11] See Rom 4:13, 16; 9:8, 29 in addition to the quotations from Scripture in Rom 4:18; 9:7.

[12] David Rhoads argues that the notion of children of Abraham is the primary lens through which the various elements of the Letter to the Galatians are seen and orga-

of Abraham because of their baptismal incorporation into Christ, there is no need for them to be circumcised as a sign of their belonging to the clan of Abraham. In 3:26 Paul argues that Christians are children of God (*hyioi theou*) because they are in Christ Jesus; three verses later he argues that Christians are the offspring of Abraham (*Abraam sperma*, 3:29) because they are in Christ Jesus. Their belonging to Christ is the key to the Galatians being members of God's family as well as the key to their being members of Abraham's family. The argument of 3:25-29 is all about belonging to the family.

Earlier on in his letter Paul affirmed, "[T]hose who believe are the descendants of Abraham [*hyioi . . . Abraam*]" (3:7). In this passage Paul uses the more common "sons" (*hyioi*)[13] rather than the biblical and Semitic buzzword "seed of Abraham," but his point remains the same: all Christians, Jews and Gentiles alike, are the children (descendants) of Abraham.

The apostle continues to develop his argument, using the family motif, in chapter four. Reflection on the Spirit-inspired "Abba" prayer allows Paul to affirm that we are children of God (4:7). An extended allegory on Hagar and Sarah and their two sons, Ishmael and Isaac,[14] leads him to write, "[Y]ou, [brothers and sisters],[15] are children of the promise [*epangelias tekna*]" (4:28). His allegory concludes with this inference: "So then, [brothers and sisters],[16] we are children [*tekna*], not of the slave but of the free woman" (4:31).

Having argued that believers are "descendants [*hyioi, sperma*] of Abraham" in Galatians 3, Paul argues that believers are children (*tekna*) of Sarah and children of the promise in chapter 4. In the family reflections of these chapters, Paul employs five related but not identical terms to speak about offspring: *sperma*, "seed," in 3:16 [3x], 19, 29; *teknon*, "child," in 4:19, 25, 27, 28, 31; *hyios*, "son," in 3:7, 26; 4:4, 6 [2x], 7 [2x], 22, 30 [3x, citing Gen 21:10]; *hyiothesia*, "adoption as a son," in 4:5; and *nēpios*, "infant" or "minor" [NRSV] in 4:1, 3. In Galatians 3–4 Paul teases out the implications of the vertical relationships that can be subsumed under the rubric of "descent." Paul acknowledges that the Scriptures (Gen

---

nized. See Rhoads, "Children of Abraham, Children of God: Metaphorical Kinship in Paul's Letter to the Galatians," *CurTM* 31 (2004): 282–97.

[13] The editors of the NRSV use the gender-neutral "descendants" to translate the *hyioi* of 3:7.

[14] Paul cites neither the name of the son of Hagar nor the name of the free woman.

[15] "Friends," NRSV.

[16] "My friends," NRSV. "My" (*mou*) does not appear in the Greek text.

21:9-10) speak of the two sons (*dyo hyioi*) of Abraham (4:22), but that is not his linguistic preference. Paul prefers to use the word *teknon*, "child," to speak about the sons of Abraham. Paul uses "child" to speak about the children of Sarah (4:27, citing Isa 54:1), Jews as children of Hagar (4:25), believers in Christ (4:28, 31), and the Galatians, Paul's children (4:19). *Teknon*, a somewhat bland term, does not enjoy the affective and legal connotations of *hyios*, "son."

In contrast with "child" (*teknon*), "son" (*hyios*) is a highly evocative term. The Jewish Scriptures used the noun to speak of the children of Abraham, but in Paul the term properly designates the Son of God (1:16; 2:20; 4:4). By extension the term can be used of those who belong to *the* Son. Believers have been adopted as sons (*hyiothesia*, 4:5) through faith and the gift of the Spirit of the Son (3:26; 4:6); they have become sons in the Son (3:26; 4:6, 7). Because the Son of God, born of a woman, is the seed (*sperma*) of Abraham, the adopted sons of God are also descendants of Abraham (3:7).

Being a minor (*nēpios*, 4:1, 3) suggests a state of subservience and dependence; a minor has not yet come of age. That was the status of the Galatians before they became sons in the Son. Paul compares and contrasts the minor and the child with good effect in this letter. Those who have become sons in the Son through adoption (4:5) are no longer minors. The minor is no better off than a slave since minors are under guardians (*epitropous*) and trustees (*oikonomous*), the latter term being generally used of the head slave in the Greco-Roman household, the steward of the household.

Before coming to faith and being adopted as sons, the Galatians were minors because they "were enslaved to the elemental spirits of the world [*stoicheia tou kosmou*]" (4:3). The word *stoicheia* describes things that keep people in line; in the context of Paul's letter, the *stoicheia* are most likely to be understood as fundamental religious principles.[17] Judaizers would make the Galatians subservient to such fundamentals as the law, circumcision, dietary prescriptions, along with the Sabbath and festal observances that enslaved the Galatian Christians. Subservience represents the *then* of the Galatians' experience, their past; *now* they are adopted children. Their status as minors has come to an end; they should not return.

A close reading of Galatians suggests that the family relationships mentioned in the Scriptures were an important element of Paul's

---

[17] See Timothy Ashworth, *Paul's Necessary Sin: The Experience of Liberation* (Aldershot, UK: Ashgate, 2006), 49. Cf. LSJ, *s. v.*, 4; Frank J. Matera, *Galatians*, SP 9 (Collegeville, MN: Liturgical Press, 1992), 155.

rhetorical *heurēsis*, his plan for developing an argument that would be convincing in the situation that he had to confront. His argument was about family ties and how families are formed. Arguing that circumcised and non-circumcised believers alike belong to the family of Abraham and Sarah, Paul addresses the Galatians as his brothers and sisters. He does so twice in the passage in which he speaks about the Galatians as children (*tekna*) of the promise and children (*tekna*) of the free woman (Sarah). As children and offspring of the same set of parents, all Galatian believers are heirs to the promise made to Abraham.

Paul's allegorical midrash[18] on the biblical story of Sarah and Hagar includes a quotation from Isaiah 54:1:[19]

> Rejoice, you childless one, you who bear no children,
>> burst into song and shout, you who endure no birthpangs;
> for the children of the desolate woman are more numerous
>> than the children of the one who is married. (Gal 4:27)

The Scripture is the first verse of a song to Zion, Isaiah 54:1-17, celebrating the "sacred marriage" of YHWH with Zion/Jerusalem, his spouse. With allusions to her barrenness and her historic nomadic state the Scripture evokes the image of Sarah, previously mentioned in Isaiah 51:1-2. Mentioning "enduring birthpangs" (*ōdinousa*) and "children" (*tekna*), Isaiah 54:1 is singularly important in Paul's appeal to the Galatians.

Just before his exposition of the Sarah-Hagar allegory, Paul writes to the Galatians as a frustrated mother might do: "My little children [*tekna mou*],[20] for whom I am again in the pain of childbirth [*ōdinō*] until Christ is formed in you, I wish I were present with you now and could change my tone, for I am perplexed about you" (4:19-20).

In 1 Thessalonians Paul used the image of a nursing mother[21] to speak of his affection for the Thessalonians and the extent of his dedication to

---

[18] Anne Davis ("Allegorically Speaking in Galatians 4:21–5:1," BBR [2004]: 161–74) argues that this is not the best way to describe Paul's argumentation in 4:21–5:1 but it remains the common way of describing the pericope's literary genre.

[19] See also the citation of Gen 21:10 in 4:30.

[20] Cf. 1 Cor 4:14, where Paul calls the Corinthians "my beloved children," a formula of direct address that expresses not only Paul's affection but also his need to talk to them as a father does to the children whom he is about to admonish.

[21] With regard to the use of this image, see further Beverly R. Gaventa, "The Maternity of Paul: An Exegetical Study of Galatians 4:19," in Robert T. Fortna and Beverly R. Gaventa, eds., *The Conversation Continues: Studies in Paul and John. In Honor of J. Louis Martyn* (Nashville: Abingdon, 1990), 189–201.

them (1 Thess 2:7-8); now he uses the image of a mother[22] to speak about his pain and frustration. Paul is suffering the pains of prolonged labor[23] because the birth of the Galatian Christians into Christ is not yet complete.[24] The image derives from Isaiah 54:1 that Paul is about to quote (4:27).

The Galatians should have grasped the brunt of Paul's remarks before he revealed the source of the scriptural allusion. The image of the pain of a woman in labor was classic in Greek literature.[25] Authors as different from one another as the poet Homer,[26] the philosopher Plato,[27] and the tragedian Sophocles[28] used the image to describe a wide variety of human experiences, from intense physical pain to profound worry or even, as in Plato, the throes of thought.

Paul's use of kinship language throughout Galatians[29] is a forceful reminder to the Galatians that they are members of a single family and that they should act accordingly. The importance of Paul's family language is underscored by his closing remarks. The final words dictated to the scribe are: "So then, whenever we have an opportunity, let us work for the good of all, and especially for those of the family of faith [*tous oikeious tēs pisteōs*]," literally, "members of the household of faith," thus, kin or family (6:10). Then, having written a final salutation in his own hand, Paul bids the Galatians farewell with this blessing: "May the grace of our Lord Jesus Christ be with your spirit, brothers and sisters. Amen" (6:18). The formula of direct address, an unusual feature of a Pauline epistolary closing, is almost a plea that arises from exasperation. The plea might be paraphrased, "After all, you are brothers and sisters. Please act accordingly." To that, Paul adds an exclamation point in the form of his final "Amen."

[22] Paul uses maternal imagery of himself in 1 Thess 2:7; Gal 4:19; and 1 Cor 3:2, but in none of these instances does he use the word "mother" (*mētēr*).

[23] Paul uses the verb, *ōdinō*, "suffer the pains of childbirth," only in 4:27 and 4:19.

[24] Gaventa holds that the image of prolonged labor reflects Paul's apocalyptic thinking. See Beverly R. Gaventa, "The Maternity of Paul," 189–201; Beverly R. Gaventa, *Our Mother Saint Paul* (Louisville: Westminster John Knox, 2007), 31–39.

[25] Paul uses the related noun, *ōdin*, "labor pains," in 1 Thess 5:3.

[26] See *Odyssey* 9.415, where Homer writes of the Cyclops's pain.

[27] Plato often used the image, especially to describe the agony of reflective thought. See, for example, *Thaetetus* 148E and *Republic* 407C.

[28] *Trachiniae* 325.

[29] Gal 1:19 is the only place in Galatians in which familial language occurs for a purpose other than Paul's overall rhetorical appeal.

## Abraham's Story

Paul introduces the story of Abraham into the Letter to the Galatians by means of the same biblical quotation that he later uses to introduce the story of Abraham into the Letter to the Romans: "Abraham 'believed God, and it was reckoned to him as righteousness'" (3:6, quoting Gen 15:6; cf. Rom 4:3). Reflecting on the biblical story at some length (3:6–4:31), Paul exploits not only the motif of Abraham's offspring but also the notion of the covenant.

Introducing the idea of the covenant, the biblical *berith*, Paul writes: "Brothers and sisters, I give an example[30] from daily life: Once a person's will has been ratified [*kekyrōmenēn diathēkēn*], no one adds to it [*epidiatassetai*] or annuls it" (3:15). The language comes from the legal domain; it evokes the idea of a last will and testament which enjoys the sanction of law. "Ratify" (*kyroō*) was often used in legal contexts, especially with regard to the ratification of laws.[31] In a legal context "adds" (*epidiatassomai*) means "add a codicil."

Scholars have sought to identify the practice to which Paul was referring in specific Greek,[32] Roman,[33] or Jewish law,[34] but the practice, with variations, is common in most cultures, especially when goods are passed along within the family.[35] Inheritance laws were part of Paul's rhetorical

---

[30] Paul's Greek reads *adelphoi, kata anthrōpon legō*. Lacking any single word that might be translated "example," Murphy-O'Connor has suggested that the Greek phrase *kata anthrōpon legō* is best translated: "according to the common estimation." See Jerome Murphy-O'Connor, "The Irrevocable Will (Gal 3:15)," *RB* 106 (1999): 224–35.

[31] Andocides, *Speeches* 1.85; cf. Demosthenes, *Speeches* 20.93. Dio Cassius uses the cognate noun *kyros*, meaning supreme power or supreme authority, in a legal sense in *Roman History* 28.27 and passim.

[32] For example, William M. Ramsay, *A Historical Commentary on St. Paul's Epistle to the Galatians*, 2nd ed. (London: Hodder and Stoughton, 1900), 349–70.

[33] See, for example, D. Walker, "The Legal Terminology in the Epistle to the Galatians," in *The Gift of Tongues and Other Essays* (Edinburgh: T&T Clark, 1906), 81–175; Greer M. Taylor says that what Paul had in mind was the testamentary device known as the *fidei commissum* ("The Function of *Pistis Christou* in Galatians," *JBL* 85 [1966]: 58–76, 65–76).

[34] See *m. Baba Batra* 8:5-7; *t. Baba Batra* 8.9-11; *b. Baba Batra* 135b, 136a-b. Bammel sought to specify the practice in the *mattĕnat bārî'* of Jewish law. See Ernst Bammel, "Gottes *diathēkē* (Gal. iii. 15-17) und das jüdische Rechtsdenken," NTS 6 (1960): 313–19.

[35] See Richard N. Longenecker, *Galatians*, WBC 41 (Dallas: Word, 1990), 128–30; Reuven Yaron, *Gifts in Contemplation of Death in Jewish and Roman Law* (Oxford: Clarendon, 1960); and Douglas Maurice MacDowell and David E. L. Johnston, "Inheritance," *OCD*, 757–58.

*heurēsis* (*inventio*). Paul returns to the idea of a bequest as he writes: "My point is this: heirs [*klēronomos*],[36] as long as they are minors, are no better than slaves, though they are the owners of all the property" (4:1).

Although Paul may not have had any specific form of testament in mind, the image of the last will and testament as a metaphor for the irrevocable will of God is powerful. Paul, however, used the image as a kind of pun. Hellenistic Jews customarily used the word *diathēkē* to render the Hebrew term, *berith*, the classic and biblical designation of the ancient covenant that God had made with Israel. Paul plays on the double entendre of *diathēkē*, moving from the image of the last will and testament to the biblical idea of God's covenant with Abraham.[37]

Before he brings his exposition of the Abraham material to a close, Paul writes about the two women who had given birth to the two sons of Abraham, commenting, "Now this is an allegory" (4:24):

> For it is written that Abraham had two sons, one by a slave woman and the other by a free woman. One, the child of the slave, was born according to the flesh; the other, the child of the free woman, was born through the promise. Now this is an allegory [*hatina estin allēgoroumena*]: these women are two covenants. One woman, in fact, is Hagar, from Mount Sinai, bearing children for slavery. Now Hagar is Mount Sinai in Arabia and corresponds to the present Jerusalem, for she is in slavery with her children. But the other woman corresponds to the Jerusalem above; she is free, and she is our mother. (Gal 4:21-26)

The verb *allēgoreō* means "speak figuratively or metaphorically." Paul seems to imply that the biblical scenario was nothing but an image,[38] but he certainly knew better. In any case, his language is careless. Paul surely knew that Sinai is located on the Egyptian peninsula, a territory then

---

[36] See also 4:7. In the example given in 4:1, Paul uses the singular number to speak of an heir, a minor (*nēpios*), slave (*doulos*), and owner (*kyrios*). The NRSV captures the generic character of the example by using the plural.

[37] Contrary to the interpretation of most contemporary commentators on Galatians, J. J. Hughes maintains that *diathēkē* should be rendered as "covenant" in 3:15 ("Hebrews ix 15ff. and Galatians iii 15ff: A Study in Covenant Practice and Procedure," *NovT* 21 [1979]: 27–96, 66–91).

[38] Paul's Greek text uses the verb *allēgoreō*, not the noun *allēgoria*. His text literally means "these things were expressed figuratively," not "these things are to be interpreted allegorically."

controlled by the Nabateans, thought to have descended from Hagar.[39] Paul relates Sinai, Jerusalem, and Hagar, but Jews were the descendants of Sarah, not Hagar. Perhaps the best way to meander through Paul's confusing language is to agree with Dean Anderson that Paul's emotion[40] led him to use the biblical story sarcastically, overturning in the process its literal meaning.[41] The sarcasm is evident in the way that he speaks about the Jewish people as children of Hagar.

## Speaking about People

Writing about people, especially those causing problems for Galatian believers, Paul often uses figurative language. In a striking affirmation of the authenticity of his ministry and his message, Paul writes: "When God, who had set me apart before I was born[42] and called me through his grace, was pleased to reveal his Son to me, so that I might proclaim him among the Gentiles, I did not confer with any human being . . ." (1:15-16). The expression rendered "human being" is literally "flesh and blood" (*sarki kai haimati*). The now common expression is rarely used in biblical literature and the New Testament.

Apart from 1 Corinthians 15:50, Paul used the synecdoche[43] only in 1:16 where the phrase emphasizes the fact that the revelation received by Paul was from God himself and not from any merely human source. Contrasting God and human beings, Paul typically juxtaposes *theos*, "God," and *anthrōpos*, "human being."[44] Since the image of "flesh and blood" underscores human creatureliness, weakness, and mortality, the phrase accentuates the contrast between God and humans more than Paul's usual language would have done.

In context, the idiom might have supplied another resonance to Paul's argument. The "Judaizers" were urging that the Gentile Christians of Galatia be circumcised,[45] a matter that directly pertained to the flesh.

---

[39] See Josephus, *Jewish Antiquities* 1.214.

[40] See 1:6, 9; 4:15, 19–20; 5:12.

[41] See R. Dean Anderson, Jr., *Ancient Rhetorical Theory and Paul*, CBET 18 (Kampen: Kok Pharos, 1996): 155–58.

[42] Literally, "from my mother's womb," "from my mother's belly," (*ek koilias mētros mou*).

[43] Cf. Sir 14:18; 17:31; *1 Enoch* 15:4.

[44] See, for example, 1:10-12.

[45] "Circumcision was the most obvious ethnic, ritual and theological identifying feature of the 'Jew' . . . and . . . it was circumcision which was at the heart of the

Paul focuses on flesh when he uses "circumcision" to refer to the Jewish people. Paul first described the gospel preached by Peter as a gospel of circumcision (*to euangelion . . . tēs peritomēs*, 2:7), an expression of God's good news that belongs to the circumcision, that is, to Jews.

Paul's metonymy is forceful and repeated. He describes Peter as one whose mission was the apostolate of circumcision (2:8).[46] The irony with which Paul writes is apparent. Describing the meeting between himself and Barnabas and the pillars of the church which led to a gentlemen's agreement, Paul wrote that he and his companion would go to the Gentiles, whereas Cephas and the pillars of the Jerusalem church would go "to the circumcision"[47] (2:9). A physical trait is used to identify collectively an ethno-religious group.[48]

Paul writes about the Jew and the Greek (*Ioudaios kai Hellēnos*) on a number of occasions,[49] but in Galatians Paul's first mention of his fellow Israelites identifies them neither by their ethnicity nor their heritage; rather, he identifies them by circumcision. Before contrasting Jews and Gentiles (2:14-15), Paul speaks about his own people as "the circumcision." Later, he will describe them as "the circumcised" (*hoi peritemnomenoi*, 6:13) but not so at the beginning of the letter. Jews are simply "the circumcision." The physicality of the metonymous expression is evident.

In Paul's simple sociology, the world is inhabited by Jews and Gentiles. Writing about the Jews as "the circumcision," Paul contrasts them with Gentiles whom he identifies as "the foreskin" (*akrobystia*, 2:7; 5:6; 6:15). Derived from the root *akr-*, "furthest," the noun is used by Paul as a form of metonymy to describe those whose skin is whole, that is, the uncircumcised. The physicality of Paul's language anticipates Paul's dismissive and crass retort, "I wish those who unsettle you would castrate themselves!" (5:12). The physicality of Paul's language also anticipates

---

dispute resolved in Jerusalem," says James D. G. Dunn, *The Epistle to the Galatians*, BNTC (Peabody, MA: Hendrickson, 1993), 107.

[46] The "non-Pauline" nature of the expressions, "gospel of the circumcision" and "apostolate of the circumcision," may suggest that the language is taken from a previously formulated official statement. See Hans Dieter Betz, *Galatians*, Hermeneia (Philadelphia: Fortress, 1979), 97–98.

[47] "To the circumcised," NRSV.

[48] See also Rom 2:26-27; 3:30. More fully, Gal 2:12 describes them as *tous ek peritomēs*, "the circumcision faction" [NRSV].

[49] See Rom 1:16; 2:9, 10; 10:12; 1 Cor 1:22-24; 10:32; 12:13.

Paul's final *ēthos* appeal, "From now on, let no one make trouble for me; for I carry the marks of Jesus branded on my body" (6:17).[50]

Virtually every time that Paul directly addresses his audience his expressions are warm and friendly, "brothers and sisters," "beloved," and so forth. One striking exception to his normal practice is to be found in 3:1 when Paul writes, "You foolish Galatians!" Even the casual reader can sense the depth of feeling with which Paul uttered these words. The Galatians are *anoētoi*, "mindless," "crazy." The apostle backs up his use of this demeaning epithet with the rhetorical question, "Who has bewitched you [*tis hymas ebaskanen*]?" What does Paul's question mean? The Greek verb, used in no other place in the New Testament, is derived from a noun that designates someone who casts a spell, *baskanos*. Paul's image is powerful. It is as if the evil eye[51] with all its harmful effects had been cast on the Galatians, driving them out of their minds. They were no longer able to act in a rational manner.

## Jesus' Crucifixion

For the most part the first two chapters of the Letter to the Galatians develop Paul's *ēthos*, establishing his authority[52] to confront the Galatians who were being weaned away from the gospel that he had preached. In 2:21–3:1, Paul challenges them to think about the death of Christ: "I do not nullify the grace of God; for if justification comes through the law, then Christ died for nothing. You foolish Galatians! Who has bewitched you? It was before your eyes that Jesus Christ was publicly exhibited as crucified [*proegraphē estaurōmenos*]!" Paul's thought moves from the thought of Christ's death to the modality of that death, crucifixion. Paul wants the Galatians to think not only about Christ's death but actually to contemplate his crucifixion. The Galatians should have been able to contemplate Christ's crucifixion because Christ had been publicly exhibited as crucified; he had been put on display as a crucified person.

As so often in the Letter to the Galatians, Paul's language is metaphorical. The basic meaning of *prographō*, "exhibit publicly," is "write before,"

---

[50] Another example of the graphic physicality of Paul's language is the way he describes how loyal the Galatians had been to him at the time of his ailment: "[Y]ou would have torn out your eyes (*ophthalmous hymōn exoruxantes*) and given them to me" (4:15).

[51] See Spicq, "*Baskainō*," *TLNT* 1:272–276.

[52] See the opening verses of the epistle, 1:1-2a.

"write previously."[53] In a technical sense, the verb was used to mean "give written notice of," that is, to set down in writing so that someone could see it. Hence, "to set forth as a public notice," the meaning of the verb in Demosthenes and Plutarch.[54]

Paul's metaphor was apropos. In the Roman world the crucifixion of runaway or rebellious slaves was intended to give notice, to alert passersby that they would be liable to similar punishment were they to commit similar crimes. Often a plaque was carried in front of the prisoner who was being led out for crucifixion. The plaque indicated the crime for which the victim was being executed. Sometimes the plaque was hung around the victim's neck. The sign could then be affixed to the cross for all to be aware of the nature of the crime whose perpetrator was being put to death in such a horrific manner. Even without the plaque, a death by crucifixion served public notice; it was a warning for all to see.

To describe the radicalism and total quality of the salvation effected in Christ, Paul draws upon the world of commerce, where buying and selling are the business of daily life.[55] The Greeks used the compound verb *exagorazō*, a compound and intensified form of the verb *agorazō*, with the meaning "buy up," "buy off," "buy from." The Greeks also used the verb to speak of slaves whose freedom might be bought when the appropriate purchase price was made to their masters. The first-century BCE historian, Diodorus of Sicily, gives an account of Plato who, when he was being sold on the slave market, was bought by his friends so that he might gain his freedom.[56] In such a scenario, the purchase of someone implied his redemption, his being set free.[57] Thus the verb was sometimes used to mean "redeem," "set free."

Writing to the Galatians, Paul uses the powerful image of believers being purchased and thus set free. He does not mention the purchase price,[58] nor does he mention to whom the price was paid, but he does

---

[53] Cf. Rom 15:4.

[54] See Demosthenes *Speeches* 47.42 and Plutarch, who uses the term with some frequency in "Themistocles and Camillus," 11 [*Parallel Lives* 2.118].

[55] Cf. 1 Cor 7:30.

[56] See Diodorus Siculus, 15.7.1.

[57] On manumission in the Greco-Roman world see, among other sources, Sam Tsang, *From Slaves to Sons: A New Rhetoric Analysis on Paul's Slave Metaphors in His Letter to the Galatians*, SBLit 81 (New York: Peter Lang, 2005), 49–58.

[58] Cf. 1 Cor 6:20; 7:23, where Paul uses a similar image, employing a form of the simple verb *agorazō* and a specific mention of the "price" (*timē*).

talk about a purchase, redemption: "Christ redeemed us from the curse of the law by becoming a curse for us" (3:13) and, again, "When the fullness of time had come, God sent his Son, born of a woman, born under the law, in order to redeem those who were under the law, so that we might receive adoption as children" (4:4-5).

The context of 4:4-5 indicates that Paul has the redemption of slaves in mind as he writes. The pericope begins with Paul talking about slaves (4:1); it ends with him saying, "You are no longer a slave [*doulos*] but a child [*hyios*], and if a child then also an heir" (4:7), using the singular to affirm that what he is saying applies to every member of the Galatian communities. To whom had they been enslaved before Christ came onto the human scene? To "the elemental spirits of the world" (4:3),[59] the law (4:5), and "beings that by nature are not gods" (4:8). Born of a woman, Jesus, too, was enslaved.[60] By his death we have all been set free; Christ's death was a death "for us" (3:13).

Paul tells the story of Jesus' redemptive death in 4:1-7. Another version of the story appeared a few verses earlier, namely, in 3:13-14,[61] a passage that unpacks the significance of the display that Paul mentions in 3:1. Galatians 3:13-14 and 4:1-7 are parallel in many respects. Both passages speak about Christ, redemption, the Spirit, and the effect of redemption. In 4:5 the result of redemption is that we receive adoption as children. In 3:14 the result of redemption is that the blessing of Abraham comes to Gentiles and that we receive the promise of the Spirit through faith:

> Christ redeemed us from the curse of the law by becoming a curse for us—for it is written, "Cursed is everyone who hangs on a tree"—in order that in Christ Jesus the blessing of Abraham might come to the Gentiles, so that we might receive the promise of the Spirit through faith. (Gal 3:13-14)

---

[59] Dunn (*Galatians*, 212–13) suggests that undue precision with regard to the meaning of the disputed phrase "elemental spirits of the world" should be avoided. Asking whether the words refer to the elements identified in early cosmology (earth, water, air, and fire), elementary forms of religion, or astral deities, Dunn responds, "The answer is probably 'All three!'" Matera (*Galatians*, 149–50) lists nine possibilities that have been advanced in the recent *Wirkungsgeschichte* of the text.

[60] This would seem to be the burden of Paul's remark that both Jesus (4:4) and we (4:5) are under the law.

[61] Richard Hays calls 3:13-14 and 4:1-7 "two tellings . . . of the same story" (*The Faith of Jesus Christ: The Narrative Substructure of Galatians 3:1–4:11*, SBLDS 56 [Chico: Scholars, 1983], 116).

To be "hung on a tree" was the way that the Bible spoke about crucifixion. Crucifixion was used as a form of punishment in the early days of Israel's history;[62] it was also employed in first-century CE Palestine.[63] Josephus says that Alexander Jannaeus used crucifixion as a form of punishment (*Jewish Antiquities* 13.380). The Qumran community stipulated crucifixion as a mode of punishment for treason, as well as for those who escaped after committing a capital crime, but otherwise eschewed crucifixion.[64] Those guilty of treason and escapees were to be "hung on a tree."[65]

As a form of punishment,[66] curses also belong to the judicial realm. Paul's Jewish readers were familiar with this form of punishment because of the Deuteronomistic tradition. In Paul's view all human beings suffer from the curse of the law (3:10).[67] So that we might be liberated from that curse, Christ became accursed. The curse was transferred from those who violated the law to Christ, who became a curse. The idea of a human being becoming a curse is decidedly not Jewish. Hellenists, however, would have been familiar with the idea. The dramatist Euripides, for example, has Medea becoming a curse.[68] Sophocles describes Oedipus praying that the curse upon Athens be transferred to him so that the city might be saved.[69]

---

[62] See Num 25:4; Deut 21:22-23; Josh 10:26-27; 2 Sam 21:6-9. Kyle McCarter argues that the verb *hôqîa'*, which appears in the Bible only in Num 25:4 and 2 Sam 21:6 and is usually translated "impale," actually means "crucify" (*II Samuel*, AB 9 [Garden City, NY: Doubleday, 1984], 442).

[63] See Joseph A. Fitzmyer, "Crucifixion in Ancient Palestine, Qumran Literature, and the New Testament," *CBQ* 40 (1978): 493–513. Haas' study of bones discovered in an ossuary found at Giv`at ha-Mivtar yields some details as to how crucifixion took place. See Nicu Haas, "Anthropological Observations on the Skeletal Remains from Giv'at ha-Mivtar," *IEJ* 20 (1970): 38–59, plates 18–24.

[64] See 4QpNah 3–4.I.7–8 [4Q169 3–4.I.7–8], apropos Nah 2:13: ". . . who hanged living men [from the tree, committing an atrocity which had not been committed] in Israel since ancient times, for it is [hor]rible for the one hanged alive from the tree." Cf. Yigael Yadin, "Pesher Nahum (4Q pNahum) Reconsidered," *IEJ* 21 (1971) 1–12; Florentino García Martínez, "4QpNah y la Crucifixión: Nueva hipótesis de reconstrucción de 4Q 169 3–4 i, 4–8," *EstBib* 3–4 (1979–1980): 221–35.

[65] See 4Q524.xiv.2–4; 11Q19.lxiv.7–12.

[66] See Kjell Arne Morland, *The Rhetoric of Curse in Galatians: Paul Confronts Another Gospel*, ESEC 5 (Atlanta: Scholars Press, 1995), 71.

[67] Cf. Deut 27:26.

[68] Euripides, *Medea* 608.

[69] See Sophocles, *Oedipus tyrranus* 1290–1293; cf. 246–54.

To explain to his Jewish readers how it is that Christ became accursed, Paul offers an aside in which for the first and only time in his writings he explicitly cites a passage from the Jewish Scriptures to speak about the death of Christ. The biblical text set down a legal prescription for the death of a person found guilty of a capital crime: "Cursed is everyone who hangs on a tree" (Deut 21:23; Gal 3:13).[70] The Qumran Temple Scroll alludes to this Scripture when it says, "Those hanged on a tree are cursed by God and man" (11Q19.lxiv.12).

Hung from the bole used as the upright piece of a cross, Jesus was cursed by humans and popularly would have been thought to be cursed by God. Paul, however, asserts that Christ actually became a curse for our sake.[71] Christ embodied the curse within himself, thereby destroying it and freeing all of us from that curse. Paul's language[72] recalls the ancient ritual of the sin offering.[73] The sinner would lay his hands upon the victim, thereby transferring his sin (*hēt'*) to the animal who was then called "sin" (*hēt'*).[74] With the death of the animal, the person's sin was destroyed. Similarly, with the crucifixion of Jesus the curse of sin has been removed; with his death our sin has been destroyed.

## Paul Crucified

Before confronting the Galatians with the reality of Christ's death on the cross, Paul alludes to the death of Christ in a powerful metaphor that he creates from that grim reality: "Through the law I died to the law, so that I might live to God. I have been crucified[75] with [*synestaurōmai*[76]]

---

[70] The Greek text of the biblical quotation has been slightly modified by Paul, perhaps under the influence of Deut 27:26.

[71] See Jer 24:9; Zech 8:13.

[72] On the possible sacrificial implications of the phrase "before the LORD" in reference to crucifixion in Num 25:4, see Baruch A. Levine, *Numbers 21–36*, AB 4A (New York: Doubleday, 2000), 285, 302.

[73] See Lev 4:1–5:13; Num 15:22-31. McLean, followed by Finlan, demonstrates that sacrificial rituals do not involve the transfer of curses. Expulsion rituals are different from sacrificial rituals. See Bradley Hudson McLean, *The Cursed Christ: Mediterranean Expulsion Rituals and Pauline Soteriology*, JSNTSup 126 (Sheffield: Sheffield Academic, 1996), 51; Stephen Finlan, *The Background and Content of Paul's Cultic Atonement Metaphors*, SBLAB 19 (Leiden and Boston: Brill, 2004), 102.

[74] In many English versions of the Bible it is identified as a "sin offering" rather than "sin."

[75] The image is the first reference to the cross in Galatians (cf. 5:11, 24; 6:12, 14).

[76] Cf. Rom 6:6.

Christ; and it is no longer I who live, but it is Christ who lives in me" (2:19-20). "Crucified with Christ" is a powerful metaphor. In the Roman world crucifixion was a punishment regularly meted out to slaves and those guilty of heinous crimes.

Those who rebelled against the empire were crucified on a row of crosses. The verb used to describe this serial punishment was *synstauroō*, "crucify with," used by Paul in 2:19.[77] Paul was not physically crucified alongside of Christ. He was alive and was scolding the Galatians for having strayed from the gospel. Paul's description of himself as having been "crucified with Christ" is figurative language. The striking image spoke, in what must have been a startling manner for Paul's Galatian readers, to the depth of Paul's identification with the crucified Jesus.

In contrast with Judaizers who boast in the mark of circumcision, Paul boasts in the cross of Christ: "May I never boast of anything except the cross of our Lord Jesus Christ" (6:14a). His handwritten postscript then mentions Paul's own crucifixion: "[by the cross of Christ] the world has been crucified to me, and I to the world [*emoi kosmos estaurōtai kagō kosmō*]" (6:14). Paul's cosmos is the present age, enslaved in sin and at enmity with God. Through the cross of Christ, that world has died; and Paul has died to that world. Between the apostle and the world there is a radical incompatibility caused by the cross of Christ. Given the fact that it is by the cross of Christ that the world has died to Paul and Paul has died to the world, Paul images the notion of death by writing about crucifixion.

Paul was not alone in his identification with the crucified Jesus. The self-referential metaphor of 6:14 is of a piece with the metaphor used in 5:24 to speak about everyone who belongs to Christ. Having contrasted the works of the flesh with the fruits of the Spirit in 5:19-23, Paul adds a parallel hortatory remark that contrasts the death of the flesh with life in the Spirit:[78] "And those who belong to Christ Jesus have crucified the flesh [*tēn sarka estaurōsan*] with its passions and desires. If we live by the Spirit, let us also be guided by the Spirit" (5:24-25). "Those who belong to Christ" implies something more than mere possession; it implies participation in the life of Christ. The tense of the Greek "crucified" implies

---

[77] In the Greek text the words translated as "I have been crucified with Christ" are the last words of verse 19 rather than being the first words of verse 20, as they appear in the English translation.

[78] See the similar antithesis in 2:19a-b.

participation in Christ's crucifixion. The flesh[79] put to death through believers' participation in the crucifixion is sinful humanity with its aberrant passions and desires. In 2:19 Paul used the image of the cross to write about his own participation in the death of Christ; in 5:24 he alludes to the crucifixion of all who belong to Christ.

To speak about himself as he comes to the end of his letter, Paul exploits another graphic image. Judaizers and those who succumbed to their argument may vaunt the mark of their circumcision; Paul does not. In a final *ēthos* appeal, he pleads: "From now on, let no one make trouble for me; for I carry the marks of Jesus branded on my body" (6:17). "Branded marks" (*stigmata*[80]) evokes the branding iron and the mark that it leaves as a sign of ownership. Paul was not physically branded nor does he specify the nature of the brand mark that he had in mind, but there is some speculation that Paul might have been thinking about some sign of the cross. Even if he had not, the image is powerful; the only physical mark that matters to Paul is a mark indicating that he belongs to Christ.

Paul's metaphoric use of the image of crucifixion is grounded in the reality of the cross of Jesus Christ. He uses various metaphors to tease out the significance of Jesus' death, exploiting the reality of the death on the cross to create a new and striking metaphor. He uses "crucify" not to say that flesh, the world, or himself had actually been nailed to a crossbeam; rather, his newly minted metaphor evocatively describes the manifold consequences of Christ's death on the cross, not only for Paul himself but also for all humanity and indeed the present order of creation.

## The Two Ages

The story of Jesus' death on the tree evokes a cosmic drama. On the one side stands the enslaving power of the law's curse and enslaved human beings; on the other side stands God who through the accursed Christ, his Son (4:4), vanquishes the power of the curse and sets us free.

From the outset of the letter, Paul's readers were aware that he was writing from an apocalyptic perspective. His reference to the "present evil age" (1:4) suggests this perspective. The phrase bespeaks an apoca-

---

[79] Paul does not speak of "flesh" as the physical component of the human being. For him "flesh" connotes human susceptibility to sin.

[80] The word occurs in no other place in the New Testament.

lyptic schema of history, the evil eon followed by the good eon, the age of deliverance. These ages are a pair of "mythico-historical periods."[81]

The argument developed in 3:22-26, with its then-now schema, presumes that Paul's audience is following his apocalyptic line of reasoning. In 3:22-26 Paul describes the "then" of human existence. Before Christ humanity was in prison:

> But the scripture has imprisoned [*synekleisen*] all things under the power of sin, so that what was promised through faith in Jesus Christ might be given to those who believe. Now before faith came, we were imprisoned and guarded [*ephrouroumetha synkleiomenoi*] under the law until faith would be revealed. (Gal 3:22-23)

Personified Scripture (cf. 3:8) has imprisoned the whole world,[82] Jews and Gentiles alike, under the power of sin. The verb *synkleiō*, whose etymology implies that it means to "shut," as it were with a key, means "confine," "lock," "lock up,"[83] or "imprison," as the NRSV renders the verb. Paul's use of the verb *phroureō*, "guard," confirms the idea of imprisonment;[84] before Christ we were imprisoned and under guard.

The notion that all people have sinned (cf. Rom 1:18-2:16) is an idea that Paul shares with other apocalyptic writers. The author of 4 Ezra, for example, writes:

> For who among the living is there that has not sinned, or who among men that has not transgressed your covenant? And now I see that the world to come will bring delight to few, but torments to many. For an evil heart has grown up in us, which has alienated us from God, and has brought us into corruption and the ways of earth, and has shown us the paths of perdition and removed us far from life—and that not just a few of us but almost all who have been created! (4 Ezra 7:46-48)

Despite Paul's pessimistic view of the present human condition, one might ask whether the confinement under sin is really a negative image. Although Dunn and Matera suggest that Paul is thinking about a kind

---

[81] Betz, *Galatians*, 175.

[82] Cf. Rom 11:32.

[83] The verb was sometimes used metaphorically to describe people hemmed in or beset by problems or worries.

[84] Thus, Betz, *Galatians*, 176, n. 125.

of protective custody in which the law serves as the custodian,[85] the image is a negative one.[86] Paul writes about the "curse of the law" (3:13). Moreover, "under the law" (3:23) should be related to other phrases used by Paul—phrases such as "under sin" (3:22; Rom 3:9; 7:14), "under a curse" (3:10), and "under the elemental spirits of the world" (4:3). These parallel constructions all have a negative connotation. In addition, Paul draws a sharp contrast between being "under the law" and "under grace" (Rom 3:19; 7:14). In Romans Paul again uses the image of imprisonment, writing: "God has imprisoned all in disobedience" (Rom 11:32). F. F. Bruce captures well the sense of Paul's vivid image; he writes: "[T]he written law is the official who locks the law-breaker up in the prison-house of which sin is the jailor."[87]

The images of apocalyptic literature are not necessarily consistent with one another nor are Paul's metaphors unmixed. Hence, following upon his reflection on the law as a power that has imprisoned us, Paul is free to write about the law as a disciplinarian (*paidagōgos*): "Therefore the law was our disciplinarian until Christ came, so that we might be justified by faith. But now that faith has come, we are no longer subject to a disciplinarian" (Gal 3:24-25). A *paid-agōgos* is, literally, a child-leader. Greek authors from Plato to Philo carefully distinguished the *paidagōgos*, the disciplinarian, from *didaskalos*, the teacher.[88] A "pedagogue" was a slave who accompanied the pupil on the way to the teacher, carrying his books and protecting the young boy from harm. For this he was often revered.[89] Portrayed in Greek drama with a rod in his hand, the "pedagogue" maintained order among the pupils. He was, in Dieter Lührmann's words, "the slave . . . who with thrashing and force held the children to the task of learning without being a teacher himself."[90] This "peda-

---

[85] Their principal argument is the image of the *paidagōgos*, "custodian," in verses 24 and 25. See Dunn, *Galatians*, 197–98, and Matera, *Galatians*, 136.

[86] Similarly, Longenecker (*Galatians*, 148) who writes: "It is difficult to interpret vv. 24-25 as assigning a positive preliminary or preparatory role to the law."

[87] F. F. Bruce, *Commentary on Galatians*, NIGTC (Grand Rapids, MI: Eerdmans, 1982), 180. See Martyn's similar phrase, "the universal prison warden" (*Galatians*, 362).

[88] See, for example, Plato, *Lysis* [208C]; Diogenes Laertius, *Lives* 3.92; Philo, *Embassy* 53.

[89] See, for example, Plato, *Republic* 5 [467D].

[90] Dieter Lührmann, *Galatians*, CC (Minneapolis: Fortress, 1992), 74–75. Cf. Albrecht Oepke, *Der Brief des Paulus an die Galater*, 3rd rev. and expanded ed. by Joachim Rohde. THKNT 9 (Berlin: Evangelische Verlagsanstalt, 1973), 87.

gogue" was akin to the teacher's aide in the contemporary classroom but, in a society where corporal punishment maintained order, Paul's pedagogue did not have to spare the rod.

Imaged as prison official and violent disciplinarian, the law delivers people over to the power of sin, to which all were enslaved. Then, all of us were enslaved (*dedoulōmenoi*) to the elemental spirits of the world (4:3). Now, "you are no longer a slave but a child" (4:7) for we are children, not of the "slave woman" (*paidiskēs*[91]) but of the "free woman" (*tēs eleutheras*, 4:31). Paul was aware that his language was metaphorical. He uses the language of slavery to underscore the idea that we have been redeemed, as it were from slavery, by Christ. Now, he says, "there is no longer slave or free" (3:28).

The institution of slavery was an integral part of the social and economic fabric of the Greco-Roman world. Hence, the baptismal formula that Paul used in 3:28 included the dichotomous "there is no longer slave or free." Slaves formed a substantial proportion of the population of the principal cities in the Roman Empire. Jews, however, valued their freedom. The annual rehearsal of the Passover story served as a reminder of the legacy of freedom that Jews enjoyed.

Apart from the reference to the institution of slavery in the baptismal formula, Paul writes about slavery in a metaphorical sense. In the then-now schema used to contrast existence before Christ and existence after baptism, Paul often writes about the kind of slavery that holds in bondage slaves and free persons alike.[92]

He introduces the topic tactfully, ironically[93] referring to himself as a "slave of Christ" (1:10),[94] perhaps the most powerful autodescriptive image in the entire letter. Then comes a subtle comparison: "Heirs, as long as they are minors, are no better than slaves" (4:1).[95] The metaphor achieves its full rhetorical effect as Paul describes the believer's pre-Christian condition: "So with us; while we were minors, we were enslaved [*dedoulōmenoi*] to the elemental spirits of the world. . . . Formerly,

---

[91] See also 4:22, 23, 30 [2x].

[92] Paul's discourse on slavery makes use of four words derived from the root *doul-*: "slave" (*doulos*) in 1:10; 3:28; 4:1, 7; "slavery" (*douleia*) in 4:24; 5:1; "be a slave" (*douleuō*) in 4:8, 9, 25; 5:13; "enslave" (*douloō*) in 4:3. Paul uses the technical term *paidiskē* to refer to a slave woman in 4:22, 23, 30, 31.

[93] Cf. 1 Cor 7:21-23.

[94] Cf. Rom 1:1; Phil 1:1.

[95] Similarly, Plato writes that a child must be treated as a slave (*Laws* 7 [808E]).

when you did not know God, you were enslaved [*edouleusate*] to beings that by nature are not gods. . . . How can you want to be enslaved [*douleuein*] to them again?" (4:3, 8, 9b). The peroration of his discourse on slavery contains a singularly powerful challenge: "Stand firm, therefore, and do not submit again to a yoke of slavery" (*zygō douleias*, 5:1). Freed from the yoke of slavery (4:7), the Galatians are never again to allow themselves to be enslaved, with but one exception. Called to freedom, they are to become slaves (*douleuete*) to one another through love (5:13).

### Baptismal Imagery

Paul explains why Christians are no longer subject to the disciplinarian about whom he has written: "For in Christ Jesus you are all children of God through faith. As many of you as were baptized into Christ have clothed yourselves with Christ. There is no longer Jew or Greek, there is no longer slave or free, there is no longer male and female; for all of you are one in Christ Jesus" (Gal 3:26-28). This is the only passage in Galatians in which Paul makes an explicit reference to baptism. The exposition of Paul's thought follows logically. Their relationship with Christ frees the members of the community of faith from the domination of the disciplinarian. This relationship is brought about through baptism into Christ with the result that divisions based on ethnicity, class, and gender have been transcended.

Verses 27-28 explain the expression "in Christ Jesus" (3:26) and recall the liturgy of baptism. Many biblical scholars consider them to be part of a pre-Pauline baptismal formula[96] which the apostle alone among New Testament writers preserves for us. James D. G. Dunn[97] suggests that "baptized into Christ" is to be taken as a metaphor for the believer's entrance into a spiritual relationship with Christ, but most scholars find

[96] So, Robin Scroggs, "Woman in the NT," *IDBSup* 996–98, 996; Longenecker, *Galatians*, 155, 157; Martyn, *Galatians*, 373, 378–83; etc. Dunn, however, maintains that the formulae which seem to have been familiar to the Galatians were a regular part of early Christian catechesis (*Galatians*, 203).

[97] James D. G. Dunn, *Baptism in the Holy Spirit: A Re-examination of the New Testament Teaching on the Gift of the Holy Spirit in Relation to Pentecostalism Today*, SBT 2/15 (Naperville, IL: Allenson, 1970), 109; "The Birth of a Metaphor—Baptized in Spirit," *ExpTim* 89 (1977–78): 134–38, 173–75; *Galatians*, 203. See further the pertinent commentary of Jung Hoon Kim, *The Significance of Clothing Imagery in the Pauline Corpus*, JSNTSup 268 (London and New York: T&T Clark, 2004), 108–33.

in Paul's mention of baptism a reference to water baptism whose explanation is given in the highly evocative metaphor of being clothed with Christ, of having "put on" Christ (*Christon enedysasthe*, 3:27).

As is the case with many metaphors, the image of being clothed with Christ can be taken in different ways, hence the power of the image and the need to understand what Paul intended when he wrote about putting on Christ. Paul's metaphor may owe its origin to the practice of believers removing their clothes, being baptized semi-naked, and putting on new clothes after emerging from the baptismal waters,[98] but there is no historical evidence that this well-attested ritual practice dates all the way back to the mid-first century CE. On the other hand, Paul might have derived his metaphor from the Hebrew Bible where there are many references to being clothed with righteousness, salvation, strength, or glory[99] or, conversely, being clothed with shame.[100] Psalm 131, for example, speaks of priests being clothed with righteousness and salvation while the enemies of the king of Israel are clothed with disgrace.

Paul's metaphor certainly implied that the newly baptized were expected to live the Christian life. Longenecker explains: "[Y]ou took on yourselves Christ's characteristics, virtues, and intentions, and so became like him."[101] Paul's Hellenistic audience might have thought of the newly baptized being so immersed in Christ that they were like actors who don the clothes of a character, enter into the role, and acquire the character's personality.[102]

Were the ethical implications of his metaphor all that Paul intended, his use of the baptismal formula would have represented a watering down of the "in Christ Jesus" formula (3:26) that he is explaining, but putting on Christ is a way for Paul to talk about incorporation into Christ. It is a way for him to write about the radical transformation that takes place in baptism, a way for him to write about one's new being in Christ.[103] Putting on Christ is giving up one's old identity to acquire a

---

[98] So, C. F. D. Moule, *Worship in the New Testament* (Richmond, VA: John Knox, 1961), 52–53; Dunn, *Baptism*, 110.

[99] See 2 Chr 6:41; Job 29:14; Ps 131:9, 16, 18; Prov 31:25; Isa 51:9; 52:1; 59:17; 61:10; Zech 3:3-5.

[100] See Job 8:22; Ps 35:26; 131:18; 1 Macc 1:28.

[101] Longenecker, *Galatians*, 157.

[102] Thus, Dunn, *Galatians*, 205.

[103] See Heinrich Schlier, *Der Brief an die Galater*, KEK. 12th ed. (Göttingen & Ruprecht, 1962), 173.

new identity in Christ.[104] In the words of Hans Dieter Betz, the image "suggests an event of divine transformation."[105] From one's new existence in Christ there flows new life in Christ.

Paul's Hellenistic audience might not have grasped the profound meaning of Paul's metaphor, but many among them would have been familiar with various practices that helped them to understand something of what Paul intended to imply. Some religious rituals had the candidates put on new garments to signify the acquisition of immortality or participation in some form of divine nature.[106] Even if those who heard Paul's message were unfamiliar with such religious practices, they would have known of people putting on different clothes as they assumed a different role in society.

### Hortatory Use of Metaphor

Paul is a master of the hortatory use of metaphor. Family images and the image of the slave serve Paul's rhetorical purpose in urging Galatian believers to accept other members of their family and cherish the freedom that is theirs. In Galatians 5 Paul employs other metaphors as he develops his thought. In 5:7, he challenges the Galatians with a rhetorical question: "You were running well; who prevented you from obeying the truth?" All eyes are focused on the runners, but the runners stop in midcourse, dropping out of the race. Why? Those who abandon the gospel are like runners who abandon the race. One can only ask, why would they do such a thing?

The image of the runner is one of Paul's favorites, appearing in Romans 9:16; 1 Corinthians 9:24 [2x], 26; and Philippians 2:16. In Galatians 2:2 Paul uses the metaphor in a description of his visit to Jerusalem. The visit was prompted by Paul's desire to be sure that his efforts on behalf of the gospel were neither meaningless nor fruitless.[107] Evoking the image

---

[104] So, Lührmann, *Galatians*, 75.

[105] Betz, *Galatians*, 187.

[106] See, among many studies, Joseph A. Fitzmyer, *Essays on the Semitic Background of the New Testament* (London: Chapman, 1971), 405–8; Betz, *Galatians*, 188.

[107] Paul indicates that the meeting went well by reporting in 2:9 that the pillars of the church in Jerusalem "gave Barnabas and me the right hand of fellowship." Paul used the expression "gave the right hand" much as we would use "shook hands" as a sign of welcome or as a sign of agreement. Such usage is well attested in classical literature and in the Bible. For example, Aristophanes, *Clouds* 81; Xenophon, *Anabasis* 7.3.1; 2 Kgs 10:15; Ezra 10:19 [= 1 Esdr 9:20, LXX]; Ezek 17:18; Lam 5:6.

of a runner who has gone down a stray path or lags so far behind as to be out of the race, Paul writes that he wanted to "make sure that I was not running, or had not run, in vain" (2:2).[108]

In 5:9 Paul moves from the stadium to the kitchen, citing the domestic maxim, "A little yeast leavens the whole batch of dough" (5:9). Also appearing in 1 Corinthians 5:6, Paul's phrase articulates a commonplace of proverbial wisdom.[109] Everyone knows that it doesn't take much yeast to make a whole batch of dough rise.[110]

Among Paul's Jewish and Hellenistic contemporaries, yeast was a symbol of evil and corruption. Thus, Plutarch, the Stoic philosopher, writes:

> Yeast is itself also the product of corruption, and produces corruption in the dough with which it is mixed; for the dough becomes flabby and inert, and altogether the process of leavening seems to be one of putrefaction; at any rate if it goes too far, it completely sours and spoils the flour. (*Roman Questions* 109 [*Moralia* 289F])

In their discussions of ritual *halakah*, ancient rabbis had much to say about the process of leavening.[111] Neither leaven nor honey were to be used in sacrificial offerings (Lev 2:11). The biblical prohibition of the use of leaven during the seven days of the Passover celebration (Exod 12:14-20; Deut 16:3-8) was important to Jews, leading them to consider leaven as a symbol for evil, something contrary to God's will for his people.[112] Coming out of the Jewish experience, Paul, too, considered leaven as a symbol of evil.

Paul's use of the household proverb suggests that the number of agitators did not have to be large in order to corrupt the entire community. The adage was so well known that Paul had no need to explain it to the Galatians. To the extent that proverbs and metaphors are transparent, they are all the more effective. Because of its transparency, the proverbial metaphor of 5:9 should have been particularly effective. Evoking the

---

[108] See Pfitzner, *Agon Motif*, 99–108.

[109] The sentence appears within quotation marks in some translations, e.g., NEB, REB, and NIV.

[110] Cf. Matt 13:33; Luke 13:21; *G. Thom.* 96.

[111] See especially *m. Orlah* 2.

[112] See Philo's allegorical interpretation of Lev 2:11 in *Preliminary Studies* 169 and *Special Laws* 1.291–293; Matt 16:6; Mark 8:15; Luke 12:1; cf. Ign. *Magn.* 10:2.

celebration of Passover, the principal Jewish feast, the metaphor of leaven was directed to those who were promoting "the Jewish cause."

Paul's sarcasm in dealing with the Judaizers who were unsettling the Galatians is patent. Defiantly he proclaims, "I wish those who unsettle you would castrate themselves!" (5:12). Sarcasm continues to ooze from the scribe's pen as Paul issues a powerful warning, "If you bite and devour one another, take care that you are not consumed by one another" (5:15). Rhetoricians often compared inappropriate behavior with the behavior of animals, but Paul's use of the metaphor is particularly graphic. He uses the rhetorical device of *klimax* as he moves from the image of animals snapping at one another and taking an occasional bite[113] out of one another's flesh to the image of these animals eating and chewing and, finally, devouring[114] their prey entirely. "The comparison," writes Betz, "describes mad beasts fighting each other so ferociously that they end up killing each other."[115]

A different kind of metaphor appears in 6:2a, 5: "Bear one another's burdens. . . . For all must carry their own loads." The parallel expressions are clearly metaphorical and seemingly contradictory. Taken literally they each refer to carrying heavy objects, respectively identified as burdens and as a load. Barkley suggests that the several maxims of 5:25–6:10 are of two kinds: those that speak of a person's corporate responsibilities and those that address personal responsibility before God.[116] Galatians 6:2a belongs to the first category, 6:5 to the second.

The pithiness of the two sayings,[117] and the fact that the virtually synonymous "burdens" (*ta barē*) and "load" (*phortion*)[118] do not elsewhere appear in Paul, suggests that the sayings are commonplace maxims which Paul adapts for his own use. They should not be taken too narrowly. The first aphorism[119] is a gnomic parallel to the love command. The second

---

[113] The verb *daknō*, "bite," does not occur elsewhere in the New Testament.

[114] The verb *analiskō*, "consume," does not appear elsewhere in Paul's letters.

[115] Betz, *Galatians*, 277.

[116] See John M. G. Barkley, *Obeying the Truth: A Study of Paul's Ethics in Galatians* (Edinburgh: T&T Clark, 1988), 149–50.

[117] 6:5a is, literally, "each will bear his (her) own load" (*hekastos gar to idion phortion bastasei*).

[118] "Load" (*phortion*) is used in a metaphorical sense by such authors as the orator Demosthenes (*Speeches* 11.14) and the fourth-century BCE dramatists Antiphanes (3, 329) and Anaxandrides (53). See, for these comic dramatists, Theodor Kock, ed., *Comicorum Atticorum Fragmenta*, 2 (Leipzig: Teubner, 1884), 12, 135.

[119] John G. Stralan ("Burden-bearing and the Law of Christ: A Re-examination of Galatians 6:2," *JBL* 94 [1975]: 266–76) assumes that the saying refers to a common

saying, whose verb in the future tense undoubtedly refers to the eschaton, suggests that each person will appear at the judgment with his or her own weaknesses and failures.

Other kinds of imagery appear in 6:7. Warning the Galatians not to be deceived, Paul says, "God is not mocked [*theos ou myktērizetai*[120]], for you reap whatever you sow." The verb in the passive voice is derived from the noun *myktēr*, "nostril." In the active voice, the verb approximates the meaning of the English-language expression "turn one's nose up at." Used in the passive voice, the image conveys the thought of being mocked, snubbed, or sneered at.[121] Perhaps the verb suggests being outwitted.[122]

Paul uses an agricultural image to explain why it is futile to mock God: "for you reap whatever you sow." The simple adage represents the proverbial wisdom of the farmer.[123] Sowing (*speirō*) and reaping (*therizō*) are a natural pair. The harvest is connatural to the seed that has been sown. The proverb was surely used in the agricultural communities ringing the Mediterranean basin.[124]

Paul clarifies the meaning of his metaphor in 6:8: "If you sow to your own flesh, you will reap corruption from the flesh; but if you sow to the Spirit, you will reap eternal life from the Spirit." As far as Paul is concerned, there are two possibilities. He imagines two fields in each of which the harvest corresponds to what has been sown. If the seed has been sown in the field of the flesh, the harvest will be nothing other than utter ruin. If a person sows in the field of the Spirit, the harvest will be eternal life. There is, however, a caveat (6:9). Just as the farmer must cultivate the field until the right moment (*kairō idiō*) for the harvest, so the believer must not grow weary in his or her efforts to do what is right. In the agricultural world and in the real world, one must take care of the field until the harvest has been reaped.

---

sharing of financial burdens. Matera (*Galatians*, 214) suggests that it is a matter of bearing with one another's temptations to sin.

[120] As with much of Paul's imaginative language in Galatians, *myktērizō* appears in the New Testament only in 6:7.

[121] See Jer 20:7.

[122] Thus, LSJ, *s.v. myktērizō*.

[123] Avoiding the pitfalls of exclusive language, the NRSV translation of the expression cloaks its proverbial nature. The generic *ho anthrōpos* ("the person who") in Paul's version of the proverb, so characteristic of expressions of traditional and common wisdom, does not appear in the NRSV translation.

[124] Cf. 1 Cor 9:11; 2 Cor 9:6.

The antithetical agricultural imagery of Paul's exhortation sheds light upon his earlier contrast between the flesh and the Spirit (5:19-23). Using a literary genre exploited by contemporary moralists, Paul gives a catalogue of vices to describe the power of the flesh in a person's life, contrasting these vices with a list of virtues that result from the power of the Spirit in one's life:

> Now the works of the flesh are obvious: fornication, impurity, licentiousness, idolatry, sorcery, enmities, strife, jealousy, anger, quarrels, dissensions, factions, envy, drunkenness, carousing, and things like these. . . . By contrast, the fruit of the Spirit is love, joy, peace, patience, kindness, generosity, faithfulness, gentleness, and self-control. (Gal 5:19-23)

The "fruit of the Spirit" (*karpos tou pneumatos*) contrasts with the "works of the flesh" (*ta erga tēs sarkos*). "Fruit of the Spirit" is an agricultural metaphor.[125] Love, joy, peace are not grown on trees or plants; rather they result from the activity of the Spirit in one's life. Antithetically paired with "fruit of the Spirit," "works of the flesh" should probably be taken as a metaphor as well. Paul is not disinclined to use the word "fruit" (*karpos*) with a negative connotation (Rom 6:21-22) but *ergon*, "work," was part of agricultural jargon. It describes a field that was recently tilled or one that was ready for tillage. Fornication, jealousy, drunkenness, and the like are not physical products. Resulting from the power of the flesh at work, they are fruits of the flesh.

Taken together, Paul's agricultural images suggest that the initial produce of the flesh is a whole series of vices while the final harvest is utter destruction. In contrast, the first produce of the Spirit consists of virtues like love, joy, and peace; the final harvest produces eternal life.

## A Metaphorical Conclusion

All of Paul's letters conclude with a salutation in the form of a blessing or wish prayer. The final words of Galatians are, "May the grace of our Lord Jesus Christ be with your spirit, brothers and sisters" (6:18). It has been noted that this epistolary closing is unique among the Pauline letters because of its use of a metaphorical "brothers and sisters." The salutation represents Paul's final attempt to appeal to their kinship, their belonging to a single family.

---

[125] Cf. Phil 1:11, 22; 4:17.

Immediately preceding the farewell greeting is a pair of verses in which metaphor plays an important role:

> As for those who follow [*stoichēsousin*] this rule—peace be upon them, and mercy, and upon the Israel of God.
> From now on, let no one make trouble for me; for I carry the marks of Jesus branded [*ta stigmata*] on my body. (Gal 6:16-17)

The penultimate blessing of 6:16 employs a verb whose primary meaning is "line up with," even though it was often used in the figurative sense of "agree with." Paul uses the verb in this applied meaning, just as he did in 5:25: "If we live by the Spirit, let us also be guided [*stoichōmen*] by the Spirit." The verb properly belongs to the military domain. Xenophon, the historian, (*Cyropaedia* 6.3.34) and Lycurgus, the orator, (*Leocrates* 77) used the verb *stoicheō* to describe soldiers standing and moving forward together in a single line. The Roman phalanx derived its strength from ranks formed and acting in this way. The armored line was almost the equivalent of a tank in modern warfare.

Having used a military image to describe the Galatians, Paul chooses an image from another domain to describe himself. He was branded, just as animals and runaway slaves[126] were branded to show that they belonged to their owner. The branding of slaves as a sign of ownership was a practice found in the East,[127] but not often in the Greco-Roman Empire. There were, however, some exceptions, and the practice became more prevalent after the New Testament period. A work by a first-century CE Alexandrian Jew condemned the practice as being contrary to the human dignity even of slaves.[128] Paul's use of the metaphor strikingly affirms that he is a slave of Christ, perhaps an unworthy one at that.[129]

The metaphors in these last few verses of Galatians are a good indication of the extent to which the expression of Paul's thought is pervaded with powerful metaphors. The images come from a wide variety of sources—commerce, agriculture, the stadium, the courtroom, the military, the family, to name but a few of the more important sources of Paul's metaphors. Similar expressions are sometimes found in classical or Hellenistic Greek; others are found in the Bible. Some are found in both Greek and Jewish sources.

---

[126] Deserters from the Roman legions were similarly branded.

[127] See *ANET* 172, 176.

[128] See Pseudo-Phocylides 225.

[129] Matera (*Galatians*, 227) notes that often persons devoted to the service of a particular temple carried a distinguishing brand mark.

Metaphors derived from the family and the household, including the guardian (*paidagōgos*) and the steward (*oikonos*), are the dominant metaphors in Paul's argument, providing the skeleton from which develops his thought. One metaphor stands out from all the others, Paul's metaphorical use of the verb "crucify" (*stauroō*). The apostle could find no precedent to describe the manifold consequences of Christ's death on the cross. So, he coined a new metaphor, one that remains part of our vocabulary to the present day.

# 6

# The First Letter to the Corinthians

In Galatians the apostle used a variety of metaphors to illustrate the reality of the cross. He developed a new metaphor to speak about the consequences of the crucifixion for those who believed in Jesus crucified. The relatively few references to the crucifixion in 1 Corinthians are straightforward references to the event.[1] Even the posing question, "Was Paul crucified for you?" (1:13), is one in which the verb is to be taken literally, not figuratively. The single passage in this letter where the "cross" is to be taken as a trope is in 1:17, ". . . so that the cross of Christ might not be emptied of its power." Of itself the wooden cross has no power; Paul uses metonymy to refer to the saving event of Christ's death on the cross.

## The Family

On the other hand, just as kinship language was used to good effect in Galatians, so too kinship language figures strongly in the rhetoric of 1 Corinthians. The familiar formula of direct address, "brothers and sisters," echoes through the letter almost as a refrain.[2] Paul emphasizes

[1] The noun *stauros*, "cross," appears in 1:17, 18; the verb *stauroō* in 1:13, 23; 2:2, 8.
[2] See 1:10, 11, 26; 2:1; 3:1; 4:6; 7:24, 29; 10:1; 11:33; 12:1; 14:6, 20, 26, 39; 15:1, 31, 50, 58; 16:15. Other instances of Paul's use of *adelphos* in this letter are in 1:1; 5:11; 6:5, 6 [2x], 8; 7:12, 14, 15; 8:11, 12, 13 [2x]; 9:5; 15:6; 16:11, 12 [2x], 20.

the relationship between himself and them by adding "my" or "my beloved" to "brothers and sisters" in 1:11 and 15:58, respectively. Paul hoped that such kinship language would be an effective rhetorical tool in calling a community that was divided over many different issues to the unity that ought to have characterized their sharing as a family (1:10).[3]

Perhaps no passage in the letter illustrates what Paul intended to achieve by calling the Corinthians "brothers and sisters" more than his use of the expression in 11:33. The formula introduces the peroration to Paul's response to the Corinthians' censurable practice of eating a meal which should have unified the family (11:17-34) in such a way that divisions within the family become apparent.[4]

Paul wants the Corinthians to celebrate their meal as a family meal and so twice tells them that their behavior is not commendable (11:17, 22). What they were doing showed contempt for the church of God and humiliated those who had nothing. Their behavior was so bad that despite their use of the ritual of the Lord's Supper, what they were doing could not be called the Lord's Supper (11:20).

What were they doing? Basically, they were letting the class divisions among them become manifest as they gathered together as a church to share a fellowship meal. Some, apparently the well-to-do, came first, eating the choice food and drinking almost all of the wine. When the slaves and the less well-off eventually made their appearance, they had only leftovers and dregs of wine.

To counter this fractious behavior, Paul retold the story of Jesus sharing the bread and the cup on the night that he was betrayed, highlighting, as he told the story, elements that he hoped would make an impression on the Corinthians.[5] To summarize and confirm his point in straightforward language, he said: "So then, my brothers and sisters, when you come together to eat, wait for one another. If you are hungry, eat at home, so that when you come together, it will not be for your condemnation" (11:33-34a-b).

Paul appeals to the Corinthians' sense of honor and shame—the apostle fully expects that they would all want to avoid condemnation—and to the bonds of kinship that tie them together as he tells them how

---

[3] See especially in this regard Mary Katherine Berge, *The Language of Belonging: A Rhetorical Analysis of Kinship Language in First Corinthians* (CBET 31. Leuven: Peeters, 2004).

[4] See the recent work of Panayotis Coutsoumpos, *Paul and the Lord's Supper: A Socio-Historical Investigation*, SBLit 84 (New York: Peter Lang, 2005), 113–16.

[5] See Collins, *First Corinthians*, 425–35.

they should act when they come together. Only then will their meal, with its memorial of the Lord and the meal that he shared with his disciples, truly be the Lord's Supper.

Paul also dealt with the issue of Christians taking one another to a secular court, "before the unrighteous," in Paul's words (6:1-11).[6] This is another passage in which the apostle's use of kinship language is crucial to his argument. Honor and shame were core cultural values in the Mediterranean world.[7] Appeals to honor and shame were an important feature of Hellenistic rhetoric; the sense of honor and a sense of shame were powerful motivational forces. Only twice does Paul tell those to whom he is writing that what he is saying is written "to their shame." One of those passages is 6:5; the other is 15:34.

Commenting on the situation in Corinth, Paul raises the issue of shame in the introduction to a rhetorical question whose purpose was to prompt the community to reflect on their shameful behavior. The question is: "Can it be that there is no one among you wise enough to decide between one believer [*adelphou*] and another, but a believer [*adelphos*] goes to court against a believer [*adelphou*]—and before unbelievers at that?" (6:5b-6).

Rendering *adelphos* as "believer," the NRSV translators have made the issue one of faith as if the basic problem was that some were taking people to court where a person without faith would be making judgment upon them. Paul's repeated use of *adelphos* shows that a judge's lack of Christian faith is only part of the problem. Equally serious is that disputes among members of the church are family affairs that ought to be resolved within the family. Bonds of kinship should prevent members of the family from washing their dirty laundry in public, letting it air in the presence of a judge.

That Paul considers family relationships to be an important aspect of the matter under consideration is almost immediately confirmed. Attempting to bring the Corinthians to their senses, Paul follows the rhetorical question of 6:5b-6 with two more rhetorical questions (6:7b-c)[8] and then confronts those who are bringing fellow believers to court with a rather blunt statement: "You yourselves wrong and defraud—and believers [*adelphous*] at that." It is bad enough that members of the Christian

---

[6] See ibid., 224–38.

[7] See John J. Pilch, *The Cultural Dictionary of the Bible* (Collegeville, MN: Liturgical Press, 1999), 36, 59–60, 129.

[8] Rhetorical questions are the backbone of Paul's argumentation in 6:1-11. In the first nine verses, the apostle asks nine rhetorical questions. The editors of the Greek text in N-A[27] have ten question marks in these nine verses.

community wrong and defraud others; it is even worse that they should do so to members of their own family.

Sibship language is also employed to good effect in the peroration of the first part[9] of an extended reflection on the matter of food offered to idols (8:1–10:33). Bringing the first part of his argument to a close, Paul writes:

> So by your knowledge those weak believers [*ho adelphos*] for whom Christ died are destroyed. But when you thus sin against members of your family [*tous adelphous*], and wound their conscience when it is weak, you sin against Christ. Therefore, if food is a cause of their [*ton adelphon mou*] falling, I will never eat meat, so that I may not cause one of them [*ton adelphon mou*] to fall." (1 Cor 8:11-13)

Wanting to avoid the repetitious "brother,"[10] the editors of the NRSV have provided their readers with a flowing translation. What the translation has gained in readability has detracted from the force of Paul's argument. The apostle is not writing about one of "them," he is talking about family relationships, albeit fictive. Four times in this relatively short passage Paul uses the term *adelphos*, "sibling." Repetition of the same word is a device used for the sake of emphasis. Paul is talking about family relationships; expectations of what it means to be members of a family is the real issue.

Paul gives himself as an example (8:13). Examples are an important element of Hellenistic rhetoric. Arguing from his own example, Paul uses an argument from ethos. His personal authority vis-à-vis the Corinthians should suffice to lead them to follow his example. Paul would not cause his own brother or sister to fall; neither should the Corinthians cause a member of their family to fall. If they do so, not only do they sin against Christ; but they are also causing serious problems within the family.

*Father and Mother*

The dynamic of honor and shame comes into play in another passage of the letter in which kinship language plays a related and complex role

---

[9] The three chapters are arranged in a chiastic pattern. What is now chapter 8 provides the A element of the pattern, chapter 9 the B element, and chapter 10 the A' element.

[10] It is more likely that men rather than women would have been in the banquet setting implied by the reference to the temple in 8:10.

(4:14-21).[11] Paul had previously chided the Corinthians for acting as if they were kings (4:8).[12] The idea that the Corinthians are acting immaturely, acting like children, will be implicit in such passages as 10:7 and 13:11. In the meantime Paul chides the Corinthians for their childish ways:

> I am not writing this to make you ashamed, but to admonish you as my beloved children [*hōs tekna mou agapēta*]. For though you might have ten thousand guardians [*paidagōgous*] in Christ, you do not have many fathers [*ou pollous pateras*]. Indeed, in Christ Jesus I became your father [*egennēsa*] through the gospel. I appeal to you, then, be imitators of me. For this reason I sent you Timothy, who is my beloved and faithful child [*mou teknon agapeton kai piston*] in the Lord, to remind you of my ways in Christ Jesus, as I teach them everywhere in every church. But some of you, thinking that I am not coming to you, have become arrogant. But I will come to you soon, if the Lord wills, and I will find out not the talk of these arrogant people but their power. For the kingdom of God depends not on talk but on power. What would you prefer? Am I to come to you with a stick [*en rapdō*], or with love in a spirit of gentleness? (1 Cor 4:14-21)

Anyone who reads this passage, paying as little attention as possible to its theological language, can recognize the voice of a father talking to his children. "I'm only doing this to help you. I really love you but I'm the father and you're the child. Look at me. Look at your older brother Timothy; he does what he is told. I'll be back. It's up to you. Do I have to get the belt?" Readers of these pages may have heard such a speech at one time or another from their own fathers. This is the kind of speech that Paul gives to the Corinthians as he brings the first section of his letter to its close.

Paul's transitional speech is a rhetorical masterpiece. Although its language is simple, the speech is woven through with contrast and ends with a pair of rhetorical questions: "What would you prefer? Am I to

---

[11] See Trevor J. Burke, "Paul's Role as 'Father' to His Corinthian 'Children': in Socio-Historical Context (1 Corinthians 4:14-21)" in Trevor J. Burke and J. Keith Elliott, *Paul and the Corinthians: Studies on a Community in Conflict: Essays in Honour of Margaret Thrall*, NovTSup 109 (Leiden: Brill, 2003), 95–113; Charles A Wanamaker, "The Power of the Absent Father: A Socio-rhetorical analysis of 1 Corinthians 4:14–5:13," in Cilliers Breytenbach, Johan Thom, and Jeremy Punt, eds., *The New Testament Interpreted: Essays in Honour of Bernard C. Lategan*, NovTSup 124 (Leiden: Brill, 2006), 339–64.

[12] See Collins, *First Corinthians*, 186–87. "Reign," "be a king" (*basileuō*) used metaphorically in Wis 6:21. Paul uses the verb metaphorically and ironically.

come to you with a stick or with love in a spirit of gentleness?" (4:14-21). The image of the father and his children[13] dominates the discourse, enhancing the powerful rhetorical force of Paul's appeal.

The apostle begins by stating that he is talking to the children whom he loves, "his beloved children." He says that he is not trying to make them ashamed—though that is precisely what he is about to do! Rather, he says, he is only going to put them on their guard; he is only going to warn them. Philosophic moralists of Paul's era often spoke about the value of admonition. The epistolary theorist Pseudo-Demetrius included the letter of admonition (*typos nouthetētikos*) as one of the recognized letter forms in the Hellenistic world. The nomenclature identifies the nature of the letter: "Admonition is instilling of sense in the person who is being admonished and teaching him what should and should not be done."[14]

Paul's admonition is framed by the mention of love, but its rhetoric is that of paternal discourse. The apostle begins by calling the Corinthians his "beloved children." They are the recipients of a father's love. Paul explains that he is their only father. As a father, he enjoys an authority over them that none of their many guardians could possibly have. Paul's fatherhood is rooted in the fact that he became their father by preaching the gospel to them.

Paul could speak in this fashion because he was a Jew. Having preached the gospel to the Corinthians and brought them to faith, Paul could speak to them with an authority similar to that of the rabbi who taught the Torah to his disciples. Perhaps Paul considered that he had to explain his use of "father" and "children" in their regard because many of them were Gentiles. The Gentile members of the Corinthian church would most likely have been unfamiliar with the apostle's Semitic metaphor. From Paul's point of view not only was he really their father, but he also enjoyed paternal authority over them. That authority far surpassed any of their tutors or guardians, perhaps an allusion to those persons in the community who might have been leading others astray.

As their father,[15] the apostle expected that they would learn from his example and follow it. Paul was not content to leave this part of his

---

[13] See the extended and comparative analysis in Gutierrez, *Paternité spirituelle*, 119–97.

[14] *Epistolary Types* 7. See Abraham J. Malherbe, *Ancient Epistolary Theorists*, SBLSBS 19 (Atlanta: Scholars, 1988), 34–35.

[15] Paul does not use the word "father" (*patēr*) of himself. The application of the epithet to himself is implied by the contrast between himself and the "many fathers"

admonition to their intuition. He became explicit: "Be imitators of me" (4:16), follow my example. If the Corinthians needed another example, they had the example of Timothy, their "big brother." Like the Corinthians (4:14), Timothy was Paul's beloved child (4:17). Unlike them, he was a "faithful" child, one who could be trusted.[16] Paul's hope was that the Corinthians would learn from Paul and become as faithful as Timothy.

Unlike 1 Thessalonians where Paul juxtaposes the images of mother and father to speak of his relationship with the community (1 Thess 2:7b-8, 11-12), Paul does not parallel his paternal relationship with the Corinthians with an explicit mention of his being like a mother to them. Nonetheless, he uses a powerful maternal image to speak of his relationship with the Corinthians: "And so, brothers and sisters, I could not speak to you as spiritual people, but rather as people of the flesh, as infants [*hōs nēpiois*] in Christ. I fed you with milk [*gala*], not solid food [*brōma*], for you were not ready for solid food. Even now you are still not ready, for you are still of the flesh" (1 Cor 3:1-3a). This passage is built on metaphor, beginning with the familiar "brothers and sisters." Immediately, Paul calls these members of his fictive family up short. He is not able to speak to them as adults; they are as yet infants, incapable of ingesting solid food. The Corinthians may have considered themselves to be fully mature (2:6), but from Paul's perspective they are hardly more than babies.

The Corinthians could hardly have failed to catch the gist of Paul's sarcastic message. The contrast between milk and solid food is classic.

---

whom the Corinthians do not have (4:15). Paternity is, in any case, an important concept in 1 Corinthians. In addition to Paul's three uses of the term *patēr* in reference to God (1:3; 8:6; 15:24), Paul uses the epithet in striking fashion in two other passages. In 5:1, Paul underscores the heinousness of the incestuous man's sin by saying that he "is living with his father's wife," *gynaika tina tou patros*, literally, "has a woman, the one who belongs to the [= his] father." Then, in 10:1, Paul writes to the largely Gentile church in Corinth: "Our ancestors [*hēmōn pateres*] were all under the cloud." Paul offers an actualizing exegesis of the Exodus story, "boldly claiming for an assorted group of Corinthian Gentiles the ancestors of Israel," as Gaventa correctly notes. See Beverly Roberts Gaventa, "Mother's Milk" in Eugene H. Lovering Jr. and Jerry L. Sumney, eds., *Theology and Ethics in Paul and His Interpreters: Essays in Honor of Victor Paul Furnish* (Nashville: Abingdon, 1996), 101–13, 108.

[16] The idea that Timothy was faithful insofar as he was faithful in his commitment to Christ is not to be totally excluded. Nonetheless, in a passage where family dynamics are involved, as they are in 4:14-21, the primary sense of *pistos*, "faithful," is trustworthiness just as it is in 4:2.

Philo, the apostle's contemporary, writes: "Souls still naked like those of mere infants [*nēpiōn*] must be tended and nursed by instilling first, in place of milk [*galaktos*], the soft food [*trophas*] of instruction given in the school subjects, later, the harder, stronger meat, which philosophy produces" (*Every Good Man Is Free* 160).[17]

Commentators frequently ask what Paul meant by the contrast.[18] Since Paul does not propose two tiers of membership in the church or two levels of preaching and acceptance of the gospel message,[19] any pursuit of specific references for "milk" and "solid food" seems to be inconsistent with his thought. Paul, moreover, does not say that he has provided solid food to anyone. The pursuit of specific references for milk and solid food is unwarranted and deprives Paul's metaphor of its rhetorical force. The contrast between milk and solid food enhances Paul's metaphorical description of the Corinthians as mere infants.[20] Proclaiming themselves to be fully mature, they are really like infants who can only drink milk, incapable as they are of eating solid food.

The nutritional metaphor projects the image of Paul as a nurturing mother who takes care of feeding the children who are incapable of taking care of themselves. With the use of an emphatic *ēgō*, "I," (3:1, 4, 6) Paul draws attention to himself and his ministry. The principal concern of the entire passage (3:1-9) is the relationship between Paul and the Corinthians.

Since popular culture in Paul's time demeaned men who looked, dressed, or acted like women,[21] his maternal metaphor not only drew attention to his care of the Corinthians, but it was also self-deprecating. In the words of Beverly Gaventa, "The metaphor expresses the bond of affection and care that characterizes the relationship and simultaneously places Paul at the margins of what is perceived to be 'genuine' manhood."[22]

---

[17] Cf. Philo, *Preliminary Studies* 19; *Agriculture* 9; *Migration of Abraham* 29; *Dreams* 2.10; Epictetus, *Discourses* 2.16.39; 3.24.9.

[18] See Wilhelm Thüsing, "'Milche' und 'feste Speise' (1 Kor 3,1f und Hebr 5,11–6,3). Elementarkatechese und theologische Vertiefung in neutestamentlicher Sicht," *TTZ* 76 (1967): 233–46, 261–80, esp. 235–38; and Gaventa, "Mother's Milk," 101–3.

[19] See Collins, *First Corinthians*, 128.

[20] The metaphorical epithet is in fact a simile. Note the comparative particle *hōs*, "as," in the phrase *hōs nēpiois*, "as infants."

[21] See, for example, Aristotle, *Physiognomonics* 807a-b; Seneca, *Epistle* 122.7; Quintilian, *Training* 11.1.3.

[22] Gaventa, "Mother's Milk," 112.

*Paul*

The self-effacing attitude transparent in Paul's description of himself as a mother also appears in other passages of the letter. Almost immediately after describing himself as a mother (3:1-2), Paul raises the question of his identity, asking, "What is Paul?" (3:5), and answering his own rhetorical question. Both he and Apollos are "servants," "*mere* servants" in Gaventa's well-turned paraphrase of Paul's words.[23]

Paul sees himself in a condition of servitude vis-à-vis God and his Christ. In fact, Paul considers himself to be among the lowest of the low in reference to God. Three metaphors make this very clear. Reflecting on the ministry of himself and Apollos among the Corinthians, the apostle asks them to ponder his role. "Think of us in this way," he says, "as servants of Christ and stewards of God's mysteries" (4:1). Paul often writes about himself as a "servant" (*diakonos*)[24] or "slave" (*doulos*),[25] but only in 4:1 does Paul describe himself and Apollos as servants (*hōs hypēretas*) and stewards (*oikonomous*). The first epithet is hapax in his writings; the second is used of himself only in 4:1-2. The unusual vocabulary, coupled with the fact that Paul employs a pair of contrasting images, leads the reader to ask what Paul had in mind as he used language that he was not otherwise accustomed to use.

"Servant" (*hypēretēs*) was commonly used in a military context to describe a military underling,[26] an ordinary soldier or armor-bearer, for instance, but it was also used to describe other functionaries, as it does in Matthew 5:25 and Luke 4:20. In common parlance it was sometimes used to describe construction workers and cultic personnel. Originally, however, the term *hypēretēs* and the related verb *hypēreteō* belonged to the nautical sphere. The noun designated a rower, especially the "under-rower" who manned the oars of a bireme or trireme; the verb meant "row" or "perform a service on board a ship."[27] Corinth was a port city located on the narrow isthmus between the Gulf of Saron and the Gulf of Corinth. The fate of slaves who, at the beat of the lash, pulled the oars on the lower deck of a rat-infested ship would have been well known to the Corinthians whose livelihood was to a large extent dominated by

---

[23] Her emphasis. See Gaventa, "Mother's Milk," 111; cf. Gordon D. Fee, *The First Epistle to the Corinthians*, NICNT (Grand Rapids, MI: Eerdmans, 1987), 129–30.

[24] 3:5; 2 Cor 3:6; 6:14; 11:23.

[25] Rom 1:1; Phil 1:1; cf. 2 Cor 4:5.

[26] The noun is so used in Matt 26:58; Mark 14:54, 65; John 18:3, 12, 18, 22, 36; 19:6.

[27] See LSJ, *s.v.*; Spicq, "*Hyperetēs*," *TLNT* 3:398–402.

the sea and the trade that it brought. Hardly could they have missed the connotations of Paul describing himself and Apollos as *hypēretas*, not only as mere servants but also as the lowest of the low.

Paul joins the nautical image to that of the steward (*oikonomos*), the rich man's chief of staff, the head slave who had the responsibility of assigning tasks and overseeing other household slaves.[28] The image is context-specific. Some members of the community were well off or of noble birth (1:26). At least one of them had a house large enough to accommodate the entire membership of the church at Corinth (11:18, 19, 20). That person may have been Gaius, whom Paul lauds as his host and host of the whole church [at Corinth] in Romans 16:23. Another member of the community was Erastus, whose position as city treasurer (Rom 16:23) would seem to indicate that he was a man of sufficient power and affluence to have had his own household and household staff. With people such as Gaius and Erastus as members of the community, the Corinthians could hardly have been unfamiliar with the power of the steward, slave though he was.

The image of Paul, the slave, occurs again in 9:16-18:

> If I proclaim the gospel, this gives me no ground for boasting, for an obligation [*anagkē*] is laid on me, and woe [*ouai*] betide me if I do not proclaim the gospel! For if I do this of my own will, I have a reward; but if not of my own will [*akōn*], I am entrusted with a commission. What then is my reward? Just this: that in my proclamation I may make the gospel free of charge, so as not to make full use of my rights in the gospel.

A clue as to the meaning of Paul's autobiographical snippet can be found in the words "entrusted with a commission" (*oikonomian pepisteuomai*). In 4:1 Paul wrote about the steward, the *oikonomos*; now he writes about the steward's task, *oikonomian*. In Paul's world household management (*oikonomia*) was the responsibility of a slave.[29] The essential quality of a steward is that he be found trustworthy (*pistos*, 4:2); Paul now uses a verb derived from that root to say that the steward's task will have been entrusted (*pepisteuomai*) to him even if he did not willingly fulfill his task.

---

[28] Derived from *oikos*, "house," and *nomos*, "law," the term *oikonomos* connotes the person who was responsible for the management of his master's household (cf. *TLNT* 2:568–75).

[29] Cf. Josephus, *Jewish Antiquities*, 12.199–200; Demosthenes, *Speeches* 36.43–44; Xenophon, *Memorabilia* 2.5.2; Luke 12:42.

A portrait of a slave emerges from 9:16-18.[30] Unable to exercise his own free will in regard to the tasks that are assigned to him, the slave labors under considerable constraint. He or she is anxious about what will happen if the assigned task is not done in the way that the master expects. In his description of the slave Paul does not use the word "slave" (*doulos*). His technique is similar to that of 3:1-2 and 4:14-21. In these passages Paul did not use the word "mother" (*mētēr*) or "father" (*patēr*);[31] rather, he let the image emerge from his descriptive language. As narratologists might say, Paul showed the metaphor rather than telling or stating it. In 9:16-18 the image is clear; Paul has effectively, and powerfully, described himself as a slave of God to whom the task of preaching the gospel has been assigned. Doing the assigned task in the way that God wants is the only reward that Paul can expect.

The image of the slave was not only self-deprecating; it also allowed Paul to identify with the slaves who constituted a good portion of the Corinthian church. Far more demeaning than the image of the slave was the way that Paul talked about himself at the end of the short fool's speech in 4:10-13.[32] The speech is a balanced three-part composition developed on the basis of a peristatic catalogue, a list of difficult situations in life. The first unit consists of a trio of circumstances contrasting the Corinthians' situation with that of Paul and Apollos (4:10). The second unit rehearses a set of six circumstances that describe the apostles' situation (4:11-12a). The third unit consists of a triad contrasting the preachers' adverse circumstances with their positive response (4:12b-13a).

Paul concludes his carefully crafted description with a startling statement: "We have become like the rubbish [*hōs perikatharmata*] of the world, the dregs [*peripsēma*] of all things, to this very day" (4:13b). The language of the simile belongs to the same semantic register as the vocabulary of Philippians 3:8 where Paul says that he considers the attributes of which he had previously boasted as rubbish (*skybala*). That he uses such demeaning language to speak about himself is remarkable. That he uses

---

[30] See Collins, *First Corinthians*, 345–49. On the meaning of *anagkē*, see further Lincoln E. Galloway, *Freedom in the Gospel: Paul's Exemplum in 1 Cor 9 in Conversation with the Discourses of Epictetus and Philo*, CBET 38 (Leuven: Peeters, 2004), 180–84.

[31] The NRSV translates the verb *egennēsa*, "I begot, as "I became your father" (4:15).

[32] Cf. the longer fool's speech in 2 Cor 11:1–12:13. The use of a circumstantial catalogue is a characteristic feature of the fool's speech (2 Cor 11:23-28), just as it is in 4:10-13.

similar language to describe not only himself but also his coworker is more remarkable still.

The words *perikatharmata*, "rubbish" or "filth," *peripsēma*, "dregs" or "refuse," and *skybala*, "rubbish" or "excrement," are vulgar and rather similar in meaning. The language is that of the street; it reeks with insult, scorn, and abuse. Classical and Hellenistic Jewish literature provide ample evidence that the terms were used in a derisive fashion. Demosthenes spoke of Euctenon as "the despicable Euctenon, that scum" (*Against Meidias* 103).[33] More than once Philo described those puffed up with pride and arrogance looking down on others and calling them names like "offscourings" (*katharmata*).[34] Epictetus describes a Cynic reflecting on the moral value of powerful people and asking, "Did Priam, who begot fifty sons, all rascals [*perikatharmata*] . . . contribute more to the common weal than did Homer?"[35]

Derived from the root *kathar-*, suggesting a cleaning process, *perikatharmata*, "rubbish," conjures up the image of garbage that is left over after someone has cleaned up after a meal or the pile of dirt and trash that is accumulated as someone cleans out a room. Since filth can be transferred from one object to another, the term was occasionally used in the secular or religious sense of "scapegoat" or even "human sacrifice."[36] The word *peripsēma*, "dregs," had a similar history in antiquity. For example, Photius's ninth-century *Lexicon* tells that the term was used of criminals tossed into the sea as an expiatory gesture to ward off public disaster.[37]

Although some commentators hesitate to exclude some sort of notion of vicarious sacrifice from Paul's use of "rubbish" and "dregs," the terms derive their meaning not from the cultic sphere but rather from the nature of the list of hardships with which they are associated. Such catalogues were used to win over the sympathy of an audience. Intended to show the miserable circumstances of an orator or author, they opened the hearts of the audience toward the speaker or writer, thus contributing to his *ēthos* appeal. Since Paul uses hardship catalogues in similar

---

[33] Cf. Demosthenes, *Crown* 128.

[34] See Philo, *Moses* 1.30; *Virtues* 174.

[35] *Discourses* 3.22.78. In a previous rhetorical question, the Cynic asked about those who sired "ugly-snouted children" (*karorygcha paidia, Discourses* 3.22.77).

[36] See Hans Lietzmann, *An die Korinther I/II*, HNT 9. 4th expanded edition by Werner Georg Kümmel (Tübingen: J. C. B. Mohr [Paul Siebeck] 1949), 20–21; C. K. Barrett, *The First Epistle to the Corinthians*, BNTC (London: Adam & Charles Black, 1968), 112–13.

[37] See Photius, *Lexicon, s.v.* "*peripsēma*."

fashion,[38] there is little reason to attribute anything but a self-deprecating meaning to Paul's use of the terms "rubbish" and "dregs" in 4:13.

Another powerful image that Paul uses to describe himself as the lowest of the low is to be found in his personal commentary on the early Christian creed (15:1-3). Rehearsing the traditional faith that Christ who had been raised was seen by Cephas [Peter] and the Twelve, Paul proclaims that Christ had also been seen by more than five hundred brothers and sisters, by James, and by all the apostles. "Last of all," Paul adds, "as to someone untimely born [*hōsperi tō ektrōmati*], he appeared also to me" (15:8).

The rare term *ektrōma* appears nowhere else in the New Testament. Meaning "stillborn child," the term appears three times in the Greek Bible, always in a comparison (Num 12:12; Job 3:16; Qoh 6:3), hence, in a figurative sense.[39] It is found in a single passage of Aristotle (*Generation of Animals* 4.5.733ᵇ18), on one Greek papyrus (*Tebtunis Papyrus* 800.30), and in the definition given by the fifth-century CE lexicographer Hesychius: "a child born dead, untimely, something cast out of the woman."[40] The image is that of a fetus born violently and before its time.

The image that Paul has used to describe his insignificance vis-à-vis the first witnesses of the risen Christ is graphic in any reading of the text. Margaret Mitchell, however, considers that Paul's use of the image is meant to convey the notion that among the apostles Paul is an abortion, that is, one that has been cast aside and rejected in much the same manner as an aborted fetus.[41] From the twelfth to the twentieth century, various commentators have suggested that the unusual simile must have first been used as a derogatory slur upon Paul.[42] Paul would have appropriated the language and then used it to his own advantage in 15:8.

---

[38] Also called peristatic catalogues, these lists of difficulties appear in Rom 8:35; 1 Cor 4:10-13; 2 Cor 4:8-9; 6:4-10; 11:23-27; 12:10; Phil 4:12.

[39] Hollander and van der Hout consider that Paul's use of the term is ultimately derived from the figurative use of *ektrōma* in the Hellenistic Jewish tradition. See Harm W. Hollander and Gijsbert van der Hout, "The Apostle Paul Calling Himself an Abortion: 1 Cor 15:8 within the Context of 1 Cor 15:8-10," *NovT* 38 (1996): 224–36.

[40] See Hesychius, *Hesychii Alexandrini lexicon recensuit et mendavit Kurt Latte, s.v.* "Ektrōma; Spicq, "Ektrōma," *TLNT* 1:464–66, 465.

[41] See Margaret W. Mitchell, "Reexamining the 'Aborted Apostle': An Exploration of Paul's Self-Description in 1 Corinthians 15.8," *JSNT* 25 (2003): 469–85.

[42] For example, Johannes Tzetzes in the twelfth century and C. K. Barrett (*The First Epistle to the Corinthians*, 344) in the twentieth.

Paul explains his simile in this way: "I am the least of the apostles, unfit to be called an apostle" (15:9). Were it possible to prove within any reasonable degree of certainty that the image of the aborted fetus as well as the images of rubbish found in 4:13 originated in derogatory remarks directed at Paul, that reality would go a long way to explain why these derogatory terms are used only once by Paul and why they are used in this particular letter. Master of rhetoric that he was, Paul could seize the opportunity provided by the language of those who attacked him to gain rhetorical advantage by using their language to enhance his own *ēthos*.

## More about the Apostle by the Apostle

Not all the images that Paul uses to describe himself in 1 Corinthians are as designedly self-deprecating as are the images of himself as mother, aborted fetus, rubbish, and dregs. Some images describe Paul as being involved in a cooperative effort which is brought to fruition by God. Such are the images of 3:5-17. In this chapter Paul's self-descriptive metaphors are related to the images that he uses to characterize the Corinthian church. First Corinthians 3:9b serves as the hinge of the pictorial diptych that Paul paints in this passage. On the one hand, there is the image of the field; on the other, there is the image of a building. As Paul moves from one image to the other, he writes: "You are God's field, God's building" (3:9b).

Juxtaposing agricultural and architectural images, Paul joins a large number of biblical, Hellenistic, and Jewish writers before him who did the same thing. Among them are Plato[43] and Philo,[44] the authors of Deuteronomy[45] and Jeremiah,[46] the evangelist Luke,[47] and the author of Qumran's *Manual of Discipline*.[48]

Paul uses the traditional pairing to make his point. Each of his metaphors is a complex metaphor, allowing for the development of submetaphors.[49] The Corinthians are comparable to a field (*geōrgion*,[50] 3:9b), but

---

[43] *Laws* 1.643B.

[44] *Allegorical Interpretation* 3.48; *Cherubim* 100–2.

[45] Deut 20:5-6.

[46] Jer 1:10; 18:7-10; 24:6; 31:28; 42:10.

[47] Luke 17:28.

[48] See 1QS 8:5; 11:5.

[49] On the notion of complex metaphors, see Zoltàn Kövecses, "The Scope of Metaphors," in Antonio Barcelona, ed., *Metaphor and Metonymy at the Crossroads: A Cognitive Perspective* (Berlin and New York: Mouton de Gruyter, 2003), 79–92.

[50] The word is hapax in the New Testament.

Paul does not dwell on the individual plants in the field; nor does he describe the variety of plants that might exist in the field he evokes. Rather, he underscores the idea that it takes more than one worker to raise a crop successfully. These coworkers (3:9a) must work together, each doing his own task if the crop is to grow: "I planted [*ephyteusa*], Apollos watered [*epotisen*]. . . . The one who plants [*ho phyteuōn*] and the one who waters [*ho potizōn*] have a common purpose" (3:6, 8). Paul pictures himself as a farmer whose work is foundational; he is the planter. Seed will not grow without being watered. Another farmer must enter the picture. That is Apollos who follows up Paul's work by watering the seed that has been planted. Human effort is, nonetheless, for naught unless God makes the seed grow. So Paul notes that in the field that belongs to God, it is God who makes the seed grow (3:6c).

Drawing the readers' attention to an imaginative building (*oikodomē*, 3:9) that belongs to God, Paul makes a somewhat similar but different point. His role in the church of Corinth is foundational. Comparing the church to a building under construction, Paul says of himself, "like a skilled master builder [*hōs sophos architektōn*] I laid a foundation" (3:10).[51] Thereafter it is the responsibility of a number of specialized craftsmen working with different building materials to construct the building. With language similar to that employed in a fourth-century BCE description of the construction of the temple of Athena, Paul mentions the quality control that takes place.[52] When the building has been completed through the cooperative effort of many workers, the owner can "move in." The building then becomes God's temple: "Do you not know that you are God's temple [*naos theou*] and that God's Spirit dwells [*oikei en hymin*] in you?" (3:16). The Corinthians are expected to answer with a heartfelt "Yes, we know."[53]

The church as the building in which God dwells through his Spirit provides Paul with the metaphor describing himself and Apollos as "stewards" (*oikonomous*) of God's mysteries (4:1). The image of the household manager draws attention to the singular importance of Paul and

---

[51] In Rom 15:20 Paul writes that he preaches the gospel where it has not yet been preached "so that I do not build on someone else's foundation."

[52] See C. D. Buck, *Greek Dialects* (Chicago: University of Chicago Press, 1955), 201–3; Jay Y. Shanor, "Paul as Master Builder: Construction Terms in First Corinthians," *NTS* 34 (1988): 461–71; Collins, *First Corinthians*, 149–51.

[53] On the moral significance of Paul's temple metaphor, see Charles A. Wanamaker, "Metaphor and Morality: Examples of Paul's Moral Thinking in 1 Corinthians 1–5," *Neot* 39 (2005): 409–33.

Apollos in the house of God. Paul's listeners would have recognized in his metaphor an allusion to the chief slave within a great household who not only had responsibility for coordinating and supervising the work of lesser slaves but who also had access to the paterfamilias, like a chief of staff, privy to the master's needs and plans. As stewards of the mysteries of God, Paul and Apollos have a unique relationship with God.[54] Paul's writing to the Corinthians about their responsibilities for and in the house of God was an exercise of the supervisory role that was his as a steward of the mysteries of God (3:10-17; cf. 12:4-30).

Later in the fourth chapter Paul turns his attention from the household to the public arena: "God has exhibited us apostles as last of all, as though sentenced to death, because we have become a spectacle to the world, to angels and to mortals" (4:9). The image is that of the amphitheater. "Exhibited" (*apedeixen*), "spectacle" (*theatron*), and "sentenced to death" (*epithanatious*) is language that pertains to the public arena; it does not appear elsewhere in Paul's extant writings.

"Spectacle" (*theatron*) is part of a word group that pertains to the sense of sight. A spectacle is a show to be watched; watching the show is the audience. Sitting in the stands of Paul's theater are the world, angels, and mortals. Paul's picture almost conveys the image of these different groups of attendees sitting in different parts or perhaps different tiers of the amphitheater.

Shows like that described by Paul were familiar to his Greco-Roman audience. Victorious generals often returned to the imperial or provincial capital with a parade. Bringing up the rear of the victory parade were the prisoners, fodder for the swords of the gladiators whom they were soon to face.[55] As Paul asks the Corinthians to conjure up the image that he is sharing with them,[56] he suggests that he and his fellow missionaries brought up the rear of the parade. Coming at its tail end, they were "last

[54] As Paul wrote about himself and Apollos being stewards of the mysteries of God, the apostle was primarily thinking in the first instance of their ministry of the word. See Collins, *First Corinthians*, 172. It is, however, not unlikely that the Corinthian audience probably assumed that Paul and Apollos had special access to God that enabled them to know about God's "secrets" and convey that knowledge to others.

[55] See Philo, *Embassy* 368.

[56] Pfitzner (*Paul and the Agon Motif*, 189) notes that the image was also used by the philosophic moralists: "Seneca and Epictetus wish to glorify the sage with this picture. . . . Paul, on the other hand, uses the picture to illustrate the humility and indignity to which the apostles, as the servants of God, are subjected."

of all," the position of those under sentence of death (*epithanatious*).[57] They were on display (*theatron*) for all the world to see, its angelic and its human populations alike.

Ironically, at least to those who read Paul's text today, the one who presided over this show is not one of the Roman emperors, like Nero or Domitian; rather, the one who has put on the show is God himself. It is, in Paul's words, God who "has exhibited us apostles as last of all."

Later in the letter, in chapter 9, Paul returns to the subject of himself in a long rhetorical digression in his discussion of food offered to idols. For the most part, the chapter is a dramatic *apologia* in which Paul pleads for his apostolic rights, only to say that he is willing to forgo those rights for the sake of the apostolic mission. As a lawyer pleading his case, Paul asks the jury a series of rhetorical questions intended to elicit from the jury, his Corinthian audience, the conviction that Paul was indeed entitled to his rights.

His series of rhetorical posers is virtually a chain of metaphors. Most of the metaphors belong to the domain of agriculture, but the first and the last derive from the military and cultic spheres, respectively:

> Who at any time pays the expenses for doing military service? Who plants a vineyard and does not eat any of its fruit? Or who tends a flock and does not get any of its milk? . . . Does not the law also say the same? For it is written in the law of Moses, "You shall not muzzle an ox while it is treading out the grain." . . . For whoever plows should plow in hope and whoever threshes should thresh in hope of a share in the crop. If we have sown spiritual good among you, is it too much if we reap your material benefits? . . . Do you not know that those who are employed in the temple service get their food from the temple, and those who serve at the altar share in what is sacrificed on the altar? (1 Cor 9:7-13)

Having teased the imagination of his audience with this series of questions, Paul does not hesitate to tell the Corinthians in plain language what he was trying to get them to conclude through this exercise in stretching the imagination: "In the same way, the Lord commanded that

---

[57] V. Henry R. Nguyen ("The Identification of Paul's Spectacle of Death Metaphor in 1 Corinthians 4.9," *NTS* 53 [2007]: 489–501) sees in Paul's metaphor a reference to the Roman practice of a public spectacle in which condemned criminals (*noxii*) were put to death in the arena.

those who proclaim the gospel should get their living by the gospel" (9:14).

Each of Paul's metaphors, taken by itself, is simple enough. The complexity of the series of metaphors calls for some comment. Paul's letters generally indicate that he was most at home in the large cities of the Greco-Roman Empire. His metaphors are typically drawn from the experience of life in the city. In 9:7-13, however, Paul's metaphors offer a panorama of life in an agricultural area. He writes about the vinedresser, the shepherd, the ox tethered to the mill, the plower, the sower, and the reaper.

Had Paul added to his list a question about the one who plants an olive tree, he would have pretty much encompassed the variety of forms of life on the farm. It may be that the omission of the olive tree owes as much to Paul's knowledge of life on the farm as it does to anything else. Olive trees are legendary in that they continue to produce olives long after those who planted them had died. This being the case, the link between activity and reward is not as apparent with regard to the olive tree as it is with regard to the various forms of agricultural life that Paul has mentioned.

A striking feature of the agricultural metaphors employed by Paul is the single reference to an animal. Paul makes reference to an item of agricultural law (Deut 25:4) embedded among legal prescriptions that regulate interhuman conduct. The law stipulates that an ox must be allowed to eat if it is expected to turn the mill. Using the kind of *a fortiori* reasoning that would be known as the rabbinic *Kal va-homer* principle of biblical interpretation, Paul suggests that as the ox tethered to the grinding mill deserves his wages, his food, so the laborer deserves his wages. Paul's citation of Scripture suggests that his Jewish heritage is the source of the agricultural imagery. Rabbis often compared animals with human beings in their attempts to tease *halakah* from their reading of Scripture.[58]

Although the citation of Deuteronomy 25:4 suggests that Paul's rural images derive from his Jewish and biblical heritage, the fact is that the soldier, the vinedresser, and the shepherd were also stock figures in Hellenistic rhetoric. The soldier frequently appears in texts that make use

---

[58] See, for example, *b. Baba Mesiʾa* 87a–91b; *m. Yadayim* 4:7; Philo, *Virtues* 145. See also D. Instone Brewer, "1 Corinthians 9:9-11: A Literal Interpretation of 'Do not muzzle the Ox,'" *NTS* 38 (1992): 554–65. Philo also reflected on the significance of Deut 25:4. See Philo, *Virtues* 145.

of the *agōn* motif, an important tool among the argumentative techniques of the philosophic moralists. Paul echoed their technique when using the panoply of other military metaphors to speak about the believer's battle to live a fully Christian life or about the evangelist's struggle on behalf of the gospel.[59] In 9:7a Paul did not use the military metaphor in typical fashion. He asks only if the soldier should expect to receive proper rations as recompense for his soldiering. Does not the soldier have a right to provisions? "Who serves as a soldier at his own expense?" is the gist of the challenge that Paul first tosses at the Corinthians.

Having evoked the image of the soldier who expects to receive his rations and having employed a variety of agricultural images, Paul turns his attention to the cult: "Do you not know that those who are employed in the temple service get their food from the temple, and those who serve at the altar share in what is sacrificed on the altar?" (9:13). Over and over again, Paul's biblical tradition taught and legislated that a portion of the animal or grains sacrificed to YHWH were to be set aside for the use of the priests.[60]

The parallel cultic questions may reflect the two classes of temple service within the Jewish tradition, namely, priests and Levites. Paul's temple metaphor should have had a powerful appeal for the Christian Jews in Corinth; the metaphor was directed not to one or another peripheral activity of their lives but to their religious tradition, a defining element of their identity as Jews. On the other hand, even Gentile Christians would have been able to grasp the meaning of Paul's metaphor. Cosmopolitan Corinth was a city with many and diverse forms of worship (10:18-20), among which was the cult of Asklepios, known for its cures and its sacrificial offerings.[61]

With the last of the nineteen questions in 1 Corinthians 9, Paul turns to another domain to enhance his imaginative argument: "Do you not know that in a race the runners all compete, but only one receives the prize?" (9:24). References to athletic competition were an important part of Paul's rhetorical strategy. After the Olympic games themselves, the biennial Isthmian Games, held on the outskirts of Corinth, were probably the most renowned athletic event in ancient Greece. The games were

---

[59] Thus, 1 Thess 5:8; Phlm 2.

[60] See Lev 2:10; 5:13; 6:16-18, 22-23; 7:6-10, 14, 30-36; 10:12-15. Cf. Josephus, *Jewish Antiquities* 3.224–236.

[61] With regard to the cult of Asklepios, see C. A. Meier, "Asklepios," *ER* 1:463–66, and Collins, *First Corinthians*, 462, 466.

inaugurated by Lucius Castricius Regulus between 7 and 3 BCE, some fifty years before Paul first preached in Corinth. By Paul's day, these games had been enhanced by a preliminary event, the Caesarean Games. Big-time athletic competition was something with which the Corinthians were fully aware.[62]

Paul shows himself to be fairly familiar with athletic events and what it takes to win. He writes about running and boxing. He knows that some are crowned winners and that some are disqualified. He knows about the discipline and training that are necessary if winning is to be a possibility:

> Do you not know that in a race [*stadiō*] the runners [*trechontes*] all compete, but only one receives the prize [*brabeion*]? Run [*trechete*] in such a way that you may win it. Athletes [*agōnizomenos*] exercise self-control [*enkrateuetai*] in all things; they do it to receive a perishable wreath [*stephanon*], but we an imperishable one. So I do not run [*trechō*] aimlessly, nor do I box [*pykteuō*] as though beating the air; but I punish my body and enslave it, so that after proclaiming to others I myself should not be disqualified [*adokimos*]. (1 Cor 9:24-27)

These eight Greek words belong to the jargon of the athletic event, its preparation and its coronation. Not only is the athletic imagery patent, Paul's argument is crafted in a vocabulary that he otherwise uses infrequently or not at all.[63]

Stoics employed the military battle and the athletic contest as metaphors to describe the struggle to achieve a goal, be that a life devoid of pathos or the acquisition of truth. Paul opts for athletic imagery to achieve his purpose.[64] Having asked the Corinthians to think about a

---

[62] "Do you not know [*ouk oidate*]?" is a typical feature of Paul's style. The disclosure formula introduces an appeal to the experience of those who listen to Paul's message.

[63] Three words are New Testament hapax legomena: "race" (*stadiōn*), "box" (*pykteuo*), and "enslave" (*doulagōgeō*). To these can be added the expression, "beating the air" (*aera derōn*), a great image for shadowboxing or sparring. Two words occur only twice in the New Testament, both times in Paul: "prize" (*brabeion*; cf. Phil 3:14) and "punish" (*ekratuomai*, 1 Cor 7:9). "Punish" (*hypōpiazō*) occurs in only one other New Testament passage, Luke 18:5. Two words occur elsewhere in the New Testament but are hapax in the undisputed Pauline corpus, namely, "athletes" (from the verb *agonizomai*) and "disqualified" (*adokimos*). "Crown" (*stephanos*) is a word that Paul uses only three times, here and in Phil 4:1, 1 Thess 2:19.

[64] Cf. Stephan Joubert, "1 Corinthians 9:24-27: An Agonistic Competition?" *Neot* 35 (2001): 57–68. Joubert contends that Paul has been criticized for not accepting

runner running the race in order to win, Paul challenges them to run the race in such a way that they finish as winners.[65] Their crown of victory will not be a perishable leafy garland; it will be the imperishable crown of eternal life. Paul wants the Corinthians to be eager and steadfast in living the Christian life.

To make his argument even more forceful, he turns the imagery upon himself, depicting himself as a runner or boxer preparing for the big event. Doing so, Paul accomplishes a remarkable rhetorical feat. He uses the *agōn* motif in an appeal from *ēthos*, offering himself as an example for the Corinthians to follow. He portrays himself as a runner who must stay the course, as a boxer engaged in shadowboxing, "beating the air," in Paul's words. The rigorous training that he faces for his imaginative bout in the ring or sprint on the track demands considerable physical discipline. "I punish my body and enslave it" is the way that Paul describes the rigor of his imaginary athletic training. Similar discipline was necessary were he to be successful in his apostolic mission. This kind of discipline is also necessary if the Corinthians are to respond to Paul's exhortation and try to be winners in the pursuit of the Christian life.

## Sounds of Music

Paul again offers himself as an example to the Corinthians in an *ēthos* appeal which serves as the introduction to the magnificent encomium on love in 1 Corinthians 13:

> If I speak in the tongues of mortals and of angels, but do not have love, I am a noisy gong or a clanging cymbal. And if I have prophetic powers, and understand all mysteries and all knowledge, and if I have all faith, so as to remove mountains, but do not have love, I am nothing. If I give away all my possessions, and if I hand over my body so that I may boast, but do not have love, I gain nothing. (1 Cor 13:1-3)

In these verses Paul is writing about himself, not some generic "I." The apostle enjoyed the gift of tongues (14:6, 13, 18) and the gift of prophecy (14:6, 19); he was able to understand something of the mysteries of God (2:7, 12-13).

---

financial support from the Corinthians. Defending his apostolic integrity, he employs the agonistic motif.

[65] "Run" (*trechete*, 9:24) is in the plural.

To show the singular importance of the greatest of all charisms, Paul states that no matter the number and diversity of charisms that have been given to him, if he does not have the most basic of all charisms, the gift of love, he is worthless. To drive home the point, Paul enhances the argument with metaphor.

His first metaphor appeals to the sense of sound; he writes about angelic sounds, the tongues of angels. The metaphor is obviously intended to put into perspective and thereby diminish in importance the speaking in tongues which some Corinthian Christians valued so highly. Their doing so was tantamount to creating a two-class church, those who spoke in tongues and those who did not.

In chapter 12 Paul puts speaking in tongues in its place by citing it at the end of all three lists of spiritual gifts (12:10, 29, 30) and juxtaposing it with the gift of interpretation of tongues, without the benefit of which speaking in tongues is so much gibberish (14:23). In 13:1 Paul relativizes the value of speaking in tongues by comparing that form of human speech, albeit Spirit-inspired, with the speech of angels. The imagery comes from Paul's Jewish background; the Hellenistic Jewish *Testament of Job* compares the ecstatic speech of Job's daughters with that of angels, archons, and the cherubim.[66] Were Paul's speech to be truly heavenly, yet were he to lack the fundamental charism of love, Paul's value would have been that of a worthless sound-maker.

Paul's metaphors generally appeal to the sense of sight but Aristotle teaches that metaphor appeals to any one of the senses and specifically mentions the beauty of its sound.[67] The rhetoric which Paul uses when he argues about speaking in tongues (1 Cor 12–14) almost requires that Paul appeal to his audience through the sense of hearing. In 13:1a Paul evokes the sound of angelic voices; in the second part of the verse he draws his audience's attention to the sounds created by human beings on instruments. The noisy gong and clanging cymbal of 13:1c enables a contemporary reader of 1 Corinthians to join with Paul's audience as it listened to the sounds that Paul is creating. If Paul does not have the fundamental charism of love, he is hardly better off than an inert instrument that produces noise rather than musical tones.

"A noisy gong or a clanging cymbal," the NRSV translation of 13:1c, captures the main thrust of Paul's argument, but it does not capture the

---

[66] See *T. Job* 48:3; 49:2; 50:2. Written in either the first century BCE or the first century CE, the document was more or less contemporary with Paul and would have reflected Jewish ideas that were in the air at the time.

[67] See Aristotle, *Rhetoric* 3.2.13.

full range of his sonorous metaphor. "Noisy gong" (*chalkos ēchōn*) is better translated as "resounding brass." Earlier in the letter, Paul asked his readers to consider him as a sight in the amphitheater (4:9). In theaters the sounds of center stage were enhanced by means of echo chambers strategically placed in niches around the theater.[68] These practical acoustical devices were generally made of bronze. In all likelihood Paul is comparing a loveless exercise of the gift of tongues to a piece of bronze that merely echoes sound coming from elsewhere. The echoed sound is hardly comparable to the sound of a fine musical instrument, like that which comes from a resounding cymbal.[69] Thus, a better translation of Paul's Greek might be: "I have become sounding brass rather than a resounding cymbal."[70] In Paul's biblical tradition[71] and in the Hellenistic world, the cymbal was considered to be a fine musical instrument.

Thinking of the cymbal as a musical instrument rather than as a simple noisemaker is consistent with the digressive nature of chapter 13. Chapter 14 urges that all charisms be exercised in such a way that the church is built up, just as the various parts of the body must function in harmony if the body is to be healthy and functional (12:12-26). Between chapters 12 and 14, chapter 13 focuses on love which builds up the community (8:1). In Paul's world harmonious sound was a well-known metaphor for the community whose members worked as a team in harmony with one another.[72] Were Paul's speech to be compared with that of a resounding cymbal, he effectively tells the Corinthians that his speech-based witness to Christ functions like that of the harmonious sound of a resounding cymbal.

Having completed the rhetorical digression, Paul returns to speaking in tongues in chapter 14. He tries to make the Corinthians understand the relative value of the gift of tongues by returning to the analogy of musical instruments:

> If I come to you speaking in tongues, how will I benefit you unless I speak to you in some revelation or knowledge or prophecy or teaching? It is the same way with lifeless instruments that produce

[68] See Vitruvius, *Architecture* 5.3.8.

[69] Cf. Ivor H. Jones, "Musical Instruments," *ABD* 4:934–39, 935.

[70] See Collins, *First Corinthians*, 475.

[71] See, for example, 1 Chr 25:1 where it is stipulated that Levitical singers, whose responsibility was to offer constant praise to Yahweh, were to be appointed "who should prophesy with lyres, harps, and cymbals."

[72] See, for example, 3 Macc 13:8; Plutarch, "On Brotherly Love," *Moralia* 478D–479B.

sound, such as the flute or the harp [*eite aulos eite kithara*]. If they do not give distinct notes, how will anyone know what is being played? And if the bugle gives an indistinct sound, who will get ready for battle? . . . There are doubtless many different kinds of sounds in the world, and nothing is without sound. If then I do not know the meaning of a sound, I will be a foreigner to the speaker and the speaker a foreigner to me. (1 Cor 14:6-11)

To the echoing brass and the resounding cymbal, Paul now adds the flute, the harp, and the bugle. The NRSV's "know what is being played" synthesizes Paul's to *auloumenon ē to kitharizomenon*, literally, "what is being played on the flute or what is being played on the harp." Using a participle that is cognate with the name of the instrument allows Paul to put into consideration the fact that each musical instrument produces its own distinctive sound; the flute "flutes" and the harp "harps," as it were.

The flute has a distinctive sound; the harp has another.[73] The beauty of sound can be appreciated only to the extent that the listener is able to discern the sound of the flute and the strain of the harp in what is being played. As Paul says, "If they do not give distinct notes [*distolēn*[74] *tois phthongois*, literally, "a distinction in sounds"], how will anyone know what is being played?"

As a human being produces the different sounds appropriate to different musical instruments by playing the flute, harp, or some other instrument, so God produces different effects (12:6) by the distribution of charisms to different people within the church. Paul does not complete his argument by saying that the sounds produced by different musical instruments contribute to the music produced by an orchestra, but the image was so common that it could hardly have been far from his own mind and that of his audience. Just as the sound produced by different musical instruments contributes to the beautiful sound of a harmonious composition, so the different effects of the various charismatic gifts within the community produce a harmonious community.

With his mention of the bugle (*salpinx*, generally translated as "trumpet" in its numerous appearances in the New Testament) in 14:8 Paul moves from the sounds produced by beautiful musical instruments to

---

[73] Cf. 15:39-41.

[74] The word *distolēn* does not connote clarity of sound in contrast with a muffled or indistinct sound; rather, the noun connotes the difference between one sound (of one musical instrument) and another (of a different musical instrument).

sounds heard on the battlefield. The military metaphor might lead the reader to think that Paul is using the agon motif. The way that Paul refers to the bugle does not, however, stress the effort or struggle that is to follow. The image no more stresses the consequences of the blare of the bugle than do his other uses of the image of the trumpet. In these passages, 1 Thessalonians 4:16 and 1 Corinthians 15:52, the sound of the trumpet indicates a transition from one moment in time to another. Despite the fact that the bugle is a piece of military equipment,[75] the metaphor of 14:8 implies only that a sound must be distinctly heard in order to produce the intended effect: "If the bugle gives an indistinct sound [*adelon*[76] *phōnēn*], who will get ready for battle?"

The sound of the bugle must be loud and clear if the army is to prepare for battle, but this is not Paul's point. His point is that they recognize the sound *of the bugle*. If soldiers are to prepare for battle, the sound that they hear must be identifiably that of the bugle. If the sound is indistinct, if it does not sound like the sound of the bugle, no response will be forthcoming. As with the flute and the harp, Paul's metaphor bears upon the distinctive sound of each instrument being recognized by the hearer. Such is the situation of charismatics and their charisms. Each must be recognized in its distinctiveness so that the church can function as church.

Continuing his discourse on the comparative importance of prophecy and tongues, Paul adds an autobiographical reflection: "I will pray with the spirit, but I will pray with the mind also; I will sing [*psalō*] praise with the spirit, but I will sing praise [*psalō*] with the mind also" (14:15). Elsewhere Paul uses the verb "sing praise" only in Romans 15:9, where it appears in a citation of Psalm 18:49. The verb, whose primary meaning is pluck, was used for pulling taut the string of a bow in order to shoot an arrow or for pulling taut a plumb line whose impression a carpenter could follow to create a straight line. Mostly, however, the verb was used for pulling the strings of a harp with one's fingers. By extension the verb came to connote singing to the accompaniment of a harp. In this sense it was used in the Psalms.[77]

---

[75] The Bible often mentions the sound of the trumpet as the declaration that the battle is about to begin. See Num 10:9; Josh 6:4-20; Judg 3:27; 6:34; 1 Sam 13:3; Isa 18:3; 27:13; 58:1; Jer 4:5, 19, 21; 51:27.

[76] "Indistinct" (*adēlon*) appears elsewhere in the New Testament only in Luke 11:44.

[77] Cf. Ps 7:18; 9:12 [LXX], etc.

Since Paul was well aware that there are many different kinds of sounds in the world and that nothing is without sound (14:10), it is remarkable that music is so rarely heard in Paul's letters. On no other occasion—at least in the extant correspondence—does Paul mention either the flute or the harp.[78] It is, however, hardly coincidental that Paul's rhetoric employs the metaphor of sound as he writes about the gifts of the Spirit. Music and musical instruments were a feature of the Hellenistic topos on the phenomenon of mantic "inspiration."

Writing about mantic inspiration, Plutarch uses the image of the flute and the harp, along with that of the trumpet and the lyre: "Wherefore it is not possible . . . to make a cylinder in motion behave in the manner of a sphere or a cube, nor a lyre like a flute, nor a trumpet like a harp. No, the use of each thing artistically is apparently no other than its natural use" ("Oracles at Delphi" 21, *Moralia* 404F). Plutarch wrote about the lyre, the flute, the trumpet, and the harp, emphasizing, as did Paul, the distinct and characteristic sound produced by different instruments.

The geographer Strabo also wrote at length about music. He noted the importance of music, and especially the music produced by the flautist, in symposia and those religious rites in which enthusiastic inspiration has a role to play.[79] Music, said Strabo, puts people in touch with the divine:

> Music, which includes dancing as well as rhythm and melody, at the same time, by its artistic beauty, brings us in touch with the divine, and this for the following reason; for although it has been well said that human beings then act most like the gods when they are doing good to others, yet one might better say, when they are happy; and such happiness consists of rejoicing, celebrating festivals, pursuing philosophy, and engaging in music. (*Geography* 10.3.9)

## Pictures of Paul

Offering himself as an example to teach the Corinthians about the relative value of spiritual gifts, Paul introduced the sounds of music, but

---

[78] The flute (*aulos*) is not otherwise mentioned in the New Testament. The harp (*kithara*) appears only in the book of Revelation's description of the heavenly liturgy (Rev 5:8; 14:2; 15:2). The cognate verbs *auleomai*, "play the flute" (Matt 11:17; Luke 7:32; 1 Cor 14:7) and *kitharizō*, "play the harp," (1 Cor 14:7; Rev 14:2) are rarely used in the New Testament.

[79] See Strabo, *Geography* 10.3.9-19.

he also wrote about a faith that would be strong enough to move mountains (*hōste orē methistanai*, 13:2). This imaginative description of charismatic faith[80] seems to echo a saying of Jesus to which Matthew 17:20; 21:21 and Mark 11:23 bear witness. The powerful picture that Paul has cleverly implanted in his readers' imagination is an example of hyperbolic rhetoric, conveying the idea that no matter the degree of dramatic power seen in the exercise of a charismatic gift, the gift is as nothing in the absence of the fundamental gift of love.

Paul's autobiographical introduction (13:1-3) to the paean on love is powerful; it exudes passion as it leads up to an emotional climax where the apostle writes that even if he were to give up his all, to hand his body over to be burned[81] and did not have love, he would still be nothing. Paul's hyperbole is a kind of metaphor, described by Aristotle as the fruit of passion:

> Approved hyperboles are also metaphors. . . . There is something youthful about hyperboles; for they show vehemence. Wherefore those who are in a passion most frequently make use of them:
>
>> Not even were he to offer me gifts as many in number as the sand and dust . . . but a daughter of Agamemnon, son of Atreus, I will not wed, not even if she rivalled golden Aphrodite in beauty, or Athene in accomplishments.
>
> (Attic orators are especially fond of hyperbole.) Wherefore it is unbecoming for elderly people to make use of them. (*Rhetoric* 3.11.15-16 [1413a-b])

Aristotle's example of hyperbole as a form of metaphor is phrased in the first person, as is Paul's use of hyperbole in 13:2b. Paul writes to the Corinthians with youthful passion and irony.

---

[80] Although Paul does not elsewhere focus on his charismatic faith, he cites the working of miracles, "signs and wonders and mighty works" among the "signs of a true apostle" (2 Cor 12:12). The "mighty works" are *dynameis*, "acts of power." Paul knows full well that he is an apostle and so describes himself in writing to the Corinthians (1:1; 9:1-2). Luke describes Paul and Barnabas reporting to the Jerusalem assembly about "the signs and wonders that God had done through them among the Gentiles" (Acts 15:12) and gives several examples of Paul working miracles (Acts 19:11-12; 20:9-12; 28:8).

[81] On the text-critical issue as to whether the Greek reads "so that I may boast" (*hina kauthēsomai*) or "so that I burn" (*hina kauchēsomai*) and an exegesis of the passage, see Collins, *First Corinthians*, 476–77.

The apostle is convinced that the various charisms are so many different manifestations of the fundamental gift of love (Rom 5:5). Someone who does not have the gift of love does not have the spiritual gifts of speaking in tongues, prophecy, knowledge, and faith to which Paul makes reference in 13:1-2, no matter the outward appearances. Paul knew that not every extraordinary phenomenon that appeared to be a spiritual manifestation was actually a charismatic gift and tried to explain this to his audience. He begins his disquisition on "spiritual gifts" (*pneumatika*) by telling his readers that they should realize that not all wonderful phenomena are gifts (*charismata*) of the Holy Spirit.[82]

Another tack taken by Paul to show that love is the gift par excellence and that it surpasses in importance any of the individual gifts is his reflection on the charisms in light of eternity. He begins: "Love never ends. But as for prophecies, they will come to an end; as for tongues, they will cease; as for knowledge, it will come to an end" (13:8) and ends with these words: "And now faith, hope, and love abide, these three; and the greatest of these is love" (13:13). To highlight the radical difference between time and eternity, Paul employs another metaphor: "Now we see in a mirror [*di'esoptrou*], dimly [*en ainigmati*], but then we will see face to face" (13:12a). He reiterates the idea and continues to use the classic rhetorical technique of the then and now schema with a specific reference to himself as he continues, "Now I know only in part; then I will know fully, even as I have been fully known" (13:12b).

The image of the mirror comes from the Hellenistic world[83] in which authors used the figure to illustrate how little humans really understand about the divine. Thus, Plutarch, Paul's philosophic contemporary, wrote:

> If, then, the most noted of the philosophers, observing the riddle of the Divine in inanimate and incorporeal objects, have not thought it proper to treat anything with carelessness or disrespect, even more do I think that, in all likelihood, we should welcome those peculiar properties existent in natures which possess the power of perception and have a soul and feeling and character. It is not that we should honor these, but that through these we should honor the Divine, since

---

[82] See 12:1-4. On the other hand, Paul also reminds his readers that not everything that a charismatic person does proceeds from his or her charismatic gift. See 14:29; 1 Thess 5:21.

[83] Both "mirror" (*esoptrou*) and the expression *en einigmati*, translated as "dimly," are not to be found elsewhere in Paul's extant correspondence.

they are the clearer mirrors [*hōs enargesterōn esoptrōn*] of the Divine by their nature also, so that we should regard them as the instrument or device of the God who orders all things. ("Isis and Osiris" 76, *Moralia* 382A-B)

A mirror offers only a reflection; the natural or poorly made mirrors of two thousand years ago provided only a fuzzy reflection of the object that was mirrored. Plutarch argued that all things mirror the divine but that to the extent that they are animate and alive, they more clearly mirror the divine. Paul takes a somewhat different tack, arguing that the image reflected by a mirror is of very poor quality compared to the vision that results from a face-to-face encounter. Paul's point is that the charismatic experience, whether in the form of prophecy, tongues, or knowledge, is a minimal experience of God compared to the experience of God that lies in that future where love continues to abide.

Paul typically writes in a personal style in the letters, sharing with his readers his travel plans and various greetings. Sometimes the apostle signs the letter and adds a few words in his own hand. In the final chapters of 1 Corinthians Paul writes some more about himself. Sometimes he uses appropriate metaphors, the most graphic of which is a reference to fighting with wild animals at Ephesus: "If with merely human hopes I fought with wild animals at Ephesus, what would I have gained by it?" (15:32).

For centuries Roman politicians enjoyed themselves by watching the "hunts" (*venationes*), including those in which criminals did battle with fierce animals in the amphitheater.[84] Some older and not-so-old commentaries take Paul's reference to the hunts as a denial of a rumor that Paul had been tossed into an amphitheater, there to do battle with one or another ferocious animal.[85] Paul's words should, however, be taken in a figurative sense;[86] he says that he is speaking in common language.[87]

---

[84] See Nicholas Purcell, "*Venationes*," *OCD* 1586. The verb used to describe criminals condemned to provide this kind of entertainment was *thēriomacheō*, "fight with wild beasts," the word used by Paul in 15:32. On Paul's use of the image, see Abraham J. Malherbe, "The Beasts at Ephesus," *JBL* 87 (1986): 71–80; reprinted in *Paul and the Popular Philosophers* (Minneapolis: Fortress, 1989), 79–89.

[85] See Dennis R. MacDonald, "A Conjectural Emendation of 1 Cor 15:31-32: Or the Case of the Misplaced Lion Fight," *HTR* 73 (1980): 265–76.

[86] See 4:9.

[87] The Greek words translated in the NRSV as "if with merely human hopes" are *ei kata anthrōpon*, literally, "if according to a human." The phrase makes no mention

It may be that Paul is speaking about the Asian affliction described in 2 Corinthians 1:8-10. As is the case with many of Paul's metaphors, the imaginative expression "I fought with wild animals" (*ethēriomachēsa*) does not occur elsewhere in Paul's correspondence; nor does it occur elsewhere in the New Testament.

The reference to the wild beasts occurs in the last of the series of four rhetorical questions in 15:29-32a. Rhetorical questions are one of the striking features of the Stoic diatribe, a rhetorical technique often used in 1 Corinthians (1:13, 20; etc.). The Stoics used the agon motif to win adherents to their point of view; Paul similarly used the agon motif at various points in this letter. Fighting with wild beasts is a motif that belongs to this kind of argumentation. Use of the image was fairly wide-spread in the agonistic literature of the Stoics and Cynics.[88] Philo used the image to describe cruel Egyptian masters oppressing the Israelites just before the Exodus.[89] The metaphor was later exploited by Ignatius, Paul's devotee, who, fully expecting to be condemned to a struggle with wild beasts,[90] wrote of his journey to Rome as a prisoner, "I am fighting wild beasts from Syria to Rome, through land and sea, by night and day, bound to ten leopards—which is a company of soldiers—who when well treated become worse" (Ign. *Rom.* 5:1).[91]

Another mention of Ephesus in the closing verses of 1 Corinthians provides a happier, if not totally happy, picture: "I will stay in Ephesus until Pentecost, for a wide door for effective work has opened to me, and there are many adversaries" (16:8-9). The image of the open door conveys the idea of accessibility; it speaks of opportunities that lie ahead. The words *thyra megalē*, "wide door," can be translated as "big door" or "great door." The size of door suggests the abundance of opportunities that continue to await Paul in Ephesus.

Paul does not, however, imply that he himself opened the door. The door lay open before him. The image recurs in 2 Corinthians 2:12 where Paul uses the passive voice, a theological passive, to suggest that the door has been opened by the agency of God through the Lord: "When I came to Troas to proclaim the good news of Christ, a door was opened

---

of hope; thus I have rendered the expression "if, humanly speaking." See Collins, *First Corinthians*, 556.

[88] See Malherbe, "The Beasts at Ephesus."

[89] See Philo, *Moses* 43–44.

[90] See Ign. *Eph.* 1:2; *Trall.* 10.

[91] See William R. Schoedel, *Ignatius of Antioch*, Hermeneia (Philadelphia: Fortress, 1985), 178–79.

[*thyras aneōgmenēs*] for me in the Lord." The Lord opened the door by making the hearts of those to whom Paul preached receptive to his word. The existence of a house church in the home of Aquila and Prisca in Ephesus (16:19) is an indication of the success of Paul's mission in Ephesus;[92] the mention of the struggle with the beasts indicates that the mission was not accomplished without some difficulty.

### The Body of Christ

Paul used appropriate metaphors to speak of his foundational role with regard to the community of faith in Corinth when he pictured the church as a field and as a building. He portrayed himself as a planter (3:6) and skilled master builder (3:10). Emphasis on Paul's foundational role is absent from the third extended ecclesial metaphor in 1 Corinthians, namely, the body of Christ.

Like the field and the building, the body is a complex metaphor. Paul develops the image in a discrete literary unit embedded within his discussion of charisms. The literary technique of ring construction helps Paul set this foundational concept within the argumentation of which it is an essential part. He begins: "For just as the body [*to sōma*] is one and has many members, and all the members of the body [*sōmatos*], though many, are one body [*hen sōma*], so it is with Christ [*ho Christos*]" (12:12). He concludes: "Now you are the body of Christ [*sōma Christou*] and individually members of it" (12:27; cf. 6:15a).

As these enveloping sentences suggest, Paul's use of the image of the body of Christ as a description of the church is intended to highlight not only the fact that the church is "of Christ" but also that the church is both one and many. This is the idea with which Paul begins his presentation of the body. As he fills in the details of the picture, Paul clearly has something more in mind than the mere fact of the multiplicity of members within the church. His portrait of the body suggests that the many members have a diversity among themselves, that they are mutually interdependent, and that, under God, they each deserve appropriate respect:

> Indeed, the body does not consist of one member but of many. If the foot were to say, "Because I am not a hand, I do not belong to the body," that would not make it any less a part of the body. And if the

---

[92] See also Acts 19:1-20.

ear were to say, "Because I am not an eye, I do not belong to the body," that would not make it any less a part of the body. If the whole body were an eye, where would the hearing be? If the whole body were hearing, where would the sense of smell be? But as it is, God arranged the members in the body, each one of them, as he chose. If all were a single member, where would the body be? As it is, there are many members, yet one body. The eye cannot say to the hand, "I have no need of you," nor again the head to the feet, "I have no need of you." On the contrary, the members of the body that seem to be weaker are indispensable, and those members of the body that we think less honorable we clothe with greater honor, and our less respectable members are treated with greater respect; whereas our more respectable members do not need this. But God has so arranged the body, giving the greater honor to the inferior member, that there may be no dissension within the body, but the members may have the same care for one another. If one member suffers, all suffer together with it; if one member is honored, all rejoice together with it. (1 Cor 12:14-26)

The image of the body was a classic topos in ancient rhetoric; it served as a model for the unity and harmony of a social and political group. The philosopher Dio Chrysostom asserts that the fabulist Aesop used the image.[93] Livy's *History of Rome* describes the Roman Senator Menenius Agrippa exploiting the image and urging the Roman people to forgo sedition and instead work together in harmony. Menenius Agrippa is reputed to have told the story of hands, mouth, and teeth revolting against the belly with the result that the whole body was impaired.[94] The widely used image of the body as a model for social harmony is also found in the writings of Plato, Cicero, Seneca, Dio Chrysostom, Philo, and Josephus.[95] Seneca, for example, wrote:

What if the hands should desire to harm the feet, or the eyes the hands? As all the members of the body are in harmony one with another because it is to the advantage of the whole that the individual members be unharmed, so mankind should spare the individual man, because all are born for a life of fellowship, and society can be kept unharmed only by the mutual protection and love of its parts. (*Anger* 2.31.7)

[93] *Discourses* 33.16.
[94] See Livy, *History of Rome* 2.32.7–33.1.
[95] See Collins, *First Corinthians*, 458–60.

In many respects Seneca's use of the body image is similar to Paul's. Like Paul, Seneca writes about the feet, eyes, and hands. Like Paul, Seneca personifies the members of the body.[96] Like Paul, he refers to the many and the one. Like Paul, he stresses the good of the whole, the interdependence of the parts, and the respect that the parts must accord to one another. And, like Paul, Seneca wrote about what happens to the whole when one part suffers harm.

Although the topos was common in first-century rhetoric, two features of Paul's use of the image[97] stand out as particular to him. The first is that the order of the one body with its several different and interdependent members is the work of God. The other is that Paul speaks about the honor to be accorded to the weaker (*asthenesthera*, v. 22), "less honorable" (*atimotera*, v. 23), and "inferior" (*tō hysteroumenō*, v. 24) members of the body. The imagery is graphic. The language that he used may have evoked thoughts of the male sexual organ, the "necessary member" of the body according to some of the ancients,[98] and the organs of excretion, less honorable members of the body.

When Paul's use of the topos is compared with that of other ancient rhetoricians, the features of the body that Paul emphasizes undoubtedly owe to the purpose for which Paul used the image. From the very beginning of his exposition on the spiritual gifts Paul stressed that God, through the Spirit, allotted to each individual the charism that the Spirit chose (12:6, 11). Hence, he highlights the idea that the members of the body have been arranged by God. Paul's focus on the less honorable parts of the body[99] was prompted by the situation at Corinth. Those who possessed the gift of speaking in tongues had inflated egos; they considered their own gifts (12:1) to be the most important of the spiritual realities within the church.

The fact that the image of the body was such a common topos in the rhetoric of the first century CE and in the rhetoric of Hellenism in general

---

[96] Ancient authors commonly personified the members of the body. In addition to Menenius's description of the hands, mouth, and feet revolting against the belly and Seneca's idea that the hands might want to harm the feet or the eyes the hands, see, among other authors, Dionysius of Halicarnassus, *Roman Antiquities* 6.86.2.

[97] Paul does not explicitly mention Christ as he develops the metaphor. The encompassing verses, 12:12 and 12:27, tell the reader that the image that he is developing before their eyes is an image of the body of Christ.

[98] See, for example, Artimedorus, *Dream Handbook* 1.45, 79, 80.

[99] A considerable part of the image, verses 22-24, is devoted to the less seemly members of the body.

made this topos exceptionally advantageous to use as Paul pleaded with the Corinthians to strive for that harmony that should be characteristic of fellowship in Christ (1:9-10). The image was all the more appropriate in that there existed at Corinth a major sanctuary in honor of Asklepios, the god of healing. Archeological excavations at the site have discovered a large number of terra-cotta images of various parts of the human body. These served as ex-votos offered to Asklepios by his devotees who attributed to the god the healing of one or another organ or limb of their body.[100]

Like Seneca, Paul enhances the complex metaphor of the body with the personification of some of its members. He lets his audience listen to talking feet, ears, and eyes. He writes about a talking head. Earlier in the letter, he underscored the importance of love by using personification. "Love builds up," he says in 8:1. The heart of 1 Corinthians 15 is a classic piece of personification in which the apostle uses fifteen verbs to paint a portrait of personified love: "Love is patient;[101] love is kind; love is not envious or boastful or arrogant or rude. It does not insist on its own way; it is not irritable or resentful; it does not rejoice in wrongdoing, but rejoices in the truth. It bears all things, believes all things, hopes all things, endures all things" (1 Cor 13:4-7).

### Christ

Paul's purpose in writing to the Corinthians, stated at the beginning of the letter, was to urge them to live in harmony with one another so that they might really be God's holy people (1:2), a community in Christ (1:9): "Now I appeal to you, brothers and sisters, by the name of our Lord Jesus Christ, that all of you be in agreement and that there be no divisions among you, but that you be united in the same mind and the

---

[100] Cf. Carl A. Roebuck, *The Asklepieion and Berna: Based on the Excavations and Preliminary Studies of F. J. de Waele* (ASCS [Athens], Corinth 14. [Princeton: American School of Classic Studies in Athens, 1951]); Andrew E. Hill, "The Temple of Asclepius: An Alternative Source of Paul's Body Theology," *JBL* 99 (1980): 437–39; C. G. Garner, "The Temple of Asklepius at Corinth and Paul's Teaching," *Buried History* 18 (1982): 52–58. A display case in the museum in Ancient Corinth contains examples of these ex-votos, two ears, two feet, two sets of male genitalia, and a woman's breast.

[101] Each of the verbs is in the present tense. The NRSV and other versions render some of Paul's verbs by means of the verb to be and an adjective, for example, "love is patient." While creating a text that is easy to read in translation, the rendition weakens the force of Paul's personification.

same purpose" (1:10).[102] This intention lies in the background of Paul's use of the images of the field, the building, and the body to describe harmony in the community.

Keenly aware that he was the apostle to the Corinthians (1:1; 9:1), Paul also used a large number of images to enhance his *ēthos* appeal. His rhetorical focus led to the selection of metaphors liberally distributed throughout the letter. He employed figurative language to underscore the importance of Christ in the life of the Corinthian church. Two images in particular stand out, Christ our paschal lamb (5:7) and Christ the first fruits (15:20, 23).

The image of the paschal lamb occurs in a parenetic section of the letter in which the apostle challenges the Corinthians to clean up their act (1 Cor 5). The issue at hand was that one of their number was having sexual relations with a woman who was his father's wife.[103] That was inappropriate, but what was even more scandalous was that the community was complacent about this egregious behavior, apparently even boasting about it. What they should have done was to remove the incestuous individual from their holy community (5:2).

To make his point, Paul refers to Christ's death in a striking metaphor. Elsewhere in the letter he also uses Christ's death as a motivational force in parenetic exhortations, appealing to his death when dealing with the issue of food offered to idols (8:11). He also appeals to Christ's death in dealing with the Corinthians' scandalous celebration of the fellowship meal in which they celebrated the twin ritual of the bread and the cup (11:23-26).

The image of Christ's death used in 1 Corinthians 5 is that of the paschal lamb. Urging the Corinthians to shun the sinner, Paul alludes to the Exodus story (cf. 10:1-11). The slaughter of the paschal lamb and the eating of the Passover supper were highlights of the commemorative festival. Ancient rhetors frequently used historical examples to make their point. Paul does so in 1 Corinthians 5. The festival's slaughter of the lamb allowed Paul to describe Christ's death as the slaughter of the

---

[102] Wanamaker ("Morality and Metaphor," 420–21) correctly notes that "divisions" (*schismata*) is a metaphor. The word properly refers to the tearing or splitting of a physical object. In the positive expression of his plea, Paul uses "say the same thing" (*to auto legēte*) as a metaphor with the meaning "be in agreement."

[103] Lev 18:7-8 (cf. Lev 20:11) distinguishes between incest with one's mother and incest with the father's wife.

paschal lamb[104] and evoke that memory as an argument to urge the Corinthians to have nothing to do with the man who so blatantly had an incestuous relationship with his father's wife.

He shows his familiarity with Jewish Passover customs as he writes:

> Do you not know that a little yeast leavens the whole batch of dough? Clean out the old yeast so that you may be a new batch, as you really are unleavened. For our paschal lamb [*to pascha*], Christ, has been sacrificed. Therefore, let us celebrate the festival [*heortazōmen*], not with the old yeast, the yeast of malice and evil, but with the unleavened bread of sincerity and truth. (1 Cor 5:6b-8)

The extended metaphor hearkens back to the Passover festival (*to pascha*). The Greek *pascha* is a transliteration of the Aramaic term used in reference to the festival of unleavened bread (Exod 23:15), the first of Israel's great pilgrimage feasts. The term generally described the entire seven-day festival, but it was also used in the Bible and in the New Testament to designate the Passover meal, the Seder, which was the highlight of the feast. On the occasion a lamb was to be slain and eaten along with the unleavened bread. Some descriptions of the ritual celebration of the Exodus used *pascha* to refer to the lamb that was slaughtered,[105] the paschal lamb.

As is the case with many of Paul's metaphors, much of the language of 5:6b-8 does not occur elsewhere in his correspondence. Only in this passage does Paul use "paschal lamb" (*to pascha*) and "celebrate the festival" (*heortazōmen*). The verb "sacrifice" (*etythē*, 5:7) appears in 10:20, but otherwise the word does not appear again in the extant correspondence. Other language found nowhere else in Paul's letters fleshes out Paul's evocation of the Passover celebration, including "batch of dough" (*phyrama*, vv. 7, 8) and "clean out" (*ekkathairō*, v. 7). "Yeast" (*zymē*) appears in verses 6, 7, 8 as well as in Galatians 5:9, but "unleavened" (*azymos*, vv. 7, 8) is not used in any of the other letters.

Paul contrasts the presence of yeast with yeast-less, that is, unleavened bread. The contrast calls to mind the Festival of Unleavened Bread whose celebratory meal included bread that was unleavened. Were yeast present in the mound of dough, the dough would rise and the bread would be

---

[104] Paul's use of "sacrifice" apparently hearkens back to the biblical phrase "sacrifice the paschal lamb" (Exod 12:21).

[105] See, among several places in the Bible, Exod 12:21 (cf.Mark 14:12; Luke 22:7).

unacceptable for use in the Passover feast. So, the use of yeast was to be avoided during the Passover festival.

Paul urges the Corinthians to shun the man who dared to sleep with his father's wife in the same way that faithful Jews shunned the use of yeast during the Passover celebration. The point of Paul's exhortation is clear: the church at Corinth is not to tolerate the presence of a sexually immoral person in its midst. Making his point, Paul created an unusual metaphor to describe the Corinthian church. Its members are "a new batch" (*neon phyrama*) since they are unleavened (*azymoi*). The use of a singular "new batch," and a plural "unleavened," to describe the church echoes the idea of the one and the many that emerges from Paul's use of the body image in 12:12-26.[106]

"Precisely because the church is God's new batch of dough," says Karl Donfried, "the apostle can urge: 'Clean out the old yeast.'"[107] Paul wants the members of the church of God at Corinth to be what they are, to live as the holy people of God that they are and are called to be. The image of the church as an unleavened batch of dough—to be ranked alongside the great ecclesial images of 1 Corinthians, the field, the temple, and the body of Christ—symbolizes not only its incorrupt nature but also the possibility of its sharing in the Passover celebration with Christ the Passover lamb.

Jewish worship may have been the source of another important christological image, first fruits. According to Leviticus 23:10-14 the first fruits of the harvest were to be brought to the priest and an unblemished lamb was to be offered as a holocaust. These first fruits were the priests' portion (Num 18:13; Deut 18:4; 2 Chr 31:4-5; cf. Deut 26:2, 10). Paul, the zealous Jew, was familiar with the cultic connotations of "first fruits" but he does not exploit the cultic nuance of the image when he describes Christ as the first fruits (*aparchē*) in 15:20 and 23.

His image is taken from the world of agriculture (cf. 3:5-9) where "first fruits" is the first crop to be harvested. Picking the first fruits is a source of hope. That some fruit has already been picked suggests that in due time other fruit will ripen; this, too, can be harvested. First fruits are a harbinger of the crop to come and a source of hope. Future salvation and hope are what Paul evokes when he describes Christ as the first fruits.

---

[106] See also 1:2, where Paul addresses "the church" (*tē ekklēsia*) in the singular with which he juxtaposes "the sanctified" (*hēgiasmenois*) and "saints" (*hagiois*) in the plural.

[107] See Karl P. Donfried, *Who Owns the Bible? Toward the Recovery of a Christian Hermeneutic*, Companions to the New Testament (New York: Crossroad, 2006), 104–5.

The image appears in Paul's rebuttal of the idea of those people who say that there is no resurrection of the dead (15:12). Paul argues that the heart of the Christian faith is the belief that Christ has been raised from the dead (15:4-8; 13-16). Christ has been raised from the dead as "the first fruits [*aparchē*] of those who have died" (15:20). The appositional phrase underscores the notion that Christ's resurrection from the dead is, like first fruits, a harbinger of things to come. Just as the harvest of first fruits suggests that additional fruit will be harvested in due time, so the resurrection of Christ presages the resurrection in God's due time of those who belong to Christ (15:20-24). Christ's resurrection is the beginning of the resurrectional sequence that God the Father effects at the appropriate time.

## Death

The context of Paul's use of the image of first fruits shows that the denial of resurrection from the dead was another issue that disturbed the unity of the church at Corinth. From the tenor of Paul's argumentation, it does not appear that these people denied Christ's resurrection; rather, they seem to have had doubts about the possibility of resurrection for other human beings.

Sophists among them might ask, "How are the dead raised? With what kind of body do they come?" (15:35). Dismissing this kind of argument as foolish,[108] Paul rebuts the objection with an analogy. Hearkening back to the creation story of Genesis 1, Paul writes:

> What you sow [*speireis*] does not come to life unless it dies. And as for what you sow [*speireis*], you do not sow [*speireis*] the body that is to be, but a bare seed, perhaps of wheat or of some other grain. But God gives it a body as he had chosen, and to each kind of seed [*spermatōn*] its own body. Not all flesh is alike, but there is one flesh for human beings, another for animals, another for birds, and another for fish. There are both heavenly bodies and earthly bodies, but the glory of the heavenly is one thing, and that of the earthly is another. There is one glory of the sun, and another glory of the moon, and another glory of the stars; indeed, star differs from star in glory. (1 Cor 15:36-41)

---

[108] He dismisses the would-be interlocutor who would pose the question as a "fool" or "senseless," (*aphrōn*, 15:36).

The imagery is complex. Paul takes the seed image from the world of agriculture[109] in which a farmer sows a seed of grain. The seed dies. The crop grows with the body that God, creator of all that is, chooses to give to it. The produce is unlike the seed which humans manipulate because it is God who brings forth the crop from the dead seed (1 Cor 3:6-7). Paul would have his imaginary interlocutor know that a human being dies with one body but that after death God will provide it with another body, just as he does with the dead seed.

Enmeshed in the imagery of the Bible, Paul's reasoning employs a kind of *Kal va-homer* reasoning commonly employed by Jewish interpreters of the Scriptures. This analogical interpretation moves from the lesser to the greater, from the minor to the major (cf. 1 Cor 9:9). So Paul argues: If the seed that humans sow rises with a different body, how much more will what God has created rise with a different body?

The idea of God as the agent who gives a new body to seed that has been sown and then died allows Paul to invite his readers to contemplate the different kinds of bodies that God has created. Paul's thought reverses the sequence of episodes in the creation story. He asks his readers to contemplate the variety of bodies that God has given to the animate creation of the sixth day; then he asks that they contemplate the bodies that God created earlier in the week of creation.

Different kinds of bodies are created by God, such as God wills. God creates living bodies from dead seed. How foolish, then, to ask with what kind of body will the dead be raised! Only God can provide the answer since it is God who creates the different kinds of bodies. The unstated conclusion of Paul's imaginative reasoning serves as a premise for his argument about the resurrection of the body. Resuming the agricultural imagery with which he began, Paul writes: "So it is with the resurrection of the dead. What is sown [*speiretai*] is perishable, what is raised is imperishable. It is sown [*speiretai*] in dishonor, it is raised in glory. It is sown in weakness, it is raised in power. It is sown [*speiretai*][110] a physical body, it is raised a spiritual body" (1 Cor 15:42-44a).

Resurrection from the dead is a Jewish idea. Rabbis speculated about the clothing to be worn by those who are raised from the dead. Even this kind of speculation is absurd in Paul's view; the bodies of those who are

---

[109] See also 3:6-9; 9:7b-c; 15:20, 23.

[110] Paul has a predilection for groups of three. Thus, it might not be coincidental that "you sow" (*speireis*) is used three times at the beginning of Paul's argument and "is sown" (*speiretai*) occurs three times at the end of the argument.

raised from the dead are clothed in imperishability and immortality: "For this perishable body must put on [*endysasthai*][111] imperishability, and this mortal body must put on [*endysasthai*] immortality. When this perishable body puts on [*endysētai*] imperishability, and this mortal body puts on [*endysētai*] immortality . . ." (1 Cor 15:53-54). Paul appropriates the language of the rabbinic discussion to create the image of the body clothed in immortality.

Apocalyptic descriptions are a product of the religious imagination and rife with imagery. Imagining the moment when the great transformation will take place, Paul describes it happening instantaneously. To capture the suddenness of it all, Paul uses language that he does not otherwise use.[112] Paul has a predilection for using groups of three for the sake of emphasis so he writes: "in a moment [*en atomō*], in the twinkling of an eye [*en ripē ophthalmou*], at the last trumpet [*en tē eschatē salpingi*]" (1 Cor 15:52a). The "moment" is an indivisible unit of time,[113] "twinkling" is rapid movement like the flutter of a bird's wings or the blink of an eye.

Master of the metaphor that he is, Paul invites his readers to employ not only the senses of sight and touch (putting on clothes) but also their sense of hearing (the sound of the trumpet) as they exercise their imaginations in contemplation of the great transformation that will take place at the parousia. The great transformation will occur "at the last trumpet. For the trumpet will sound [*salpisei*],[114] and the dead will be raised" (1 Cor 15:52). A stock image in apocalyptic literature, the sound of the trumpet was used by Paul in his depiction of the parousia in 1 Thessalonians 4:16.[115] Appealing to three of the five human senses, Paul imaginatively suggests that the entire human being will be transformed at the parousia.

Before concluding his exposition of the topos on resurrection with an exultant doxology (1 Cor 15:57), Paul hurls a taunt at (personified) death, using the imaginative language of the prophet Hosea:

[111] In Greek, the verb *endyō* means "get into clothes" or "clothe." See LSJ, *s.v.*

[112] Neither "moment" (*atomos*) nor "twinkling" (*ripē*) is to be found elsewhere in the New Testament.

[113] The word *atomos* is basically an adjective meaning "uncut."

[114] This verb occurs only here in Paul's extant writings. As is the case with the sound of the flute and the sound of the harp (14:7), the Greek uses a more simple phrase than does the English language to describe an instrument producing its sound. English needs an additional word, "play" or "sound," to capture the idea of an instrument producing sound.

[115] Cf. 14:8.

"Death has been swallowed up in victory."
"Where, O death, is your victory?
Where, O death, is your sting?" (1 Cor 15:54-55)

Paul's words are a paraphrase rather than an exact quotation of the Greek Bible's rendition of Hosea 13:14. The biblical verse, only part of which has been paraphrased by Paul, proclaims that God will redeem his people from death.[116] Behind the prophetic text may lie a Canaanite myth that portrayed personified death exerting power over people by means of plagues and destruction. Jewish monotheism proclaims that these forces are controlled by God;[117] death has no power over them.

Paul brings his disquisition on death to a close with a shout of triumph that echoes the words of the prophet. Victory over death has been assured through Jesus Christ, the Lord who has been raised from the dead. Like a lethal insect, death used the sting of sin to lead humans to death (1 Cor 15:55-56). With the resurrection of our Lord Jesus Christ, death has been conquered; its poisonous sting has been deprived of its noxious power. The insect has lost its lethal stinger. Death is, in Paul's words, "the last enemy to be destroyed" (1 Cor 15:26).

---

[116] See Hans Walter Wolff, *Hosea*, Hermeneia (Philadelphia: Fortress, 1974), 228–30; Francis I. Andersen and David Noel Freedman, *Hosea* AB 24 (Garden City, NY: Doubleday, 1980), 639.

[117] See Exodus 9–10; Hab 3:5; etc.

# 7

# The Second Letter to the Corinthians

he study of Paul's rhetorical use of figurative language in the
Second Letter to the Corinthians is complicated by the fact that
considerable scholarly disagreement exists as to whether or not
the letter is a single composition written by the Apostle Paul. There is
hardly any doubt that Paul is responsible for the letter in its entirety,
apart perhaps from 2 Corinthians 6:14–7:1. The issue is whether the
Apostle Paul himself dictated the epistle as a single piece of correspondence with the Corinthians or whether the canonical text is the work of
an anonymous editor who compiled extensive fragments from Paul's
ongoing correspondence with the Corinthians, creating from these fragments the letter such as it exists today.[1]

A radical form of the theory of the composite nature of 2 Corinthians
has been defended by Walter Schmithals.[2] A more moderate form of the
theory was presented by Hans Dieter Betz in the *Anchor Bible Dictionary*
article on the Second Letter to the Corinthians.[3] Betz opines that extant

---

[1] The theory of the composite nature of 2 Corinthians was first proposed by Johann
Salomo Semler, professor at the German University of Halle (1753–91). For a history
of the theory, see Reimund Bieringer, "Teilungshypothesen zum 2. Korintherbrief:
Ein Forschungsüberblick," in Bieringer and Jan Lambrecht, *Studies on 2 Corinthians*,
BETL 112 (Louvain: University Press–Peeters, 1994), 67–105.

[2] See, especially, Walter Schmithals, *Gnosticisim in Corinth* (Nashville: Abingdon,
1971).

[3] "Corinthians, Second Epistle to the," *ABD* 1:1148–54.

2 Corinthians is a composite of six extensive fragments: (1) a first apology, appearing in 2:14–6:13; 7:2-4; (2) a second apology, the "letter of tears" (cf. 2:3-4, 9) represented by 10:1–13:10; (3) a letter of reconciliation, now found in 1:1–2:13; 7:5-16; 13:11-13; (4) an administrative letter, 2 Corinthians 8; (5) another administrative letter, 2 Corinthians 9;[4] and (6) an interpolation (6:14–7:1).

On the other hand, the authors of two very fine recent commentaries on 2 Corinthians maintain the integrity of the canonical text.[5] In either case, we must take to heart the words of C. H. Dodd, who wrote in reference to the Fourth Gospel that the only form of the text that we know for sure actually existed is the form that we now have. Thus it is to the study of 2 Corinthians as we now have it that we turn to understand Paul's use of 2 Corinthians' metaphorical strategy.[6]

The first part of the canonical letter is devoted to what Matera has called "the crisis over Paul's apostolic integrity."[7] The crisis came to a head on the occasion of Paul's second visit to Corinth. The apostle was so fiercely attacked by a member of the community that he left town and then wrote a painful letter to the community (2:3-4, 9; 7:8, 12), a letter which has apparently been lost.[8] Notwithstanding his desire to return to the community, Paul decided to write a letter whose tone is clearly conciliatory. This first part of 2 Corinthians fits into Pseudo-Libanius's category of the conciliatory letter.[9] The name derives from its style which

---

[4] See the introductory words in 2 Cor 9:1.

[5] Jan Lambrecht, *Second Corinthians*, SP 8 (Collegeville, MN: Liturgical Press, 1999); Frank J. Matera, *II Corinthians*, NTL (Westminster John Knox, 2003). For an overview of the history of scholarly support for this position, see Reimund Bieringer, "Der 2. Korintherbrief als ursprüngliche Einheit: Ein Forschungsüberblick," in Bieringer and Lambrecht, *Studies*, 107–30. See also his defense of the literary unity of 2 Corinthians, "Plädoyer für die Einheitlichkeit des 2. Korintherbriefes: Literarkritische und inhaltliche Argumente," in the same volume, 131–79.

[6] Were 2 Corinthians a composite composition, the present study would stress the intertextuality of Paul's metaphors.

[7] See Matera, *II Corinthians*, 45.

[8] Partitionists believe that the tearful letter is presently preserved in 10:1–13:10 whose tone is decidedly different from the tone of the first part of the canonical letter. An older exegesis, represented nonetheless in a work as recent as David R. Hall's *The Unity of the Corinthian Correspondence*, JSNTSup 251 (Sheffield: Academic Press, 2004), maintained that the tearful letter is the canonical 1 Corinthians.

[9] Pseudo-Libanius, "Epistolary Style" 19. See Abraham J. Malherbe, *Ancient Epistolary Theorists*, SBLSBS 19 (Atlanta: Scholars, 1988), 76–77.

Pseudo-Libanius describes as that "in which we conciliate someone who has been caused grief by us for some reason."[10]


## A Down Payment

Defending the integrity of his apostolic mission, Paul described himself as a man of his word, just as Jesus Christ whom he preached was always "Yes" (1:17-19). God had commissioned Silvanus, Timothy, and himself for their mission: "It is God who establishes us with you in Christ and has anointed us by putting his seal on us and giving us his Spirit in our hearts as a first installment" (1:21-22).

The apostles' missioning by God was an experience that was indescribable in ordinary terms. It was not an experience that could be caught on a camcorder or on audio tape. To convey some idea of what it was, Paul resorted to three powerful metaphors. The first was that of anointing, a cultic image. As in other New Testament passages, "be anointed" (*chriomai*) refers to the reception of the Holy Spirit, but 1:21 is unique in its use of the verb to describe the Spirit being given to someone other than Christ. The verb was occasionally used as a metaphor in Greek literature, but its meaning in 1:21 derives from Paul's biblical tradition in which the verb was sometimes used to describe the commissioning of a prophet. Paul often uses language to describe himself that the Bible used in reference to one or another prophet.

Having used the metaphor of anointing to rank himself and his companions in the line of the biblical prophets, Paul asserts his authenticity, using a metaphor drawn from the legal sphere. He describes God as one who has put his seal (*sphragisamenos*) on Paul, Silvanus, and Timothy. This was a powerful image in the Hellenistic world. Seals (*sphragis*) were placed on animate and inanimate objects alike as a sign of ownership. Sealed by God, Paul and his companions were to be recognized as belonging to God.

Seals were also affixed to documents, often instead of a signature, to attest to their validity and integrity. Speaking of himself and his companions as being sealed by God, Paul may have intended not only to

---

[10] Pseudo-Libanius notes that the style is sometimes called the apologetic style (*charactēr apologetikē*). See "Epistolary Styles," 19 in Malherbe, *Epistolary Theorists*, 68–69. For more on the nature of the apologetic letter, see Pseudo-Demetrius's description and example in "Epistolary Types," 18 in Malherbe, *Epistolary Theorists*, 40–41.

affirm that they belonged to God but also that God attested to the integrity and authenticity of their message. God gave, as it were, the "Good Housekeeping Seal of Approval" to their words. The ancients used the verb in precisely this sense, indicating that upon examination something had been approved.[11]

In 1:21-22 Paul uses a third metaphor to describe the situation of himself and his companions. He affirms that God gave them "his Spirit in our hearts as a first installment [*arrabōna*]" (cf. 5:5). The image is taken from the economic sphere, the world of financial transactions, and makes use of a Semitic loanword most likely of Phoenician origin. In Hellenistic culture the term properly describes a deposit or down payment, in money or goods, made by a purchaser or contractor as a bona fide proof that they will complete the purchase or the work. Should the purchase not occur or the work be left unfinished or done unsatisfactorily, the *arrabōn* was forfeited. In the first instance the *arrabōn* would be similar to what is today called a nonrefundable deposit. As an image of the gift of the Spirit, "first installment" implies that the gift of the Spirit which has already been received is a pledge of things to come; there is more yet to happen. Paul is suggesting not only that the Spirit would continue to use Paul and his companions as instruments but also that the Spirit would continue to be operative among the Corinthians.

In this passage Paul uses legal and financial images well-known in the Hellenistic world as well as the Semitic cultic image to describe the qualifications of himself and his companions to exercise their prophetic ministry among the Corinthians. The double image of the seal and the down payment symbolize that their ministry enjoys God's seal of approval and that it entails further experiences both for Paul and for the Corinthians themselves. The prophetic calling is a spiritual reality. Tangible realities are used as metaphors to affirm its authenticity.

## The Open Door

Much of what Paul writes in 2 Corinthians is in the form of a travelogue. He describes his journeys and the trips that he intends to take, as well as those of Titus.[12] Their travels are mentioned in a brief passage of

---

[11] LSJ gives a reference to Lollius Bassus, an early first century CE author from whom we have a dozen or so extant epigrams (*AP* 9.236).

[12] See 1:15-16; 2:12-13; 7:6-7; 8:17-19; 9:3-5; 12:14, 20-21; 13:1-2, 10.

the first part of Paul's letter in which he describes his frustration at having arrived in Troas only to learn that Titus was not there, as had been expected. Paul took advantage of the absence of Titus to evangelize Troas before moving on to his next stop somewhere in Macedonia.

Although Paul's stay in Troas may have been short, his preaching of the good news of Christ was successful: "A door was opened for me in the Lord" (2:12). The open door is a metaphor still in use today. It symbolizes accessibility. Because of the Lord, Paul found the inhabitants to be accessible, their hearts open to the reception of the gospel. According to Paul, the Lord Jesus opened the door, allowing Paul's proclamation of the gospel to be effective.

Paul used the metaphor in his earlier correspondence with the Corinthians, saying that his effective ministry in Ephesus (1 Cor 16:9) was the reason he intended to stay in the provincial capital until Pentecost. Only then would he begin his return trip to Macedonia and Corinth.

Lest metaphor become allegory, metaphor generally highlights only one point of comparison between the image and that which it symbolizes. When Paul uses the image of the open door, the point of comparison is clearly the accessibility that an open door provides. It is, however, legitimate to ask if Paul's use of this powerful image may not have been due to the fact that the open doors of the householders who welcomed Paul into their homes, where he then preached the gospel, might not have provided the impetus for Paul's use of this time-honored metaphor.

### Aroma of Christ

Immediately after his expression of frustration at the absence of Titus, Paul describes his itinerant missionary trips with an image as odiferous as it is graphic. As classic rhetoricians suggest, Paul appeals to the senses of sight and smell in an imaginative attempt to allow the Corinthians to appreciate his missionary endeavors:

> But thanks be to God, who in Christ always leads us in triumphal procession [*thriambeuonti*], and through us spreads in every place the fragrance that comes from knowing him. For we are the aroma of Christ to God among those who are being saved and among those who are perishing; to the one a fragrance from death to death, to the other a fragrance from life to life. (2 Cor 2:14-16a)

The Corinthians are invited to appear as spectators, viewing a marvelous triumphal procession orchestrated by God, to whom Paul gives thanks.

The sounds of triumph are to be heard in the image. The image[13] is victorious troops, led by their standard bearer, accompanied by booty and captured prisoners. The triumphal processions of victorious Roman troops were well known throughout the Greco-Roman Empire, of which Corinth was a vital part.[14]

Arguing that *thriambeuonti* means "make known," Dautzenberg demurs from this interpretation.[15] He claims that the metaphor of a triumphal procession neither fits the Pauline context nor is otherwise used in extant Hellenistic literature. The arguments are weak. A rhetorically powerful metaphor is one that has not become trite through overuse. Moreover, Paul uses the metaphor of a triumphal procession (*parousia*)[16] to describe an eschatological event. Far from being removed from an appropriate context, the metaphor of the triumphal procession is apropos to Paul's successful proclamation of the gospel in Troas and his subsequent trip to Macedonia where he had previously been instrumental in establishing Christian communities. While it is true that there is no extant literary attestation of the verb being used as a metaphor other than in 2:14, there is also no evidence of the verb ever being used to mean "make known."

In 2:14-16, Paul appeals not only to the readers' senses of sight and sound as they capture the mental image of a great procession and hear the sounds of triumph but also to their sense of smell,[17] capturing the aromas that arise during the celebratory event. It may be that Paul is inviting the readers to ponder the image of Paul, Silvanus, and Timothy as incense bearers in the procession. The billowing smoke pervades the air with an aroma[18] that Paul describes as "the fragrance [*osmēn*] that

---

[13] In the New Testament the image occurs only here and in the deuteropauline Col 2:15.

[14] Duff has argued that the image is that of the epiphany processions of deities in the Greco-Roman world. He presents Paul and his coworkers as being part of a triumphal procession rather than as belonging to a file of prisoners of war. See Paul B. Duff, "Metaphor, Motif, and Meaning: The Rhetorical Strategy behind the Image 'Led in Triumph' in 2 Corinthians 2:14," *CBQ* 53 (1991): 79–92.

[15] See Gerhard Dautzenberg, "*Thriambeuō*," *EDNT* 2:155–56.

[16] 1 Cor 15:23; 1 Thess 2:19; 3:13; 4:15; 5:23.

[17] See Gerhard Dautzenberg, "*Euōdia . . . osmē*," *EDNT* 2:90–91, which summarizes various scholarly positions as to the origin of the metaphor in 2:14-16. Paul uses the noun *euōdia*, "aroma," only in 2:15 and Phil 4:18 (cf. Eph 5:2) and *osmē* only in 2:14, 16 (twice) and Phil 4:18.

[18] In 1 Thess 1:8 Paul uses an auditory image to speak about the spread of the gospel.

comes from knowing him." The "him" of whom Paul writes is Christ. The knowledge of Christ is the gospel message which comes from Paul and his companions, like incense rising from a thurible.

In verse 15, Paul appropriates the metaphor to himself and his companions. They are "the aroma of Christ." Reading Paul's personal appropriation of the metaphor, we can think of how the smell of strong perfume pervades the air and adheres to one's clothing, as does the smell that comes from fires, burning incense, and lit cigarettes. One cannot be certain that Paul himself made this connection, but modern readers of Paul's letter certainly will do so.

Appropriating a metaphor that appeals to the sense of smell, Paul uses the word "aroma" (*euōdia*, 2:15) whose etymology implies a pleasant smell.[19] "Fragrance" (*osmē*, 2:14, 16)[20] is used of both foul smells and pleasant aromas. The ambiguity of the term may be the reason that Paul replicates it as he writes, "to the one[21] a fragrance from death to death, to the other a fragrance from life to life" (2:16a). The doubled metaphor is used in reference to "those who are being saved" and "those who are perishing." These antithetical terms were used by Paul in 1 Corinthians 1:18. In 2:15-16a as in 1 Corinthians 1:18 Paul writes about the discriminating potential of the gospel. To those who receive it, the gospel leads to life and salvation. To those who do not accept it, the gospel leads to destruction and death.

To fully appreciate Paul's use of visual, auditory, and odorous metaphors in 2:14-16, the reader must be attentive to the eschatological dimension of Paul's thought. He writes about death and those who are perishing (*tois apollymenois*), using a verb that connotes utter destruction. Images of triumphal processions are regularly used by Paul and his disciples to speak of the eschaton. What the apostle has captured metaphorically in 2:14-16 is the spread of the gospel by Paul and the ultimate effect that the gospel has upon those who receive it and those who do not.

---

[19] The prefix *eu-* has the connotation "well" or "good" in a large number of Greek words, one of which appears in English transliteration as euphoria.

[20] Paul uses *osmē*, "fragrance," three times, once in verse 14, twice in verse 16. The noun is related to *ta osmōmena*, "the organs of smell."

[21] The explanatory chiastic structure of verse 16 is clearer in Greek than it is in the NRSV English translation. Paul's relative pronouns *hois . . . hois* are in the plural, suggesting that "to the latter . . . to the former" might be a better translation than "to the one . . . to the other."

## A Letter Written on the Heart

Almost immediately after using the powerful public image of the triumphant procession to speak of his ministry, Paul turns to the more private image of writing, writing letters and writing on the human heart. The letter of recommendation (*epistolē systatikē*, 3:1) was well known in the Hellenistic world. Its style is that in which we commend someone to someone else, says Pseudo-Libanius.[22] Pseudo-Demetrius described it as a letter "which we write on behalf of one person to another, mixing in praise, at the same time also speaking of those who had previously been unacquainted as though they were [now] acquainted."[23]

In a rhetorical question (3:1b), Paul suggests that neither the Corinthians nor himself needs a letter of recommendation;[24] they do not need to be praised by one another. The reason why this is so is that: "You yourselves are our letter, written on our hearts, to be known and read by all; and you show that you are a letter of Christ, prepared by us, written not with ink but with the Spirit of the living God, not on tablets of stone but on tablets of human hearts" (1 Cor 3:2-3). The Christian community at Corinth is the only letter of recommendation that counts.

Morna Hooker says that the letter of recommendation is a "brilliant metaphor" for Paul's ministry.[25] The existence of this living letter brings to Paul's heart a kind of joy that cannot be compared with words of praise, not even those engraved on stone. The commendation that Paul experiences comes not from his own words of self-praise but from the very Spirit of the living God. Everyone should be able to "read" the result of the Spirit of God at work in Paul, who rejoices in the Corinthian community. Conversely, the community is a letter, a letter of Christ, not

---

[22] Pseudo-Libanius, "Epistolary Styles" 8 in Malherbe, *Ancient Epistolary Theorists*, 68–69. Sometimes called the "introductory style" of letter, it is the fourth of forty-one styles of letter writing identified by Pseudo-Libanius.

[23] Pseudo-Demetrius, "Epistolary Types" 2 in Malherbe, *Ancient Epistolary Theorists*, 32–33.

[24] Matera suggests that Paul's remarks are prompted by the situation in Corinth. The intruding apostles may have arrived bearing letters of recommendation and in turn flattering the Corinthians by asking them for letters of recommendation. See Matera, *II Corinthians*, 76.

[25] Morna Hooker, "Beyond the Things That Are Written? St. Paul's Use of Scripture," *NTS* 27 (1981): 295–309, 296. See further, Scott J. Hafemann, *Suffering and Ministry in the Spirit: Paul's Defense of His Ministry in II Corinthians 2:14–3:3* (Grand Rapids, MI: Eerdmans, 1990), 189; M. Luther Sirewalt, *Paul, the Letter Writer* (Grand Rapids, MI: Eerdmans, 2003), 121–24.

written in the black ink that Paul might have employed but written by the Spirit of the living God. All Paul did was, as it were, prepare the writing tablets much in the fashion that a servant might have prepared a piece of wood or stone so that it could be used as a writing tablet.

The image of mutual letters of recommendation written by the Spirit of God on the hearts of the Corinthian Christians and on the hearts of Paul and his companions is powerful in itself. Paul enhances the image by making a contrast between letters inscribed in the heart and letters that are written on stone tablets. The vitality of letters inscribed on the heart presents a striking contrast with dead characters on a lifeless stone. Stone tablets call to mind the tablets on which the precepts of the covenantal law were written (Exod 34:28-29).[26] The writing on human hearts recalls the words of Jeremiah 31:31-33, a passage in which the prophet speaks of a new covenant and God's writing the law on the hearts of the house of Israel.

Paul prepared the tablet on which Christ's letter was written just as Moses prepared the stone tablets (Exod 34:1; Deut 10:1, 3) on which the precepts of the covenant were written. As God wrote on the stone tablets (Exod 24:12; 34:1, 27-28)[27] and promised to write on human hearts in the renewal of the covenant (Jer 31:33), Paul affirms that it is the Spirit of the living God who writes on tablets of human hearts.

Paul continues his midrash in 3:4-11, contrasting the ministry of the new covenant[28] with the ministry of Moses. He mentions the Spirit (3:8) and reprises the motif of the stone tablets with their engraved letters of the alphabet[29] (3:7). Then in 3:12-18 Paul exploits another covenant-related biblical image, that of the veil covering Moses' face when he was not receiving or communicating God's word (Exod 34:33-35), the distinctive element in Exodus 34's description of the renewal of the covenant.[30]

---

[26] Exod 34:1, 4, 28, 29; cf. Deut 9:15-17; 10:1-5.

[27] See Deut 9:10; 10:2, 4. Exod 34:27 mentions God's ordering Moses to write. Apropos this reference, Childs comments: "These words which Moses wrote . . . are distinguished from the words of The Commandments which Yahweh wrote upon the stone tablets." See Brevard S. Childs, *The Book of Exodus: A Critical, Theological Commentary*, OTL (Philadelphia: Westminster, 1974), 615. The Deuteronomic version of the rewriting of the covenant prescriptions makes no reference to any writing by Moses.

[28] See 3:6 for the expression "new covenant." Elsewhere Paul uses this expression only in 1 Cor 11:25, an etiological rendition of the institution narrative.

[29] *Gramma* is used three times in verses 6 and 7.

[30] See Childs, *Exodus*, 618, 619.

Paul writes about a veil covering the minds of Jews as they listen to the Torah being read during the synagogal service. The veil symbolizes the absence of communication with God. "Veil" (*kalymma*) appears four times in the passage (vv. 13, 14, 15, 16); "unveil" (*anakalyptō*), twice (vv. 13, 18). As is often the case with Paul's metaphors, these terms do not appear elsewhere in his correspondence.[31]

Buried within Paul's reflection on the metaphorical veil that impedes the Jews' understanding of the Torah is another biblical image. The apostle mixes metaphors as he writes about minds that "were hardened" (*epōrōthē*, 3:14; cf. Rom 11:7). Paul's language is influenced by what he had written about the stone tablets. Stones used for construction were called *poroi*. What Paul is saying about the Israelites is that their minds were petrified, they were turned into stone. In a passage replete with biblical themes the image of the petrified mind recalls the biblical image of stony hearts.[32] Paul's use of the passive voice implies that God caused minds to be hardened.

Jews who have not accepted Christ do not and cannot perceive the Torah as God's communication with them for it is in Christ that the veil is removed and divine revelation appropriated. When the veil is removed by Christ (v. 14),[33] those who believe have unveiled faces and see the glory of the Lord, albeit not directly and in its full splendor, for we see the glory of the Lord "as though reflected in a mirror" (*katoptrizomenoi*,[34] 3:18). The image evokes the attenuated experience of the Lord's glory that humans are able to perceive during their lives on earth.

## Light

In chapter 4 Paul continues to exploit the metaphor of the veil when he speaks about the possibility of the gospel itself being veiled (*kekalummenon*, 4:3). It is veiled for those who are perishing because of a lack of

[31] Neither does Paul use the verb "veil" (*kalyptō*) in his correspondence apart from its appearance in 4:3 [2x].

[32] Cf. Exod 4:21; 7:3; 14:4, 17.

[33] "In Christ" (*en Christō*) should be taken instrumentally.

[34] The verb, cognate with *esoptron*, "mirror" (1 Cor 13:12), is rarely attested in classical and Hellenistic Greek literature and is hapax in the New Testament. Used by Philo of Byzantium, a 2nd–3rd century BCE writer on technology, *katoptrizō* means "behold as in a mirror," but, as LSJ s.v. notes, the term may mean "reflected as by a mirror." The REB retains Paul's metaphor, translating the participle as "see as in a mirror." Translations found in the RSV ("beholding"), NIV ("reflect"), RevNAB ("gazing") overlook the metaphorical reference.

faith. Paul explains: "The god of this world has blinded the minds of the unbelievers, to keep them from seeing the light of the gospel of the glory of Christ" (4:4). Paul again mixes his metaphors but remains within the same semantic domain as he speaks of light and blindness. The switch of metaphors was easy to make. The biblical image of the glory of God, the divine *kabod*, evoked weight and massiveness. In the course of time the metaphor was transformed so that "glory" (*doxa*) came to evoke overwhelming luminosity.[35]

The glory of the Lord (3:18) is perceived through the light of the gospel, refracted as it were through a prism, the glory of Christ. God, who said, "Let light shine out of darkness" (4:6; cf. Gen 1:3[36]), caused light to shine in this way. The light shining in the gospel is the light of God himself for Christ is the image of God (4:4) and Christ's glory is experienced in the proclamation of the gospel. That light illumines the hearts of believers so that they have some experience of the glory of God in the face of Jesus Christ (4:6b). Were the modern reader to try to capture the communication of light about which Paul writes in 4:1-6, he or she might find a natural analogy in the light of the sun that is reflected in the moon which, passing through a prism, enlightens objects on planet earth.

Unbelievers, those who are perishing, are not caught up in this communication of light. They are blinded. For them the gospel is veiled. Satan has created a barrier that hinders them from seeing the glory of Christ; their blindness and hardness of heart and mind prevent them from seeing the glory of God.

## Clay

In 4:7 Paul describes the gospel as a "treasure in clay jars." The clay jars are Paul and his companions who maintain and transport the gospel message. What does the metaphor imply? Matera reflects:

> Paul's metaphor is open to several interpretations, since an earthen vessel is of its very nature inferior (2 Tim 2:20), ignoble (Lam 4:2), and disposable (Lev 6:28; 11:33), as well as fragile and easily broken (LXX Ps 30:13 = MT 31:12; Isa 30:14). For example, the contrast between the treasure and the earthen vessel points to the superiority of the former and the inferiority of the latter, whereas the description

---

[35] See G. Henton Davies, "Glory," *IDB* 2:401–3; cf. *DBI*, 330–31.

[36] Paul introduces the theme of the new creation in 5:17.

of Paul's apostolic sufferings in verses 8-9 suggests the notions of fragility and weakness.[37]

Matera's dilemma can be resolved when due attention is paid to the immediately preceding context.

Paul had been speaking about writing. In his world written texts were frequently preserved in earthenware jars. The discovery of the Dead Sea Scrolls a half century ago was a discovery of written texts that had been preserved for centuries in clay pots. The fragility of the pots led to the discovery of the scrolls. As the story of their discovery is told, a Bedouin boy tried to coax a goat out of a cave by throwing a stone at the animal. The stone hit and broke an earthenware vessel. The sound of the breaking clay led the boy to investigate. The rest is history, but the incident shows that texts were preserved in clay vessels and that these were fragile indeed.

The legendary fragility of clay pots makes them an appropriate metaphor for apostolic evangelizers whose personal weakness is rehearsed in the circumstantial catalogue found in 4:8-9 [10]. The rhetorical force of such a list does not lie in its enumeration of particular details; it derives from their cumulative effect. Paul's use of the hardship catalogue underscores his apostolic conviction that the power of the gospel comes not from the personal skills of the evangelists (4:7) but rather from the power of God's Spirit. As the word of God, the gospel is able to withstand every human and natural obstacle.

### The Life to Come

As he continues to exposit the idea that the instruments used by God are weak human beings, Paul uses a pair of contrasting yet related metaphors to compare human existence on earth with existence in heaven, the life to come. Someone's life on earth can be compared with life in a tent (5:1, 4),[38] where a person wears simple clothing, if anything at all (*ekdysamenoi*,[39] *gymnoi*, 5:3, 4). The image of the tent (*oikia tou skēnous*)

---

[37] Matera, *II Corinthians*, 108.

[38] Paul may have borrowed the metaphor from Wis 9:15 (cf. Isa 38:12).

[39] The NRSV translates the participle *ekdysamenoi* as "we have taken it off" (cf. RevNAB). Reading the Greek as *endysamenoi*, the reading found in the 25th and prior editions of the Nestle-Aland text, the RSV translated the participle as "by putting it on." For this latter reading, see also NIV and REB.

conjures up ideas of fragility, a lack of solid protection against the elements and animals, a transitory condition, and stark existence. In contrast, heavenly existence is comparable to life in a permanent and magnificent building that comes from God and is not made by human hands (*acheiropoiēton*, 5:1). Those dwelling in this building are fully clothed (*ependysasthai*, 5:2, 4).

Paul's vocabulary is unusual. Apart from the word *oikia*, "house" or "dwelling," and one occurrence of *gymnos*, "naked" (1 Cor 15:37), none of the highlighted words appears elsewhere in his writings. Since Paul uses the imagery of clothing to speak of the resurrected body in 1 Corinthians 15, the interpreter is tempted to use that passage as a heuristic device in order to determine the precise meaning of Paul's imagery. The search inevitably leads to reflections on Paul's anthropology and comparisons with the dualistic anthropology of Hellenistic philosophy.[40]

Seeking interpretive precision may, however, result in one's missing the point of Paul's imagery. Poetry functions in its gestalt rather than by means of an articulated rational message; metaphors function in their appeal to the senses, the impression that they convey rather than in their rationality and precision of detail. A modern reader has only to contrast life on a weeklong camping trip with life in a comfortable suburban home to catch the flavor of Paul's metaphor.

The implications of the contrasting metaphors in 5:1-5 are developed in the following pericope, 5:6-10, in which Paul repeatedly contrasts traveling abroad (*ekdēmeō*) with "living at home" (*endēmeō*). The verbs are antithetically juxtaposed three times in this short pericope (vv. 6, 8, 9), the only times that they appear in the New Testament. Hellenists would have been familiar with a metaphorical sense of *ekdēmeō*, namely, as a way of speaking about death. This is not the meaning of Paul's metaphor. Death is on the horizon of 5:1-10 but Paul writes about being away (*ekdēmoumen*) from the Lord (v. 6). He seems to be implying that life is like a pilgrimage on which the sojourner dwells in a bodily tent. When the journey comes to its end, the traveler no longer lives in the tent, rather he or she has an abode with the Lord. En route, a human being wants to be with the Lord, walking (*peripatoumen*) with the confidence generated by faith (v. 7).

---

[40] See, for example, M. Eugene Boring, et. al., *Hellenistic Commentary to the New Testament* (Nashville: Abingdon, 1995), 451–54.

## Mutual Affection

Synecdoche, the figure of speech by which the part stands for the whole, is a kind of metaphor. Thus, each of Paul's uses of "heart" (*kardia*) is metaphorical; he writes about the heart to speak about the entire human person. In 6:11-13; 7:2-4 Paul uses the word "heart" metaphorically but in a way that differs from his ordinary usage. He employs the metaphor of the human heart to speak about affection, in much the same way that the metaphor is used at the present time. Having spoken to the Corinthians as willingly and as frankly as he did—and for this Paul uses the metaphorical expression "our mouth was open" (RSV; *to stoma hēmōn aneōgen*, the NRSV's "we have spoken frankly to you")—Paul affirms that his heart was wide open to the Corinthians (*kardia hēmōn peplatuntai*, 6:11).

The intensity of Paul's affection for the Corinthians was, however, not reciprocated. Paul's rhetorical *antithesis* highlights the contrast between his unlimited affection for the Corinthians and their failure to reciprocate: "There is no restriction in our affections, but you are restricted in your own affections" (6:12, RSV).[41] Paul then pleads with the Corinthians: "Make room in your hearts for us" (7:2).[42] Their hearts are closed; his is wide open (*peplatuntai*, 6:11).

The tightly knit unit (6:11-13; 7:2)[43] in which Paul pleads with the Corinthians to reciprocate his affection demonstrates, beyond any doubt, the apostle's ability to use metaphors creatively and forcefully. Paul uses three nouns that indicate bodily organs: the mouth (*to stoma*), the heart (*hē kardia*), and the vital organs (*tois splanchnois*). Those who are attentive to the images can hardly fail to observe the progression, from the visible mouth to the heart that lies deep within and then to all the inward parts: the stomach, heart, lungs, liver, spleen, and kidneys—the whole group of vital organs[44] without whose proper function the human being cannot survive.

---

[41] The NRSV's "There is no restriction in our affections, but only in yours," failing to translate the repeated verb (*stenochōreisthe*), attenuates the contrast between Paul's two phrases and suggests that the metaphorical *en tois splanchnois* was used of Paul, whereas it is implied for Paul and explicitly stated with regard to the Corinthians.

[42] A footnote in the NRSV observes that the Greek (*chōrēsate hēmas*) lacks "in your hearts."

[43] The fact that 7:2 follows so naturally upon 6:11-13 is one reason why many commentators consider 6:14–7:1 to be a later interpolation into the letter.

[44] See Philo, *Creation* 118, *Allegorical Interpretation* 1.12, *Drunkenness* 106; cf. *Special Laws* 1.62.

Paul's verbs demonstrate a similar progression. The mouth is open (*aneōgen*). The heart is wide open (*peplatuntai*). The vital organs are not constricted in any way (*ou stenochōreisthe*). Were one to capture Paul's spatial imagery, he or she would have to think about a mouth that is agape, a heart that is enlarged, and vital organs that are ready to burst. Paul, however, is not writing about his personal physical condition. Rather, he is trying to convey to the Corinthians the intensity of his affection. The open mouth symbolizes the frankness of his speech, the wide open heart the intensity of his affection, the vital organs the expanse and limitless quality of that affection; his affection knows no bounds. Each of the metaphors used in Paul's description of his affections and throughout his poignant plea is a double metaphor, the nouns designating physical organs, the verbs referring to phenomena that can be seen with the eye.

The contrast between Paul's unrestricted emotions and the restricted emotions of the Corinthians (6:12) serves as a transition to Paul's plea that the Corinthians open up their hearts to him. The contrast talks about being "restricted" or cramped (*stenochōreōmai*). Paul is not cramped; the Corinthians are cramped. One can imagine a crowd cramped together with "no room to breathe," physical cramps, or emotions that are so pent up that they cannot be expressed. In 7:2 Paul urges the Corinthians to get rid of the cramps and open up, making room for him (*chōrēsate*) in their hearts. The verbs are related to one another; between the two there is not only verbal but also imaginative contrast. Paul wants the Corinthians to experience the same intensity of affection for him that he has for them.

The metaphors are rooted in Paul's Jewish tradition, especially the image of the inward parts. Since the vital organs are the most intimate and hidden part of the human being,[45] Jews "located" human emotions in the entrails. The Bible frequently uses the image of the inward parts to speak of pity and compassion (Gen 43:30; 1 Kgs 3:26; Jer 31:20). Later Jewish literature used the image to speak of suffering (*Psalms of Solomon* 2.15), sorrow (*Testament of Abraham.* A. 3,5), despair (Philo, *Rewards* 151), worried concern for one's child (Sir 30:7), and romantic love (*Joseph and Aseneth* 6.1). These various emotions arise from deep within the human being. Paul's plea that the Corinthians requite his love is to be situated within this rich tradition.

---

[45] See Philo, *Posterity* 118; Josephus, *Jewish War* 4.263.

## An Interruption

Paul's richly imaged plea is "interrupted" by six verses, 6:14-7:1, which urge the Corinthians to free themselves of anything that might defile them. The central section (vv. 16b-18) is a catena of biblical passages,[46] one of which contains the traditional biblical metaphor of YHWH as father and the children of Israel as God's sons and daughters.[47] Biblical language is also echoed in the metaphor that serves as the opening gambit of the pericope: "Do not be mismatched [*mē ginesthe heterozygountes*] with unbelievers" (6:14). The image is agricultural; the word *zygos* designates the yoke that binds two animals together as they are hitched to a plow. The Bible's agricultural law forbade the pairing of an ox and an ass as yokemates: "You shall not plow with an ox and a donkey" (Deut 22:10).[48] Second Corinthians 6:14 evokes this precept of agricultural law, urging readers to avoid unbelievers.

Rabbinic lore often cited biblical prohibition against mixtures. The body of laws in Deuteronomy 22:9-11 represents one small compilation of such laws, as did Lev 19:19 whose collection included the prohibition: "You shall not let your animals breed with a different kind [*heterozygō*]." In accordance with the *Kal va-homer* principle of biblical interpretation, a kind of argument from the lesser to the greater, early Jewish texts drew human inferences from laws pertaining to animals.[49] The author of the pericope[50] is well versed in the emergent traditions of first century Judaism.

The author's familiarity with Jewish teaching is also reflected in the reprise of the Pauline metaphor of the Christian community as the temple of God: "We are the temple of the living God" (6:16b). The affirmation is explained by Leviticus 26:11-12, a brace of biblical verses that spoke of God's dwelling in the tabernacle[51] and made use of the covenant

---

[46] The order in which they appear in 6:14–7:1 is: Lev 26:11-12; Ezek 37:27; Isa 52:11, 52:4; Ezek 20:34, 41; 2 Sam 7:14; and 2 Sam 7:8.

[47] 6:18 speaks explicitly about "sons and daughters" (*hyious kai thygateras*). The phrase does not appear in 2 Sam 7:14, the inspiration for the Pauline verse. "Sons and daughters" may reflect the influence of Isa 43:6 upon the Pauline catena. In any case, it represents an early expression of antisexism in the Pauline tradition.

[48] Paul uses another precept of agricultural law (Deut 25:4) to speak about his apostolic right to sustenance (1 Cor 9:9).

[49] See, e.g., *b.Baba Mesiʾa* 87a–91b; *m.Yadayim* 4:7; cf. Philo, *Virtues* 145.

[50] That is, either Paul or a later interpolator.

[51] The idea behind Lev 26:11-12 is also expressed in Exod 29:44-45 which speaks of the tent of meeting rather than the tabernacle.

formula. Second Corinthians uses the Leviticus passage to explain the incompatibility between God's dwelling place, the temple of God, and idols:[52] "What agreement has the temple of God with idols?" The implied answer is "none;" there is no agreement between God's temple and idols. The reader or listener hardly has time to formulate the answer in his or her mind before the author states: "We are the temple of the living God" (6:16b). This Pauline image, expanded by the characterization of God as "living," God's primal trait, is reprised from 1 Corinthians 3:16-17. The building in which God dwells[53] is a metaphor for the people[54] among whom God dwells.

## Ministry to the Saints

The collection on behalf of poor Christians in Judea (Gal 2:10), an endeavor to which Paul and his coworkers were committed, lasted for at least two years (8:6, 10). In 2 Corinthians 8–9[55] Paul makes a lengthy plea for the Corinthians to be generous in their support of this collection. Paul rehearses a variety of reasons why they should be generous. His appeal runs the gamut of arguments, from the example of Christ's generosity (8:9) to the Corinthians' self-interest. With regard to the latter, Paul writes: "The point is this: the one who sows sparingly will also reap sparingly, and the one who sows bountifully will also reap bountifully" (9:6), an agricultural image expressed in the form of an adage.

The use of proverbs in letter writing is lauded by Demetrius who says:

> Ornament, however, it [the letter] may have in the shape of friendly bits of kindly advice, mixed with a few good proverbs. This last is the only philosophy admissible in it—the proverb being the wisdom of a people, the wisdom of the world. But the man who utters senten-

---

[52] Cf. 1 Cor 10:14.

[53] Jacob Milgrom (*Leviticus 23–27*, AB 3B [New York: Doubleday, 2001], 2300) rightly notes apropos Lev 26:12 that the verb "to walk," reprised in 6:16c as *emperipatēsō*, implies "that God's presence is not condensed into a building, but is present everywhere among the Israelites."

[54] The use of the plural in 1 Cor 3:16 and 2 Cor 6:16b shows that the community is identified as God's temple.

[55] These two chapters may have originally been two independent "administrative" letters. See, especially, Betz, *2 Corinthians 8 and 9: A Commentary on Two Administrative Letters of the Apostle Paul*, Hermeneia (Philadelphia: Fortress, 1985).

tious maxims and exhortations seems to be no longer talking familiarly in a letter but to be speaking *ex cathedra*. ("On Style," 232)

Paul's maxim expresses the common wisdom of humankind. Appearing in Galatians 6:7 and in Cicero's *De oratore* 2.262,[56] various forms of the proverb were in common use in Mediterranean agricultural society. Aristotle, for example, criticized Gorgias's "you have sown shame and reaped misfortune" as being too much like poetry.[57] An encouraging form of the metaphor is found in the Greek Apocalypse of Baruch: "For those who have sown well, harvest well" (*3 Bar.* 15:2.3). The book of Proverbs contains similar sayings, "Those who sow righteousness get a true reward" (Prov 11:18b) and "Whoever sows injustice will reap calamity" (Prov 22:8a).

Aristotle characterizes proverbs as "metaphors from species to species,"[58] an apt description of the proverbial saying in 9:6. He also stated that proverbs are evidence,[59] classifying proverbs as a kind of witness, one of the inartificial proofs used in rhetoric.[60] Attesting to the common wisdom of humankind as they do, proverbs enjoy a rhetorical force comparable to a saying of one or another philosopher or well-known sage. Speaking of the bountiful harvest accruing to those who sow sufficiently, Paul asks the Corinthians to consider for a moment the great advantage that they will enjoy if only they invest a little something for the support of poor Christians in Judea.

The complex history of the Greek Bible sheds some light on Paul's use of the agricultural metaphor. Proverbs 11:18b [LXX][61] has a parallel in Prov 11:21b, "He that sows righteousness shall receive a faithful reward."[62] Three verses later we read, "There are some who scatter their own, and make it more; and there are some also who gather, yet have

---

[56] Cicero cites the proverb with verbs in the second person singular: "As you do the sowing, so shall you reap."

[57] See Aristotle, *Rhetoric* 3.3.4 [1406b]. Aristotle thought that the way that Gorgias used the proverb imparted a frigid quality to his prose.

[58] Ibid., 3.11.14 [1413a].

[59] Ibid., 1.15.14 [1376a].

[60] For Aristotle, inartificial proofs properly belong to forensic oratory and are five in number: laws, witnesses, contracts, torture, and oaths. See *Rhetoric* 1.15.2 [1375a].

[61] The Greek *sperma de dikaiōn misthos alētheias* can be translated "The seed of the righteous is a reward of truth" (Brenton's translation).

[62] The Greek text is different from the Hebrew which reads, "Those who are righteous will escape."

less" (Prov 11:24 [LXX]). The Hebrew text of Proverbs 11:24-25 shows that the pair of sayings is cited to make a point about generosity: "Some give freely, yet grow all the richer; others withhold what is due, and only suffer want. A generous person will be enriched, and one who gives water will get water."

The history of Proverbs 22:8a is similarly complex. The Hebrew text of Prov 22:8a reads: "Whoever sows injustice will reap calamity" [NRSV]; the Greek has been translated: "He that sows wickedness shall reap troubles."[63] The manuscript tradition of the Septuagint indicates that the saying is the second line of a two-part maxim whose first line is: "God honors a cheerful giver."[64] The variant, remarkably similar to 9:7, suggests that Paul's metaphors came from the same well as the agricultural metaphors of the book of Proverbs.

The imagery of 9:6 continues in the verses that follow. Describing the all-provident God who is able to convey blessings in abundance on the Corinthians, Paul says: "He who supplies seed to the sower and bread for food[65] will supply and multiply your seed for sowing and increase the harvest of your righteousness" (9:10). The language has a biblical ring. The idea of righteousness appears in Prov 11:18b. Paul's imagery recalls the figurative language of Hosea 10:12: "Sow for yourselves righteousness; reap steadfast love; break up your fallow ground; for it is time to seek the Lord, that he may come and rain righteousness upon you." The language of seed and bread echoes the Deutero-Isaiah, "giving seed to the sower and bread to the eater" (Isa 55:10).

Paul affirms that the Creator God has supplied the seed (9:10a); he encourages the Corinthians to sow liberally the seed with which they have been supplied. The seed (v. 6) is a metaphor for the coin of the realm, the monetary gift that the Corinthians will make in response to the apostles' plea for the support of the poor in Jerusalem. The agricultural metaphor continues in 9:10b, "[He] will supply and multiply your seed for sowing." Paul then expands on "seed for sowing" by adding another agricultural metaphor, "the harvest of your righteousness," literally, "the fruits [*genēmata*, hapax in Paul] of your righteousness" (9:10c).

---

[63] Brenton's translation of *ho speirōn phaula therisei kaka, plēgēn de ergōn autou syntelesei* simplifies the Greek. The Greek *phaula . . . kaka* is literally "bad evils," while *plēgēn de ergōn* is a "calamity of works."

[64] See R. B. Y. Scott, *Proverbs. Ecclesiastes*, AB 18 (Garden City, NY: Doubleday, 1965), 128.

[65] Note the previous reference to the manna tradition in Paul's citation of Exod 16:18 in 8:15.

Righteousness is traditional Jewish terminology for a right relationship with God and with all God's people. What the Corinthians stand to reap from their generosity to Jerusalem Christians is an increase of both material well-being and spiritual benefits.

## A Defense of Ministry

As 2 Corinthians turns from its appeal for the saints in Jerusalem (2 Cor 8–9) to the defense of Paul's ministry, the semantic domain of Paul's metaphors changes rapidly. His letter moves from the fruitful field to the battlefield as the imagery shifts from agriculture to warfare:[66]

> We do not wage war [*strateuometha*] according to human standards; for the weapons of our warfare [*hopla tēs strateias*] are not merely human, but they have divine power to destroy strongholds [*kathairesin ochyrōmatōn*]. We destroy [*kathairountes*] arguments and every proud obstacle [*hypsōma epairomenon*] raised up against the knowledge of God, and we take every thought captive [*aichmalōtizontes*] to obey Christ. We are ready to punish [*en hetoimō echontes ekdikēsai*] every disobedience when your obedience is complete. (2 Cor 10:3b-6)

Commentators frequently identify Prov 21:22, "One wise person went up against a city of warriors and brought down the stronghold in which they trusted," as the background for Paul's extended use of the military metaphor in 10:3b-6, but the density of military imagery[67] and Paul's infrequent recourse to the book of Proverbs militate against the idea that the saying of the wise man is the source of Paul's imagery. It is more likely that Paul's use of military imagery is a reflection of the agon motif, used by the Stoics and Cynics as well as by Paul to speak about the struggle on behalf of perceived truth.

Paul uses a military metaphor in 1 Thessalonians 5:8, in which he paraphrases an image taken from Isaiah 59:17, but the imagery of 2 Corinthians 10:3b-6 is unique in Paul's extant writings. Its closest parallel may well be 2:14-16, the passage in which Paul writes about a triumphal

---

[66] Military and agricultural images are also juxtaposed in 1 Cor 9:7.

[67] The seven Greek phrases incorporated into the citation of 10:3b-6 belong to the military domain. To these might be added the verb "oppose" (*tolmēsai*, 10:2), a Pauline verb (Rom 5:7; 15:18; 1 Cor 6:1; 2 Cor 10:2, 12; 11:21; Phil 1:14). Within the verb's wide range of meanings are "to dare" or "to have courage." In the latter sense the verb was used of military leaders who showed courage in the face of the enemy. Cf. Plutarch, *Sayings of Spartans* 213C.

procession, whose *Sitz im Leben* is the celebration of a military victory. In the soldier's life, the victor's triumph is celebrated after the battle. What Paul describes in 10:3b-6 is the battle plan.

The plan of attack is a siege whose success depends on three successive stages: (1) the demolition of fortifications; (2) the taking of prisoners; and (3) the punishment of resistance.[68] Roman soldiers used this classic military strategy to conquer the Greeks. They destroyed strongholds, took wives and children captive, and enslaved the troops.[69] In Paul's image the besieged city is defended by its strongholds (*ochyrōmatōn*) and its ramparts (*hypsōma*). Each of these terms is rarely used in the New Testament; the first appears only here; the second, only here and in Romans 8:39. The latter term—derived from the root *hypso-*, "high"— designates an elevation, a strategic location in battle. Paul, however, is not talking about natural elevations, but about "elevations that have been raised up." The reader must imagine towers and ramparts that have been erected.[70]

In addition to the formulation of the objective component of the military metaphor, the battle plan, there is a subjective component. Paul and his fellow missionaries are the ones who are waging war, who have a strategy (*strateuometha*) and weapons (*hopla tēs strateias*). The rhetorical force of the imagery is enhanced by the various contrasts of 10:1-4. The lowly Paul (*tapeinos*, 10:1) is able to mount a successful siege because of the weapons of war with which he has been armed. The weapons are

[68] See Abraham J. Malherbe, "Antisthenes and Odysseus, and Paul at War," *HTR* 76 (1983), 143–73, reprinted in *Paul and the Popular Philosophers*, 91–119, 112; Matera, *II Corinthians*, 223. Malherbe rightly observes that the three participles, "destroy" (*kathairountes*), "take captive" (*aichmalōtizontes*), and "ready" (*echontes*) are grammatically dependent on "wage war" (*strateuometha*), illustrating how the war is to be waged. See Malherbe, "Paul at War," 112, n. 130. On the use of the military metaphor in this passage, see also Christine Gerber, "Krieg und Hochzeit in Korinth: Das metaphorische Werben des Paulus um die Gemeinde in 2 Kor 10,1-6 und 11,1-4," *ZNW* 96 (2005): 99–125, 105–13.

[69] See 1 Macc 8:9-10.

[70] Chrysostom drew attention to Paul's use of the military metaphor and noted that Paul prolongs the metaphor. For him, Paul's *hypsōma* was equivalent to the *pyrōgma*, a defensive tower. See John Chrysostom, *In epistolam secundam ad Corinthios*, Homily 21 (PG 61.543). In Greek the word *hypsos* was more commonly used for such defensive towers. Paul's use of the rarer word, *hypsōma*, may be due to his use of a form of assonance known as homoioteleuton, a figure of speech in which a series of words have the same ending. Here, as in Rom 5:14-16, Paul uses a series of nouns ending in *ma*: *ochyrōma*, *hypsōma*, *noēma*. See BDF 488.3; Malherbe, *Popular Philosophers*, 92–93.

not ordinary weapons (*sarkika*,[71] literally, "according to the flesh"); they are weapons that have divine power (*dynata tō theō*[72]). The objective and subjective components of Paul's use of the military metaphor in defense of his proclamation is best understood by means of a comparison with the philosophic moralists, particularly those of the Cynic school.[73] Not only did these Cynics, like the Stoics, employ military metaphors in their use of the agon motif, but they also used the images in much the same way as Paul did. Thus, Antisthenes, the philosopher who wrote between the middle of the fifth century and the middle of the fourth century BCE, used the image of a soldier's military armor to speak about the garb of the legendary Odysseus, whose self-humiliation allowed him to obtain the good of his associates and save them. Rigorous Cynics claimed that their attire consisted of armaments received from the gods.[74] Cynics used a city's fortifications against a siege to describe rational faculties.[75] Similarly, Paul refers to the "arguments" and "thought" with which the wise man fortifies himself (10:4-5). Paul uses the imagery for his own purposes,[76] but his military metaphor has a place within a rich and ancient tradition of philosophic discourse.[77]

## Building Up and Tearing Down

Paul continues to defend himself in a pair of verses in which he asks the Corinthians to contemplate the church and his role in it:

> Look at what is before your eyes [*kata prosōpon*]. If you are confident that you belong to Christ, remind yourself of this, that just as you belong to Christ, so also do we. Now, even if I boast a little too much

[71] One familiar with Paul's customary usage might expect Paul to use a contrast between *sarkika*, "fleshy," and *pneumatika*, "spiritual," as the basis for his antithesis, but he does not do so.

[72] The dative *tō theō* could also be a dative of interest, meaning "in God's service." Malherbe and Lambrecht prefer that it be taken in this sense. See Malherbe, *Popular Philosophies*, 117; Lambrecht, *Second Corinthians*, 154.

[73] See Malherbe's essay, "Paul at War."

[74] See Malherbe, *Popular Philosophies*, 109–12.

[75] See ibid., 109–12.

[76] See ibid., 112–18.

[77] Paul's agonistic language is echoed in Philo's *Confusion of Tongues*. Philo speaks of reason razing to the ground cities that had been fortified to menace an unhappy soul. In his description of the conflict, he also uses the expression "destruction of a stronghold" (*tēn tou ochyrōmatos toutou kathairesin*), repeated simply as "the destruction" (*kathaireseōs*). See Philo, *Confusion of Tongues* 128–32.

of our authority, which the Lord gave for building you up and not
for tearing you down, I will not be ashamed of it. (2 Cor 10:7-8)

Paul asks the Corinthians to look at themselves and at Paul's role in
building them up as the community they have become. The introductory
gambit employs a well-known metaphor. He tells them to look at what
is facing them (*kata prosōpon*). Classic authors such as Thucydides and
Xenophon used the expression centuries before Paul did.[78]

Paul had no literary antecedent for the more striking metaphor that
he uses when he writes about the authority "which the Lord gave for
building you up and not for tearing you down." The expression was so
well cast that Paul uses it again as he brings the letter to a close: "So I
write these things while I am away from you, so that when I come, I may
not have to be severe in using the authority that the Lord has given me
for building up and not for tearing down [*eis oikodomēn kai ouk eis kathairesin*]" (13:10). Extant Greek literature offers no precedent for the use of
"tearing down" (*kathairesis*) with a figurative meaning. The word was
used to speak about the destruction or demolition of a fortified structure,
as Paul himself uses the term in the military metaphor of 10:4.

Paul contrasts tearing down with "building up" (*oikodomē*), a term
rarely used in a metaphorical sense. The word typically describes either
the act of building or the completed structure, as it does when Paul uses
the term metaphorically in 1 Corinthians 3:9 and 2 Corinthians 5:1. The
related verb *oikodomeō*, "build," was sometimes used with the metaphorical sense "build upon,"[79] but it is difficult to find an ancient author who
uses the term as Paul did when he urges the Thessalonians to "encourage
and build up [*oikodomeite*]" one another (1 Thess 5:11).[80] Paul uses the
verb in 1 Corinthians 14:4 to describe a prophet whose prophesying
builds up the metaphorical edifice which is the church: "those who
prophesy build up the church." Paul uses a related noun, "building up"
(*oikodomē*) to identify the purpose of charismatic activity in the church;
such activity should "build up" the church (1 Cor 14:3, 5, 12, 26). Paul's

[78] See Thucydides, *History of the Peloponnesian War* 1.106; Xenophon, *Cyropaedia*
1.6.43.

[79] Cf. Gal 2:18.

[80] Arguably, the ecclesial sense of "building up" as a member of the church, the
community of those who hope, is not beyond the connotation of Paul's use of *oikomeō*
in 1 Thess 5:11; 1 Cor 8:1, 10; 10:23; and 14:4, 17. The verb appears to have lost its
ecclesial connotation only in Paul's negative uses of the verb (1 Cor 8:10; 14:4).

construction imagery, build (*oikoidomeō*) and (the act of) building (*oikodomē*), coheres with his image of the church as a building (1 Cor 3:9). The construction imagery is an ecclesial metaphor.

Paul's prophetic activity was intended to build up the church. For that purpose he was empowered by Christ (10:8; 13:10); that was the purpose he pursued in his apostolate to the Corinthians (12:19). In 10:8 Paul underscores this idea by contrasting the building that he had been empowered to do with that of tearing down the edifice of the Corinthian church. The contrasting images do not occur elsewhere in Paul's letters but they are apropos; Paul had just spoken about God's power to destroy (*pros kathairesin*) strongholds (10:4).

### Foolishness

After writing about his presence among the Corinthians, in person and by letter (10:9-11), Paul articulates one of the driving principles of his choice of territories to evangelize, the principle of nonintervention: he will not go to someone else's territory (cf. Rom 15:20-24); they should stay out of his.[81] Then he begins his "fool's speech":

> I wish you would bear with me in a little foolishness [*mikron ti aphrosynēs*]. Do bear with me! I feel a divine jealousy for you, for I promised you in marriage to one husband, to present you as a chaste virgin to Christ. But I am afraid that as the serpent deceived Eve by its cunning, your thoughts will be led astray from a sincere and pure devotion to Christ. For if someone comes and proclaims another Jesus than the one we proclaimed, or if you receive a different spirit from the one you received, or a different gospel from the one you accepted, you submit to it readily enough. (2 Cor 11:1-4)

Foolishness is the antithesis of moderation or prudence (*sophrosynē*), which Plato considered to be one of the four basic virtues.[82] Paul was aware of the demeaning nature of his language. He confronted the imaginary interlocutor who questioned the possibility of resurrection from the dead by calling him a fool (*aphrōn*, 1 Cor 15:36). In a remark that reeks

---

[81] See Lambrecht, *Second Corinthians*, 165–67, 169, 170. On 10:12-18 whose Greek is difficult to translate into English, see also Raymond F. Collins, "'The Field That God Has Assigned to Us' (2 Cor 10:13)," in *Orientale Lumen VII Conference 2003 Proceedings* (Fairfax, VA: Eastern Christian Publications, n.d. [2004]), 123–42, 125–30.

[82] See Plato, *Protagoras* 332e.

with sarcasm and stings all the more because of its use of antithesis, Paul calls rival apostles fools: "You gladly put up with fools, being wise yourselves!" (11:19).[83]

The language of "fools" and "foolishness" is scattered throughout chapters 11 and 12 of 2 Corinthians: "fool" (*aphrōn*) in 11:16 [2x], 19; 12:6, 11; "foolishness" (*aphrosynē*) in 11:1, 17, 21; "madman" (*paraphronōn*) in 11:23.[84] This kind of language is all the more striking because it is not the kind of language that Paul ordinarily uses. First Corinthians 15:36 is a rare instance of Paul calling anyone a fool.

Because of the density of the language of foolishness in 2 Corinthians 11–12 and because Paul repeatedly says that he is speaking like a fool, it is customary to describe 11:17–12:13 as "the fool's speech." The title is appropriate; Paul says that he is speaking as a fool (*en aphrosynē legō*, 11:21) and talking like a madman (*paraphronōn lalō*,[85] 11:23). The speech begins in 11:17 where Paul says: "What I am saying in regard to this boastful confidence, I am saying not with the Lord's authority, but as a fool (*en aphrosynē*)."

Second Corinthians 11:1-16 functions as an extended introduction to the speech. Paul begins by asking the Corinthians to put up with a little foolishness because he is going to boast about himself[86] and only a fool would do that. It concludes with an apologetic remark, "Let no one think that I am a fool [*aphrona*]; but if you do, then accept me as a fool [*hōs aphrona*], so that I too may boast a little" (11:16).

A classic ploy in Hellenistic rhetoric was for the speaker to demean himself so as to win the sympathy of his audience.[87] This was essentially an argument from *ēthos* in which a rhetor spoke of himself in such a way as to obtain a favorable hearing on the part of his audience. Paul used

---

[83] In Paul's text "fools" (*aphronōn*) and "wise" (*phronimoi*) appear side by side, thereby making the remark all the more biting.

[84] "Madman" does not appear in any other passage of the New Testament. Apart from 2 Corinthians 11–12, Paul does not otherwise speak of "foolishness." Elsewhere he uses the word "fool" only in Rom 2:20 and 1 Cor 15:36.

[85] The noun is hapax in the New Testament.

[86] This boasting is different from the way that Paul boasted about his ministry in 10:8, 12-18.

[87] See, for instance, *Rhetoric to Alexander* 29.30–37, "To an audience neither hostile nor friendly . . . we must employ self-depreciation, saying: 'I have risen owing not to confidence in my own ability, but in the belief that the proposal which I am about to introduce is advantageous for the community'" (Aristotle, to whom the *Rhetoric* is falsely attributed, 1354b).

this kind of argument in his earlier correspondence with the Corinthians in which he wrote about himself as a slave and as an aborted fetus.

In 11:17–12:13 Paul says that he is talking like a fool.[88] We would not consider Paul to have been a fool; neither, in fact, would he have considered himself to be a fool (11:16a). He was, however, content to allow himself to be considered a fool in order to establish his[89] authority in the eyes of the Corinthians. He enhances this portrayal of himself by repeatedly describing his weakness.[90] Doing so, Paul has added a stone of another color to the complex mosaic of the self-image that emerges from his letters. Demetrius wrote that a letter should be strong in characterization. Paul's Second Letter to the Corinthians does not fail in that regard.[91]

Paul's emotions are perhaps most apparent when he writes, "Who is made to stumble [*skandalizetai*], and I am not indignant [*poroumai*]" (11:29). He is on fire (*poroumai*) when he becomes aware of someone failing in regard to their Christian commitment because of the activity of false teachers. To "make stumble" is to lead someone to trip over a stone, a *skandalon*. Paul uses the image repeatedly in the Letter to the Romans, both in his paraenesis[92] and in his reflections on Israel's lack of faith.[93] In 2 Corinthians the image serves to describe someone who is weak with regard to his or her faith and trips up in the Christian way of life because of what someone else has done. This causes Paul to burn. He is on fire with his emotions; he is angry and indignant about what has happened.[94]

---

[88] See, especially, the parenthetical remark in 11:21, "I am speaking like a fool."

[89] Lambrecht says that "'weakness' summarizes all sorts of situations wherein Paul feels himself helpless but assisted by God" (Lambrecht, *Second Corinthians*, 195).

[90] See the use of words the root *asthen-* in 11:21, 29 [2x], 30; 12:5, 9 [2x], 10 [2x].

[91] See Demetrius, *On Style*, 227. Cf. Cicero, *Epistulae ad familiares* 16.16.2; Seneca, *Epistle* 40.1; Philostratus, *Epistles* 2.257.30.

[92] Rom 14:13, 21; 16:17; cf. 1 Cor 8:13 [2x].

[93] Rom 9:33; 11:9.

[94] See 1 Cor 7:9 for a similar metaphorical use of the verb "burn." There the verb suggests being on fire with sexual passion. See Collins, *First Corinthians*, 269. Similar usage is attested in classical Greek. In 2 Cor 11:29 the emotion that is enkindled is indignation (cf. 2 Macc 4:38; 10:35; 14:45; 3 Macc 4:2), though some commentators observe that the metaphor may refer to Paul's love which would make him burn with a desire to set the situation right (thus, Ralph P. Martin, *2 Corinthians*, WBC 40 [Waco, TX: Word, 1986], 282–83).

## Marriage and Betrothal

Embedded within his introduction to the fool's speech is a powerful image of the church that at this point in history had not yet appeared in Christian literature—the image of the church as the bride of Christ:[95]

> I feel a divine jealousy for you, for I promised you in marriage [*hērmosamēn*] to one husband, to present [*parastēsai*] you as a chaste virgin to Christ. But I am afraid that as the serpent deceived Eve by its cunning, your thoughts will be led astray from a sincere and pure devotion to Christ. (2 Cor 11:2-3)

The image reflects Jewish marriage customs in which betrothal, with its solemn promise, preceded marriage, when the bride is introduced into her husband's home. The betrothal period sometimes lasted several years, as it did when a father promised a young daughter in marriage to her future husband long before either of them reached the age of puberty. The bride-to-be was considered to belong to the groom during the betrothal period; any voluntary sexual intercourse on her part was adultery.

The Jewish practice of betrothal followed by a period of betrothal before the consummation of the marriage was used by Paul to describe the eschatological condition of the Corinthians.[96] Betrothed to Christ through Paul's preaching of the gospel and baptism, the Corinthians await the consummation of their relationship with Christ in the parousia yet to come. Paul presents himself as the matchmaker between Christ and the Corinthian community.[97] Subsequently, he carefully watches over the Corinthian church like a father watches over his daughter in order to be able to hand her over as a virginal bride to her husband when she is introduced into his house.[98] Paul's jealousy, as Lambrecht notes,[99] is God's jealousy; God himself is involved in the matter. Wanting the church to remain unsullied until the parousia,[100] Paul is on guard lest his

---

[95] See, especially, Gerber, "Krieg und Hochzeit," 113–25.

[96] See, especially, Renzo Infante, "Imagine nuziale e tensione escatologica nel Nuovo Testamento. Note a 2 *Cor.* 11,3 e *Eph.* 5,25-27," *RivB* 33 (1985) 45–61.

[97] See further Gerber, "Krieg und Hochzeit," 113–25.

[98] See Deut 22:13-21.

[99] See Lambrecht, *Second Corinthians*, 173.

[100] Cf. 1 Thess 3:13; 5:23.

opponents lead the church to a liaison with a Jesus other than the Jesus whom Paul proclaims (11:4).

As is the case with many of Paul's metaphors, the language that Paul uses to speak of the promise of betrothal does not occur elsewhere in Paul's letters nor, for that matter, does it occur elsewhere in the New Testament.[101] The image derives from Paul's biblical tradition as the example of Eve indicates. "Betrothed" as it were to Adam (Gen 2:23-24), Eve was seduced from her fidelity to God by a wily serpent (Gen 3:1-6). In similar fashion, Paul warns, the Corinthian church could be seduced by the clever speech of the false apostles. Paul would do all that he could to prevent that from happening, even to the point of demeaning himself by talking like a fool.

The marriage imagery used by Paul to speak of the unique and unsullied relationship that ought to exist between the church and Christ also has its roots in the biblical tradition where Israel was pictured as the bride of YHWH . The image received dramatic expression in the allegorical account of Hosea's marriage to Gomer (Hos 1–3), but it is found in other prophetic texts as well, including Isaiah 51, 54; Jeremiah 3; and Ezekiel 16. Paul is the first New Testament author to use this kind of imagery to speak about the relationship between Christ and the church. Later New Testament texts exploit the image,[102] but with reference to the "universal" church rather than to a local church like the church at Corinth.

### Robbing the Churches

Another image appears in the lengthy introduction to the fool's speech. Paul writes:

> Did I commit a sin by humbling myself so that you might be exalted, because I proclaimed God's good news to you free of charge? I robbed [*esylēsa*] other churches by accepting support [*opsōnion*] from them in order to serve you. And when I was with you and was in need, I did not burden anyone, for my needs were supplied by the friends who came from Macedonia. So I refrained and will continue to refrain from burdening you in any way. (2 Cor 11:7-9)

---

[101] Paul used the verb *hērmosamēn*, a word that etymologically means "fit together."

[102] Eph 5:25-27; Rev 19:7-8; 21:2, 9; 22:17.

That Paul refused to accept any material support from the Corinthians seems to have been a source of tension (1 Cor 9:11-12, 15). In the Hellenistic world teachers were generally supported by their students; messengers who carried good news were generally "tipped" for their service.[103] Paul, however, refused to be supported by those to whom he preached the gospel.[104] Some may have thought less of him because he wanted to preach the gospel free of charge.

To defend himself, Paul uses language often used in military circles. The verb "rob" (*sylaō*) was originally used in reference to taking a bow from its case or uncovering a quiver of arrows. In Homer and in later usage the verb was used to describe soldiers seizing the arms of their enemies, despoiling the bodies of the fallen, or pillaging cities and towns that had been captured.[105] "Wages" (*opsōnion*) describes the rations that a soldier received during military service. As is often the case with the imaginative language of Paul's metaphors, the characteristic vocabulary of 11:8 rarely occurs in the New Testament. "Rob" is a New Testament hapax;[106] "wages" is elsewhere used by Paul only in 1 Corinthians 9:7.

Paul's use of a military metaphor in defense of his apostolate is consistent with his use of the agon motif in 10:3-6, where military imagery is used in Paul's self-defense. Spicq, however, suggests that Paul's imaginative language is best understood against another background, namely, the legally recognized right of seizure as an exercise in legitimate retaliation.[107] In exceptional cases it was considered neither dishonorable nor illegal to seize another's property as a form of retaliation. Thus, "[a] private individual who considers himself the victim of a tort by a foreigner . . . will take justice into his own hands . . .; he will seize the person or property of a fellow citizen of his adversary."[108] From this perspective, Paul's defense would have been an attempt not only to defend himself but also to shame the Corinthians from whom he did not receive the subsistence that he deserved.

---

[103] The "tip" was often called *euangelion*.

[104] Cf. 1 Thess 2:9.

[105] See LSJ, *s.v. sylaō*; Spicq, "*Sylaō, TLNT* 3:312–16, 312–13.

[106] In the Greek Bible, the verb occurs only in the Epistle of Jeremiah: "the priests make their temples secure with doors and lock and bars, in order that they may not be plundered [*sylēthōsi*] by robbers" (Ep Jer 18).

[107] See Spicq, "*Sylaō*," 313–16.

[108] Philippe Gauthier, *Symbola: les Etrangers et la justice dans les cités grecques*, Annales de l'Est 42 (Nancy: Université de Nancy, 1972), 212, cited by Spicq, "*Sylaō*," 315–16.

## Wild Beasts

An argument from pathos appears in the body of the fool's speech. Telling the Corinthians that they ought to be ashamed of themselves, Paul writes:

> You gladly put up with fools, being wise yourselves! For you put up with it when someone makes slaves of you [*katadouloi*], or preys upon you [*katesthiei*], or takes advantage of you [*lambanei*], or puts on airs [*epairetai*], or gives you a slap in the face [*eis prosōpon hymas derei*]. (2 Cor 11:19-20)

The irony and sarcasm of verse 19 continues in verse 20 as Paul "explains" what really happens when the Corinthians fall victim to the seduction of the false teachers. Metaphor upon metaphor contributes to Paul's graphic description of the Corinthians' situation. "Each clause of this splendid series of anaphorae," says Windisch, "operates as a whiplash."[109] Paul's description exudes action and abasement. The Corinthians have become enslaved; they are preyed upon and taken advantage of; false teachers put on airs and slap them in the face. The inhabitants of the proud city of Corinth have become slaves.[110] They have not lost their civic freedom, but they have become subservient to false teachers.

It is not bad enough that the Corinthians are enslaved by these false teachers; they are being eaten alive. The basic sense of "preyed upon" (*katesthiei*) is to be "eaten up," especially by wild animals. Such was the meaning of the verb when it was used by Homer (*Iliad* 17.542); such, too, was its meaning when it was used metaphorically by Paul in Galatians 5:15.[111]

"Take advantage of" is an overly cautious translation of *lambanei*, a verb meaning "take hold of," "seize," used in classical Greek in reference to eagles and lions grabbing hold of their prey and carrying it away.[112]

---

[109] Hans Windisch, *Der zweite Korintherbrief*, KEK 6. 9th ed. (Göttingen: Vandenhoeck und Ruprecht, 1970), 347, cited in translation by Lambrecht, *Second Corinthians*, 189.

[110] In Rom 6:6, 16-20 Paul uses slavery as a metaphor for subservience to sin and impurity. According to Donfried (*Who Owns the Bible?*, 102) "Paul uses the term 'slavery' to define the human situation. One is a slave either to the power of sin or to the power of the Spirit."

[111] 2 Cor 11:20 represents the only other occurrence of the word in Paul's letters.

[112] See, for example, Homer, *Iliad* 11. 114; 17.678; 24.43, 46; 52.316; *Odyssey* 6.142; Pindar, *Nemean Odes* 3.81.

Used of humans, it meant "seize by violence" or "take as prize or booty."[113]

That graphic metaphor is followed by another in which Paul presents the false teachers as "putting on airs" (*epairetai*). The apostle used the same language when he described the false teachers rising up, almost militantly, against the true knowledge of God (10:5).[114] Now he presents those same false teachers smugly puffed up, gloating with pride and elation over what they had done to the Corinthians.[115]

The description of the false teachers giving the Corinthians a slap in the face (*eis prosōpon hymas derei*) is almost a letdown after the violent and graphic images that Paul used to describe the havoc that his opponents were wreaking upon the Corinthians who thought themselves to be so wise.

### Thorn in the Flesh

The apostle's use of hardship catalogs to describe the difficulties that he has encountered in preaching the gospel is one of the striking features of 2 Corinthians.[116] Urging the Corinthians to contemplate the image of a man truly devoted to the task at hand, the lists enhance Paul's *ēthos* appeal. A tantalizing description of one such difficulty appears in 12:7: "To keep me from being too elated, a thorn [*skolops*] was given me in the flesh, a messenger [*angelos*] of Satan to torment me, to keep me from being too elated."

Paul's personification of the affliction adds to the intrigue of identifying the thorn in his flesh. The affliction is Satan's angel, Satan's messenger. Paul attributed whatever it was that he suffered to the malevolence of God's cosmic adversary. He sees Satan as God's agent in keeping him humble and attentive to his mission.

"Thorn" appears in no other place in Paul's writings; nor does it occur elsewhere in the New Testament. The word properly describes any

---

[113] See, for example, Homer, *Iliad* 5.273; 8.191; Herodotus, *Histories* 4.130; Sophocles, *Philoctetes* 68.

[114] See Udo Borse, "*Epairō*," *EDNT* 2:17.

[115] For this use of the verb *epairō*, see Herodotus, *Histories* 5.81; 9.49; Xenophon, *Memorabilia* 1.2.25. Ancient physicians used the verb to describe a physical swelling. Thus, Hippocrates, *Use of Liquids* 2, and Galen in K. G. Kuhn, *Claudii Galeni Opera omnia* (Leipzig: Cnobloch, 1825) 6. 264.

[116] See 4:8-9; 6:4-5, 8-10; 11:23-28; 12:10.

pointed object, but most commentators take it to mean "thorn" or "splinter," the meaning that the term commonly has in the Greek Bible.[117] Commentators sometimes refer to Numbers 33:55 where the phrase "barbs [*skolopes*] in your eyes and thorns [*bolides*] in your sides" is used to refer to the enemies of Israel.[118]

Other commentators take the word *skolops* to mean "stake," seeing in the stake an instrument of torture that has been (figuratively) driven into Paul's body.[119] Understood in this fashion, the image would underscore the intensity of Paul's suffering. Verena Jegher-Bucher finds in Paul's use of the metaphor an echo of Aristotle, who described the inept orator as one who spoke as if he had swallowed a ruler.[120]

Most commentators are at a loss in trying to identify the referent of Paul's metaphor. They contemplate the possibility[121] of psychological difficulties, sexual desires, pangs of conscience, or the frustration arising from Paul's inability to bring his fellow Jews to believe in the gospel. Others see the thorn as a reference to Paul's enemies in general or, specifically, to the false teachers in Corinth. Still others take the image to be some sort of physical ailment, such as headaches, eye problems, or epilepsy. Clavier once noted that the list of possibilities reads like a medical dictionary.[122]

---

[117] See Num 33:55; Ezek 28:24; Hos 2:6; Sir 43:19.

[118] Hos 2:6 [2:8 LXX] uses the term "thorn" with a different figurative meaning. God punishes Gomer who has been running after her adulterous lovers: "I will hedge up her way with thorns [*en skolopsin*]." Because of the figurative use of thorn in the Greek Bible, Thomas argues that there is some sort of cooperation between God and Satan and that God's power is manifest in the faithfulness of those who suffer for the sake of Christ. See John C. Thomas, "An Angel from Satan: Paul's Thorn in the Flesh (2 Corinthians 12.7-10)," *JPT* 9 (1996): 39–52.

[119] Thus, for example, David M. Park in "Paul's *skolops tē sarki*: Thorn or Stake? (2 Cor. xii 7)," *NovT* 22 (1980): 179–83, 181–83.

[120] See Verena Jegher-Bucher, "Der Pfahl im Fleisch: Überlegungen zu II Kor 12,7-10 im Zusammenhang von 12,1-13," *TZ* 52 (1996): 32–41. Jegher-Bucher sees in the reference to the messenger of Satan an allusion to Num 22:22-35 where an angel of the Lord prevents Balaam from speaking.

[121] See the useful survey of opinions in Margaret E. Thrall, *2 Corinthians 8–13*, ICC (London and New York: T&T Clark, 2000), Excursus XV, 809–18.

[122] See Henri Clavier, "La santé de l'apôtre Paul," in Jan N. Sevenster and Willem C. van Unnik, *Studia Paulina in honorem Johannis de Zwaan* (Haarlem: Bohn, 1953), 66–82, 66.

Reversing the emphasis, Abernathy suggests that Paul suffered from some sort of harassment from a physical demon.[123] In the end most commentators agree that it is all but impossible to know what Paul intended by means of this metaphor. In fact, although letters presume more than they actually state, with the result that the recipient could often understand what the author meant even if modern commentators cannot, it is not altogether certain that even the Corinthians would have understood what Paul really meant by this intriguing image.

### The Family

A different image of Paul emerges from 12:14-15, that of Paul as a parent. For the most part kinship language does not play an important role in the rhetoric of 2 Corinthians. Rarely does Paul address the Corinthians as "brothers and sisters."[124] The apostle uses kinship language to speak of his coworkers, Timothy (1:1) and Titus (2:13), and trusted emissaries (8:18, 22, 23; 9:3, 5; 11:9; 12:18), but he hesitates to use this language in reference to the Corinthians. His reticence speaks volumes about his strained relationship with the Corinthians. The lack of kinship language contrasts with the relatively warm tone of 1 Corinthians, in which "brothers and sisters" is repeated almost as a refrain.

Only once in 2 Corinthians does Paul speak to the Corinthians as to his children and that is to chide them for the immaturity of their emotions (6:13). Parental imagery does, however, occur in 12:14-15. Paul writes not about father or mother but about the generic parent, using parental imagery in what was for him a novel way: "I will not be a burden [*katanarkēsō*] to you because I do not want what is yours but you; for children ought not to lay up for their parents [*goneusin*], but parents [*goneis*] for their children. I will most gladly spend [*dapanēsō*] and be spent [*ekdapanēthēsomai*] for you." Paul's language is unusual,[125] as is so often the case when the apostle uses figurative language. Defending himself from accusations that he was not a proper preacher because he

---

[123] David Abernathy, "Paul's Thorn in the Flesh: A Messenger of Satan?" *Neot* 35 (2001): 69–79.

[124] The formula appears just three times, twice in a disclosure formula (1:8; 8:1) and once in the letter's closing farewell (13:11).

[125] In addition to 11:9, Paul uses "be a burden" only in 12:13-14. He uses "parent" only in 12:14 where the word appears twice. He uses "spend" only in the same verse, where the word also appears twice.

did not accept a stipend, he tells the Corinthians that he had no intention of being a burden to them.

Among New Testament authors only Paul uses the verb "be a burden" (*katanarkaō*); he does so only in 2 Corinthians (11:9; 12:13, 14).[126] His verb is a compound form, an intensive form of the verb *narkaō*, "benumb." Both the compound and the simple form of this verb belong to the medical field, where each of them means "anesthetize." Each of the words is used by Hippocrates.[127] The NRSV and most modern versions translate Paul's verb as "be a burden," but the image is that of a person so benumbed, anesthetized, perhaps even comatose, that he or she needs to be taken care of. That is not Paul's situation; he does not need to be taken care of. He is self-supporting and proud of it. He is like a parent who must work and take care of small children.[128]

Paul uses the generic word "parent" only in 12:14. He associates being a father with working[129] and being a mother with nurturing the children, pouring out her heart and soul on their behalf.[130] In 12:14-15 Paul wants to defend his track record as a working father, all the while affirming that, like a mother, he pours himself out for his Corinthian children. He will, he says, gladly spend and be spent on their behalf.

"Spend" (*dapanaō*) is a word that properly belongs to the field of financial transactions. Mark uses the verb to describe the woman who had spent all that she had on medical expenses (Mark 5:26). James uses it to describe those who dissipate their fortune while living a dissolute life (Jas 4:3), as does Luke (Luke 15:14), who also uses it of those who pay for a ritual haircut (Acts 21:24). In the New Testament Paul alone uses the verb in the figurative sense of generously spending time and energy.

Paul's *apologia pro vita sua* includes a pair of metaphors taken from another semantic domain. Peppering his audience with a series of rhetorical questions, Paul asks, "Did we not conduct ourselves [*periepatēsamen*] with the same spirit? Did we not take the same steps [*ichnesin*]?" (12:18c-d). The figurative use of "walk" (*peripateō*), apparently influenced by Semitic usage, is common in Paul's letters, not so, however, the

---

[126] In 12:16 Paul uses the term *katebarēsa*, a common word meaning "be a burden [to]."

[127] See Hippocrates, *Liquids* 1.3, 6-23 for *narkaō*, *Epidemics* 6.7.3 for *katanarkaō*.

[128] Cf. 1 Cor 3:1-3.

[129] See 1 Thess 2:9-12.

[130] See 1 Thess 2:7-8.

figurative use of "steps." The Greek term means footsteps or footprints. In 12:18d the term is used in a metaphorical sense as it is in Romans 4:12, Paul's only other use of the term.[131]

As Paul's letter draws to a close, the apostle shares with the Corinthians the reason why he is writing to them: "I write these things while I am away from you, so that when I come, I may not have to be severe in using the authority that the Lord has given me for building up [*oikodomēn*] and not for tearing down [*kathairesin*]"[132] (13:10). Rhetorical antithesis gives added strength to the construction metaphor which is virtually the final use of figurative language[133] in this complicated letter. The construction imagery recalls the extended metaphor that Paul had developed toward the beginning of 1 Corinthians (1 Cor 3:10-17). Before closing his last (extant) letter to the Corinthians, the apostle reminds them that he is a builder, not a wrecker.

Paul's farewell begins with the familiar "brothers and sisters" (13:11). Earlier in the letter he used this form of address only in 1:8 and 8:1. The infrequent use of this form of address is a telltale sign of the strained relationship that then existed between Paul and the Corinthians. The metaphors that he uses evidence the strain. He writes about a procession of prisoners, stony hearts, military battles, fools, a thorn in the flesh, and tearing down—sure signs that all was not well between Paul and the church of God in Corinth.

---

[131] All three New Testament uses of the term are metaphors. Cf. 1 Pet 2:21.

[132] The only other use of this term in the New Testament is in 10:4, where it also has a figurative meaning.

[133] See the use of the familiar vocative *adelphoi* in 13:11.

# 8

# The Letter to the Romans

E very letter is unique, a one-time communication from someone
to someone else in a very determined set of circumstances. Despite
the unique character of each of Paul's letters, the Letter to the
Romans stands out from among the other letters in the Pauline corpus
as being radically different from the rest. The root of the difference is
that instead of having been written to a community or communities that
Paul had evangelized on a topic of mutual concern, Romans was written
to a community that Paul had not evangelized nor even visited (Rom
1:10-13; 15:22). Various Christian churches had developed informally in
Rome[1] because of settlement by Christians coming from other parts of
the Empire and the return to Rome of traveling merchants who learned
about the Christian faith during the course of their journeys.[2]

Paul's letter reveals a trace of his pride in not having preached the
gospel in Rome. His ambition was to preach the gospel where it had

---

[1] Romans 16 suggests that there were at least five house churches in Rome: (1) Prisca,
Aquila, and the church in their house (16:3-5); (2) the family of Aristobulus (16:10);
(3) those in the Lord who belong to the family of Narcissus (16:11); (4) Asyncritus,
Phlegon, Hermes, Patrobas, Hermas, and the brothers and sisters who are with them
(16:14); and (5) Philogus, Julia, Nereus and his sister, and Olympas, and all the saints
who are with them (16:15).

[2] See C. E. B. Cranfield, *The Epistle to the Romans*, 1, ICC (Edinburgh: T&T Clark,
1975), 16–17; Joseph A. Fitzmyer, *Romans*, AB 33 (New York: Doubleday, 1993), 30–31;
Brendan Byrne, *Romans*, SP 6 (Collegeville, MN: Liturgical Press, 1996), 10.

never before been preached (15:20-22). Often reflecting on his apostolic calling in the light of the Deutero-Isaian Servant canticles (Isa 42:1-4; 49:1-7; 50:4-11; 52:13-53:12), Paul found in Isaiah 52:15 a Scripture that helped him to make sense of his apostolic mission to Gentiles among whom the good news had not been proclaimed.

That Paul did not preach the gospel in Rome does not mean that the apostle had no desire to go to Rome nor does it mean that he was un-acquainted with the Christians of Rome. The long series of greetings in Romans 16 is a litany of Roman Christians with whom Paul was ac-quainted. He mentions twenty-six of them by name, along with the mother of Rufus (16:13) and the sister of Nereus (16:15).

Despite the fact that Paul knew as many Roman Christians as he did, the tone of his letter suggests that he had no experience of the community of Roman Christians as such. Unlike his letters to the Thessalonians, Philippians, Galatians, and Corinthians, the letter to the Romans is not addressed to a "church," a gathering. The language of "church" is absent from the Letter to the Romans until the long list of greetings in Romans 16, where Paul makes reference to the church at Cenchreae (v. 1), the churches of the Gentiles (v. 4), the church in the house of Prisca and Aquila (v. 5), the churches of Christ (v. 16), and the whole church in Gaius's house in Corinth (v. 23).

The familiar "brothers and sisters" which punctuated Paul's letters to the church of the Thessalonians and the church at Corinth and which served as the linchpin of the argument of Galatians is relatively absent from the long letter to the Romans. When the formula of direct address does appear, it does so for the most part in stereotypical formulas like the disclosure formulas of 1:13 and 11:25, "I want you to know, brothers and sisters,"[3] or the hortatory formula of 12:1, 15:30, and 16:17, "I appeal to you, brothers and sisters." Other than in its appearance in these ready-made formulas, the vocative *adelphoi* of direct address occurs only in 7:4, 8:12, 10:1, and 15:14.

We do not know whether Paul, a Roman citizen, had a tourist's desire to visit the imperial capital or not, but we do know that for a long time he had wanted to visit Christians living in Rome (1:10-13; 15:23). Acts 27–28 describes Paul arriving in Rome as a prisoner, but that was not what Paul had in mind. By his own account, Paul hoped to pass through Rome on his way to Spain, where he intended to continue his apostolic

---

[3] Cf. Rom 7:1.

mission of proclaiming the gospel there where it had not previously been proclaimed (15:23-24). A stop in Rome would provide him with the opportunity of visiting Christians living in Rome, gathering support from them as they sent him on his way east. Paul may have expected Phoebe, deacon of the church at Cenchreae (16:1-2), then at Rome, to take charge of gathering provisions for his trip to Spain.

Paul wrote the Letter to the Romans to prepare for his arrival in Rome. Intended as a kind of introduction of the apostle to God's holy people in Rome (1:7), the letter does not treat specific issues like those addressed in his letters to the churches in Corinth, Galatia, Philippi, Thessalonica, and Philemon's house in Colossae. Romans is rather like a letter treatise in which Paul considers the related issues of justification by faith and the relationship between Gentile and Jewish Christianity. Its Roman destination probably explains why Paul includes a fairly long exhortation on civil obedience (13:1-7), the only time that he writes in this manner in the extant correspondence.

Paul, then, was not an apostle to the Romans in the same sense that he had been an apostle to the church in Corinth (1 Cor 9:2),[4] but he did expect that his visit to Rome would provide some occasion for his missionary efforts to be successful, even among the Romans. Accordingly, he wrote them with the news that he intended to visit them, "in order that I may reap some harvest [*karpon schō*] among you as I have among the rest of the Gentiles" (1:13). Paul uses this agricultural image in Philippians 1:22 (cf. 1 Cor 3:6-9) to describe the results of his apostolic work. Because his presence in Rome was not to be an occasion for a pioneering proclamation of the gospel, we cannot be sure whether Paul simply meant to imply that he thought that his presence would strengthen the faith of the Romans or whether he thought that God might possibly raise up neophyte Christians through his work in Rome.

## Gentiles

Romans is a powerful rhetorical composition whose strategically placed metaphors enable Paul to achieve his purpose. The body of the letter begins in earnest with proclamation of the power of the gospel to

---

[4] See 1:5; 15:16-19. Paul considers the apostle to be one who has been sent to a specific group of people in order to preach the gospel among them and thus establish a community of believers. It is for this reason that Paul, in his only enumerated list of charisms, cites "apostles" as the first of the charisms (1 Cor 12:28).

effect salvation for all, both Jew and Gentile (1:16-17). The sequence of negative (1:18-3:20) and positive arguments (3:21-31) lays the stress on the latter. First, however, Paul appeals to the bias of Jews with regard to the sexual mores of Gentiles. Paul confirms the Jewish conviction that Gentiles are reprobate idolaters because they engage in homosexual conduct and all kinds of deviant behavior (1:18-31). Applauding this way of life, Gentiles condone and encourage such misconduct (1:32).

They act as they do because "their senseless minds were darkened," *eskotisthē hē asynetos autōn kardia*, literally, "their foolish hearts were plunged into darkness" (1:21). "Heart" describes the core of the human being especially in its thinking, self-determining, and emotional reality. The idea that a heart not yet penetrated by the light of the gospel lies in darkness is rooted in Paul's biblical background. Speaking of the latter times, an Isaian oracle says of the Gentiles: "The people who walked in darkness have seen a great light; those who lived in a land of deep darkness—on them light has shined" (Isa 9:2; see Matt 4:15-16). Paul uses the darkness metaphor again in 11:10 to describe unrepentant Israel, quoting Ps 69:24, "let their eyes be darkened [*skotisthētōsan*] so that they cannot see."

In the crescendo of his *pathos* appeal to Christian Jews, Paul describes males being "consumed [*exekauthēsan*] with passion [*orexei*] for one another" (1:27).[5] The imagery comes from the Hellenistic world. Hellenists often described people as burning with all sorts of emotion[6]—hope, passion, pride, anger, curiosity, to mention only a few of the strong emotions that can "enflame" a human being. Paul's "passion" describes a strong and, in this case, disordered emotion. In the unfolding of his rhetoric the word evokes the notion of a strong sexual desire gone awry.

The images of darkness and the burning fire are sufficiently removed from one another in the text to suggest that Paul may not have consciously juxtaposed the metaphors. Nonetheless, the combination of the two images creates a graphic and dramatic scene. Because of idol worship, Gentiles are plunged into darkness unto the very core of their being. From the darkness emerges the flame of their passion. The darkness accentuates the power of the flame. The single flame that breaks the darkness is the flame of passion that leads some to abandon sexual inter-

---

[5] Paul uses neither the metaphor nor "passion" elsewhere in his letters.

[6] See, for example, Polybius, *Histories* 3.3.3, 5.108.5 with regard to hope; Dionysius of Halicarnassus, *Roman Antiquities* 7.35 for passion; Plutarch, *Fabius Maximus* 7 for wrath; Herodas, "Women Making a Dedication and Sacrifice to Asclepius," 4.49, for anger; and Lucian, *Alexander* 30, for curiosity.

course with women in their lust for other men. The flame of that lust burns bright against the darkness of their hearts.

## Jews

Having convinced Christian Jews of the perversity of Gentiles, Paul turns the tables. In no uncertain terms he tells the Jews that despite the advantage that they might have had from the covenant and the law, they were no better off than idol-worshiping Gentiles: "You, the judge, are doing the very same thing" (2:1). He goes on to tell them, "By your hard and impenitent heart[7] you are storing up wrath for yourself on the day of wrath" (2:5).

Paul's imaginative language is telling. The Jewish image of the hardened heart can be compared with the image of the darkened heart used to describe the situation of Gentiles who had not embraced the gospel. The contrast is striking. The darkness of the heart signifies the ignorance of the Gentiles with regard to God and God's will for them; hardness of heart evokes the idea of resistance. Jews steeled themselves against God's will; they did not conduct themselves in the way required by the covenant.

The image of the hardened heart often appears in the Bible,[8] particularly in reference to Israel stubbornly refusing to listen to YHWH. The Greek Bible coined a new word to describe the condition, *sklērokardia*, "hardness of heart," cardiosclerosis, a condition mentioned in passages that recall the biblical call to circumcise the foreskin of one's heart, Deuteronomy 10:16 and Jeremiah 4:4, for example. Paul exploits this topos, closing his indictment of the Jews with a plea that they circumcise their hearts: "Real circumcision is a matter of the heart [*peritomē kardias*]" (2:29). The biblical idiom[9] recalls unrepentant Israel whom YHWH called to repentance and conversion. Jews who had the law but did not observe

---

[7] Literally translated, the Greek *kata de tēn sklērotēta sou kai ametanoēton kardian* means "because of your hardness and unrepentant heart." The noun *sklērotēta*, "hardness," is hapax in the New Testament.

[8] See, for example, Ps 95:8; Prov 28:14; Ezek 3:7. The Letter to the Hebrews repeatedly cites Ps 115:8, "Do not harden your hearts" (Heb 3:8, 15; 4:7). A similar image, the "stiff-neck," appears in such passages as Exod 33:3, 5; 34:9; Deut 9:6, 13. A draft animal, such as a horse or an ass, tightens its neck when it does not want to work—hence, it becomes an image of stubborn resistance—but Paul does not use this related biblical image.

[9] See also 9:18; 11:25, where Paul similarly describes Israel as being "hardened."

it did not have that circumcision which entails observance of the law; their only distinguishing factor was physical circumcision.

Instead of storing up treasure, Jews were storing up (*thēsaurizeis*, 2:5) God's wrath as a result of their cardiosclerosis. The accumulated wrath will be revealed on the day of wrath (1:18; 2:8), when God's righteous judgment becomes manifest. Paul's irony adds a striking tone to the image of Jews accumulating divine wrath in a storehouse where one expects the fruits of one's labors to be stored.

Describing what lies ahead for unrepentant Jews, then for Gentiles (2:9), Paul uses the image of physical pressure exerted on someone confined in a narrow space. We might think of being caught between a rock and a hard place, with the rock pushing toward the hard place. The "anguish and distress" (*thlipsis kai stenochōria*) experienced by the unrepentant in 2:9 corresponds to the divine "wrath and fury" of 2:8. The words translated as "anguish" and "distress" are metaphorical. "*Thlipsis*" means pressure but the term was commonly used in Hellenistic parlance, in the Greek Bible, and in the New Testament as a metaphor connoting anxiety or tribulation. "*Stenochōria*," literally a narrow, confined space, was used to speak about various kinds of difficulty.[10] Found in Isaiah 8:22; 30:6 and Deuteronomy 28:53, 55, 57, the "protological pair" describes the result of God's displeasure.[11] Should one think it necessary to distinguish one term from the other, one might think of *thlipsis* as connoting outward affliction, while *stenochōria* connotes inner distress.

Paul rubs salt on the wounds of the Jews as he contrasts their conduct with the conduct of those Gentiles who do what the law requires:

> When Gentiles, who do not possess the law, do instinctively what the law requires, these, though not having the law, are a law to themselves. They show that what the law requires is written on their hearts, to which their own conscience also bears witness; and their conflicting thoughts will accuse or perhaps excuse them on the day when, according to my gospel, God, through Jesus Christ, will judge the secret thoughts of all. (Rom 2:14-16)

Doing what the law requires, albeit not possessing the written law, some Gentiles do the law and will be justified (2:13). Explaining how Gentiles

---

[10] The word *stenochōria* appears in a number of Paul's hardship catalogs (8:35; 2 Cor 6:4; 12:10).

[11] See Fitzmyer, *Romans*, 303.

can do what the law requires without having the written law, Paul employs figurative language (2:14-16), one metaphor explaining another. Paul says that the Gentiles constitute a law to themselves (*heautois eisin nomos*),[12] an idiomatic and figurative expression known to Hellenists who used it in reference to a virtuous person who does not need written guidelines or external sanctions to motivate his or her behavior.[13] To explain this figure of speech, Paul resorts to Jewish imagery: the works of the law are written on their hearts (*to ergon tou nomou grapton en tais kardiais autōn*, cf. 2 Cor 3:3). Implying participation in the covenant, the image hearkens back to Jeremiah 31:33, "I will put my law within them, and I will write it on their hearts; and I will be their God, and they shall be my people."[14] Law-abiding Gentiles are a law to themselves insofar as the demands of the law[15] are engraved deep within the core of their very being.

As he continues his rhetorical appeal, Paul talks about the Jew who has the law and thinks that he can teach it to others. This hypothetical Jew considers himself to be a "guide to the blind, a light to those who are in darkness, a corrector of the foolish, a teacher of children" (2:19-20).

The entire phrase is an extended metaphor. This teacher of the law might consider himself to be a guide to the blind. The metaphor is apt for a teacher but "blind" is a frequently used biblical metaphor for those who do not see the ways of the Lord. This figurative use of "blind" continues in the New Testament, where "blindness" characterizes those whose conduct impedes discipleship.[16] Paul's Jew might think of himself in biblical terms as "a light to those who are in darkness" (*phōs tōn en skotei*). Paul shares the traditional view that Gentiles are in the dark, their hearts plunged into darkness (1:21). The Servant of YHWH is a "light to the nations" (Isa 42:6; 49:6). Isaiah 42:7 describes the Servant opening the eyes of the blind and bringing from prison those who sit in darkness.

---

[12] See, Fitzmyer, *Romans*, 310: "Paul uses *nomos* in a figurative sense. . . . Pagans are themselves a way of knowing some of the things prescribed or proscribed by the Mosaic law."

[13] Aristotle, for example, writes, "The cultivated gentleman will therefore regulate his wit, and will be as it were a law to himself" (*Nichomachaen Ethics* 4.8.10 [1128a]).

[14] Cf. Isa 51:7; 2 *Bar.* 57:2.

[15] On the meaning of "what the law requires," *to ergon tou nomou*, literally, "the work of the Law," see Fitzmyer, *Romans*, 311.

[16] See Matt 15:14 [4x]; 23:16, 17, 19, 24, 26; John 9:39, 40, 41; 2 Pet 1:9; Rev 3:17.

Jews have a similar role;[17] a righteous Jew can consider himself privileged to teach the law to the Gentiles.[18]

Continuing his list of the Jew's self-referential attributes, Paul says that the Jew considers himself to be a "corrector of the foolish" (*aphronōn*). The foolish are those who are senseless or crazy. Judaism's wisdom tradition considered wisdom to consist of knowledge and observance of the law. Gentiles are "foolish" insofar as they do not observe the law. Idol worship is a striking manifestation of their foolishness.[19]

The apostle adds to these metaphorical descriptions of the teacher of the law that he is a "teacher of children" (*didaskalon nēpiōn*). A father had a duty to teach his sons the Torah; the rabbi who taught the Torah to a young adolescent was considered to be like a father to him.

The Jew who relies on the law can consider himself to be a guide to the blind, a light to those who are in darkness, a corrector of the foolish, and a teacher of children (2:19-20) because he has the Book of the Law, the embodiment[20] of knowledge and truth, but Jews break the law. The breaking of the law allows Paul to contrast Jews and Gentiles using the language of circumcision and uncircumcision (2:25-26) that he uses in Galatians.

Each of the pair of antithetical nouns has any one of three connotations.[21] "Circumcision" (*peritomē*) is the act of circumcision, the state of being circumcised, and, collectively, the population that has been circumcised, namely, Jews. Similarly, "uncircumcision" (*akrobystia*) denotes the male foreskin, the state of having a foreskin, and, collectively, those who possess the foreskin, namely, Gentiles. Paul teases the imagination of the reader with the interchange of the second and third meaning of the two words.[22]

---

[17] See Scot McKnight, *Light Among the Gentiles: Jewish Missionary Activity in the Second Temple Period* (Minneapolis: Fortress, 1991), 104–6. Among the texts that may be cited are Philo, *Abraham* 98; Josephus, *Against Apion* 2.279–295; *Sibylline Oracles* 3.195; *Testament of Levi* 14:4; 1 *Enoch* 105:1; 4 *Ezra* 14:20-21.

[18] Cf. Wis 18:4.

[19] See Wis 12:23-24; 15:14-17; Deut 6:4; *Sibylline Oracles* 3:722, etc.

[20] The Greek *morphēsin*, which appears only twice in the New Testament, basically means shaping, but it can also mean form or semblance. For the rendering "embodiment" or "formulation," see BAGD 528.

[21] See Otto Michel, *Der Brief an die Römer*, KEK 4, 12th ed. (Göttingen: Vandenhoeck und Ruprecht, 1963), 90–91; Cranfield, *Romans*, 1.171 n.4, 172–73; *Romans*, 322; Byrne, *Romans*, 105.

[22] The third meaning of each of the words is found in 3:30; 4:9; in 4:11 the terms are to be taken in their second sense.

He states that in the case of the lawbreaker circumcision becomes uncircumcision (2:24). Paul concludes with an imaginative portrayal of a real Jew: "A person is a Jew who is one inwardly, and real circumcision is a matter of the heart—it is spiritual and not literal" (2:29). The language derives from the Bible's prophetic tradition where passages such as the oracle of Jeremiah 9:24-25 similarly contrast the circumcised with those who are not circumcised. Deuteronomy encourages Jews to circumcise their hearts (Deut 10:16)[23] and proclaims that "the Lord your God will circumcise your heart and the heart of your descendants, so that you will love the Lord your God with all your heart and with all your soul, in order that you may live" (Deut 30:6).[24] The Book of Jubilees' vision of the restoration of Israel includes the promise: "I shall cut off the foreskin of their heart and the foreskin of the heart of their descendants" (*Jubilees* 1:23). Portraying the real Jew as one who has a circumcised heart, Paul immerses himself within this Jewish tradition.

### Universality of Sin

To prove that everyone is a sinner, Paul brings his argument to a climax in 3:10-18, saying that the Jewish Scriptures testify to the universality of human sin. Scripture's witness is Paul's strongest argument, the witness of the word of God itself. One of the remarkable features of the catena of scriptural passages in 3:10-18,[25] the longest chain of biblical passages in the New Testament, is its reference to various parts of the human anatomy:

> "Their throats are opened graves;
>      they use their tongues to deceive."
> "The venom of vipers is under their lips."
>      "Their mouths are full of cursing and bitterness."
> "Their feet are swift to shed blood;
>      ruin and misery are in their paths,
> and the way of peace they have not known."
>      "There is no fear of God before their eyes." (vv. 13-18)

---

[23] Similarly, Jer 4:4.

[24] 1QpHab 11:13, a commentary on Hab 2:16, speaks of the priest who did not circumcise his heart and would therefore be consumed by God's anger.

[25] Fitzmyer (*Romans*, 334), following Dibelius, Keck, and van der Minde, opines that the catena is a pre-Pauline list that may have been derived from a liturgical setting.

The apostle's portrayal of universal sin mentions throats, tongues, lips, mouths, feet, and eyes,[26] parts of the anatomy that appear in these biblical passages: Psalms 5:10; Psalms 140:3 [139:4 LXX]; 10:7; Isaiah 59:7-8/Proverbs 1:16;[27] and Psalms 35:2 [34:2 LXX].

The psalmist characterizes his enemies with strong metaphors. Their harmful speech is such that their throats are comparable to wide-open graves (Ps 5:10).[28] They are like venomous snakes whose poison is lethal (Ps 139:4 [LXX]). Their mouths are full of bitterness (*pikrias*), that is, bitterness to taste used as a metaphor for embittered speech (Ps 10:7).

Another part of the anatomy and another image speak about violence. The image is that of running feet, the feet of those bent on shedding innocent blood, eager to wreak violence on another human being. Blood that has been shed is blood poured out on the ground,[29] the hands of the perpetrator bloodied.[30]

Having used anatomical imagery to describe two of the many forms of sin that affect humankind, Paul continues with physical imagery in his description of God's judgment on sin in the following verse. The law speaks as it does, "so that every mouth may be silenced [*hina pan stoma phragē*], and the whole world may be held accountable [*hypodikos*] to God" (3:19). Accountability brings the reader into the courtroom. Paul's image is that of a defendant unable to speak in his own defense,[31] let alone boast before the judge. The inability to speak comes from the weight of the evidence brought against him.[32] The contrast is powerful, the irony patent. The mouth that was rampantly destructive falls silent in the presence of the divine judge.

Paul's linking judicial and anatomical images is inspired by his biblical source material. In the Bible each of the conflated passages that speaks about running feet is linked to a judicial scene. Proverbs 1:16 is closely related to Proverbs 6:16-19 and lists false witness after shedding blood and running feet. Isaiah 59:7 belongs to a pericope that speaks about

[26] Prov 6:16-19 similarly uses various parts of the body, the eyes, tongue, hands, heart, and feet, to describe people who act perversely.

[27] The two passages are almost identical. Cf. Prov 1:11; 6:17-18.

[28] Dahood's translation of the Hebrew text suggests that Ps 5:10c and 5:10d are in a relationship of synonymous parallelism. See Mitchell Dahood, *Psalms I: 1–50*, AB 16 (Garden City, NY: Doubleday, 1966), 35.

[29] Cf. Gen 4:10-11; Isa 26:21.

[30] Cf. Isa 1:15; 59:3.

[31] Cf. Ps 38:14b.

[32] So Cranfield, *Romans*, 1.196–197.

lies[33] and false suits (Isa 59:1-8). The sage and the prophet precede Paul in linking the courtroom with feet running to shed blood.

## *Justification*

Paul's use of the image of human speech to speak of the universal human experience of sin and the indefensibility of the sinner who stands speechless before God leads to Paul's proclamation of the sinner's "vindication," that is, his justification through the mercy of God: "all have sinned . . . [and] are now justified by his grace as a gift, through the redemption that is in Christ Jesus, whom God put forward as a sacrifice of atonement [*hilastērion*, hapax in Paul] by his blood" (3:23-25). The images probably derive from a pre-Pauline justification formula used as a creed or in a covenant renewal or eucharistic liturgical setting.[34]

The images are mixed, the vocabulary rare.[35] "Redemption" (*apolytrōseōs*) evokes the emancipation of prisoners of war or the sacral manumission of slaves. This is the image that comes to the minds of Corinthians who hear that Jesus Christ was their redemption (1 Cor 1:30); this would have been the image that engaged the imagination of the Romans when they heard Paul's words about "the redemption of our bodies" (8:23). For the Christian Jews among them the image may also have evoked the Greek Bible's idea of YHWH (re)acquiring Israel at various moments in its history, including the liberation from Egypt, the return from the Babylonian captivity, and at the eschaton.[36] From this perspective the image of redemption evokes the idea of God's definitive acquisition of humanity as his own people.

---

[33] Joseph Blenkinsopp (*Isaiah 56–66*, AB 19B [New York: Doubleday, 2003], 188) opines that this false and perverse utterance can be understood in a forensic sense as bringing false charges or as the issuance of an unwarranted summons or subpoena.

[34] See Karl Kertelge, *"Rechtfertigung" bei Paulus: Studien zur Struktur und zum Bedeutungsgehalt des paulinischen Rechtfertigungsbegriffs*, NTAbh, n.s. 3. 2nd ed. (Münster: Aschendorff, 1967) 48–62; and John Reumann, "The Gospel of the Righteousness of God: Pauline Reinterpretation in Romans 3:21-31," *Int* 20 (1966), 432–52, 436–38, repeatedly echoed in Fitzmyer, *Romans*, 342–54.

[35] Elsewhere Paul uses the word "redemption" (*apolytrōseōs*) only in 8:23 and 1 Cor 1:30.

[36] See Fitzmyer, *Romans*, 122–23.

In the Greek Bible the *hilastērion* was the mercy seat, an important feature of the liturgy of the Day of Atonement.[37] Philo writes about the lid of the ark of the covenant, "the mercy seat" that represents God's gracious power.[38] The Dead Sea Scrolls' "Melchizedek" (11QMelchizedek) describes an eschatological Day of Atonement liturgy. Paul evokes the liturgy of the Day of Atonement with an image of God setting forth the crucified Jesus[39] as the mercy seat, the sign of God's mercy on sinful humanity. Imaging Christ as the mercy seat[40] (*hilastērion*, "sacrifice of atonement" [NRSV]), Paul describes God putting Christ on display as the means of expiating human sin. The significance of the mercy seat, a sign of God's graciousness, would not have escaped the Jews to whom Paul is directing his appeal.

The image of the sinner standing speechless before the divine tribunal and the language of accountability brings the reader into the courtroom (3:19), introducing the judicial imagery that dominates 3:21-26. Paul writes about the disclosure of the "righteousness of God":

> But now, apart from law, the righteousness [*dikaiosynē*] of God has been disclosed, and is attested by the law and the prophets, the righteousness [*dikaiosynē*] of God through faith in Jesus Christ for all who believe. For there is no distinction, since all have sinned and fall short of the glory of God; they are now justified [*dikaioumenoi*] by his grace as a gift, through the redemption that is in Christ Jesus, whom God put forward as a sacrifice of atonement by his blood, effective through faith. He did this to show his righteousness [*eis endeixin dikaiosynēs autou*], because in his divine forbearance he had passed over the sins previously committed; it was to prove [*pros endeixin dikaiosynēs autou*] at the present time that he himself is righteous [*dikaion*] and that he justifies [*dikaiounta*] the one who has faith in Jesus. (Rom 3:21-26)

In just six verses, "righteousness" (*dikaiosynē*, meaning justice, the business of the judge in a court of law) occurs four times, "justify" (*dikaioō*,

---

[37] See Lev 16:2, 12-15; cf. Exod 25:17-22. For a recent study of the *hilastērion* in Rom 3:25, see Stephen Finlan, *The Background and Content of Paul's Cultic Atonement Metaphors*, 123–62.

[38] See Philo, *On Flight and Finding* 100; cf. *Cherubim* 25; *Moses* 2.95, 97.

[39] Cf. Gal 3:1.

[40] "We must not deprive Paul of the possibility of using 'mercy seat' in a symbolic or figurative sense, which is precisely what he seems to be doing, even though he insists as well on the public display of Christ crucified" (Fitzmyer, *Romans*, 350).

set right or, in the court of law, pronounce someone as righteous, that is, as vindicated, as having acted in accordance with the law and therefore innocent of any crime) once, and "just" (*dikaios*, properly describing those who obey the law) once.

Judicial imagery continues in the following pericope, 3:27-31, where "justify" occurs twice: "a person is justified by faith . . . [God] will justify the circumcised on the ground of faith and the uncircumcised through that same faith" (3:28, 30). It is regrettable that the NRSV translates the phrase *pros endeixin dikaiosynēs autou* in verse 26 with an overly simple "prove."[41] The phrase is almost identical to the similar phrase, *eis endeixin dikaiosynēs autou*, in verse 25 and has the same meaning, "to show his righteousness." Verse 26 virtually defines what Paul means by God's righteousness: not only is God righteous in himself, but God also demonstrates his righteousness by justifying sinners who believe.

The imaginative scenario evoked by Paul's judicial imagery is enhanced by his discourse on the law. Writing about the judicial process in 3:21-31, Paul mentions the law (*nomos*) seven times.[42] This is not surprising; the law is the standard on the basis of which an impartial judge makes his judgment.

Paul often speaks about the law in Romans, some sixty-six times in Romans 1–8 alone. By "law" (*nomos*) Paul generally means the Torah, the Law of Moses, albeit with different nuances here and there throughout the letter.[43] "Law" designates the Mosaic law in 3:21, 28, 31 but has another connotation in verse 27: "What becomes of boasting? It is excluded. By what law [*dia poiou nomou*]? By that of works? No, but by the law of faith [*dia nomou pisteōs*]."

Posing a rhetorical question, Paul uses the word "law" (*nomos*) in its generic sense (4:15). The word describes any law, any standard by which the licitness of human conduct can be judged. Answering his question with "by the law of faith," Paul uses "law" in a figurative sense.[44] The

---

[41] This translation is also found in the RSV. Other translations provide a fuller rendition of the Greek phrase in verse 26. Thus, the NIV and REB which read "to demonstrate his justice," and the RevNAB which reads "to prove his righteousness." All three of these versions translate the parallel phrases in verses 25-26 in identical fashion.

[42] Twice in verses 21, 27, and 31; once in verse 28.

[43] See Hans Hübner, *Law in Paul's Thought*. Studies of the New Testament and Its World (Edinburgh: T&T Clark, 1984); Fitzmyer, *Romans*, 131–35.

[44] Fitzmyer considers the expression to be an oxymoron since "Paul contrasts law and faith, which is in reality no law at all" (*Romans*, 363; cf. p. 131). Both Fitzmyer

metaphor is striking and unique within the Pauline corpus.[45] There is no way in which "faith" is "law." Nonetheless, Paul wants to make a point. Faith replaces the law with another standard of behavior. It entails a relocation of the believer from the sphere of law to the sphere of God's righteousness. The "law of faith" removes any ground for a person's boasting about his or her own righteous deeds; any righteousness that they might have results from the gratuitous gift of God.

### Abraham: Justified, Counted, and Sealed

As he does in Galatians (Gal 3:6-18 [29]), Paul offers Abraham as an example of justification (Rom 4). The story of Abraham shows that God justifies Gentiles as well as Jews. There is a before and after in Abraham's adult life, a time when he was not circumcised and a time when he was circumcised. Accordingly, Abraham is uniquely situated in the history of salvation to serve as a paradigm both for those who are uncircumcised (Gentiles) and for those who are circumcised (Jews).

Using scriptural language, Paul speaks about Abraham. He reminds Christian Jews at Rome that Abraham is the great patriarch, "our ancestor according to the flesh" (4:1). Speaking about his righteousness, Paul says: "If Abraham was justified [*edikaiōthē*] by works, he has something to boast about, but not before God. For what does the scripture say? 'Abraham believed God, and it was reckoned to him as righteousness [*elogisthē autō eis dikaiosynēn*]'" (Rom 4:2-3).

Genesis 15:6, the Scripture cited by Paul, reappears in 4:22-23,[46] the peroration of Paul's discourse on Abraham. Scripture's affirmation of Abraham's righteousness brackets the entire chapter, setting it apart as a discrete unit within the letter. The righteousness motif is sprinkled throughout the exposition. Paul uses "righteousness" ("justification") not only in the bracketing verses, 4:3, 22, but also in verses 6, 9, 11 [2x], and 13.

Genesis 15:6 provides another metaphor that the apostle uses in his portrayal of Abraham. The image is taken from the world of commerce,

---

and Byrne (*Romans*, 139) describe *nomos* as meaning "principle" in 3:27. A similarly figurative use of *nomos* appears in 8:2: "The law of the Spirit of life in Christ Jesus has set you free."

[45] The greatest similarities are with "the law of the Spirit of life in Christ Jesus" (8:2) and "the law of Christ" (Gal 6:2).

[46] See also Rom 4:9 and Gal 3:6.

where numbers, goods, and wages are counted. The Scripture says that Abraham's trust in God was "reckoned [*elogisthē*] to him as righteousness." "Reckon," meaning "count" or "calculate," is a term that properly belongs to the business world, as Paul knows well: "To one who works, wages are not reckoned [*logizetai*] as a gift but as something due [*opheilēma*]" (4:4). In Paul's implied and extended metaphor, wages are counted and owed, but the righteousness accorded by God is something different; it is not owed and cannot be counted as wages.

Sins, on the other hand, can be counted, but God chooses not to count the sins of believers. Paul cites David, the "author" of Psalm 32, as an authority on this point:

> Blessed are those whose iniquities are forgiven,
>     and whose sins are covered;
> blessed is the one against whom the Lord will not reckon sin.
>         (Ps 32:1-2; Rom 4:7-8)

Wages can be counted; sins can be counted. Righteousness cannot be counted. Yet Paul would have his readers think of God doling out righteousness in amounts vastly superior to any wages that are due or sins that can be counted. The imagery appears repeatedly throughout Romans 4. Over and over again (vv. 3, 5, 6, 9, 10, 11, 22, 23) Paul says that Abraham's faith was reckoned to him as righteousness.

If Abraham's faith was reckoned to him as righteousness before he was circumcised, what is the purpose of circumcision? Capitalizing on "*peritomē*" as describing the state of being circumcised, Paul responds to his own question by describing circumcision as a "seal" (*sphragida*)[47] of righteousness (4:11). A "seal" is an instrument that makes an impression, for instance, a signet ring, an embosser, or a sealing cylinder, or the impression that remains behind after the use of a seal.

Abraham's circumcision is the seal of his righteousness, the official confirmation and visible guarantee of the righteousness reckoned to him (4:11). Circumcision is God's guarantee that Abraham was in a right relationship with him. The image derives from the court of government. Abraham was justified by God before and after being circumcised. Circumcision is but a guarantee of his righteousness.

---

[47] Paul uses "seal" as a metaphor on each of the two occasions that it appears in his correspondence. See 1 Cor 9:2.

Using an image of people walking in the footsteps of Abraham[48] (*stoichousin tois ichnesin*), Paul explains:

> The purpose was to make him the ancestor of all who believe without being circumcised and who thus have righteousness reckoned to them, and likewise the ancestor of the circumcised who are not only circumcised but who also follow the example of the faith[49] that our ancestor Abraham had before he was circumcised. (Rom 4:11-12)

Summing up his exegesis of the story of Abraham, Paul comments on the scriptural verse which serves as the linchpin of his argument: "Now the words, 'it was reckoned to him,' were written not for his sake alone, but for ours also. It will be reckoned to us who believe in him who raised Jesus our Lord from the dead, who was handed over to death for our trespasses and was raised for our justification" (Rom 4:23-25).

Using the familiar technique of actualizing exegesis (1 Cor 9:10; 10:6), Paul affirms that just as the faith of Abraham was reckoned to him as righteousness before he was circumcised, so the faith of Christian believers is reckoned to them as righteousness,[50] whether or not they are circumcised.

## Freedom and Slavery

In Romans 5–8 Paul develops the idea that justification brings with it the sure hope of salvation and freedom from death, sin, self, and the law. Personification is used to make the ideas come alive. Personified law enters (*pareisēlthen*) the human scene (5:20). It wages war (*antistrateuomenon*)[51] and takes prisoners (*aichmalōtizonta*,[52] 7:23). The figurative use of these military terms is rarely attested before Paul.[53]

---

[48] See Ashworth, *Paul's Necessary Sin*, 40–41.

[49] The NRSV translation of *stoichousin tois ichnesin*, "follow the example," deprives Paul's idiom of its figurative value.

[50] With regard to the notion of righteousness, see the bibliographies in Fitzmyer, *Romans*, 144–46, 151–54 as well as the classic study of Karl Kertelge, *"Rechtfertigung" bei Paulus*, and the summary in Fitzmyer, *Romans*, 105–7.

[51] The verb is hapax in the New Testament. Paul, however, uses a simple form of the verb *strateuomai*, "fight militarily," in a figurative sense in 2 Cor 10:3.

[52] Paul's only other use of the verb "take captive" is in 2 Cor 10:5, where it also has a figurative meaning.

[53] See, however, Aristaenetus 2.1 for an instance of the metaphorical use of "wage war" (*antistrateuomai*).

Personified law is the agent of sin in 5:20 and 7:23 while in other passages Paul speaks of the law as an impersonal instrument used by sin in doing its dirty work. Paul personifies both sin and death acting in concert with one another. In a seemingly self-reflective and autobiographical manner Paul writes that sin, "seizing an opportunity in the commandment [law], deceived me and through it killed me" (7:11). He repeats the idea that sin is a killer in verse 13 before twice pointing to "sin that dwells [*oikousa*] within me" (7:17, 20; cf. 7:18). As an unwanted visitor, sin makes its home[54] within the human person. Personified sin lives in its adopted home, it seizes available opportunities, it deceives, and it kills. It is like a cancer, seated deep within a person and ultimately causing the person to die.

Above all, however, sin, like death, rules over human beings. Paul attributes imperial power to death when he describes death as "reigning" (*ebasileusen*) over humans. Death had dominion over humanity from the time of Adam until the time of Moses (5:14, 17). Death is the agent of sin;[55] so Paul can say that sin exercised dominion through death (5:21). Because Christ has been raised from the dead, death no longer reigns (*ouketi kyrieuei*, 6:9).

As he did with death, Paul contrasts the reign of sin with the time in which sin will no longer reign. There was a time when sin had dominion over human beings; there will be a time when sin will reign no longer. Having urged the Romans, "Do not let sin exercise dominion [*mē oun basileuetō*] in your mortal bodies" (6:12), Paul proclaims, "Sin[56] will have no dominion [*ou kyrieusei*] over you, since you are not under law but under grace" (6:14).

The imperial metaphors come from the political world of the Greco-Roman Empire. The dominant civil authorities were emperors or kings and lesser lords. The emperor "reigned" over his subjects; the lord "had dominion" over his subjects. The Greek verbs are related to the respective nouns. To "reign" (*basileuin*) is to act as an emperor (*basileus*); to "have dominion" (*kyrien*) is to act as a lord (*kyrios*). Since the emperor was occasionally called lord, the verbs "reign" and "have dominion" are

---

[54] Note the root *oik-*, "home," in the participle, *oikousa*.

[55] Cf. 8:10: "the body is dead because of sin [*nekron dia hamartian*]."

[56] For Paul's personification of sin, see also 6:13, "No longer present your members to sin as instruments of wickedness."

virtually interchangeable.[57] Paul's imperial imagery was highly evocative in the Greco-Roman Empire where the emperor reigned supreme, ruling with ultimate authority and exercising dominion through provincial governors.

Paul rarely[58] uses the political imagery at the core of Jesus' preaching, the coming of the kingdom of God, but his political metaphors provide a contrast between the reign of sin and death and the dominion that occurs with righteousness through Jesus Christ: "If, because of the one man's trespass, death exercised dominion through that one, much more surely will those who receive the abundance of grace and the free gift of righteousness exercise dominion in life through the one man, Jesus Christ" (Rom 5:17). Again, "grace might also exercise dominion [*basileusē*] through justification leading to eternal life through Jesus Christ our Lord" (5:21). Through Jesus Christ, through grace, humans who are made righteous share in the reign of Christ.

## From Political to Social Conditions

Lords have slaves; slaves have lords. If someone or something has dominion (*kyrioō*) over another, then someone or something else is enslaved (*douleuō*). If sin exercises dominion (*ebasileusen*) over human beings through death (5:21), the implication is that humans are slaves to sin. Paul does not leave the suggestion to the imagination of his readers. Repeatedly he reminds them that they were once slaves to sin (6:6, 17, 20).

The antithesis of being enslaved is to be free. The Romans to whom Paul is writing are now freed from sin (*eleuterōthentes*, 6:18, 22).[59] They have been freed from the law (8:2) which exercises power through sin

---

[57] The NRSV underscores the synonymity of the verbs *basileuein* and *kyrien* by translating their appearances in 5:14, 17; 6:9, 12, 14 as "exercise/have dominion." The NIV and the RevNAB maintain the lexical distinction between the two words. The NAB translates the former verb by "reign" and the latter by "be master/have mastery;" the RevNAB translates the former "reign" and the latter "have power." The REB is inconsistent, translating the former by "hold sway" and "establish dominion," the latter by "[be under] dominion" and "be master."

[58] Paul mentions the kingdom of God only in 14:17; 1 Cor 4:20; 6:9, 10; 15:24, 50; Gal 5:21; and 1 Thess 2:12.

[59] Cf. 6:7, "Whoever has died is freed from sin (*dedikaiōtai apo tēs hamartias*)." The judicial imagery means "pronounced innocent of sin."

and death.[60] Freedmen are not, however, totally free. They always remain subject to the imperial lord, the emperor. Those who have been freed from sin are now slaves to God: "Now that you have been freed from sin and enslaved [*edoulēthentes*] to God, the advantage you get is sanctification. The end is eternal life" (6:22).

Slaves rightly expect to receive some benefits, some advantage, from their masters; at the very least they could expect food and lodging. What is the benefit that results from being a slave to sin? Death, says Paul (6:21). What is the benefit that results from being a slave to God? Eternal life, says Paul (6:22). Posing these questions and offering his answers, Paul uses the agricultural image of "fruit," *karpos*, which the NRSV translates as "advantage" (6:21, 22).

Paul interrupts the flow of his agricultural imagery with the analogy of the married woman bound by law (7:1-3) but returns to it in 7:4-5, contrasting life freed from the law with life under the law: "You have died to the law . . . in order that we may bear fruit for God. . . . our sinful passions, aroused by the law, were at work in our members to bear fruit for death" (7:4-5; cf. 7:11). Paul often uses the image of fruit (1:13, etc.) but only in 7:4-5 does he employ the evocative verb "bear fruit" (*karpophoreō*). The image is that of a tree laden with ripe fruit in an orchard of similar trees.

Those who once were slaves to sin have become slaves to righteousness through Christ Jesus: "You, having been set free from sin, have become slaves of righteousness" (6:18). Believers are slaves (7:6) in the new life in the Spirit, slaves (7:25) to the law of God. All their members are slaves to righteousness (*doula tē dikaiosynē*, 6:19).[61] Since righteousness is the antithesis of sin, Paul asks: "Do you not know that . . . you are slaves of the one whom you obey, either of sin, which leads to death, or of obedience, which leads to righteousness?" (6:16) and says, "When you were slaves of sin, you were free in regard to righteousness" (6:20).

Steeped in the biblical tradition, Paul shared the Semitic understanding of the symbiotic relationship between human beings and creation. So he writes about the enslavement of creation, the corollary of human enslavement to sin, and about the freedom of creation, corollary to the human freedom effected through Jesus Christ: "Creation itself will be set free

---

[60] See 7:25; 8:2.

[61] In this verse Paul contrasts righteousness with impurity (*akatharsia*) and iniquity (*anomia*).

from its bondage [*eleutherōtēsetai apo tēs douleias*] to decay and will obtain the freedom [*eleutherian*] of the glory of the children of God" (8:21).

Highlighting the relationship between humanity and creation as he does, Paul accentuates the symbiotic relationship by personifying creation. He begins to do so in verse 19 when he writes: "Creation waits with eager longing [*apokaradokia*] for the revealing of the children of God."

Creation's passage from slavery to freedom is not easy.[62] Paul uses the image of the pains of childbirth to illustrate just how difficult and painful the process will be: "The whole creation has been groaning in labor pains [*systenazei kai synōdinai*] until now" (8:22). Paul compares creation to a mother about to give birth. Each of the verbs in his hendiadys is hapax in the New Testament.[63] The compound form of these verbs, with the prefix *syn*, "with," stresses that all creation shares in the pains, including humans: "Not only the creation, but we ourselves . . . groan inwardly [*stenazomen*]" (8:23).

Labor pains are a powerful metaphor.[64] The image is that of the entire creation moaning as a woman moans and groans as she is about to give birth. Similar imagery is exploited in Jewish[65] literature to describe the sufferings of the messianic times that precede the age to come.[66]

Paul uses a different female image to help his audience understand the relationship among the law, death (the death of Jesus that effects righteousness, 7:4), and sin. To clarify the relationship Paul describes the situation of a married woman (7:1-4). She is under the law and bound to her husband until death intervenes. Once he has died, she is free to be married again. As all analogies, this one limps. Nonetheless, in his extended metaphor Paul has made his point: death frees a person who has been under the law.

### The Peroration

Romans 1:16–8:39 is the heart of Paul's magnificent letter to the Romans; 8:31-39 is the peroration of its extended and intricate argument. Paul appeals to the audience by means of a series of rhetorical questions

---

[62] Cf. Gal 4:19; 1 Thess 5:3.

[63] Paul uses the simple verb *ōdinō* in Gal 4:19, 27 and the related noun *ōdin* in 1 Thess 5:3. The usages in Gal 4:19 and 1 Thess 5:3 are figurative.

[64] Similarly, Horst Balz, "*Systenazō*," *EDNT* 3:313–314, 313.

[65] Cf. Isa 26:17-18; Mic 4:9-10; *b. Sanh.* 98b.

[66] Cf. 4 Ezra 4:40-43; 5:44-55.

which invite the listener to participate in the discourse and make a judgment on what he has to say. Metaphors are an integral element of the argument.

The rhetorical questions of the first section of the peroration (8:31-34) evoke a court of law.[67] Paul writes about accusation (8:31b, 33) and defense (8:31b), pleas (8:34, where one might think of a witness for the defense), condemnation (8:34), and acquittal (8:32,[68] 33).

The peroration increases in intensity when Paul asks his final rhetorical questions: "Who will separate us from the love of Christ? Will hardship, or distress, or persecution, or famine, or nakedness, or peril, or sword?" (8:35). Personification adds a dramatic element to Paul's peroration. He asks, Who (*tis*) will separate us from the love of Christ? Repeating the question and fleshing it out by giving different examples, Paul personifies hardship, distress, persecution, famine, nakedness, peril, and the sword.

Paul further intensifies the threat of these perils by citing an imaginative verse of Scripture that points to the constant and death-threatening nature of these perils: "For your sake we are being killed all day long; we are accounted as sheep to be slaughtered" (Ps 44:22 [43:23 LXX]). The image was well known to those who knew the Scriptures.[69]

Paul's positively phrased questions call for a negative answer; none of the personified realities can separate us from the love of Christ. Paul nevertheless answers his own question. He affirms his conviction that none of these earthly realities can separate us from Christ, no matter how these personified realities might be manipulated by superhuman

---

[67] Cf. Fitzmyer, *Romans*, 529; Byrne, *Romans*, 276–77; Tobin, *Paul's Rhetoric* in its contexts: The Argument of Romans (Peabody, MA: Hendrickson, 2004), 322–23. Fitzmyer comments: "The setting for the passage is that of a lawcourt, as in Job 1–2 and Zechariah 3, in which a prosecutor accuses a justified Christian."

[68] The NRSV's "give us everything" renders the Greek *ta panta hēmin charisetai*. The words *charis* and *charizō*, a noun and a verb whose basic meaning is "favor," were used in a wide variety of contexts in the Hellenistic world, including the legal and judicial context. The word *charis*, for example, is used in a legal sense in the Oxyrhynchus (*POxy* 273.14 9) and Grenfell Papyri (*PGrenf* 2.70.5). The verb has a legal sense in Plato (*Apology of Socrates* 35c) and Plutarch ("Tiberius and Gaius Gracchus" [*Lives* 10] 4). The verb *charizō* is used in a strange manner in Acts 25:11, 16 in Paul's apology before Festus where he implicitly compares Roman and Jewish law. Fitzmyer comments: "The verb *charizesthai* actually means 'to favor, gratify.' The procurator cannot gratify the Sanhedrin as he proposes" (Fitzmyer, *The Acts of the Apostles*, AB 31 (New York: Doubleday, 1998), 745.

[69] Cf. Isa 53:7; Zech 11:4, 7.

forces: "I am convinced that neither death, nor life, nor angels, nor rulers, nor things present, nor things to come, nor powers, nor height, nor depth, nor anything else in creation, will be able to separate us from the love of God in Christ Jesus our Lord" (8:38-39). Personified death appears in the first place on this list of malevolent powers; personified death also appears in 1 Corinthians 15:26, where it is described as the last enemy to be destroyed.

Often overlooked in the theological discussion of Paul's discourse on justification in Romans 1–8 is that the theological exposition hinges on Paul's ability to personify the mysterious powers of sin and death and to create a picture using a variety of meaningful metaphors. The key metaphors come from the socio-juridico-political world in which Paul lived. Without these metaphors, and a variety of supporting metaphors, Paul might well have been unable to articulate what would become a touchstone of the Christian message throughout the ages.

Among Paul's metaphors are those found in compound verbs where the prefix *syn* ("with" or "co-") highlights the union that exists between the believer and Christ. For example, Paul writes, "We have been united with [*symphytoi*] him [Christ] in a death like his" (6:5). The verbal adjective, hapax in the New Testament, is properly used in horticulture where it describes plants that have grown together, either in the sense of having grown alongside one another or in the sense of having been organically fused into one, as would be the case when a branch of one tree is grafted onto another.

Other compound verbs pertain to death and burial. Paul writes that the "old self was crucified with [*synestaurōthē*] him" (6:6; cf. Gal 2:19) and that "we have been buried with him [*synetaphēmen*]" (6:4). Believers have not hung on a cross alongside of Christ nor were they entombed in the sepulcher that held the body of the dead Jesus. Paul is using graphic images that point to the shared lot of believer and Jesus: the believer participates in the death and burial of the Christ. For Paul that is the heart of the message, his *homilia*.

### The Potter

Paul begins an extensive reflection on the fate of Israel in salvation history (Rom 9–11) with an exposition of the gifts that God has given to Israel: adoption, glory, the covenants, the law, worship, promises, the patriarchs, and the Messiah (9:4-5). Paul then argues that God has a plan in which he acts freely (9:6-29). Even though Israel has rejected the gospel

(9:30–10:21), it will ultimately be included in the mystery of salvation (11:1-32). One dominant image focuses Paul's thought in each of the three parts of his exposition.

The potter working his clay is the key image in Paul's description of God's freedom at work in the divine plan of election (9:6-29). As a potter can make whatever he wants to make out of his clay, so God can do as he wills with his creation and the chosen people:

> Will what is molded say to the one who molds [*erei to plasma tō plasanti*] it, "Why have you made me like this?" Has the potter [*kerameus*] no right over the clay [*pēlou*], to make out of the same lump [*phyramatos*] one object [*skeuos*] for special use and another for ordinary use? (Rom 9:20-21)

The image is quite ordinary. Every village and town, depending upon its size, would have a potter or two who would shape, spin, and bake the vessels that villagers used. Cooking and storage pots as well as lamps were among them, while other vessels were used for waste. Paul's image would have struck home to every Roman who had stopped to observe the potter at work, as would most who had bought a pot or two. The potter made his pots and sold them in a workshop on the agora. The key words in the picture that Paul paints, "what is molded", "mold," "potter," and "clay," do not appear elsewhere in Paul's letters. Their appearance in the Greek Bible suggests that Paul's imagery may have been biblically inspired, notwithstanding his own experience of a potter working in another shop on the agora while he plied the leatherworker's trade in Prisca and Aquila's shop on the agora.[70]

The image of the potter and his clay is common in the Bible's prophetic[71] and sapiential literature,[72] appearing in the Dead Sea Scrolls as well.[73] Appearing in Romans 9's tapestry of biblical citations, Paul's image of the potter is constructed from a collage of biblical motifs. One passage is Isaiah 29:16[74] (9:20), which features a potter and a talking piece

---

[70] Some of the pottery made on the Corinthian agoras in Paul's day is on display in the museum of Ancient Corinth.

[71] Isa 29:16; 41:25; 45:9; 64:7; Jer 18:1-12.

[72] Ps 2:9; Job 10:8-9; Sir 33:13; Wis 15:7.

[73] 1QS 11:22; 1QH 1:21; 3:20-21, 23-24; 4:29; 11:3; 12:26, 32; 18:12.

[74] "Shall the potter [*kerameōs*] be regarded as the clay [*pēlos*]? Shall the thing made say of its maker [*erei to plasma tō plasanti*], 'He did not make me'; or the thing formed say of the one who formed it, 'He has no understanding?'" The NRSV does not

of pottery. Another passage comes from Jeremiah, one of the apostle's favorite biblical books. The Lord commanded Jeremiah to go to a potter's home and observe the potter at work. An accompanying oracle uses vocabulary that Paul will use: "'Can I not do with you, O house of Israel, just as this potter [*kerameus*] has done?' says the Lord. 'Just like the clay in the potter's hand [*pēlos tou kerameōs*], so are you in my hand, O house of Israel'" (Jer 18:6).

Paul speaks about the value of different pieces of pottery, distinguishing those that are for special use (*eis timēn*, literally, "for honor") and those that are for ordinary use (*eis atimian*, "for dishonor").[75] The distinction derives from Wisdom 15:7, which made the distinction with reference to the production of clay: "A potter [*kerameus*] kneads the soft earth and laboriously molds [*plassei*] each vessel for our service, fashioning out of the same clay [*pēlou*] both the vessels that serve clean uses and those for contrary uses."

Paul's image of the potter describes what the potter makes as a vessel (*skeuos*, "object" in the NRSV), the kind of pottery that most likely consumed most of the potter's time, effort, and care and provided him with his biggest source of income. In 9:21 Paul uses "vessel" in its proper sense. The potter makes vessels for honorable use and others for less noble uses (9:21). In the potter's shop, a vessel of wrath would be something made by the potter with which he was extremely dissatisfied, a vessel that made him angry and was about to be tossed into the scrap pile.

God makes vessels of wrath and vessels of mercy (9:22-23). "Vessel" is a metaphor. Jeremiah uses "vessels of wrath" to describe the instruments of war used by an angry God against the Chaldeans (Jer 50:25 [Jer 27:25 LXX]). Yahweh's wrath is like a curse.[76] The implication of Paul's metaphor might be that unbelieving and unrepentant Israel is destined for destruction (*eis apōleian*), a manifestation of God's eschatological wrath (1:18). As the potter does not immediately throw into the scrap heap pieces of pottery with which he is not satisfied, so God delays the display of his wrath to manifest his patience.

---

identify Isa 29:16 as a direct citation. What Paul has done is recognized in N-A[27] and by many commentators. So, Fitzmyer, *Romans*, 568, and, with nuance, Byrne, *Romans*, 300.

[75] Cf. 1 Cor 12:23-24.

[76] See Jack R. Lundbom, *Jeremiah 37–52*, AB 21C (New York: Doubleday, 2004), 405.

The biblical imagery from which Paul has shaped the image of the divine potter allows him to portray the freedom with which God accomplishes the eschatological plan of salvation and the purpose of election. The allusions to the biblical imagery are so evident that they could hardly have failed to make an impression on Christian Jews listening to the reading of Paul's letter. They were prepared for these allusions by the many biblical citations and scriptural references with which Paul constructs his exposition of the elective pattern in God's activity.

Some of these passages use traditional imagery. The descendants of Abraham are called his seed (*sperma*) in 9:7-8, echoing the language of Genesis 21:12 cited by Paul in verse 7. The image of Pharaoh's hardened heart echoes throughout the Exodus story.[77] In the midst of it all is the image of the runner (9:16),[78] which Paul uses not in the customary mode of the agonistic topos but as a simple image of human effort. No amount of human striving, says Paul, can accomplish God's elective plan of salvation: "It depends not on human will or exertion [*trechontes*], but on God who shows mercy" (9:16).

## The Stumbling Block

Paul continues his reflection on the divine plan of salvation in 9:30–10:21, another tapestry of biblical citations with which Paul writes about Israel's rejection of the gospel. They did not strive for righteousness on the basis of faith. Rather, they sought to attain righteousness through the law and were not able to do so. Paul repeatedly mentions righteousness (*dikaiosynē*, 9:30, 31; 10:3 [3x], 4, 5, 6, 10), but he does not really exploit the motif nor does he use any of the other terms in the word group. The image of God, the generous judge, hardly emerges from his discourse. Paul's focus is on unbelieving Israel that has not received righteousness.

Toward the beginning of the exposition Paul offers a startling image of Israel rushing ahead madly,[79] then tripping and falling to the ground. The image, he reminds his readers, is drawn from the Scripture itself: "They have stumbled over the stumbling stone, as it is written, 'See, I am

---

[77] Exod 4:21; 7:3; etc.

[78] On this metaphor and the metaphor of the olive tree in Romans 11, see F. Scott Spencer, "Metaphor, Mystery and the Salvation of Israel in Romans 9–11: Paul's Appeal to Humility and Doxology," *RevExp* 103 (2006): 113–38.

[79] Thus, Fitzmyer, *Romans*, 579.

laying in Zion a stone that will make people stumble, a rock that will make them fall, and whoever believes in him will not be put to shame'" (Rom 9:32-33). In its pursuit of righteousness through the works of the law Israel has tripped up.

The Hebrew text of the Scripture cited by Paul reads, "See, I am laying in Zion a foundation stone, a tested stone, a precious cornerstone, a sure foundation: 'One who trusts will not panic'" (Isa 28:16). The imagery of the construction of a new building in Zion contrasts dysfunctional society with a new social order based on the righteousness and justice of God.[80]

Paul cites the Scripture according to the Greek Bible which is not always a literal translation of the Hebrew. The final phrase of the Greek text reads, "Whoever believes in him will not be put to shame" not "One who trusts will not panic."[81] The apostle further modifies the prophetic text by adding the qualifying phrase, "that will make people stumble, a rock that will make them fall" (*proskommatos kai petran skandalou*, literally, "that one strikes against, that is, a stumbling rock"). The prophet's foundation stone has become Paul's stumbling block.

Interpreting Isaiah, Paul uses a well-known principle of rabbinic exegesis, the *gezerah shavah* principle. Inference from the analogy of words allowed the interpreter to use one scriptural passage to explain another in those cases where the two passages had identical words or phrases.[82] Paul found the expressions "a stone that will make people stumble" and "rock" in Isaiah 8:14: "He will become a sanctuary, a stone one strikes against [*lithou proskommati*]; for both houses of Israel he will become a rock one stumbles over [*petras*]."[83] With this trove Paul says that the rock that tripped up Israel was Christ; the Israelites did not believe in him.[84]

---

[80] See Joseph Blenkinsopp, *Isaiah 1–39*, AB 19 (New York: Doubleday, 2000), 392–93.

[81] With regard to the differences between the two versions of Isa 28:16, see the discussion in Cranfield, *Romans*, 2.511–12.

[82] Tobin observes with respect to 9:33 that the Greek texts of both Isa 28:16 and Isa 8:14 have words meaning stone as well as a reference to someone believing or trusting. See Tobin, *Paul's Rhetoric*, 342.

[83] Blenkinsopp (*Isaiah 1–39*, 242) comments: "The 'rock of stumbling' figure combines a poetic image of the strong God of Israel, of frequent occurrence in heroic poetry (e.g., Deut 32, 2 Sam 22), with that of a stumbling block, used elsewhere with reference to idols (Ezek 7:20; 14:3, 4, 7; 44:12)."

[84] Lindars opines that the stone was belief in Christ, rather than Christ himself. The nuance may be helpful. See Barnabas Lindars, *New Testament Apologetic: The*

Hellenistic Judaism interpreted Isaiah 28:16 in a messianic sense;[85] Paul provides his readers with his own spin on the idea.

The image of a stone or rock used in reference to Christ was common in early Christianity. Paul employs rock as an image of Christ in 1 Corinthians 10:4 and refers to Christ as a "foundation" (*themelion*, a key word in Isa 28:16 [LXX]) in 1 Corinthians 3:11. The image of Christ as a rock also appears in Mark, Q, Luke's special material, Paul, and 1 Peter.[86] The image imparted to Jesus the qualities of solidity, stability, and reliability that were associated with the image used of YHWH in the biblical tradition.

The image also allowed early Christian apologists to make use of the Scripture in "explaining" why Israel for the most part did not accept Jesus. For Paul, that was a matter of Israel having tripped up. Ironically, the rock that should have provided stability became the rock over which Israel stumbled.

Pursuing his biblical reflection on Israel's failure to come to belief in Christ, Paul puns on the idea of a stone at the beginning of chapter 11: A chosen remnant obtained what they were seeking; "the rest were hardened" (11:7). They became like stone (*epōrōthēsan*),[87] petrified, insensitive and unable to move. The theological passive implies that God was the agent who hardened them.[88]

Another stony image appears almost immediately afterwards: "David says, 'Let their table become a snare and a trap, a stumbling block [*skandalon*; cf. 9:33] and a retribution for them'" (11:9, citing Ps 69:22-23). With "Let their table be a trap for them, a snare for their allies" (Ps 69:22 [Hebrew]), the psalmist curses those who place obstacles in the way as he

---

*Doctrinal Significance of Old Testament Quotations* (London: SCM, 1961), 175–77, 177. Lindars' suggestion is certainly more apropos than are the suggestions of Meyer and Barrett who take "stone" to refer to the Torah. See Paul W. Meyer, "Romans 10:4 and the 'End' of the Law," in James L. Crenshaw and Samuel Sandmel, eds., *The Divine Helmsman: Studies on God's Control of Human Events. Presented to Lou H. Silbermann* (New York: Ktav, 1980), 59–78, 65; C. K. Barrett, "Romans 9:30–10:21: Fall and Responsibility of Israel," in Lorenzo de Lorenzi, ed., *Die Israelfrage nach Röm 9–11*, Benedictina: Biblical-Ecumenical Section 3 (Rome: St. Paul's Abbey, 1977), 99–130, 112.

[85] See the addition of "in him," *ep'autō*, in the Greek text and the footnoted observation of Cranfield, *Romans*, 2.511.

[86] See Matt 21:44 (par. Luke 20:18); Mark 12:10 (par. Matt 21:42; Luke 20:17); Acts 4:11; 1 Pet 2:4, 6-8 (incorporating Isa 28:16 and Isa 8:14).

[87] Cf. 2 Cor 3:14. See also Rom 2:5, albeit with a different verb.

[88] Cf. 9:18.

tried to live as one consumed with zeal for the house of the Lord (Ps 69:9 [69:10 LXX]). In his complex image the table evokes an altar of sacrifice on which were placed the bread and meats to be offered to idols. The table is then compared to a trap in which the vittles serve as bait. When an animal comes to eat the food, the trap springs shut, catching the animal in its grasp.[89]

The Greek Bible used by Paul omits "for their allies" from the Hebrew text and adds "retribution" (*antapodosin*) and "stumbling block" (*skandalon*). Paul cites these added words in reverse order. Doing so, he accentuates the image of the stumbling block. A tablecloth (table) lying on the ground[90] is the obstacle that leads Israel to trip and become ensnared in the net.

The image of the stumbling Israel continues as Paul addresses the Gentiles[91] with a rhetorical question:

> So I ask, have they stumbled [*eptaisan*] so as to fall [*pesōsin*]? By no means! But through their stumbling [*paraptōmati*] salvation has come to the Gentiles, so as to make Israel jealous. Now if their stumbling [*paraptōma*] means riches for the world, and if their defeat means riches for Gentiles, how much more will their full inclusion mean! (Rom 11:11-12)

Hellenists as early as the dramatist Aeschylus and the philosopher Plato used the verb "stumble" to describe someone tripping over a stone.[92] Paul uses the same verb—one that he uses only here—to describe the mass of Israel tripping over the stumbling block that is Christ. He continues the image by mentioning Israel's stumbling, *paraptōma*, a Greek word meaning "false step" or "slip" but often used in a metaphorical sense to describe a mistake, an error, or transgression. Paul himself ordinarily uses the term in this manner,[93] but in 11:11-12 the image of the misstep enhances his figurative description of a stumbling Israel.

---

[89] See the description and representative drawings in Frank-Lothar Hossfeld and Erich Zenger, *Psalms 2*, Hermeneia (Minneapolis: Fortress, 2005), 182.

[90] See Fitzmyer, *Romans*, 608.

[91] See 11:13.

[92] Aeschylus, *Prometheus Bound*, 926; Plato, *Republic* 553b. See also Theocritus, *Idylls* 7.26.

[93] See 4:25; 5:15,16, 17, 18, 20; 2 Cor 5:19; Gal 6:1. Hence, the NRSV footnotes at Rom 11:11, 12, "Greek *transgression*."

The image of a person stumbling draws attention to the feet. In 11:8-10 the image of stumbling feet is sandwiched between images of eyes that cannot see: "God gave them a sluggish spirit, eyes that would not see and ears that would not hear, down to this very day" (a conflation of Deut 29:3 and Isa 29:10; Rom 11:8) and "Let their eyes be darkened [*skotisthētōsan*, another theological passive] so that they cannot see and keep their backs forever bent" (Ps 69:23; Rom 11:10a). The image of eyes that cannot see allows Paul to group the two passages together on the basis of their analogy of words.

The catena of biblical citations with anatomical references in 11:8-10 recalls the similar but longer scriptural sequence in 3:8-18. The composite image of a body whose parts do not function properly, with spirits that are sluggish, eyes that cannot see, ears that cannot hear, feet that trip, and a hunched back,[94] is a graphic representation of Israel totally out of kilter.

## The Olive Shoot

Paul begins to speak to the Gentile members of the Roman community in 11:11, addressing them in earnest as of 11:13: "Now I am speaking to you Gentiles. Inasmuch then as I am an apostle to the Gentiles." The Gentiles who were listening to the reading of Paul's letter had heard that God had rejected Israel, that this rejection was for the salvation of the world, and that this rejection was not definitive. How then should the Gentiles think about Israel? To answer the question Paul uses an agricultural analogy.

He begins with a mixed metaphor: "If the part of the dough offered as first fruits [*aparchē*] is holy, then the whole batch [*phyrama*] is holy;[95] and if the root [*rixa*] is holy, then the branches [*kladoi*] also are holy" (11:16). The image of the first fruits[96] belongs to the cultic domain, the image of roots and branches to horticulture.

---

[94] The Greek words "back" (*nōton*) and "bent" (*synkampson*) appear in the New Testament only in 11:10, Paul's citation of Ps 69:23.

[95] The Greek is turned in a phrase that is more simple than its English translation. The Greek reads simply, "If the first fruits are holy, the dough is holy."

[96] On the images in 11:16, see Anthony G. Baxter and John A. Ziesler, "Paul and Arboriculture: Romans 11.17-24," *JSNT* 24 (1985): 25–32; Karl H. Rengstorf, "Das Ölbaum-gleichnis in Röm 11:16ff," in Ernst Bammel, ed., *Donum gentilicum: Studies in Honour of David Daube* (Oxford: Clarendon, 1978): 127–64.

First fruits offered to God must be unblemished or unadulterated so that they can be sanctified. Only if a batch of dough is unadulterated—that is, without yeast[97]—could the portion taken for an offering be holy. At the time of the Exodus YHWH instructed Moses about the first batch of dough:

> From your first batch of dough [*aparchēn phyramatos*] you shall present a loaf as a donation; you shall present it just as you present a donation from the threshing floor. Throughout your generations you shall give to the Lord a donation from the first of your batch of dough [*aparchēn phyramatos*]. (Num 15:20-21)

In Philo's allegorical interpretation of this passage "batch" (*phyrama*) means the Jewish people,[98] much in the same way that it does in Romans.

In Paul's horticultural image (11:16b), the roots are the patriarchs;[99] the branches, individual Israelites. Agricultural imagery used of the patriarchs is also found in *1 Enoch* 93:5, "Then after that at the completion of the third week a (certain) man shall be elected as the plant of the righteous judgment, and after him one (other) shall emerge as the eternal plant of righteousness." Ethiopian commentators hold that the first man is Abraham; the other, Isaac.

The image of the root and branches provides a transition to the allegory of the wild olive shoot grafted onto an old olive tree. Verbs in the passive voice attribute the pruning and grafting to God. God removes unwanted branches from the cultivated olive tree and replaces them with branches taken from a wild olive:

> But if some of the branches [*kladōn*] were broken off, and you, a wild olive shoot [*agrielaios*], were grafted in their place to share the rich root [*rixēs*] of the olive tree [*elaias*], do not boast over the branches

---

[97] See 1 Cor 5:6; Gal 5:9.

[98] See Philo, *Sacrifices of Abel and Cain* 107–108. Cf. Philo, *Special Laws* 1.132; Josephus, *Jewish Antiquities* 4.71.

[99] This is the opinion of virtually all the commentators, including Byrne, Cranfield, Fitzmyer, Michel, Pesch, Sanday and Headlam, Wilckens, and Ziesler. Cf. 11:17, 28. Exploiting the parallelism between Paul's two metaphors, some commentators opine that the first fruits of 11:16 is also a reference to the patriarchs. Cranfield and Fitzmyer, however, divide the two images, seeing in the "first fruits" a reference to the remnant of Israel which accepted Christ. See Cranfield, *Romans* 2, 564; Fitzmyer, *Romans*, 614.

[*kladōn*]. If you do boast, remember that it is not you that support the root [*rixan*], but the root [*rixa*] that supports you. You will say, "Branches [*kladoi*] were broken off so that I might be grafted in." That is true. They were broken off because of their unbelief, but you stand only through faith. So do not become proud, but stand in awe. For if God did not spare the natural branches [*kladōn*], perhaps he will not spare you. Note then the kindness and severity of God: severity toward those who have fallen, but God's kindness toward you, provided you continue in his kindness; otherwise you also will be cut off. And even those of Israel, if they do not persist in unbelief, will be grafted in, for God has the power to graft them in again. For if you have been cut from what is by nature a wild olive tree [*agrielaiou*] and grafted, contrary to nature, into a cultivated olive tree [*kallielaion*], how much more will these natural branches be grafted back into their own olive tree [*elaia*]. (Rom 11:17-24)[100]

The olive tree appears as a symbol of Israel in Jeremiah 11:16. Paul's use of the image reflects a Jewish topos in which the metaphor of a plant serves to explain God's disciplining and restoration of Israel. Not only does the image occur in *1 Enoch*, but it also appears in a passage in which Philo allegorizes on Jewish eschatological expectations. Concluding his treatise "On Rewards and Punishments," Philo writes, "For just as when the stalks of plants are cut away, if the roots are left undestroyed, new growths shoot up" (*Rewards* 172).[101]

The practice of rejuvenating an old olive tree by grafting onto it a shoot of a hearty, wild olive tree is attested by Lucius Iunius Moderatus Columella, a contemporary of Paul and the author of the most complete extant Roman agricultural manual.[102] The practice had a twofold result: the engrafted branch bore fruit because it drew its life from the roots, and the rejuvenated old tree was able to bear fruit once again.[103]

---

[100] The key words of this allegory are used by Paul only in reference to it. Thus, branches (*kladoi*) in 11:16, 17, 18, 19, 21; root (*rixa*) in 11:16, 17, 18 [see, however, the appearance of the word in Paul's citation of Isa 11:10 in 15:12]; olive tree (*elaia*) in 11:17, 24; wild olive tree (*agrielaios*) in 11:17, 24; cultivated olive tree (*kallielaios*) in 11:24.

[101] Philo then segues to the image of a seed and writes about the soul that is renewed as long as a tiny seed remains. See Tobin, *Paul's Rhetoric*, 365–66.

[102] See Columella, *De re rustica* 5.9.16–17.

[103] See Baxter and Ziesler, "Paul and Arboriculture," and Ziesler, *Paul's Letter to the Romans*, TPINTC (London: SCM and Philadelphia: Trinity Press International, 1989), 279.

Paul's image illustrates God's plan to save Israel despite its apparent rejection. The "hardening" of Israel was only temporary: "Hardening [*pōrōsis*][104] has come upon part of Israel until the full number of Gentiles has come in" (11:25). En passant, the image reminds Gentile Christians[105] that they draw their life from the roots of the old olive tree; Israel remains the bearer of life and salvation to the world.

The image also contains a warning: Gentile Christians must not become complacent in their faith. If God had previously cut (unbelieving) branches from the tree, there is no reason why he might not do so again. Moreover, Gentiles must not boast of their position vis-à-vis the fruit-bearing natural branches of the olive tree; they have no right to boast at the expense of Israel or of Christian Jews, from whom they draw their life.

After the allegory, Paul concludes his scriptural meditation on the fate of Israel with a pair of biblical catenae. Romans 11:26-27 uses Isaiah 59:20; Jeremiah 31:33-34; and Isaiah 27:9 to speak about God's promise to Israel. Isaiah 40:13 and Job 15:8 are cited in 11:34 in reference to the inscrutability of the mind of God. An expression of awe (11:33) recalls Paul's words in 1 Corinthians 2:16 and 2 *Baruch* 14:8-9.[106] In awe and in gratitude, Paul then breaks into his final paean of praise: "For from him and through him and to him are all things. To him be the glory forever. Amen" (11:36).

## A Living Sacrifice

Romans 12–15, the explicitly hortatory section of the letter, begins with a general exhortation that speaks about the human body, the place and means of a person's activity in the world:

> I appeal to you therefore, brothers and sisters, by the mercies of God, to present your bodies as a living sacrifice, holy and acceptable to God, which is your spiritual worship. Do not be conformed to this

---

[104] Literally, petrification. Rom 11:25 is the only time that Paul uses the noun *pōrōsis*, cognate with the verb *epōrōthēsan* of 11:7.

[105] Similarly, Tobin (*Paul's Rhetoric*, 259, 263) speaks of a "representative Gentile." This passage, directed to Gentiles, is the longest passage in Romans 9–11 that is totally devoid of explicit scriptural references.

[106] "O Lord, my Lord, who can understand your judgment? Or who can explore the depth of your way? Or who can discern the majesty of your path? Or who can discern your incomprehensible counsel? Or who of those who are born has ever discovered the beginning and the end of your wisdom?"

world, but be transformed by the renewing of your minds, so that
you may discern what is the will of God—what is good and acceptable and perfect. (Rom 12:1-2)

Addressed to Paul's siblings, the introduction abounds in cultic imagery.
Paul writes about "offering" (*parastēsai*), "sacrifice" (*thysian*), being "holy
and acceptable to God" (*hagian euareston tō theō*), and "worship"
(*latreian*).

Having the general meaning of "place before [someone]," "place at
the service of [someone]," the verb "offer" connotes in a cultic setting
offering in sacrifice.[107] What Christians are to offer to God is not the
animal or grain sacrifices that Gentiles offered in their temples or Jews
offered in the temple of Jerusalem. Rather, believers should offer themselves as a living sacrifice. A sacrifice that is alive contrasts with the
slaughtered animals and harvested grain that are offered in temple worship. Animals are put to death; the grain no longer lives; believers are a
living sacrifice.

Echoing the prophets,[108] Paul describes this living sacrifice as "holy
and acceptable to God."[109] Sacrifice offered in this fashion is "spiritual
worship" (*logikēn latreian*[110]), an unusual turn of phrase that appears in
no other passage of Paul's extant writings. The phrase adds to the idea
of living sacrifice that this kind of worship conforms to the rational
nature of the human being.

Mention of bodies offered as sacrifice to God enables Paul to speak of
the "one body" (*hen sōma*, 12:4, 5) with its several interrelated members
and their different functions. The striking metaphor, lacking any explicit
ecclesial reference[111] but with an accompanying list of spiritual gifts
(*charismata*), is a condensed and non-polemical cameo of the thought
expressed in 1 Corinthians 12. Fitzmyer opines that the image "probably

[107] See Josephus, *Jewish War* 2.89; *Jewish Antiquities* 4.113. Cf. Lucian, *Sacrifices*, 13.
BGDF 629 describes the word as a technical term in the language of sacrifice.

[108] Thus, Byrne, *Romans*, 363, with reference to Hosea and Amos, Isaiah and Jeremiah.

[109] Cf. 15:16.

[110] The noun *latreia* appears elsewhere only in 9:4 where "worship" is identified as
one of the privileges of Israel. In 12:1, Paul's qualifying adjective is not *pneumatikē*,
"spiritual," but *logikē*, "rational." Hapax in Paul, the adjective is difficult to translate.
Many commentators note the use of the adjective in Stoic literature.

[111] In Romans "church" (*ekklēsia*) first appears in the list of greetings in Romans 16
(vv. 1, 4, 5, 16, 23).

does not suggest anything more than a moral union of the members who work together for the common good of the whole, as in the body politic."[112]

A trace of the agon motif can be found in the images that Paul uses as he urges the Romans to work zealously for the common good: "Outdo [*proēgoumenoi*] one another in showing honor. Do not lag [*skēroi*] in zeal" (12:10-11).

Immediately afterwards Paul urges the Romans, "Be ardent [*zeontes*] in spirit" (12:11). Recalling the exhortation "Do not quench the Spirit," of 1 Thessalonians 5:19, the image is of fire[113] that causes something to boil and bubble, a bustle of activity. Another fiery image is introduced when Paul cites Proverbs 25:21-22 in his paraenesis: "If your enemies are hungry, feed them; if they are thirsty, give them something to drink; for by doing this you will heap burning coals on their heads." The figurative expression most probably referred to some form of torture, but it is impossible to ascertain what specifically the sage had in mind when he wrote about the pile of burning coals on a person's head.[114] It is even more difficult to determine what Paul meant by the appropriation of the image. Neither "pile" (*sōreuseis*) nor "coals" (*anthrakas*) appear elsewhere in the extant correspondence.

The final image of chapter 12 is a parenetic use of the agon motif: "Do not be overcome [*nikē*] by evil, but overcome [*nika*] evil with good" (12:21). The image is that of the athletic contest or the battle. Who will win? Evil or good?

## Night and Day

Biblical scholars generally agree that Paul's appeal to the eschaton as a motivation for appropriate behavior is couched in motifs associated with early Christian baptismal catechesis and the baptismal ritual.

---

[112] Fitzmyer, *Romans*, 648.

[113] Although *zeō* properly means "boil," "seethe," Gerhard Schneider renders Paul's phrase "aflame in the Spirit." See Schneider, "*Zeō*," *TDNT* 2:99–100, 99.

[114] A survey of the different opinions is to be found in Arndt Meinhold, "Der Umgang mit dem Feind nach Spr. 25:21f. als Masstable für das Menschsein," in Jutta Hausmann and Hans-Jürgen Zobel, eds., *Alttestamentlicher Glaube und biblische Theologie: Festschrift Horst Dietrich Preuss zum 65. Geburtstag* (Stuttgart: Kohlhammer, 1992), 244–52.

Scholars such as Schlier, Wilckens, Byrne, and Tobin opine that the material contained in 13:11-12 is essentially a baptismal hymn:[115]

> It is now the moment for you to wake from sleep; . . .
> the night is far gone, the day is near.
> Let us then lay aside the works of darkness
> and put on the armor of light. (13:11ab, 12)

Breaking the rhythm of the hymn, 13:11c, "For salvation is nearer to us now than when we became believers," is an interpolated interpretive comment that recalls the moment of baptism.

Contrast and temporal images dominate 13:11-12 much as they do in 1 Thessalonians 5:1-11. Romans and 1 Thessalonians share the introductory observation that the audience knows about the time, the significant time.[116] Both speak about night[117] and day,[118] darkness[119] and light.[120] The contrast between night and day, darkness and light, appears in 13:12 and 1 Thessalonians 5:4. The antithesis yields parenetic inferences. Night is the time when, under the cover of darkness, evil activity takes place (13:13; 1 Thess 5: [4], 7). In Paul's imagery light is caused by the coming of day, a cipher for the Day of the Lord. Activity taking place in the light is influenced by the coming of the Day of the Lord.

Romans 13:11-14 and 1 Thessalonians 5:1-11 share other similarities as well. Both make reference to sleeping, albeit with different terminology: the noun *hypnou* in 13:11, the verb *katheudōmen* in 1 Thessalonians 5:6, 7 [2x]. Both draw upon the analogy of clothing oneself (*endysōmetha*, 13:12, 14; 1 Thess 5:8) and speak of military accoutrements, armor (*hopla*)[121] in 13:12, a breastplate (*thōraka*) and helmet (*perikephalaian*) in 1 Thessalonians 5:8. Both passages speak about drunkenness (*methais*,

---

[115] See Ernst Käsemann, *Commentary on Romans* (Grand Rapids, MI: Eerdmans, 1980), 362; Henrich Schlier, *Der Römerbrief*, HTKNT 6 (Freiburg im Briesgau: Herder, 1977), 395–96; Ulrich Wilckens, *Der Brief an die Römer*, 3, EKKNT 6 (Zurich: Benziger, 1982), 74–75; Byrne, *Romans*, 398; Tobin, *Paul's Rhetoric*, 403. Fitzmyer (*Romans*, 682) considers that the hypothesis is possible.

[116] In Greek, *chronos*, "time," designates chronological time; *kairos*, the word used in 13:11a; 1 Thess 5:1 denotes significant time, especially feasts, holidays, and specific opportunities.

[117] *Nyx* in 13:12; 1 Thess 5:2, 5, 7 [2x].

[118] *Hēmera* in 13:12; 1 Thess 5:2, 4, 5, 8.

[119] *Skotous* in 13:12; 1 Thess 5:4.

[120] *Phōtos* in 13:12; 1 Thess 5:5.

[121] Cf. 2 Cor 6:7; 10:4.

13:13; *methyskomenoi, methyousin,* 1 Thess 5:7)[122] as a kind of conduct to be avoided by the Christian.

It is likely that Paul uses images that early Christian catechesis associated with baptism in both passages. This is especially the case with the reference to putting on clothing, a baptismal ritual (Gal 3:27; cf. Eph 4:24). The wearing of baptismal robes symbolizes the newly baptized putting on Christ,[123] the new person, a motif closely associated with Adam-Christ typology. With the coming of day, the "clothing" that is to be put on is Jesus Christ, that is, Christ as Lord.[124]

Although 13:11-14 shares much of the imagery of 1 Thessalonians 5:1-11, the Romans passage highlights the urgency of the eschaton. Using a greater variety of words with temporal connotations than he did in the earlier missive, Paul systematically arranges the vocabulary to capture the urgency of the moment. He writes about time (*kairos*), the day (*hēmera*), the hour (*hōra*),[125] and now (*nyn*)! For Paul, now is the critical moment; now it is day, the time when it is light.

Being dressed for the day means putting on the armor of light. Paul joins the idea of putting on the armor of light with the idea of laying aside the works of darkness.[126] The notion that a change of clothing symbolizes a change in behavior appears in the legendary Jewish tale of Aseneth's conversion (*Joseph and Aseneth* 10:10-16). That the Christian should wear military armor as he or she strives to live the Christian life, the life of Christ who has been put on (13:14), is consistent with the way that the Stoics used the agon motif to image the struggle for the virtuous life. In the Judeo-Christian tradition the struggle also reflects the battle that precedes the imminent eschaton.

---

[122] In 13:13 "drunkenness" is a vice among several others, whereas in 1 Thess 5:7 "drunkenness" is a metaphor for the various kinds of immoral behavior associated with the night. There, drunkenness is contrast with sobriety, a contrast that does not appear in the paraenesis of 13:11-14.

[123] Cf. 13:14. With regard to the clothing imagery of 13:12, 14, see, especially, Kim, *Clothing Imagery,* 135–51.

[124] The similar image in Gal 3:27 does not use "Lord" (*kyrios*), a title that Paul often associates with the coming of Jesus at the parousia.

[125] The NRSV translates *hōra* as "moment" in 13:11.

[126] One need not belabor the point that the ancients did have a set of bedtime clothes and a set of daytime clothes as we do. One can, however, note that armor would have been added to the soldiers' garb when it was time to do battle.

## The Weak and the Strong

In Romans 14:1–15:13 Paul writes about the responsibility of the strong toward those who are weak. The gist of his exhortation is that "[w]e who are strong [*dynatoi*] ought to put up with the failings of the weak [*asthenēmata*[127] *tōn adynatōn*]" (15:1). The weak are those who are weak with regard to their faith. These are Christian Jews in Rome who continue to observe dietary laws and religious festivals. Paul urges the strong to bear with the weak and not despise them.

The extended paraenesis of 14:1–15:13 incorporates a number of metaphorical expressions. Many of the images had previously been used but none of them is key to Paul's argument. Parenetic discourse does not attempt to explain its reasons why, even though it may cite any number of motivational factors. For example, Paul writes about the judgment seat (*bēmati*, 14:10) of God. The image is that of God, the eschatological judge.[128]

As is his wont, Paul uses the traditional Semitic idiom "walk" (*peripatēsōmen*, 13:13; 14:15) as a synthetic description of a person's behavior. He urges the Romans not to put a stumbling block or hindrance (*proskomma . . . skandalon*, 14:13) in someone else's path, using the image of Isaiah 28:16 that he uses apropos of Israel in 9:33. It is wrong to make others fall (*proskommatos*, 14:20);[129] it is good not to do anything that causes another to stumble (*proskoptei*, 14:21).

Other familiar metaphors also occur in the letter's final paraenesis, especially the judicial metaphor of "righteousness" (*dikaiosynē*) and the synecdochic use of "circumcision" (*peritomē*). "Righteousness" is cited as a quality of the kingdom of God in 14:7. Christ is identified as a servant of the circumcised in 15:8. Another metaphor familiar to the readers of this letter is that of the root, previously used in reference to the patriarchs (11:16-18) and now used in reference to Christ: "The root of Jesse[130] shall come, the one who rises to rule the Gentiles" (15:12, with reference to Isa 11:10).

---

[127] This word belongs to the same word group as the "weak," *asthenounta*, a participle that appears in 14:1, 2. The verb also appears in some manuscript readings of 14:21, including P[46], the Codex Vaticanus, and the majority of minuscules; this reading is reflected in the KJV, JB, and NJB.

[128] Cf. 2 Cor 5:10, where Paul writes about the judgment seat of Christ.

[129] The noun *proskomma*, "stumbling block," and the verb *proskoptō*, "stumble," belong to the same word group.

[130] 15:12 is the only New Testament passage that mentions the root of Jesse.

Romans 15:14-16 is typically understood by commentators as an introduction to the travelogue that follows (15:17-33). Another reading of the text might find in these verses a transitional passage. As such the passage is both the peroration of Paul's paraenesis, forming a literary inclusion with the liturgical language of 12:1, and an introduction to what follows. The passage speaks about Paul's ministry in cultic terms:

> . . . the grace given me by God to be a minister [*leitourgon*][131] of Christ Jesus to the Gentiles in the priestly service [*hierourgounta*] of the gospel of God, so that the offering [*prosphera*] of the Gentiles may be acceptable [*euprosdektos*], sanctified [*hēgiasmenē*] by the Holy Spirit. (15:15c-16)

Paul's description of himself in cultic terms is unique; only rarely does he use the terminology. "Priestly service" is not otherwise mentioned in the New Testament. "Offering" appears in no other passage of Paul's extant correspondence. "Sanctified" appears only here in the letter to the Romans. Paul occasionally uses the words "minister" and "acceptable" but rarely does he do so.[132]

In 15:15c-16 Paul compares the work of evangelization with that of priests and Levites[133] officiating in the Jerusalem temple. Those ministers sacrificed animals in the temple, making them holy. Paul prepares Gentiles as an offering; previously they were unclean but through the preaching of Paul they have been made holy by the Spirit. The cultic language of the passage (cf. Phil 2:17) is consistent with an early Christian tendency to describe the Christian community as an eschatological community in terms that properly refer to Israel's worship.[134]

Having described his ministry to the Gentiles in cultic terms, Paul reaffirms his intention to visit the Romans, noting, however, that he has no desire to build on another's foundation (15:20; cf. 1 Cor 3:10). Before going to Rome, he must take the collection for the Christian poor in Jerusalem to the Holy City. Then he would be free to go.

---

[131] This word often has a secular meaning, connoting a functionary who serves the people, as, for example, in 13:6. In passages such as Isa 61:6; Neh 10:39; and Heb 8:2 (in reference to Christ, the high priest) the term bears a specifically cultic meaning.

[132] "Minister" in 13:6; Phil 2:25; "acceptable" in 2 Cor 6:2; 8:12.

[133] With regard to Levites, see Cranfield, *Romans* 2.755.

[134] So, Byrne, *Romans*, 435.

## Farewell

For the most part the language of the final chapter of Paul's Letter to the Romans is matter of fact. Metaphorical expressions rarely interrupt the business at hand. Greeting Prisca and Aquila, Paul says, however, that they "risked their necks" (*trachēlon upethēkan*, 16:4) for him. Paul does not elsewhere use either of the words that comprise this graphic metaphor. The verb means "place under," but it was commonly used in the Hellenistic world to mean risk or venture.[135] Today we might say that they put their necks on the line. We would love to know what it was that Prisca and Aquila had done for Paul that was so dangerous. We can speculate that it was something that happened at Ephesus but neither 1 Corinthians 15:32 nor 2 Corinthians 1:8-9 provides sufficient information for the contemporary reader to know what it was that Prisca and Aquila did.

Romans' exhortation employs other bodily images. Addressing Roman Christians as "brothers and sisters" one last time, Paul writes:

> I urge you, brothers and sisters, to keep an eye on [*skopein*] those who cause dissensions and offenses [*skandala*], in opposition to the teaching that you have learned; avoid them. For such people do not serve our Lord Christ, but their own appetites [*koilia*], and by smooth talk [*chrēstologias*] and flattery they deceive the hearts [*kardias*] of the simple-minded [*akakōn*]. (16:17-18)

The imagery of this short exhortation is striking, not only because of Paul's recourse to kinship language, but also because of the way he plays with physical imagery. He encourages the Romans to be on the lookout, as if with their eyes,[136] for people who are arranging stumbling blocks on the path that others trod. He urges them to be wary of people's pleasing words, the kind of sweet talk that is deceptive.[137] He reminds them that some people are addicted to their own lusts, their bellies,[138] rather

---

[135] So, for instance, Plato, *Protagoras* 313a; Plutarch, *Crassus* 7.

[136] Paul's Greek does not use the word "eye." He uses the verb *skopeō* in its proper, physical sense, in 2 Cor 4:18 and in an extended sense in Gal 6:1; Phil 2:4 (cf. Phil 3:17).

[137] The word *chrēstologia*, "pleasing speech," is hapax in the New Testament. Paul uses the term with a negative connotation. Greeks, however, generally used the term to describe those who spoke well.

[138] Cf. Phil 3:19.

than serving Christ, while others lead astray the hearts of those who are naive.

Drawing his letter to a close, Paul describes God as the God of peace, as he did in 1 Thessalonians 5:23, writing, "The God of peace will shortly crush Satan under your feet" (16:20). Alluding to Genesis 3:15 and using human anatomy to construct his image, Paul utters a solemn promise. He expresses the common belief of Christians and apocalyptically oriented Jews alike that the end time will bring with it the cosmic victory of God and the suppression of Satan, the great adversary.

## Summing Up

The Letter to the Romans is often considered to be Paul's chef d'oeuvre. In terms of its systematic and well-balanced presentation, that may well be the case. The apostle would not, however, have been able to achieve what he did in the letter were it not for his skillful use of metaphor. In the letter's first eight chapters Paul builds a case for the universality of human sin with anatomical imagery, including the image of the hardened heart and the darkened mind. He builds his case for the gratuity of grace with imagery drawn from the courtroom, using the language of justification and acquittal.

Dealing with the fate of Israel in the second large unit of his letter essay, chapters 9–11, Paul puns with stony imagery and capitalizes on his knowledge of botany to speak about the renewal of Israel and the salvation of Gentiles. The extended exhortation that constitutes the third major unit of Romans, chapters 12–15, opens on a liturgical note, but Paul could not have been as effective as he was had he not had some recourse to the agonistic motif and found in the clothing that one puts on at daylight a remarkable image for new life in Christ.

Without metaphor Romans would not be the chef d'oeuvre that it is.

# 9

# Paul's Use of Metaphor

A ristotle writes that we must make use of appropriate metaphors and epithets.[1] Paul's epistolary rhetoric, intended to persuade the congregations to which he wrote, was effective. Those early churches persevered in their faith commitment and preserved the letters as a legacy for the believing congregations of our generation. The metaphors that enhanced Paul's letters are an integral part of his rhetorical appeal. He does not use metaphor for the sake of metaphor nor did he use it for the sake of mere ornament. His images were part of the very fabric of his argument, to make the appeal or to clarify his point.

The images were drawn from a wide variety of semantic fields and different areas of human discourse. It is difficult to say that one field was more important than another because Paul, master of the art of rhetoric, chose his images according to the circumstances of his intended audience and the point that he was trying to make.

## Kinship

Robert Banks writes that the use of *adelphoi*, "brothers and sisters, is "far and away Paul's favorite way of referring to the members of the communities to whom he is writing."[2] One can reasonably argue that family relationships are the primary area from which Paul took his most

---

[1] See Aristotle, *Rhetoric* 3.2.9 [104b].

[2] Robert J. Banks, *Paul's Idea of Community: The Early House Churches in Their Historical Setting* (Grand Rapids, MI: Eerdmans,1980), 50–51.

significant metaphors. That might be true for Paul's letters to the Thessalonians, Galatians, and Philemon, but it is less so for 1 Corinthians and hardly the case at all for 2 Corinthians, Romans, and Philippians.

The family relationship is particularly important in the first of Paul's letters. The letter to the church of the Thessalonians is characterized by the frequency with which Paul appeals to the Thessalonians as his "brothers and sisters." Relative to its size, no other letter uses that formula of direct address as often as does that first letter; none use it in quite the same way.

When Paul writes to the Thessalonians as his siblings, he imparts a warm and friendly tone to his letter. Using the relationship to encourage the Thessalonians, Paul urges them to follow his example and heed his fraternal advice. The Thessalonians to whom he writes are not only his siblings, but they are also siblings among themselves. Paul encourages them to continue in their love for one another and uses their relationship as an argument for why they ought not offend or take advantage of one another (1 Thess 4:6).

Paul also uses paternal and maternal images to describe the warm positive relationship that exists between himself and the Thessalonians. Like a mother, he has nurtured them and poured himself out for them. Working night and day, he instructed them as a father does his children. To be sure, Paul is not always consistent in his use of metaphors. Thus, still speaking about the quality of his relationship with the Thessalonians, Paul is able to describe himself as a little infant and as a virtual orphan when he is separated from them.

Sibling and paternal metaphors are otherwise important in the Letter to Philemon. From the outset of this short note, Paul builds up a *pathos* appeal to Philemon by affirming that there exists among Timothy, Apphia (perhaps Philemon's wife), Philemon, and himself a sibling relationship. The strength of that appeal is increased with Paul's specific reference to the gathering in Philemon's home. Paul writes to Philemon asking that Onesimus be accepted into the family circle as one of them, one of the group of siblings.

The reason why Paul makes bold with this request is that he, Paul, had become a father to Onesimus during the time of his imprisonment. The paternal metaphor is predicated upon Paul's evangelization of the slave who had come to him, hoping to find in him an *amicus domini*.

Kinship metaphors also play an important role in the Letter to the Galatians. The letter is limned by the idea of the relationship among siblings (Gal 1:2; 6:18). Relatively bereft of one of Paul's favorite forms of direct address, "brothers and sisters,"[3] the sheer abundance of parental, both paternal and maternal, and filial vocabulary, including the idea of generation, indicates that Paul is putting the notion of the family at the heart of his letter. His basic argument is that Jews and Gentile believers alike are children of Abraham. Gentile believers are children of Abraham because they are in Christ Jesus who is of the seed of Abraham who is, in Paul's words, *the* seed of Abraham. As children of a common father and mother (Gal 4:26), they belong to the same family and should act accordingly.

In this letter paternal imagery figures principally in Paul's description of Abraham, the common ancestor of Jews, Christ, and Gentile believers. The apostle does not use paternal imagery of himself, but he does use the figure of the mother to describe himself. The image is that of a woman in the throes of labor pains, suffering and perplexed because the pregnancy has not yet come to term (Gal 4:19-20).

Various images provide the color and verve of the complex argument in 1 Corinthians. Among them are paternal and maternal images, as well as the use of "brothers and sisters" as a formula of direct address. The use of this form of direct address is to be expected in a missive whose major theme is an appeal for harmony within the community. Paul lays the groundwork for the appeal by mentioning the Corinthians' fellowship (1 Cor 1:9); he follows this up with a statement of his purpose directed to the Corinthians as "brothers and sisters" (1 Cor 1:10), the first among twenty uses of the vocative *adelphoi* in the letter. Apart from the *ēthos* and *pathos* appeal implicit in this formula of direct address, Paul does not use the sibling relationship in his argument except for 1 Corinthians 8:11-13. No more than they would dare inflict further suffering on a sibling who was ill should the Corinthians sin against a brother or sister who has a weak conscience.

Images of parent and child, on the other hand, are an important part of the argument that Paul makes in the first part of the letter. As a mother feeds her infant children with milk, so the Corinthians are like infants who are not yet ready for solid food (1 Cor 3:1-3). In 1 Corinthians 4:14-21 Paul reminds the Corinthians that he is their father since he had evangelized them, just as he had Timothy. Timothy was a beloved and faithful child, whereas they were in danger of receiving the rod.

---

[3] The formula appears only in Gal 4:12; 5:13; 6:18.

## The Body

One of the most striking images of 1 Corinthians is Paul's use of the figure of the body, the one body with its many members, the many members of the one body, to portray the dynamic and interactive unity of the church (1 Cor 12:12-26). Paul writes about the eye, the ear, and the weaker and less respectable members of the body without focusing on any one of them. His point is simply that all members must function harmoniously if the body is to function well. Paul also uses the image of the body in Romans but he does not mention any specific parts of the body as he makes his point (Rom 12:4-5).

Earlier in Romans Paul mentions specific parts of the body: throats, tongues, lips, mouths, and feet (Rom 3:13-15). The images served Paul's portrayal of the universality of human sin. Using their throat, tongue, mouth, and lips, humans are capable of sinning in speech. With their feet they are able to run, positioning themselves to inflict violence on others. On the other hand, the feet of a runner enable him to announce good news, the "gospel" in its root sense, in various places (Rom 10:15). With the foot, a person is able to crush things that are annoying and irksome. Thus, Paul describes God as putting his various enemies and all things under the feet of Christ at the eschaton (1 Cor 15:25, 27) or, again, the God of peace putting Satan under the feet of those who obey the gospel (Rom 16:20).

Paul took this figurative use of the parts of the human anatomy from his biblical tradition. His mentions of feet are for the most part found in biblical quotations or allusions. Anatomical imagery was also mediated to Paul through Hellenistic culture. The figure of the body was an important *topos* in political discourse; rhetors used the image to urge social harmony.

A feature of Paul's references to parts of the body that are visible to the naked eye is his use of personification. Developing the image of the body in reference to the church at Corinth in 1 Corinthians 12:12-26, Paul describes feet, ears, eyes, and head that speak. Aristotle notes that one of the features of metaphor is that it strikes the audience because it is unusual or out of the ordinary. The speaking body parts enjoy this quality of the metaphor. Similarly striking is Paul's description of feet that are swift to shed blood (Rom 3:15), though this figure of speech is more properly synecdoche than an example of metaphor.

Parts of the anatomy also feature in the rhetoric of 2 Corinthians. Paul hopes that the Corinthians will reciprocate the depth of his affection for them (2 Cor 6:11-13). To speak of the frankness of his speech, he uses the image of a mouth that is wide open. To speak of his warm affection for the Corinthians, he uses the image of the heart. To speak of the depth and unconditional nature of his affection, Paul writes about his gut, the vital organs. In return, Paul hopes that the Corinthians will open up their hearts to him.

For the most part Paul's bodily language reflects his Semitic and biblical holistic anthropology. Contemporary readers may interpret "flesh," "flesh and blood," and "heart" as examples of figurative language, synecdoche in which a part is used to designate the whole. Semites, including Paul, typically used such terms to designate the whole human person. Thus, "flesh" designates the whole human person as a created being, in solidarity with other humans, and prone to weakness, sickness, and sin. The heart, on the other hand, designates the entire human person in the depths of its humanity, particularly highlighting the idea that a man or woman is a person with will and emotions.

Semites typically used various parts of the anatomy to speak of various emotions. Philo, a Hellenistic Jew, describes the "belly" as the seat of lust and irrational craving.[4] Paul may well have shared this view of the belly since he tells the Philippians that those who are opposed to the cross of Christ have their belly as god (Phil 3:19). He warns the Romans to be on the lookout for those who serve their bellies rather than the Lord Christ (Rom 16:18).

A particularly striking example of Paul's indebtedness to this kind of Semitic usage is the way in which he speaks of the "gut" (*splanchnon*). We moderns will occasionally speak of a gut reaction; Paul uses the idiom in 2 Corinthians and the letters from prison, Philippians and Philemon. In 2 Corinthians Paul writes about his own emotions in this way (2 Cor 6:11) and uses similar language to speak about the emotions of Titus (2 Cor 7:15). In Philippians Paul writes about Christ's gut (Phil 1:8) and his own gut (Phil 2:1) as he compares the depth of his own feeling with that of Christ. Paul's relatively brief note to Philemon is one extended *pathos* appeal. Not surprisingly, then, Paul uses the image of the gut more often than he does in the longer letters. He uses the image twice in reference to his own emotions (Phlm 12, 20) and also to speak about the emotions of a larger group with whom he is associated (Phlm 7).

---

[4] See Philo, *Allegorical Interpretation* 3.115–16.

## The Senses

Aristotle wrote about the beauty of the metaphor, noting that metaphorical speech appeals to the senses. Paul was well aware of the importance of the senses. He invites his readers to smell the aroma and fragrance wafting through the air as the gospel spreads as a result of his ministry (2 Cor 2:14-16). He asks the Philippians to smell the sweet aroma of the gifts that they had sent to him as they might smell the aroma of a fragrant sacrifice (Phil 4:18).

The Galatians can hear the voice of a previously barren woman singing and shouting over her numerous progeny (Gal 4:27). Paul invites the readers of 1 Corinthians to hear the sounds of the flute and the harp (1 Cor 14:7), the sound of the gong (1 Cor 13:1), and the cacophonous or complementary sound of the tinkling cymbal (1 Cor 13:1). He asks that they hear the sound of angelic voices (1 Cor 13:1) and the sound of a voice raised in a song of praise (1 Cor 14:15). And certainly the Corinthians should know the difference between the sound of the voice of a child speaking about childish things and the sound of the voice of adults who speak of more serious matters (1 Cor 13:11).

He would have his readers listen for the sound of the bugle that announces that the battle is about to begin (1 Cor 14:8). Earlier in his ministry he suggested that his readers await the sound of the trumpet announcing the imminent appearance of the Lord—a sound that will be accompanied by a cry of command and the call of the archangel as the great parade is about to begin (1 Thess 4:16). The sounding trumpet also appears in the eschatological scenario sketched by Paul in 1 Corinthians 15:52.

Other sounds are less welcome—like the sounds of the voices of those who speak but the listener is unable to understand (1 Cor 14:11) or the sounds of outsiders calling Christians crazy, out of their minds, because of the incomprehensible babble that arises from within the congregation (1 Cor 14:23).

There is the sound that arises from within us when we are lost for words, not knowing how to pray, while the Spirit intercedes with sighs too deep for words (Rom 8:26). There are the Spirit-prompted groans, like those of a woman in labor, that arise from within as we await the birth that consists of the redemption of our bodies (Rom 8:23). Indeed, all creation groans with the pangs of birth as it awaits the freedom of the glory of the children of God (Rom 8:21-22).

Paul does not often tantalize the taste buds of his readers and when he does so his speech is not usually metaphoric. One exception would be when he compares the Corinthians' immaturity in faith to children whose diet consists only of milk because they are not yet ready for solid food (1 Cor 3:1-2). Despite the relative absence of an appeal to the sense of taste in Paul's letters, the apostle urges the Corinthians to think about the Israelites eating and drinking at the time of the Exodus (1 Cor 10:3-4, 7). He asks them to think about their own eating and drinking, about how getting a head start on the food and drinking more than sufficient wine while others go hungry and thirsty is a sign of contempt for the church of God (1 Cor 11:21-22). He asks them to think about how their eating a meal in the precincts of the temple of an idol might destroy a member of the family for whom Christ had died (1 Cor 8:10-11).

Great rhetoricians like Aristotle and Cicero, and the anonymous author of the *Rhetorica ad Herennium,* write about the importance of a speaker putting things in front of the eyes of his audience so that they can visualize what he is talking about. Paul reminded the Galatians that the crucified Christ stood out like a placard before their eyes (Gal 3:1) as he hung on the cross accursed (Gal 3:13). Together with angels, other human beings, and the entire world, the Corinthians are like spectators sitting on the benches of the theater looking at Paul and his fellow apostles paraded before their eyes as if they were on display (1 Cor 4:9). Later, Paul would ask the Corinthians to think about the Israelites who were unable to gaze on the glory of Moses' face (2 Cor 3:7, 14).

A mirror helps a person to see but the image, particularly in the more primitive mirrors of Paul's day, is somewhat distorted. Thus, at the present time we can see only as if in a mirror (1 Cor 13:12); we can see the glory of the Lord as though it were reflected in a mirror (2 Cor 3:18).[5] When, however, the eschaton arrives, then we shall see face to face, no longer in need of a mirror to catch but a glance.

## Life Cycles

Paul uses the image of the woman about to give birth in various ways. The image first appears in the Letter to the Thessalonians, when Paul provides his readers with a picture of a pregnant woman suddenly overcome by labor pains (1 Thess 5:3). Paul draws attention to the suddenness of the onset of the pains in his attempt to rouse the Thessalonians from

---

[5] Paul uses the image of the mirror twice, but he uses two different words for mirror, *ainigma* in 1 Cor 13:12, *katoptron* in 2 Cor 3:18.

whatever complacency might affect them as they hear people talk about "peace and security."

Paul writes about the prolonged labor pains that he experiences because the Galatians are not fully formed as a Christian community: "My little children, for whom I am again in the pain of childbirth until Christ is formed in you, I wish I were present with you now and could change my tone" (Gal 4:19-20). The image is all the more striking insofar as birth pains are attributed to a male, rather than to a woman for whom labor pains are a normal part of life's experience.

Equally striking is Paul's writing about personified creation's labor pains. In symbiotic relationship with the humanity which inhabits creation, creation itself groans with labor pains along with human beings as it awaits the freedom of the glory of the children of God (Rom 8:21-23). As he often does, particularly when using biological relationships in a figurative manner, Paul mixes his metaphors. What human beings groaning with labor pains along with creation expect is not birth, but adoption (Rom 8:23). "Adoption" can be listed among the privileges of Israel (Rom 9:4); applied to believers, "adoption" is one of the effects of the Spirit acting within believers. The Spirit brings about their adoption as children of God[6] (Rom 8:15, 23; Gal 4:5-6).

Not all labor pains terminate with the birth of a healthy child. Sometimes labor pains issue forth in a premature abortion or a stillborn child. Paul uses the former idea when he speaks about himself as "one untimely born," an "aborted fetus" (*ektrōmati*) in 1 Corinthians 15:8.

As people pass through their lives they clothe themselves, but they are sometimes naked. Clothing oneself, taking off one's clothes, and being naked come together in a complex passage in which a tent and a heavenly house are the items of clothing in Paul's metaphorical wardrobe: "[I]n this tent we groan, longing to be clothed with our heavenly dwelling—if indeed, when we have taken it off we will not be found naked. For while we are still in this tent . . . we wish not to be unclothed but to be further clothed" (2 Cor 5:2-4). A related image appears in 1 Corinthians where the wardrobe consists of imperishability and immortality rather than a tent and a heavenly dwelling (1 Cor 15:53-54).

Putting on a set of clothes occasionally symbolizes the assumption of an office or a rite of passage. Paul uses the image of a person clothing

---

[6] For the designation "children of God" (*tekna theou*) used of believers, see Rom 8:16, 21; 9:8; Phil 2:15.

himself or herself with military armor (Rom 13:12; 1 Thess 5:8) as an expression of the agonistic motif, but he also speaks about "putting on" Christ. Paul refers to the baptismal ritual of putting on a new garment when he uses this language in Romans 13:14 and Galatians 3:27.[7]

Putting on specific kinds of clothing is often a rite of passage, but sleeping and waking are daily activities. Life cannot go on without sleeping and waking. The images served Paul's paraenesis very well. Using the verb *katheudō*, Paul writes about sleep in 1 Thessalonians 5:6, 7, 10. In 1 Thessalonians 5:6-7, he writes about sleepers sleeping, contrasting that experience with the experience of those who are awake and alert. Sleepers are those who can be caught off guard, as by a thief in the night, whereas those who are fully awake are vigilant, ready for the unexpected.

The apostle creates a similar verbal contrast in 1 Thessalonians 5:10 but the referent of the paired metaphor has changed. Now "sleeping" appears as a euphemism for "being dead" and "being awake" connotes those who are alive. In the immediately preceding pericope, 1 Thessalonians 4:13-18, Paul had used the verb *koimomaō*, a Greek synonym of *katheudō*[8] and, like it, also meaning sleep, to speak about those who had died (1 Thess 4:13, 14, 15). When Paul returns to the subject of the resurrection of Jesus and our resurrection in 1 Corinthians 15, he repeatedly uses this idiom to speak about the sleep of death (1 Cor 15:6, 18, 20, 51). When Paul's principal concern is the resurrection of the dead, the use of "sleep" as a euphemism for death has the additional connotation that sleep is not the end of the story. One wakes from sleep. With respect to death, waking from "sleep" occurs in the resurrection from the dead.

A different connotation attaches to the verb *koimomaō* as a way of speaking about death in two earlier passages of Paul's First Letter to the Corinthians. There, in 1 Corinthians 7:39, "death" suggests some finality. When a man dies (*koimēthē*), the marital bond between him and his wife is severed and she is free to marry again. In 1 Corinthians 11:30, dying (*koimōntai*, "have died") is understood in a typically Jewish fashion, namely, as the ultimate punishment inflicted on those who have sinned.

In Romans, Paul uses the image of being awake to describe the vigilance of those who are prepared for the parousia. The image appears almost unexpectedly in the letter's extensive paraenesis. Paul's pointed reminder comes in these words: "You know what time it is, how it is

---

[7] The baptismal allusion is patent in Gal 3:27.
[8] Paul uses this verb only in 1 Thessalonians.

now the moment for you to wake from sleep (Rom 13:11). The vocabulary of this particular image is unusual for Paul. Only here does he employ the noun "sleep" (*hypou*); the verb that he uses, "wake" (*egerthēnai*), appears elsewhere in his letters as a way of speaking about the resurrection from the dead.

Finally, although people do not often talk about them, and when they do they speak euphemistically, bowel movements are part of the rhythm of life. Reflecting on his own acceptance of the gospel in Philippians 3, Paul tells his readers that he now regards all things that he previously valued as "rubbish" (*skybala*) so that he can gain Christ. The King James Version of the Bible caught the nuance of Paul's language when it rendered Paul's Greek as "[I] count them but dung, that I may win Christ." The New King James Version, however, euphemistically renders Paul's *skybala* as "rubbish," as do most contemporary translations.

## Walking and Stumbling

One of the most common metaphors used by Paul—indeed, the most common metaphor in his writings—is that of "walking" as a description of human conduct. With the exception of the note to Philemon, this metaphor appears in all of Paul's letters. The first attested instances are, of course, to be found in the Letter to the Thessalonians. This letter provides a clue as to how Paul understands the metaphor. In 1 Thessalonians 2:12, Paul portrays himself as a father who teaches his children how to "walk worthily of God."[9] The image recalls the Jewish father who was under obligation to teach his sons the Torah, along with its *halakah*. The *halakah*, "walking," were the rules of behavior derived from the Torah.

This Jewish background also explains Paul's use of the metaphor in 1 Thessalonians 4:1, a passage in which Paul reminds the Thessalonians that he had taught them how "to walk" and tells them that they were "walking" as he had taught them to. That the image is to be understood in Jewish fashion is all the more important when one realizes that the Thessalonians are portrayed as having "received" this teaching from Paul. The verb used by Paul is the Hebrew equivalent of the verb used in rabbinic circles to describe students who have "received" the traditional lore that the rabbis had "delivered" to them.

---

[9] The literal translation of *peripatein . . . axiōs tou theou* which the NRSV renders as "lead a life worthy of God."

For Paul, "walking" is a matter of living one's life in a manner consistent with the gospel. There are, however, stumbling blocks (*skandala*). So Paul urges the Romans not to put a stumbling block in another's path (Rom 14:13) and to be on the lookout for those who position stumbling blocks in opposition to the teaching that they had learned (Rom 16:17).

The biggest stumbling block was, however, the stumbling block that the Jewish people had to face. That was Christ; indeed, Christ crucified (1 Cor 1:23). Using passages from their very own Scriptures, especially Isa 8:14; 28:16; and Ps 69:22-23, Paul offers a graphic description of Israel stumbling over the Christ (Rom 9:33; 11:9). Tripping over Christ as they do, the Jewish people were not following in the way of the Lord. Yet, there was hope for the nation, as Paul would explain before he finished his long disquisition on the fate of Israel in Romans 9–11.

## Running and Fighting

Writing to Christians at Corinth, where the biennial Isthmian Games were an important feature of social life, Paul invites the Corinthians to think about some of the athletic contests with which they were familiar (1 Cor 9:24-27). He asks them to think about the runner straining to win the race, about the discipline that an athlete imposes upon himself while he is in training, and about the punishment that a boxer's body receives not only when he is in training but also during the course of a bout. And, of course, Paul reminds them that following the rules of the particular contest is important because failure to do so brings disqualification. All the training, all the discipline, all the effort would then be for naught. On the other hand, a laurel wreath, the victor's crown, awaits those who win.

Paul does not write in this fashion because he wanted to promote the Isthmian Games. Rather, he used these images to speak about his own efforts on behalf of the gospel. Doing so, he was making use of the agon motif, a well-known rhetorical device in the Hellenistic world. The *agōn*, a "contest," was principally of two sorts, the athletic event and the military battle. Philosophic moralists contemporary with Paul used images drawn from these two spheres of activity to speak of efforts that must be made in pursuit of the truth and/or in the attempt to lead a moral life. Paul used similar imagery in much the same fashion, but for him the truth was the gospel message and the moral life was life as a Christian.

Some use of the agonistic motif appears in each of the seven undisputed Pauline letters, from 1 Thessalonians 2:4 to Romans 13:12. Paul uses the term *agōn*, a "contest," in 1 Thessalonians 2:4 and Philippians 1:30 and the related verb *agōnizomai*, "contest," in 1 Corinthians 9:25. As far as athletic contests are concerned, Paul's most common image was that of the runner. Not only does the image occur in 1 Corinthians 9:24, but it also appears in the letters to the Philippians (Phil 2:16), Galatians (Gal 2:2; 5:7), and Romans (Rom 9:16; 12:11). The image of the victor's wreath is the background which explains why Paul can call the Thessalonians and the Philippians his crown and joy (Phil 4:1; 1 Thess 2:19).

A striking image is that of teammates, fellow-athletes, striving together to win. Paul uses the image twice in his Letter to the Philippians: "striving side by side [*synathlountes*] with one mind for the faith of the gospel" (Phil 1:27) and "they have struggled beside me [*synēthlēsan*] in the work of the gospel" (Phil 4:3). Among Paul's several athletic images, the image of struggling teammates perhaps represents Paul's most transparent use of the agonistic motif.

Paul's use of athletic imagery generally appears when he is writing about the gospel. When, however, he is writing about the Christian life, the military metaphor dominates Paul's use of the agon motif. In 1 Thessalonians 5:8, Paul urges the Christians of Thessalonica to get ready to do battle: "Put on the breastplate of faith and love, and for a helmet the hope of salvation." Paul urges the Romans to "put on the armor of light" (Rom 13:12). He concludes the long series of parenetic exhortations in Romans 12:21 with the summarizing exhortation, "Do not become overcome [*nikō*] by evil, but overcome [*nika*] evil with good," a final exhortation speaks of the victory of good over evil.

The longest circumstantial catalogue in Paul's letters includes the expression, "with the weapons of righteousness[10] for the right hand and for the left" (2 Cor 6:7). Second Corinthians, in fact, contains Paul's most sustained use of the military metaphor. Paul offers a scenario in which he writes about waging war, ordinary weapons and powerful weapons, battlements and strongholds, and taking prisoners (2 Cor 10:3-6). Paul's struggle on behalf of the truth of the gospel is a real battle.

## Occupations

Those who gathered in Philemon's home as they listened to the reading of Paul's letters heard the apostle address one of them, Apphia, as a member of the family, a "sister." Next in line to be addressed by Paul

---

[10] A similar phrase appears in Rom 6:13.

was Archippus, whom Paul describes as "our fellow soldier" (Phlm 2) as if Paul and Archippus were Roman legionnaires. Similarly, Paul refers to Epaphroditus as his fellow soldier (Phil 2:25). It is hardly likely that Paul, Archippus, and Epaphroditus were pursuing a military career. At the very least and even without the silent evidence of his letters, Paul as a Jew would have been exempt from military service.

Neither Archippus nor Epaphroditus was any more of a soldier than was Paul, even though Paul called each of them a "fellow soldier." The image, derived from the Stoic agonistic motif, describes Paul's fellow evangelists, those who were engaged with him in promoting the truth of the gospel despite the obstacles that had to be overcome.

This metaphorical nuance is not present when Paul writes about the one who soldiers in 1 Corinthians 9:7. The image appears in a series of examples of people with different occupations, identified by means of a verb rather than a noun, who deserve appropriate payment for their work. Payment for the work is described in terms appropriate to the task at hand. Paul's rhetorical questions suggest that a soldier deserves his rations, a farmer enjoys some of the fruit that he has raised, and the shepherd drinks the milk of the animals that he is tending. No less than the soldier, farmer, or shepherd, Paul and his companions deserve compensation for their work.[11]

Earlier in 1 Corinthians Paul writes about his ministry in terms of two other occupations. He describes himself as a planter (1 Cor 3:6, 8) and as a master builder who lays the foundation of a building (1 Cor 3:10). While those involved in each of these occupations make an indispensable contribution to the end product, neither of them, by himself, achieves the final result. So Paul describes Apollos as one who waters (1 Cor 3:6, 8) and speaks of the builder who constructs the edifice on the foundation that has been laid (1 Cor 3:10, 12, 14).

Like the soldier, farmer, and shepherd, the builder receives appropriate wages for a job well done (1 Cor 3:14). Received wages are an important feature of Paul's occupational metaphors. Paul echoes the notion when he writes about himself having been paid in full in Philippians 4:18.

---

[11] Paul often uses "work" (*ergon*) as a technical term meaning evangelization. Epaphroditus is described as Paul's coworker (*synergos*, Phil 2:25) as is Philemon (Phlm 1). Among his other coworkers, Paul mentions by name Aquila and Prisca (Rom 16:3), Urbanus (Rom 16:9), Timothy (Rom 16:9), Titus (2 Cor 8:23), Clement (Phil 4:3), Mark, Aristarchus, Demas, Luke, (Phlm 24), and, arguably, Apollos as well (1 Cor 3:9).

"Wages" is a metaphor in its own right when Paul writes about the wages of personified sin: "The wages of sin is death" (Rom 6:23).

Paul refers to himself as a worker, soldier, planter, and as a master builder who lays a foundation. In 1 Corinthians 4:1 he uses other occupational images to describe his ministry when he asks the Corinthians to think of him and Apollos as "servants [*hyperētas*] of Christ and stewards of God's mysteries." The first image is nautical; the second comes from the household. In a port city like Corinth everyone would appreciate the lot of the "under-rower" (*hyperētēs*) who manned the oars on the lowest deck of a mighty trireme. In any cosmopolitan city, people would know about the power exercised by the "steward" (*oikonomos*), the chief of a household staff. The positions of under-rower and steward were filled by slaves, but their use by Paul reminds us that even slaves had different occupations in the Greco-Roman world. Some had demeaning positions, while others enjoyed prominence and power.

Another occupation to which a slave might be assigned was that of the pedagogue, the disciplinarian and tutor who, in each of these capacities, effectively functioned as a teacher's aid in assuring the education of the sons of the wealthy. To describe his unique role as the evangelist of the Corinthians, Paul describes himself as their father, contrasting his relationship with that of the myriad of pedagogues (*paidagōgous*) that they might have had in Christ (1 Cor 4:15).

Paul's most powerful use of the image of the pedagogue is undoubtedly to be found in Galatians 3:23-24. The apostle describes personified law as being the pedagogue of Jews who had not yet embraced the faith. In this passage the coercive dimensions of the pedagogue's role come to the fore; Paul complements the image of the pedagogue with that of the jailer who imprisons people under lock and key (Gal 3:22, 24).[12] God has allowed the law to function in this fashion. In Romans, Paul uses the image of the jailer to describe God, writing, "God has imprisoned all in disobedience so that he may be merciful to all" (Rom 11:32).

The thief is engaged in an occupation that is less than honorable. Rabbis taught that a man who fails to teach his son a trade teaches him to be a thief. Paul considered thieves and robbers to be among those excluded from the kingdom of God (1 Cor 6:10), people whom believers are to avoid. Despite his negative evaluation of thievery, Paul did not

---

[12] The verb used by Paul is *synkleiō*, a compound verb derived from the noun *kleis*, originally denoting the bar or bolt on a door or gate but later used to mean "key."

hesitate to make use of the image of the thief. A nocturnal figure who comes upon unwary folks while they are asleep, the image of the thief serves Paul's rhetoric as an example of the surprise with which the parousia will come upon the unsuspecting and unaware (1 Thess 5:2, 4).

A striking occupational metaphor used by Paul in reference to God himself is that of the potter. Paul developed the image in Romans 9:20-21 to speak about God's freedom to do with the humanity that he has created whatever he wills, choosing some for a special purpose and others for an ordinary existence. The potter at work with his clay can do whatever he wants with it. A particular twist in Paul's image of the potter at work is his portrayal of a piece of personified pottery saying to the potter, "Why have you made me like this?" (Rom 9:20).

## Agriculture

Paul is often portrayed as an educated city dweller or as an artisan plying his leatherworker's trade in a shop along the agora of the cities along the principal trade routes linking Asia, Macedonia, and Achaia. This portrayal suggests to many that Paul would not have been acquainted with life in rural areas. His portrayal of himself as one who plants, while another waters, and God makes the seed to grow (1 Cor 3:6-9) suggests, however, that he had at least some awareness of life on the farm. Indeed, he compared the church at Corinth to a planted field (*geōrgion*).

An image that appears in several of Paul's letters is that of fruit (*karpos*). Many Christians who have attended catechism or Sunday school can recite by heart the list of the fruits of the Spirit mentioned by Paul in Galatians 5:22-23. In Philippians Paul used the image of fruit to speak of the results of his apostolic endeavors (Phil 1:22), the benefits that accrue to the Philippians because of his efforts (Phil 4:17), and the fruit of righteousness that they will receive on the day of Christ if they persevere in a life of love (Phil 1:11). Similar imagery appears in Romans as Paul writes about his apostolic endeavors (Rom 1:13) and the results of the collection for the saints in Jerusalem (Rom 15:28). Fruit is a metaphor applied to the sanctification received by those who have been freed from sin and enslaved to God (Rom 6:22). Paul writes about this "fruit" in contradistinction to the "fruit" that is produced by things of which believers are now ashamed (Rom 6:21).

As a good Jew, Paul was fully aware that the first fruits (*aparchē*) were something special. They were the harbinger of the full crop and were to be offered to God in thanksgiving (Rom 11:16). Paul uses the image of the first fruits to portray Christ as the first fruits of those who have died (1 Cor 15:20) and the first fruits of those who have been raised from the dead (1 Cor 15:23). The household of Stephanas was the first fruits of Paul's missionary activity in Achaia (1 Cor 16:15), while Epaenetus was the first fruits of his activity in Asia Minor (Rom 16:5). Moreover, while the redemption of creation is not yet complete, believers have received the first fruits of the Spirit (Rom 8:23).

First fruits are the harbinger of the harvest to follow but fruit is the product of a seed and a seedling. Seeds decompose before they come to life, grow into seedlings, and then into plants that produce fruit or grain. Paul uses the image of the seed that is sown and the grain that arises as a result of divine activity[13] when he writes about the age to come in 1 Corinthians 15:36-38.

Earlier in 1 Corinthians, Paul uses a different but related image of the growth of a crop. In the apologia on behalf of his ministry, proffered as an example to be followed by the Corinthians whom he urges to forgo some of their "rights," Paul uses a variety of images to speak about the laborer being worthy of his hire. He writes about the vintner and the shepherd (1 Cor 9:7). Paul follows these images with that of the farmer at work (1 Cor 9:10). A panorama of ordinary human activities shows that those who work should receive their pay.

In 2 Corinthians, Paul again uses the image of the seed that is sown and of God who provides the crop to be harvested. As was the case with the image of the seed that is sown in 1 Corinthians 15, Paul develops the agricultural image at some length in the second letter. The application of the metaphor is, however, quite different from that of the metaphor in 1 Corinthians. In 2 Corinthians Paul uses the image of the seed to encourage the Corinthians to give generously to the collection on behalf of the saints in Jerusalem. Sowing seed and reaping a good harvest (*genēmata*, a Pauline hapax) is the leitmotif of the paraenesis of 2 Corinthians 9:6-10.

The most striking of all of Paul's agricultural images may well be the arboricultural imagery developed in Romans 11:16-24. The imagery is complex. Paul begins with the image of a tree whose roots are holy. These holy roots give rise to a tree that is holy. Some of its branches have been broken off. Paul then identifies the tree as an olive tree. The broken

---

[13] Cf. 1 Cor 3:6-7.

branches are replaced by a wild shoot whose engrafting reinvigorates the tree. The renewal of the tree's life occurs despite the lack of connaturality between the cultivated tree and the wild tree from which the olive shoot has been taken. Having constructed the image of a flourishing olive tree, Paul uses a typically Jewish *Kal va-homer* kind of reasoning to conclude, "how much more will these natural branches be grafted back into their own olive tree" (Rom 11:24). The reinvigorated tree will easily receive back the engrafting of its own, connatural branches, communicating the sap of its new life to them. This fully developed image serves as an allegorical reflection on the role of Israel in the history of salvation.

Cultivated by God, some of the branches of the tree (Israel) are temporarily cast aside only to be regrafted after the tree has been invigorated by the engrafting of the wild olive shoot (the Gentiles). No other agricultural image serves Paul's theological reflection as well as does the allegory of the olive tree.

## Animals

Paul, the cosmopolitan urbanite, is reasonably versed in rural life and its agriculture. He does not, however, seem to be as well acquainted with the dimension of husbandry that deals with animals. Domestic animals are mentioned only in 1 Corinthians 9 and Romans 8. In 1 Corinthians 9:7c-9 Paul gives the example of a shepherd tending sheep, fully expecting to receive some of the milk that the sheep produce.[14] The image serves as an argument for Paul's contention that the apostle has a right to be provided for. The next image of a domestic animal is that of the ox, tethered to a millstone. Paul cites an item from Jewish agricultural law (Deut 25:4) to remind his readers that even an ox deserves to eat while he is engaged in grinding the grain. In Romans 8:36 Paul uses to good advantage the scriptural image of sheep led to slaughter. Psalm 44:22 [43:23 LXX] furnishes Paul with this image as he passes in review a series of unrelenting and death-threatening hostile powers that might possibly separate us from the love of Christ.

Paul's other references to the animal kingdom are of a different sort. Three of the references are to a pack of wild and destructive animals. One occurs in 1 Corinthians 15:32 where Paul conjures up the image of

---

[14] The verb "shepherd" (*poimainō*) is hapax in Paul at 1 Cor 9:7c. The noun "flock" [of sheep] (*poimnē*) occurs but twice in his writings. Both occurrences are in 1 Cor 9:7c.

a slave brought into the amphitheater and battling with wild animals for the entertainment of the crowds: "I fought with wild animals [*ethēriomachēsa*][15] at Ephesus." The image is graphic, but exegesis is at a loss when it comes to determining what it was that happened to Paul at Ephesus.

Paul is even more graphic in his use of this kind of imagery in his Letters to the Philippians and to the Galatians. In Philippians, he warns the congregation against Judaizers who sought to circumcise even the Gentiles who did not require circumcision for salvation's sake. Paul's warning is abrupt: "Beware of the dogs [*kynas*]" (Phil 3:2). The pointed warning could hardly fail to make an impact among people who considered dogs to be wild and vicious animals. In 2 Corinthians, Paul evokes the specter of animals preying upon the Corinthians as they fall victim to false teachers (2 Cor 11:20).

Another graphic image occurs in Galatians 5:15. It, too, has reference to the problems caused by false teachers. Judaizers' intrusion into the churches of Galatia was harmful to those Christian communities. The Judaizers' actions, supposedly in fidelity to the law, were in blatant opposition to the love command, in which the whole law is summed up (Gal 5:14). How does Paul describe the havoc wreaked within the community as a result of the activity of these Judaizers? "You bite and devour one another" (Gal 5:15). The Galatians run the risk of acting like a pack of wild animals.

The Scriptures provide Paul with yet another image of the destructive and even lethal force of an untamed animal. Psalm 140:3 [139:4 LXX] mentioned those who had the venom of vipers under their lips. Paul borrowed this Scripture (Rom 3:13c) for use in the mosaic of scriptural passages that he had put together in Romans 3:10-18 to portray the universality of sin.

Thus, although Paul appears to be relatively unfamiliar with the animal world, he was sufficiently aware of it to use images of animals in four of his letters, those to the Romans, Galatians, Philippians, and the First Letter to the Corinthians. Only the Second Letter to the Corinthians and the relatively short letters to the Thessalonians and to Philemon are completely lacking in images drawn from the animal kingdom.

---

[15] This is the only time that Paul uses the root *thēri-*, "wild animal," in his extant writings.

## Construction

Paul seems relatively well acquainted with the world of agriculture but he is equally at home when it comes to urban construction. The language of his most extensive use of construction imagery, 1 Corinthians 3:10-17, echoes the technical language of the labor contracts of his time. Paul knows that the construction of a building begins with the laying of a well-placed foundation. He is the wise architect (*sophos architektōn*) who lays the foundation, Christ. Other construction workers build on the foundation that Paul has laid. Without intending to be exhaustive, Paul passes in review a variety of materials that enter into the construction of a magnificent new building: gold, silver, precious stones, wood, hay, straw. A variety of appropriately skilled artisans are required to work with these materials. Toward the end of the construction, there is an inspection, a kind of quality control. If the building does not measure up, the workers are docked of some of their pay.

The pictorial portrayal of the local church as a building that Paul developed at length in 1 Corinthians 3:10-17 is reflected in Romans 15:20, where Paul explains that his specialty is laying the foundation of new buildings. He had not yet visited the Christians in Rome because it was his desire to proclaim the gospel where it had not previously been proclaimed, "so that I do not build on someone else's foundation."

Although mention of the foundation of a building occurs only in 1 Corinthians 3:10, 11, 12 and Romans 15:20, construction imagery appears in several other passages in Paul's letters. Paul uses the verb "build" (*oikodomeō*) and the related noun "building" (*oikodomē*), denoting the activity of constructing something. Only in 1 Corinthians 3:9 and 2 Corinthians 5:1 does *oikodomē* mean building in the sense of a piece of construction that has been finished, an edifice, a building. In 1 Corinthians 3:9 Paul uses the term *oikodomē*, juxtaposed with the image of the field, to speak of the church at Corinth as "God's building." The "building" of 2 Corinthians 5:1 is likewise something that God has constructed. This building has, however, been erected not in an earthly city like Corinth but in heaven.

Paul exploits the image evoked by "build" and "building" to speak about activity that "builds up" the church. Emphasizing the point by means of the rhetorical contrast with "tearing down," Paul tells the Corinthians that his role is building up, not tearing down (2 Cor 10:8; 12:19; 13:10). In Galatians, having confessed that by persecuting the church of God he was trying to destroy it (Gal 1:13), Paul reminds his readers that he was later involved in building up what he had once torn down (Gal 2:18).

The extended construction imagery of 1 Corinthians 3:10-17 reminds the Corinthians that many hands must be at work in the construction of an edifice. In 1 Corinthians 14 Paul uses construction imagery to characterize prophetic activity within the church. First Corinthians 14:4 encapsulates his thought: "those who prophesy build up the church."[16] Other charismatics also serve to build up the church (1 Cor 14:12, 26). Even one who speaks in tongues can build up the church, provided that the glossolalia is accompanied by the activity of someone who interprets the tongues (1 Cor 14:5). The danger is that, without the complementary action of a person who has the gift of interpretation, those who speak in tongues build up themselves rather than build up the church (1 Cor 14:4).

The metaphorical use of this kind of construction language appears earlier in 1 Corinthians when Paul states as a principle that "love builds up" (1 Cor 8:1). It can be argued that Paul is here talking about building up the church, but it might also be argued that he is using the terminology in reference to building up the individuals within the church.

A peculiarly Pauline use of the construction metaphor is to be found in those passages of the letters in which the apostle uses the verb "build" in the sense of building up one's self (1 Cor 10:23; 14:4) or in the sense of edifying, strengthening, or encouraging one another as in 1 Thessalonians 5:11, "Therefore encourage one another and build up each other." Similar usage occurs in 1 Corinthians 14:17 and in Romans 14:19; 15:2.

Paul's particular spin on the word "build" is also reflected in 1 Corinthians 8:10, where, in Paul's discourse about eating foods offered to idols, the verb "build" is used with a negative connotation: ". . . might they not . . . be encouraged [*oikodomēthēsetai*] to the point of eating food sacrificed to idols?"

While Paul draws attention to the laying of the foundation as his particular role in building up the church (Rom 15:20; 1 Cor 3:10), he mentions another part of the building in reference to his apostolic ministry in 1 Corinthians 16:9 and 2 Corinthians 2:12. God's "open door policy" enabled Paul to proclaim the gospel both in Ephesus (1 Cor 16:9) and in Troas (2 Cor 2:12).[17] The success of his ministry in the Asian capital is reflected in the observation that the door that God had opened for him

---

[16] Cf. 1 Cor 14:3.

[17] In the extant correspondence the word "door" appears in only these two verses.

in Ephesus was a "wide door," a "big door." As the Corinthians heard Paul refer to his ministry in this way, they might have imagined the doors of the homes in Ephesus and Troas that had been opened so that Paul's work of evangelization could be successful.

Paul typically uses construction imagery with regard to the church and his ministry. In 2 Corinthians 5:1-4 he uses construction to make another point, contrasting our earthly home (*hē epigeios hēmōn oikia*) in a tent (*skēnous*) with the heavenly building (*oikodomēn*) that God has made. God's building is a permanent construction; tenting is an occasional and transitional activity.

Another construction image is reflected in Romans 9:33. Paul cites a few words from Isaiah 28:16, "See, I am laying in Zion a foundation stone, a tested stone, a precious cornerstone, a sure foundation." Pointedly, Paul omits from his quotation of the Scripture the qualifying characteristics of the stone. Paul cites the oracle only insofar as it says, "See, I am laying in Zion a stone." For Paul, the stone that ought to have served as a foundation stone has become a stumbling block. Christian Jews, familiar with the Scriptures, would presumably have grasped Paul's point. Christ, who should have been the foundation stone has become a stumbling block.

## The Temple and Its Cult

The construction of the grand building that Paul describes in 1 Corinthians 3:10-17 morphs into a temple at the end of his exposition: "Do you not know that you are God's temple and that God's Spirit dwells in you? If anyone destroys God's temple, God will destroy that person. For God's temple is holy, and you are that temple"[18] (1 Cor 3:16-17). The building that is the church of God at Corinth becomes God's temple because the Spirit dwells within it.

The imagery is reprised in Paul's rejoinder to the community that tolerated and even encouraged the presence of the incestuous man: "Do you not know that your body[19] is a temple of the Holy Spirit within you?" (1 Cor 6:19). A similar reminder is found in 2 Corinthians 6:16:

---

[18] The Greek text does not repeat the use of the word "temple;" it reads simply "which you are." The word "temple" occurs in Paul's writings only in 1 Cor 3:16-17 and 2 Cor 6:16, where the word is used twice.

[19] "Body" is singular, whereas the qualifying pronoun *hymōn*, "of you" ["yours"], and the following pronoun are in the plural.

"We are the temple of the living God." The passage emphasizes the temple imagery by means of a contrast with a temple in which idols have been placed.

Specific temple language, that is, the use of the word *naos*, appears only in the two Corinthian letters. Cultic imagery is, however, fairly common throughout Paul's writings. Among the several examples that he gives of people who are worthy of their hire is that of the priest (1 Cor 9:13).

Two Jewish feasts, the Passover and the Day of the Atonement, play an important role in Paul's metaphorical rhetoric. In parenetic yet judgmental remarks addressed to the Corinthians who were boasting, Paul evoked the celebration of the Passover (1 Cor 5:6-8). An essential part of the ritual was the eating of unleavened bread after leavened bread, with its yeast, had been set aside. Paul urges the Corinthians to get rid of the incestuous man in a way that would imitate Jews casting yeast aside as they prepared to celebrate Passover. The church in Corinth is invited to celebrate the festival without the yeast of malice and evil. The yeast had to be completely removed because even a little yeast would cause the whole loaf to rise. And why should the Christians of Corinth celebrate this festival? Paul's answer, "Our paschal lamb, Christ, has been sacrificed" (1 Cor 5:7).

Paul's exhortation to the Galatians includes a similar reference to yeast, albeit without specific reference to the Feast of Unleavened Bread. Urging the Galatians to be on their guard against those who were persuading them to turn from the truth, Paul quoted a familiar proverb, "A little yeast leavens the whole batch of dough" (Gal 5:9). The household maxim is a commonplace in traditional wisdom. Among Jews and Greeks the yeast that can transform a whole batch of dough was a symbol of the power of evil. It is more than likely that among Hellenistic Jews, at least, the Passover observance of a yeastless festival served as a reminder that God's people was a holy people, within which there was no place for evil.

An implicit reference to the Passover festival might be found in Paul's mention of the "cup of blessing that we bless" (1 Cor 10:16). The cup of blessing, as a symbol of salvation, was an element in the paschal ritual. The blessing of the cup was not, however, exclusively found in the paschal festival nor was it reserved to the celebration of major feasts. A cup of blessing was drunk as often as wine was served during a Jewish meal, even the common meals of every day.[20]

---

[20] See Collins, *First Corinthians*, 379.

The Letter to the Romans exploits a different celebration, that of the Day of Atonement. Paul uses the mercy seat (*hilastērion*, Rom 3:25), an important feature of the Atonement ritual, as a figure for Christ who has been showcased by God. The writings of Philo and the Qumran scrolls indicate that at the time of Paul, both Hellenistic and Palestinian Jews were thinking about the rituals of that feast. Paul's allusive reference to the mercy seat derives from a similar kind of thinking.

The parenetic section of Romans (Rom 12–15) also makes pointed use of cultic language. Paul introduces his hortatory remarks with a poignant plea: "I appeal to you therefore, brothers and sisters, by the mercies of God, to present your bodies as a living sacrifice, holy and acceptable to God, which is your spiritual worship" (Rom 12:1). The language is thoroughly cultic. "Present," "sacrifice," "holy," "acceptable to God," and "worship" is vocabulary that properly belongs to the sphere of liturgy. Paul would have the Romans consider that the kind of lives that they lead as a result of their faith is an expression of that same faith, their relationship with God, just as formal liturgical action is an expression of a relationship with God.

Using much of the same vocabulary, the cultic imagery of Philippians is of a different order. Paul contemplates the possibility of dying as a prisoner, writing, "even if I am being poured out as a libation over the sacrifice and the offering of your faith" (Phil 2:17). In the event that Paul should die for the sake of the gospel, the Philippians are urged to consider his death as a sacrifice.

In the Letter to the Romans, the apostle indicates that he considers his apostolate to the Gentiles, his work of evangelization, as a priestly service: "a minister of Christ Jesus to the Gentiles in the priestly service of the gospel of God, so that the offering[21] of the Gentiles may be acceptable, sanctified by the Holy Spirit" (Rom 15:16). The cultic vocabulary is clustered, just as it is in Romans 12:1 and Philippians 2:17. Toward the end of the Letter to the Philippians, in a guarded but sincere expression of thanks, Paul turns his thoughts to God and to the gifts that he had received from the Philippians through Epaphroditus, describing those gifts as "a fragrant offering, a sacrifice acceptable and pleasing to God" (Phil 4:18). In this case the gifts that the Philippians had given to Paul to support him in his imprisonment and the ministry that he exercised while in prison are compared to a sacrificial offering.

---

[21] The word *prosphora* remains to this day as the technical term for the loaf of leavened bread that is used for the celebration of the eucharist in Byzantine churches.

"First fruits" (*aparchē*), as has been noted, is a cultic term denoting the offering of the first results of one's labor to God. Paul is well aware of the cultic implications of the term, as he indicates on a couple of occasions in writing to the Romans (Rom 8:23; 11:16). He uses this term as a metaphor to describe his first converts in Asia (Rom 16:5) and in Achaia (1 Cor 16:15), thereby complementing his portrayal of himself as a person engaged in a kind of priestly ministry. A striking use of "first fruits" is in reference to Christ whose death and resurrection are the first fruits of the death and consequent resurrection of believers (1 Cor 15:20, 23).

## Finances

Mark Kiley once observed that a feature of Paul's authentic letters is his mention of finances.[22] The observation is correct; the indisputably Pauline letters speak about the collection on behalf of the saints in Jerusalem, Paul's support, or both. On the other hand, the observation was deficient insofar as Kiley did not attend to the number of important financial metaphors that appear in Paul's letters. With the exception of the Letter to the Thessalonians, Paul uses the language of financial transactions as a metaphor in each of the extant letters.

The language of profit and loss appears in both Philippians 1:21-22 and Philippians 3:7-8. The technical terms for profit and loss, *kerdos* and *zēmia*, respectively, appear in the latter passage: "Yet whatever gains I had, these I have come to regard as loss because of Christ. More than that, I regard everything as loss because of the surpassing value[23] of knowing Christ Jesus my Lord. For his sake I have suffered the loss of all things" (Phil 3:7-8). Earlier in this same letter Paul used one of these technical terms, complementing "gain" (*kerdos*) with the image of "fruit" (*karpon*), as he explains a personal dilemma: "For to me, living is Christ and dying is gain. If I am to live in the flesh, that means fruitful labor for me; and I do not know which I prefer" (Phil 1:21-22). "Loss" also appears in 1 Corinthians 3:15, where it refers to a worker's having his

---

[22] See Mark C. Kiley, *Colossians as Pseudepigraphy*, Biblical Seminar 4 (Sheffield: JSOT, 1986), 46–51, 98–118.

[23] Among many connotations of the term *hyperechon*, including "hold above," "rise above," "outflank," is its use as a financial term to designate lending on the basis of excess value of the security, as an Ephesian inscription of the third century BCE indicates (see *SIG* 364.33).

pay docked or even, and more likely, having to pay a penalty because the job was not done in timely or satisfactory fashion.

Accounting practice is the background against which Paul writes, "To one who works, wages are not reckoned [*logizesthai*] as a gift but as something due [*opheilēma*]. But to one who without works trusts him who justifies the ungodly, such faith is reckoned as righteousness" (Rom 4:4-5). The language of Genesis 15:6, "The Lord reckoned it to him as righteousness," which Paul quotes in Galatians 3:6 and Romans 4:3, 9, runs throughout much of what Paul writes about justification. Readers of his letters can think of the ledger lying on the desk of an old-time bookkeeper.

The apostle also made use of the idea of a down payment, a kind of nonrefundable deposit, as a pledge of full payment to come. Second Corinthians speaks about the Spirit in this fashion. God has given us the Spirit as a "first installment" or guarantee (*arrabōn*, 2 Cor 1:22; 5:5).

Toward the end of the Letter to the Philippians Paul entered into the world of finance as he reflected on the fiscal and physical support that the Philippians had given him: "I seek the profit that accumulates to your account. I have been paid in full and have more than enough; I am fully satisfied. . . . And my God will fully satisfy every need of yours according to his riches in glory in Christ Jesus" (Phil 4:17-19). Accounts and full payment belong to the world of finance. This image of a three-party transaction twice uses "satisfy," a verb (*plēroō*) that often meant "pay in full."

The short note to Philemon includes a brief statement in which Paul plays with the idea of paying a financial debt. Referring to whatever possible financial obligations Onesimus might have incurred vis-à-vis his master, Paul writes, "If he owes you anything, charge that to my account" (Phlm 18). A handwritten postscript contains Paul's personal guarantee, "I will repay it" (Phlm 19b). Paul then quips, "I say nothing about your owing me even your own life" (Phlm 19c). Paul's pun is apropos but it, too, comes from the world of financial obligation.

Finances also appear in 2 Corinthians. As in the Letter to Philemon, Paul cleverly contrasts the real world of finance with the figurative. He writes, "Children ought not to lay up [*thēsaurizein*] for their parents, but parents for their children. I will most gladly spend [*dapanēsō*] and be spent [*ekdapanēthēsomai*] for you" (2 Cor 12:14-15). In the real world parents save up for their children and spend their money on them. Paul considers himself like currency that was willingly spent for the sake of his children, the Corinthians.

The way that Paul writes about redemption might be his most telling use of financial language. From the time of Homer, a town's marketplace was known as the agora; the verb *agorazō* meant to buy in the marketplace.[24] A compound verb, *exagorazō*, meant to buy from or redeem. Paul uses this verb to speak about our redemption in Galatians 3:13, "Christ redeemed us," and Galatians 4:5, "sent . . . in order to redeem those who were under the law." In 1 Corinthians 6:20; 7:23, using the simple words "buy" (*agorazō*) and "price" (*timē*), Paul writes about us as having been bought and paid for.

In 1 Corinthians 7:23, Paul implies that our freedom has been purchased, using vocabulary in a way similar to the way language was used in regard to the manumission of slaves. A related idea was reflected in the word *apolytrōsis*, a word that properly meant redemption, that is, the payment of a ransom for prisoners or slaves. This is the way that the common folk of Paul's era would have understood the term. Paul appropriates the terminology to speak about redemption by Christ (Rom 3:24; 8:23; 1 Cor 1:30).

## Social Status

Slavery was a fact of life in the Greco-Roman world, a reality of its economic life. Much of Paul's use of figurative language relates to the institution of slavery. Employing a variety of images, the apostle uses the idea of slavery to speak about his ministry and the reality of the Christian life.

Paul calls himself a slave of Christ for the first time in Galatians 1:10. The designation recurs in the *intitulationes* of Philippians and Romans (Rom 1:1; Phil 1:1). In Galatians Paul uses the image to remind the Galatians that, as a slave of Christ, his job is to please God. He need not be concerned about pleasing (other) people. As a slave of Christ, he bears the marks of Jesus on his body (Gal 6:17). The brand seared into his body is a permanent physical sign of his belonging to Jesus.

Describing his ministry in 1 Corinthians 4:1, Paul juxtaposes two tasks normally assigned to slaves. He says that he and Apollos are "servants of Christ and stewards of God's mysteries." The latter image underscores his loyalty and the trust that God has put in him. Slaves must fulfill their tasks. Paul alludes to this constraint when he describes his proclaiming

---

[24] Cf. 1 Cor 7:30.

the gospel in 1 Corinthians 9:16: "An obligation is laid on me, and woe to me if I do not proclaim the gospel!" Like the slaves of Jesus' gospel story, Paul could say of himself and his fellow evangelists, "[W]e are worthless slaves; we have done only what we ought to have done!" (Luke 17:10).

Paul considers himself to be a slave of Jesus Christ; he also considers himself to be the slave of those whom he has evangelized: "We do not proclaim ourselves; we proclaim Jesus Christ as Lord and ourselves as your slaves for Jesus' sake" (2 Cor 4:5). In Galatians, where the opposition between slavery and freedom provides substance for a good part of Paul's rhetoric, Paul urges his readers to become slaves to one another through love (Gal 5:13). The exhortation is addressed to them at a time when they are no longer slaves (Gal 4:7). They had previously been enslaved to the elemental spirits of the world (Gal 4:3, 9). Now, children of the free woman (Gal 4:31), they are never again to submit themselves to the yoke of slavery (Gal 5:1).

In many ways the principal argument of Romans parallels that of Galatians. As in Galatians, the image of slavery plays an important role in the rhetoric of Romans. Paul repeatedly reminds the Romans that they had been slaves to sin (6:16, 17, 20; 7:6, 25). The Jews among them are enslaved to the law; all are subject to death. Among other consequences of their enslavement is that their members were enslaved to impurity (Rom 6:19). Creation, which is in a symbiotic relationship with human beings, is being held in slavery to corruption (Rom 8:21).

It is against the background of Paul's creative use of the reality of slavery in Galatians and Romans that his use of the image of the manumission of slaves is to be seen. Human beings, slaves to the elemental spirits of the universe and enslaved to sin, have been redeemed by Christ. In 2 Corinthians Paul reminds his addressees that the false teachers among them would take away their freedom and make them slaves (2 Cor 11:20).

Social class and gender tend to create social divisions. Baptismal incorporation into Christ means that the divisions caused by these social markers are transcended (Gal 3:28). Ethnicity is the third constant in social division. Paul's social construct of ethnicity was relatively simple: there are Jews and Gentiles. Paul uses the terms "circumcision" and "foreskin" to designate Jews and Gentiles. Since metonymy is a kind of metaphor, this use of "circumcision" and "foreskin" must be included under the rubric of Paul's use of figurative language. As one might expect, these ethnicity-designating terms are found in both Galatians and

Romans. Thus, Jews are designated by "circumcision" in Galatians 2:7, 8, 9, 12 and Romans 3:30; 4:9, 12; 15:8 while Gentiles are called "foreskin" in Galatians 2:7 and in Romans 2:26, 27; 3:30; 4:9, 12. In Romans, Paul uses the image of circumcision in another figurative sense. Capitalizing on the teaching of the biblical prophets, Paul speaks about a kind of "spiritual circumcision," the circumcision of the heart (Rom 2:28, 29).

Age is not as graphic a reminder of a person's social status as gender, class, and ethnicity, but it is an important social marker. For the most part, age distinctions do not play an important role in Paul's letters. In Galatians, however, Paul uses the figure of a minor who is owner and heir but is no better off than a slave (Gal 4:1-2). A minor is not able to use what he owns and is even under the control of slaves in much of what he does. Paul uses the image principally to speak about Jews to whom the inheritance belongs but who are not able to take advantage of it.

## Public Life

Paul's favorite title for Jesus, *kyrios*, "Lord," merits a study unto itself, but there are a number of other images in Paul's letters which refer to the political, public, and judicial spheres and also merit attention. Luke depicts Paul as an individual who was willing to stand on his Roman citizenship (Acts 25:10-12), but Paul appears to be more proud of his Jewish ancestry than he does of his Roman citizenship (2 Cor 11:22; Phil 3:4-6).

The city (*polis*) was the center of political life in the world in which Paul lived. In Philippians, written to a city whose inhabitants were retired members of the Roman military to some large extent,[25] Paul uses civic imagery to good advantage. He urges the Philippians to live like good citizens in accordance with the gospel of Christ, as if the gospel were the constitution or basic law of the Christian community: "Live your life [*politeuesthe*] in a manner worthy of the gospel of Christ" (Phil 1:27). The Roman inhabitants of Philippi were citizens of Rome, a place far removed from the Macedonian city in which they lived. So it was also with believers who are citizens of heaven: "Our citizenship [*politeuma*] is in heaven, and it is from there that we are expecting a Savior,[26] the Lord Jesus Christ" (Phil 3:20).

[25] At the end of the letter, Paul conveys greetings on behalf of members of "the emperor's household" (*kaisaros oikias*).

[26] Hapax in the indisputable Pauline letters, the title *sōtēr* plays an important role in the christology and soteriology of the Pastoral Epistles.

To portray the apocalyptic scenario, Paul evokes the memory of the populace leaving the city to extend a solemn welcome to a visiting monarch or conquering general. Conferring benefaction on the city, the visitor is hailed as savior and revered as benefactor. Paul's scenario: "The Lord himself, with a cry of command, with the archangel's call and with the sound of God's trumpet, will descend from heaven, and the dead in Christ will rise first. Then we who are alive, who are left, will be caught up in the clouds together with them to meet the Lord" (1 Thess 4:16-17).

A different public event serves Paul's rhetoric in 1 Corinthians 4:9. Paul invites the Corinthians to think about the spectacular events that took place in the theater, particularly the spectacle of prisoners being led into the arena in much the same way that a procession of bulls precedes an afternoon of bullfighting in Spain. For all practical purposes the bulls are doomed to death; so, too, were the prisoners, clearly underdogs in the gladiatorial role that they were to play before the day was over. Such is the scene that Paul evokes when he asks the Corinthians to contemplate the hardships of the apostolic ministry: "I think that God has exhibited us apostles as last of all, as though sentenced to death, because we have become a spectacle to the world, to angels and to mortals" (1 Cor 4:9).

## The Courtroom

Paul was familiar with the legal system and the venue in which judgment took place. He observed that the Lord rather than any human court would be his judge (1 Cor 4:3-4). Paul knew how to distinguish small claims from felonies (1 Cor 6:1-6). He knew about heirs and their inheritance (Rom 4:13,[27] 14; 8:17; Gal 3:18, 29; 4:7) and that minors were not able to make use of the inheritance which was theirs (Gal 4:1). Paul knew that a seal (*sphragis*) served as an authenticating sign or guarantee. Thus he could write about the Corinthians being the seal of his ministry (1 Cor 9:2) and the gift of the Holy Spirit as God's guarantee to us (2 Cor 1:22).[28] Paul also knew that a woman was legally bound to her husband as long as he was alive (1 Cor 7:39).

---

[27] Paul uses the language of "heir" and "inheritance" to speak of the covenant benefits that accrue to believers. Apart from Rom 4:13, the notion of inheritance is always closely linked to that of descent. In Rom 4:13, Abraham is said to receive an "inheritance" as a result of a promise rather than as a consequence of ancestry.

[28] In 2 Cor 1:22, Paul explains believers being sealed by means of the impress on their hearts of the gift of the Holy Spirit, which he describes as an *arrabōn*, a down payment.

Paul's most striking use of judicial imagery occurs in Galatians and in Romans, where Paul develops his notion of justification. The forensic language of *dikaiosynē*, "righteousness/justification," *dikaios*, "righteous/just/innocent," and *dikaioō*, "to find righteous/justify/declare innocent," echoes throughout these letters.[29]

The image that pervades these letters is that of God the divine judge sitting in judgment on human beings. God is characterized by righteousness; God manifests his righteousness in the way that he judges sinners. All human beings are sinners, Jews and Gentiles alike. Nonetheless, God declares righteous those who believe in Christ.

Divine jurisprudence was established in a telling precedent, to which the Scriptures attest, namely, the justification of Abraham: "Abraham believed God and it was reckoned to him as righteousness" (Gen 15:6). Paul cites this precedent in developing the rhetorical argument of both Galatians and Romans (Gal 3:6; Rom 4:3).

A related concept is that of prison to which the guilty are confined. Prior to the death and resurrection of Jesus, the righteous God demonstrated this aspect of righteousness: "God has imprisoned all in disobedience so that he may be merciful to all" (Rom 11:32). Commenting on the situation of Jews as sinners, Paul personified the law as the bailiff and warden who metes out the imprisonment that God decrees: "The scripture has imprisoned all things under the power of sin . . . before faith came, we were imprisoned and guarded under the law" (Gal 3:22-23).

### And the Cosmos

Paul does not often write about the cosmos, the universe in which we live. One passage in which he does so is Philippians 2:14-18, where Paul combines an image taken from the cosmos with images that derive from the stadium and from the temple. The temple metaphor pertains to Paul's apostolic ministry; the cosmos is used in reference to believers and the way that they stand out in the world in which they live: "[Y]ou shine," Paul writes, "like stars in the world" (Phil 2:15).

Heavenly bodies come again to the fore in Paul's response to those who would try to deny the resurrection of the body with a *reductio ad*

---

[29] The word *dikaiosynē* appears 33 times in Romans and 4 times in Galatians; *dikaios* 7 times in Romans, once in Galatians; *dikaioō*, 15 times in Romans and 8 times in Galatians.

*absurdum* kind of argument. Paul's imaginary interlocutor asks, "With what kind of body do they [those who have been raised from the dead] come?" Paul responds: "Not all flesh is alike, but there is one flesh for human beings, another for animals, another for birds, and another for fish. There are both heavenly bodies and earthly bodies, but the glory of the heavenly is one thing, and that of the earthly is another. There is one glory of the sun, and another glory of the moon, and another glory of the stars; indeed, star differs from star in glory" (1 Cor 15:39-41). The diversity among bodily forms both in the proximate part of the cosmos and in the heavens above provides Paul with an analogy that enables him to put the potential objection to rest. Basically, the apostle responds that it is foolish to argue about the form of the resurrected body; God makes all sorts of bodies, just as God wills.

Surprising in the light of Paul's many sea voyages is the fact that he makes little use of the sea in his figurative language. True, the Genesis-inspired vision of the cosmos reflected in 1 Corinthians 15:39-41 leads him to mention fish (1 Cor 15:39), but that is the only mention of fish in the extant correspondence.

Writing to the Philippians, an inland community, when Paul speaks about his imprisonment and his desire to leave this life (Phil 1:18-26), Paul uses a pair of images that evoke a journey by sea. In their origins, the Greek terms translated as "turn out for deliverance" (Phil 1:19) and "depart" (Phil 1:23) evoke the images of someone disembarking from a ship and of a person setting sail. Paul would like to safely disembark from the present journey and set his sails heavenward.

One nautical image that may well have had an impact on those who lived by or from the sea is found in 1 Corinthians 4:1: the image of the under-rower. Because of the ports nearby to the east and to the west, Corinth was a thriving mercantile community. It was also a convenient stopping point for those traveling to and from Rome to Ephesus, the capital of the province of Asia. The under-rower was the slave who pulled the lowest tiers of oars on a multitiered ship.

A cosmic phenomenon that plays a major role in Paul's rhetoric is the contrast between night and day, light and darkness. Paul particularly exploits this contrast in the parenetic section of his letters, beginning with 1 Thessalonians: "You are all children of light and children of the day; we are not of the night or of darkness" (1 Thess 5:5). A similar assemblage of images occurs in Romans 13:12: "The night is far gone, the day is near. Let us then lay aside the works of darkness and put on the armor of light."

Paul's mention of the nearness[30] of the day is an indication that he considers the "day" to be the Day of the Lord. Paul uses "day" to refer to the twenty-four-hour day and in reference to days of observance, but as part of his eschatological jargon "day" is a technical term to refer to the "Day of the Lord,"[31] a biblical expression found in a number of equivalent phrases in Paul's letters. When Paul tells the Romans that day is nearing and when he tells the Thessalonians that they are "children of the day," he is telling them that the coming of the Day of the Lord impinges on who they are. The coming of the Day of the Lord provides an eschatological dimension to their being, transforming their entire existence.

Whereas "children of the day" describes the very being of the Thessalonians, "children of the light" points to the activity of the Thessalonians. Those who are armed for the day are clothed with faith, love, and hope (1 Thess 5:8), and the armor of light (Rom 13:12). Children of the light are to avoid activities that properly belong to the night, activities concealed under the cloak of darkness.[32] The thief does his thievery at night (1 Thess 5:2). Unaware of what is happening around them, the inebriated get drunk at night (1 Thess 5:7). Those who engage in works of darkness[33] are given over to revelry, drunkenness, debauchery, licentiousness, quarreling, and jealousy (Rom 13:13). Such conduct is inconsistent with putting on the Lord Jesus Christ, the believer's daytime clothing, as it were.

## Paul's Sources

A survey of the various semantic domains from which Paul took his imagery shows that Paul was a man with a rich and varied experience. It also confirms something revealed by a close reading of each of Paul's letters, namely, that he has taken his figurative language not only from

[30] Paul's verb, *engiken*, appears in the Synoptics' description of the proclamation of the kingdom: "The kingdom of God has come near" (*engiken*, Mark 1:15; Matt 4:17; cf. Matt 3:2; 10:7).

[31] Cf. 1 Cor 1:8; 5:5; 2 Cor 1:14; Phil 1:6, 10; 1 Thess 5:2.

[32] Cf. 1 Cor 4:5. A rhetorical question in 2 Cor 6:14 expresses the radical incompatibility of light and darkness: "What fellowship is there between light and darkness?" The verse belongs to a passage that has probably been interpolated into Paul's letter.

[33] The reference to darkness in Rom 2:19 evokes the biblical notion of darkness being an area of unbelief.

the Hellenistic culture within which he lived but also from the Jewish tradition in which he was reared.

Biblical imagery, often embedded within scriptural passages that Paul cites in a fashion analogous to the way that Hellenistic orators cited the dicta of statesmen, sages, and poets, appears in many of Paul's letters. This type of imagery appears chiefly, but not exclusively, in letters to the Romans and to the Galatians, missives that address the "Jewish Question." These letters are largely the product of scriptural argumentation and include a plethora of scriptural citations. The images that arise from Paul's use of Scripture in these two letters range from a passing reference to the venom of vipers (Rom 3:13; Ps 5:10 [LXX]) to the pregnant imagery of the "seed of Abraham" (Gal 3:16; Gen 13:15) and the all-important judicial and financial imagery of "Abraham believed God and it was reckoned to him as righteousness" (Rom 4:3; Gal 3:6; Gen 15:6).

In addition to the images taken over verbatim from the Scriptures, Paul employs a number of images whose figurative connotations are best understood in the light of his familiarity with the Jewish Scriptures. A striking example of this sort of imagery would be that of the Day of the Lord, a prophetic motif that shapes Paul's vision of the eschaton even if he did not actually cite any biblical texts that use the phrase. Similarly, Paul used the biblical idea of "first fruits" to good advantage in articulating his soteriology.

Judaism, particularly in the form of the emergent rabbinism of Paul's day, also contributed to the range of Paul's metaphors. Most common among this kind of imagery was his frequent use of "walk" to talk about a life that is in accord with faith in God and commitment to Christ. Reflecting on his ministry, Paul was able to exploit the image of a father teaching a son the Torah as a way of speaking about the apostolic ministry of evangelization, a ministry that allowed Paul to describe himself as a father.

No less important in providing Paul with images than the biblical and Jewish tradition was the Hellenistic culture of his addressees and the institutions of the Greco-Roman world in which they and he lived. With Paul they were invited to listen to the roar of the crowd in the stadium and contemplate the spectacle before their eyes. Writing about the age to come, Paul asked them to think about the grand event that was the arrival in town of a reigning emperor or conquering general.

Beyond these magnificent images, Paul is able to write about the nitty-gritty of life in the Greco-Roman world, about down payments and payment in full. He urged his audience to think about citizenship and what it meant to live as a citizen. With them he could talk about being and acting like a Christian in terms of slavery and its various forms. This would have been the lot of many of them in those early Christian congregations. Some of them had undoubtedly been manumitted while others yearned for freedom. Their experience provided Paul with the image of redemption that was such a prominent element in his soteriology.

Previous generations of biblical scholars were wont to write about Paul's Jewish background or about the Hellenistic background of Paul's letters. In fact, the biblical and Jewish tradition as well as Hellenistic culture were the context within which Paul wrote. His imagery came from Judaism and Hellenism alike, the Bible and the Greco-Roman world. Paul's personal experience was the common element within his Jewish tradition and his ongoing encounter with the Hellenistic world. His personal experience was a third source of his metaphors. His experience of family, of the human body, of its various members, and all its senses provided him with any number of images by means of which he was able to proclaim the gospel of God in all its fullness.

## Personification

Paul drew his figures from his experience, his culture, and his religious tradition. A feature of his use of figurative language that merits particular notice is his frequent and broad use of personification. *Prosōpoia*, "personification" or "dramatization," was well known to cultured Hellenists. With the use of this term they meant putting speeches into the mouths of certain characters. Demetrius, the fourth-century BCE rhetorician, knew of this figurative technique as did Philodemus, the first-century BCE philosopher.[34] The art of *prosōpoia* was practiced by dramatists and historians alike.

Paul's use of *prosōpoia* is reflected in the speaking foot, the speaking ear, the speaking eye, and the speaking head that appear in his use of the body image in 1 Corinthians 12:12-26. Apart from Romans 9:20, where a piece of talking pottery appears, Paul's description of the talking parts of the anatomy in 1 Corinthians 12:14-21 is the only place in his correspondence in which the apostle presents personified realities taking part in a conversation or dialogue. The apostle himself, however, addresses

---

[34] See Demetrius, *Style* 5; Philodemus, *On Poems* 5.12.

personified death in 1 Corinthians 15:55, taunting the ultimate enemy with these words: "Where, O death, is your victory? Where, O death, is your sting?"

Paul uses personification, as we moderns understand the figure of speech, to great rhetorical advantage in 1 Corinthians. Love is personified in 1 Corinthians 8:1 and 13:4-7. Parts of the body are personified in 1 Corinthians 12:12-26. Paul personifies death in 15:26, referring to death as the enemy, and animates death in 15:55-56a, comparing it to a lethal insect.

In Philippians 4:7 Paul describes God's peace as guarding hearts and minds. In Galatians 3:22-23 he writes about Scripture and the law as a bailiff, putting people in prison and standing guard over them. In 2 Corinthians 12:7 he speaks of the enigmatic thorn in the flesh as being a messenger of Satan.

It is, however, in the Letter to the Romans that Paul makes the greatest use of personification. Not only does he describe a talking piece of pottery in Romans 9:20, but he also personifies the law, sin, and death with great rhetorical effect. The law enters in, wages war, and takes prisoners (Rom 5:20). Sin dwells, seizes opportunities, deceives, and kills (Rom 7:11, 17, 20). Sin also takes slaves (Rom 6:6, 17, 20). Through its agent, death, sin reigns (Rom 5:21; 6:12, 14). Death, the agent of sin, also reigns (Rom 5:17). In contrast with the malevolent reign of the law, sin, and death there is a benevolent reign. That is the reign of grace which exercises dominion through justification (Rom 5:21; cf. Rom 5:17).

Other malevolent actors on the stage of the drama of salvation are personified hardship, distress, persecution, famine, nakedness, peril, and the sword. All of these seek to separate us from the love of Christ (Rom 8:35-39), as does personified death itself (Rom 8:38).

Romans 8 provides Paul's readers with a dramatic portrayal of personified creation. Creation had been subjected; it was enslaved to corruption (Rom 8:21). Now it hopes and eagerly waits for freedom, the freedom of the glory of the children of God (Rom 8:19, 20-21). Paul likens the process of creation's obtaining this freedom to a woman giving birth: as a woman about to give birth, creation groans with labor pains.

## Mixed Metaphors

Another feature of Paul's use of figurative language that deserves to be noted is his tendency to mix metaphors. Contemporary grammarians often say that a writer ought not to mix metaphors. Poets, however, often mix their metaphors in order to create a surplus of meaning. Similarly, Paul creates new meanings as he mixes together elements from different metaphoric terms. He creates new notions of substitution, for example, by combining elements from two or three of the following: payment, punishment, heroic substitution, and the scapegoat.[35]

The mixing of metaphors is found throughout Paul's letters from the first to the last. In his first letter, he describes himself and his fellow-evangelists, Silvanus and Timothy, by means of parental images but also portrays them and himself as infants (1 Thess 2:7b-12). He calls the Corinthians his brothers and sisters but then addresses them as his children, not yet ready for solid food (1 Cor 3:1-2). He mixes the dominant judicial metaphors of Romans 3:21-26 with images drawn from cult and the financial transaction involved in the manumission of slaves.

Philippians 3:17–4:1 contains a striking blend of familial, anatomical/physiological, and political images. Galatians 3:22-26 combines the imagery of a bailiff and his prisoner with that of the pedagogue and the student. Galatians 5:7-9 invites the reader to quickly shift thought from the runner in the stadium to the yeast in the kitchen. In 2 Corinthians 4:4-6 Paul writes about the blindness of unbelievers, juxtaposing this imagery with the contrast between light and darkness. The light created by God makes the handicap of blindness all the more regrettable. Between these two images, however, comes that of slavery (2 Cor 4:5) used to portray Paul and Timothy, his loyal companion in the work of evangelization.

## Hapax Legomena

A final particularity to be noted in Paul's use of metaphorical and figurative language is that the images which he uses and, even more often, the vocabulary[36] that he employs in the composition of these images often occur only a single time in the extant correspondence.

The many occurrences of this once-only phenomenon are too numerous to mention. They occur in each of Paul's letters. They range from the financial term "benefit" (*onaimēn*) in Philemon 20 to the cultic "sacrifice of atonement" (*hilastērion*) in Romans 3:25. They include such full-blown images as that of the joyful reception of a savior in 1 Thessalonians

---

[35] See Finlan, *Paul's Cultic Atonement Metaphors*, 191.

[36] Many but not all of the Pauline or New Testament hapax legomena that occur in these images are cited in the footnotes of this study.

4:15-17, with its singular and characteristic terminology, and the anatomically and theologically significant image of the body in 1 Corinthians 12:12-26, with its sensitive and socially correct euphemisms.

Some of the one-time images that Paul uses have been mediated to him through the Scriptures. Thus he writes about the venom of vipers in Romans 3:13 (Ps 140:3 [139:4]) and the seed of Abraham in Galatians 3:16 (Gen 13:15; 17:8). Other images come from his desire to appeal to the people to whom he was writing in terms of their own experience. Thus, writing to inhabitants of the port town of Corinth, site of the biennial Isthmian Games, Paul writes about the under-rower (1 Cor 4:1), the runner running a race (1 Cor 9:24-26), and the boxer preparing for a bout (1 Cor 9:26-27).

Some of Paul's images are similar to those used by contemporary authors; others are without parallel in extant Hellenistic literature. These latter derive from his rich and inspired imagination. Whether he has created his images *de novo* or not, there can be little doubt that Paul was a master of metaphor.

# Epilogue

I n his classic series of essays on metaphor, the French Philosopher
Paul Ricoeur quoted some of the last words of Aristotle's *Poetics*:

> The greatest thing by far is to be a master of metaphor. It is the one
> thing that cannot be learned from others; and it is also a sign of genius,
> since a good metaphor implies an intuitive perception of the similarity
> in dissimilars. (*Poetics* 24)[1]

If ever there was a master of metaphor in the history of early Christianity,
that master was Paul of Tarsus. In the human order, he was a genius in
bridging two cultures and radically changing those to whom he spoke
and wrote. In the religious order, he was an inspired genius, who used
his literary talent and intuitive perception in the service of his prophetic
calling. A metaphor, like a poem, articulates an affective value. Paul was
well aware of his own affect and strove to shape the affective values of
those to whom he wrote.

Jew that Paul was, he believed in the transcendent God of Israel. He
wanted to speak about that God and his Christ and found a way to do
so in the use of metaphor. An important function of metaphor is that it
allows mere mortals to name the unnameable and speak of the unspeakable. God had revealed his name to Moses at the burning bush, but there
was much about the Transcendent One that was indeed unnameable and
almost impossible to articulate. Paul's use of metaphor enabled him to

---

[1] This translation, cited in Paul Ricoeur, *The Rule of Metaphor: Multi-disciplinary
Studies of the Creation of Meaning in Language* (London: Routledge & Kegan Paul, 1978),
differs from that given in the most recent LCL (1995) edition of the *Poetics*.

speak about his God and the Christ and move the hearts of those to whom he wrote.

The length of the present study did not permit the in-depth analysis of some of Paul's most significant metaphors, his choice of "Father" to speak of God and of "Lord" to speak of the Christ; nor did it allow the analysis that Paul's resurrectional language richly deserves. Those topics warrant further study because in the choice of Paul's figurative language those rich metaphors both reveal and conceal the heights and depths of his theology.

Metaphor, Ricoeur wrote, "is defined in terms of movement."[2] In the case of Paul, the use of metaphor represented not only movement in his thought but also an attempt to move his audience from the complacency of their status quo. At the conclusion of this study of Paul's use of metaphor, I can only hope that Paul's metaphors will continue to move those who read his words from their own status quo to the Transcendent Father.

[2] Ricoeur, *Rule of Metaphor*, 17.

# General Bibliography[1]

Aasgaard, Reidar. *"My Beloved Brothers and Sisters!" Christian Siblingship in Paul.* Early Christianity in Context. London and New York: T&T Clark, 2004.

———. "Paul as a Child: Children and Childhood in the Letters of the Apostle." *JBL* 126 (2007): 129–59.

Abernathy, David. "Paul's Thorn in the Flesh: A Messenger of Satan?" *Neot* 35 (2001): 69–79.

Aejmelaeus, Lars. *Wachen vor dem Ende: Die traditionsgeschichtlichen Wurzeln von 1 Thess 5:1-11 und Luk 21:34–36.* SESJ 44. Helsinki: Finnische Exegetische Gesellschaft, 1985.

Anderson, R. Dean, Jr. *Ancient Rhetorical Theory and Paul.* CBET 18. Kampen: Kok Pharos, 1996.

Ashworth, Timothy. *Paul's Necessary Sin: The Experience of Liberation.* Aldershot, UK: Ashgate, 2006.

Baldanza, Giuseppe. "La portata teologica di *osmē euōdias* in Fil 4,18." *Laur* 47 (2006): 161–85.

Bammel, Ernst, ed. *Donum gentilicum: Studies in Honour of David Daube.* Oxford: Clarendon, 1978.

———. "Gottes *diathēkē* (Gal. iii. 15-17) und das Jüdische Rechtsdenken." *NTS* 6 (60): 313–19.

Banks, Robert J. *Paul's Idea of Community: The Early House Churches in Their Historical Setting.* Grand Rapids, MI: Eerdmans, 1980.

———. "Walking as a Metaphor of the Christian Life." In Conrad and Newing, *Perspectives on Language and Text*, 303–13.

Barkley, John M. G. *Obeying the Truth: A Study of Paul's Ethics in Galatians.* Edinburgh: T&T Clark, 1988.

---

[1] This bibliography does not include commentaries on the individual books of the Bible, articles in the standard reference works, and editions of ancient authors.

Barrett, C. K. "Romans 9:30–10:21: Fall and Responsibility of Israel." In de Lorenzi, *Die Israelfrage nach Röm 9–11*, 99–130.

Baxter, Antony G. and John A. Ziesler. "Paul and Arboriculture: Romans 11.17-24." *JSNT* 24 (1985): 25–32.

Berge, Mary Katherine. *The Language of Belonging: A Rhetorical Analysis of Kinship Language in First Corinthians*. CBET 31. Leuven: Peeters, 2004.

Betz, Hans Dieter. "The Foundation of Christian Ethics According to Romans 12:1-2." In Devenish and Goodwin, *Witness and Existence*, 55–72.

Bieringer, Reimund and Jan Lambrecht. *Studies on 2 Corinthians*. BETL 112. Leuven: University Press–Peeters, 1994.

Blocker, H. "Biblical Metaphors and the Doctrine of the Atonement." *JETS* 47 (2004): 629–45.

Boring, M. Eugene, et. al. *Hellenistic Commentary to the New Testament*. Nashville: Abingdon, 1995.

Brewer, D. Instone. "1 Corinthians 9:9-11: A Literal Interpretation of 'Do not muzzle the Ox.'" *NTS* 38 (1992): 554–65.

Brewer, Raymond R. "The Meaning of *Politeuesthe* in Philippians 1:27." *JBL* 73 (1954): 76–83.

Brown, Alexandra R. *The Cross and Human Transformation: Paul's Apocalyptic Word in 1 Corinthians*. Minneapolis: Fortress, 1995.

Brown, Raymond E. *The Death of the Messiah: From Gethsemane to the Grave*, 2. ABRL. New York: Doubleday, 1994.

———. *An Introduction to the New Testament*. ABRL. New York: Doubleday, 1997.

Brummett, Barry. "Gastronomic References, Synecdoche, and Political Images." *Quarterly Journal of Speech* 67 (1981): 138–45.

Buck, C. D. *Greek Dialects*. Chicago: University of Chicago Press, 1955.

Burke, Trevor J. *Family Matters: A Socio-historical Study of Fictive Kinship Metaphors in 1 Thessalonians*. JSNTSup 247. London and New York: T&T Clark, 2003.

Church, F. Forrester. "Rhetorical Structure and Design in Paul's Letter to Philemon." *HTR* 71 (1978): 17–33.

Clavier, Henri. "La santé de l'apôtre Paul." In Sevenster and van Unnik, *Studia Paulina*, 66–82.

Collart, Paul. *Philippes, ville de Macédoine depuis ses origines jusqu'à la fin de l'époque romaine*. École française d'Athènes: Travaux et Mémoires 5. Paris: E. de Boccard, 1937.

Collins, Raymond F. "Apropos the Integrity of 1 Thess." *ETL* 65 (1979): 67–106.

———. *The Birth of the New Testament: The Origin and Development of the First Christian Generation*. New York: Crossroad, 1993.

———. "'The Field That God Has Assigned to Us' (2 Cor 10:13)." In *Orientale Lumen VII Conference 2003 Proceedings*. Fairfax, VA: Eastern Christian Publications, n.d. [2004]. 123–42, 125–30.

———. *Letters That Paul Did Not Write: The Epistle to the Hebrews and the Pauline Pseudepigrapha*. GNS 28. Wilmington, DE: Glazier, 1988.

————. *Studies on the First Letter to the Thessalonians.* BETL 66. Leuven: University Press–Peeters, 1984.

————, ed. *The Thessalonian Correspondence.* BETL 87. Leuven: University Press, 1990.

Conrad, E. W. and E. G. Newing, eds., *Perspectives on Language and Text.* Winona Lake, IN: Eisenbrauns, 1987.

Conzelmann, Hans. *An Outline of the Theology of the New Testament.* NTL. London: SCM, 1969.

Crawford, Charles. "The 'Tiny' Problem of 1 Thessalonians 2,7: The Case of the Curious Vocative." *Bib* 54 (1973): 69–72.

Crenshaw, James L., and Samuel Sandmel, eds. *The Divine Helmsman: Studies on God's Control of Human Events. Presented to Lou H. Silbermann.* New York: Ktav, 1980.

Davies, W.D. *The Setting of the Sermon on the Mount.* Cambridge: University Press, 1964.

Davis, Anne. "Allegorically Speaking in Galatians 4:21–5:1." *BBR* 14 (2004): 161–74.

Delobel, Joël. "One Letter Too Many in Paul's First Letter? A Study of *(n)ēpioi* in 1 Thess 2:7." *LS* 20 (1995): 126–33.

de Lorenzi, Lorenzo, ed. *Die Israelfrage nach Röm 9–11.* Benedictina: Biblical-Ecumenical Section 3. Rome: St. Paul's Abbey, 1977.

————, ed. *Paul de Tarse.* SMBen 1. Rome: Benedictina, 1979.

Denis, Albert-Marie Denis. "La fonction apostolique et la liturgie nouvelle en esprit. Étude thématique des métaphores pauliniennes du culte nouveau." *RSPT* 42 (1958): 401–36, 617–56.

Devenisch, Philip E. and George L. Goodwin, eds. *Witness and Existence: Essays in Honor of Schubert M. Ogden.* Chicago: University of Chicago, 1989.

Dodd, C. H. "The Mind of Paul." *BJRL* 17 (1933): 91–105, reprinted in *New Testament Studies.* Manchester: University Press, 1953, 67–82.

Donfried, Karl P. *Paul, Thessalonica, and Early Christianity.* Grand Rapids, MI: Eerdmans, 2002.

————. *Who Owns the Bible?* Companions to the New Testament. New York: Crossroad, 2006.

Donfried, Karl P., and Johannes Beutler, eds. *The Thessalonians Debate: Methodological Discord or Methodological Synthesis?* Grand Rapids, MI: Eerdmans, 2000.

Dunn, James D. G. *Baptism in the Holy Spirit: A Re-examination of the New Testament Teaching on the Gift of the Holy Spirit in Relation to Pentecostalism Today.* SBT 2/15. Naperville, IL: Allenson, 1970.

————. "The Birth of a Metaphor—Baptized in Spirit." *ExpTim* 89 (1977–78): 134–38, 173–75.

Dupont, Jacques. *Gnosis: La connaissance religieuse dans les épîtres de saint Paul.* Bruges and Paris: Desclée de Brouwer, 1949.

Finlan, Stephen. *The Background and Content of Paul's Cultic Atonement Metpahors.* SBLAB 19. Leiden and Boston: Brill, 2004.

Fitzmyer, Joseph A. "Crucifixion in Ancient Palestine, Qumran Literature, and the New Testament." *CBQ* 40 (1978): 493–513.

———. *Essays on the Semitic Background of the New Testament.* London: Chapman, 1971.

Focant, Camille. "Les fils du Jour (1 Thes 5,5)." In Collins, *The Thessalonian Correspondence*, 348–55.

Fortna, Robert T., and Beverly R. Gaventa, eds. *The Conversation Continues: Studies in Paul and John. In Honor of J. Louis Martyn.* Nashville: Abingdon, 1990.

Galloway, Lincoln E. *Freedom in the Gospel: Paul's Exemplum in 1 Cor 9 in Conversation with the Discourses of Epictetus and Philo.* CBET 38. Leuven: Peeters, 2004.

Garner, C. G. "The Temple of Asklepius at Corinth and Paul's Teaching." *Buried History* 18 (1982): 52–58.

Gauthier, Philippe. *Symbola: les Etrangers et la justice dans les cités grecques.* Annales de l'Est 42. Nancy: Université de Nancy, 1972.

Gaventa, Beverly Roberts. "The Maternity of Paul: An Exegetical Study of Galatians 4:19." In Fortna and Gaventa, *The Conversation Continues*, 189–201.

———. "Mother's Milk." In Lovering and Sumney, *Theology and Ethics in Paul and His Interpreters*, 101–13.

———. *Our Mother Saint Paul.* Louisville: Westminster John Knox, 2007.

Gempf, Conrad. "The Imagery of Birth-Pangs in the New Testament." *TynBul* 45 (1994): 119–35.

Gerber, Christine. "Krieg und Hochzeit in Korinth: Das metaphorische Werben des Paulus um die Gemeinde in 2 Kor 10,1-6 und 11,1-4." *ZNW* 96 (2005): 99–125.

Gillman, John. "Signals of Transformation in 1 Thessalonians 4:13-18." *CBQ* 47 (1985): 263–81.

Gillman, Florence Morgan. *Women Who Knew Paul.* Zacchaeus Studies: New Testament. Wilmington, DE: Glazier, 1992.

Gribomont, Jean. "Facti sumus parvuli: La charge apostolique (1 Thess 2,1-12)." In de Lorenzi, *Paul de Tarse*, 311–38.

Gundry, Robert H. *SOMA in Biblical Theology: With Emphasis on Pauline Anthropology.* SNTSMS 29. Cambridge: University Press, 1976.

Gutierrez, Pedro. *La Paternité spirituelle selon saint Paul.* EBib. Paris: Gabalda, 1968.

Haas, Nicu. "Anthropological Observations on the Skeletal Remains from Giv`at ha-Mivtar." *IEJ* 20 (1970): 38–59.

Hafemann, Scott J. *Suffering and Ministry in the Spirit: Paul's Defense of His Ministry in II Corinthians 2:14–3:3.* Grand Rapids, MI: Eerdmans, 1990.

Hall, David R. *The Unity of the Corinthian Correspondence.* JSNTSup 251. Sheffield: Academic Press, 2004.

Harnisch, Wolfgang. *Eschatologische Existenz: Ein exegetische Beitrag zum Sachan-liegen von 1. Thessalonicher 4,13–5,11.* FRLANT 110. Göttingen: Vandenhoeck & Ruprecht, 1973.

Hartman, Lars. *Prophecy Interpreted: The Formation of Some Jewish Apocalyptic Texts and the Eschatological Discourse Mark 13 Par.* ConBNT 1. Lund: Gleerup, 1966.

Hausmann, Jutta, and Hans-Jürgen Zobel, eds. *Alttestamentlicher Glaube und biblische Theologie: Festschrift Horst Dietrich Preuss zum 65 Geburtstag.* Stuttgart: Kohlhammer, 1992.

Hays, Richard B. *The Faith of Jesus Christ: The Narrative Substructure of Galatians 3:1–4:11.* SBLDS 56. Chico: Scholars, 1983.

Hendrix, Holland Lee. "Archaeology and Eschatology at Thessalonica." In Pearson, *The Future of Early Christianity,* 107–18.

Hill, Andrew E. "The Temple of Asclepius: An Alternative Source of Paul's Body Theology." *JBL* 99 (1980): 437–39.

Hollander, Harm W. and Gijsbert van der Hout, "The Apostle Paul Calling Himself an Abortion: 1 Cor. 15:8 within the Context of 1 Cor. 15:8-10." *NovT* 38 (1996): 224–36.

Hooker, Morna. "Beyond the Things That Are Written? St. Paul's Use of Scripture." *NTS* 27 (1981): 295–309.

Horrell, David G. "From *adelphoi* to *oikos theou*: Social Transformation in Pauline Christianity." *JBL* 120 (2001): 293–311.

Hübner, Hans. *Law in Paul's Thought.* Studies of the New Testament and Its World. Edinburgh: T&T Clark, 1984.

Hughes, J. J. "Hebrews ix 15ff. and Galatians iii 15ff: A Study in Covenant Practice and Procedure." *NovT* 21 (1979): 27–96.

Infante, Renzo. "Imagine nuziale e tensione escatologica nel Nuovo Testamento. Note a 2 *Cor.* 11,3 e *Eph.* 5,25-27." *RivB* 33 (1985): 45–61.

Jegher-Bucher, Verena. "Der Pfahl im Fleisch: Überlegungen zu II Kor 12,7-10 im Zusammenhang von 12,1-13." *TZ* 52 (1996): 32–41.

Jewett, Robert. *Paul's Anthropological Terms: A Study of Their Use in Conflict Settings.* AGJU 10. Leiden: Brill, 1971.

Joubert, Stephan J. "1 Corinthians 9:24-27: An Agonistic Competition?" *Neot* 35 (2001): 57–68.

Kertelge, Karl. *"Rechtfertigung" bei Paulus: Studien zur Struktur und zum Bedeutungsgehalt des paulischen Rechtfertigungsbegriffs.* NTAbh, n.s. 3. 2nd ed. Münster: Aschendorff, 1967.

Kiley, Mark C. *Colossians as Pseudepigraphy.* Biblical Seminar 4. Sheffield: JSOT, 1986.

Kim, Jung Hoon. *The Significance of the Clothing Imagery in the Pauline Corpus.* JSNTSup 268. New York: T&T Clark, 2004.

Krentz, Edgar M. "Military Language and Metaphors in Philippians." In McLean, *Origins and Method,* 105–27.

Lambrecht, Jan. "Our Commonwealth Is in Heaven." *LS* 10 (1984–85): 199–205.

———. *Pauline Studies.* BETL 115. Leuven: University Press–Peeters, 1994.

———. *The Wretched "I" and Its Liberation: Paul in Romans 7 and 8.* LTPM 14. Leuven: Peeters, and Grand Rapids, MI: Eerdmans, 1992.

Lindars, Barnabas. *New Testament Apologetic: The Doctrinal Significance of Old Testament Quotations.* London: SCM, 1961.

Lovering, Eugene H., Jr. and Jerry L. Sumney, eds. *Theology and Ethics in Paul and His Interpreters: Essays in Honor of Victor Paul Furnish.* Nashville: Abingdon, 1996.

Lövestam, Evald. "1 Thessalonians 5:1-11." In *Spiritual Wakefulness in the New Testament.* LUÅ 1.55.3. Lund: Gleerup, 1963.

MacDonald, Dennis R. "A Conjectural Emendation of 1 Cor 15:31-32: Or the Case of the Misplaced Lion Fight." *HTR* 73 (1980): 265–76.

Malherbe, Abraham J. *Ancient Epistolary Theorists.* SBLSBS 19. Atlanta: Scholars, 1988.

———. "Antisthenes and Odysseus, and Paul at War." *HTR* 76 (1983): 143–73.

———. "The Beasts at Ephesus." *JBL* 87 (1968): 71–80.

———. *Paul and the Popular Philosophers.* Minneapolis: Fortress, 1989.

Martin, C. J. "The Rhetorical Function of Commercial Language in Paul's Letter to Philemon (Verse 18)." In Watson, *Persuasive Artistry*, 321–37.

März, Claus-Peter. "Das Gleichnis vom Dieb: Überlegungen zur Verbindung von Lk 12,39 par Mt 24,43 und 1 Thess 5,2.4." In van Segbroeck et al., *The Four Gospels*, 635–48.

Maysz, Piotr J. "Paul's Use of the Imagery of Sleep and His Understanding of the Christian Life: A Study in the Thessalonian Correspondence." *CTQ* 67 (2003): 65–78.

McCarthy, Dennis J. "Further Notes on the Symbolism of Blood and Sacrifice." *JBL* 92 (1973): 205–10.

———. "The Symbolism of Blood and Sacrifice." *JBL* 88 (1969): 166–76.

McKnight, Scot. *Light Among the Gentiles: Jewish Missionary Activity in the Second Temple Period.* Minneapolis: Fortress, 1991.

McLean, Bradley Hudson. *The Cursed Christ: Mediterranean Expulsion Rituals and Pauline Soteriology.* JSNTSup 126. Sheffield: Sheffield Academic, 1996.

———, ed. *Origins and Method: Towards a New Understanding of Judaism and Christianity. Essays in Honor of J. C. Hurd.* JSNTSup 86. Sheffield: JSOT Press, 1993.

Meinhold, Arndt. "Der Umgang mit dem Feind nach Spr. 25:21f. als Masstable für das Menschsein." In Hausmann and Zobel, *Alttestamentlicher Glaube und biblische Theologie*, 244–52.

Merk, Otto. "1 Thessalonians 2:1-12: An Exegetical-Theological Study." In Donfried and Beutler, *The Thessalonians Debate*, 89–113.

———. *Handeln aus Glauben: Die Motivierungen der paulinischen Ethik.* MTS 5. Marburg: Elwert, 1968.

Metz, Annette. "Why Did the Pure Bride of Christ (2 Cor. 11.2) Become a Wedded Wife (Eph. 5.22-33)? Theses about the Intertextual Transformation of a Metaphor." *JSNT* 23 (2000): 131–47.

Metzger, Bruce. *A Textual Commentary on the Greek New Testament*. 2nd ed. Stuttgart: Deutsche Bibelgesellschaft, 1994.

Meyer, Paul W. "Romans 10:4 and the 'End' of the Law." In Crenshaw and Sandmel, *The Divine Helmsman*, 59–78.

Mitchell, Margaret W. "Reexamining the 'Aborted Apostle': An Exploration of Paul's Self-Description in 1 Corinthians 15.8." *JSNT* 25 (2003): 469–85.

Morland, Kjell Arne. *The Rhetoric of Curse in Galatians: Paul Confronts Another Gospel*. ESEC 5. Altanta: Scholars Press, 1995.

Moule, C. F. D. *Worship in the New Testament*. Richmond: John Knox, 1961.

Murphy-O'Connor, Jerome. "The Irrevocable Will (Gal 3:15)." *RB* 106 (1999): 224–35.

Nguyen, V. Henry R. "The Identification of Paul's Spectacle of Death Metaphor in 1 Corinthians 4.9." *NTS* 53 (2007): 489–501.

Osty, Émile. "Pour une traduction plus fidèle du N.T." In [Institut catholique de Paris], *Mémorial du Cinquantenaire 1914–1964*. Travaux de l'Institut catholique de Paris 10. Paris: Bloud & Gay, 1964, 81–96.

Park, David M. "Paul's *skolops tē sarki*: Thorn or Stake? (2 Cor. xii 7)." *NovT* 22 (1980): 181–83.

Pearson, Birger A., ed. *The Future of Early Christianity: Essays in Honor of Helmut Koester*. Minneapolis: Fortress, 1991.

Petersen, Erik. "Die Einholung des Kyrios." *ZST* 7 (1930): 682–702.

Pfitzner, Victor C. *Paul and the Agon Motif*. NovTSup 16. Leiden: Brill, 1967.

Plevnik, Joseph. "The Parousia as Implication of Christ's Resurrection (An Exegesis of 1 Thess 4, 13-18)." In Plevnik, *Word and Spirit*, 199–277.

———. *Paul and the Parousia: An Exegetical and Theological Investigation*. Peabody, MA: Hendrickson, 1997.

———, ed. *Word and Spirit: Essays in Honor of David Michael Stanley on His 60th Birthday*. Toronto: Regis College, 1975.

Rengstorf, Karl H. "Das Ölbaum-gleichnis in Röm 11:16ff." In Bammel, *Donum gentilicum*, 127–64.

Reumann, John. "The Gospel of the Righteousness of God: Pauline Reinterpretation in Romans 3:21-31." *Int* 20 (1966): 432–52.

———. "Philippians 3.20-21—A Hymnic Fragment?" *NTS* 30 (1984): 593–609.

Rhoads, David. "Children of Abraham, Children of God: Metaphorical Kinship in Paul's Letter to the Galatians." *CurTM* 31 (2004): 282–97.

Ricoeur, Paul. *The Rule of Metaphor: Multi-disciplinary Studies of the Creation of Meaning in Language*. London: Routledge & Kegan Paul, 1978.

Robbins, Vernon K. *The Tapestry of Early Christian Discourse: Rhetoric, Society and Ideology*. New York: Routledge, 1996.

Roebuck, Carl A. *The Asklepieion and Berna: Based on the Excavations and Preliminary Studies of F. J. de Waele*. ASCS (Athens), Corinth 14. Princeton: American School of Classic Studies in Athens, 1951.

Russell, D. S. *The Method and Message of Jewish Apocalyptic*. NTL. London: SCM, 1964.

Sevenster, Jan N., and Willem C. van Unnik, *Studia Paulina in honorem Johannis de Zwaam*. Haarlem: Bohn, 1953.

Shanor, Jay Y. "Paul as Master Builder: Construction Terms in First Corinthians." *NTS* 34 (1988): 461–71.

Sirewalt, M. Luther. *Paul, the Letter Writer*. Grand Rapids, MI: Eerdmans, 2003.

Smith, Jay E. "Another Look at 4Q416 2ii.21, a Critical Parallel to First Thessalonians 4:4." *CBQ* 63 (2001): 499–504.

———. "1 Thessalonians 4:4: Breaking the Impasse." *BBR* 11 (2001): 65–105.

Spencer, F. Scott. "Metaphor, Mystery and the Salvation of Israel in Romans 9–11: Paul's Appeal to Humility and Doxology." *RevExp* 103 (2006): 113–38.

Stralan, John G. "Burden-bearing and the Law of Christ: A Re-examination of Galatians 6:2." *JBL* 94 (1975): 266–76.

Taylor, Greer M. "The Function of *Pistis Christou* in Galatians." *JBL* 85 (1966): 58–76.

Tellbe, Mikael. *Paul Between Synagogue and State: Christians, Jews, and Civic Authorities in 1 Thessalonians, Romans, and Philippians*. ConBNT 34. Stockholm: Almqvist & Wiksell, 2001.

Thomas, John C. "An Angel from Satan: Paul's Thorn in the Flesh (2 Corinthians 12.7-10)." *JPT* 9 (1996): 39–52.

Thüsing, Wilhelm. "'Milche' und 'feste Speise' (1 Kor 3,1f und Hebr 5,11-6,3). Elementarkatechese und theologische Vertiefung in neutestamentlicher Sicht." *TTZ* 76 (1967): 233–46.

Tobin, Thomas H. *Paul's Rhetoric in Its Contexts: The Argument of Romans*. Peabody, MA: Hendrickson, 2004.

Tsang, Sam. *From Slaves to Sons: A New Rhetoric Analysis on Paul's Slave Metaphors in His Letter to the Galatians*. SBLit 81. New York: Peter Lang, 2005.

van Segbroeck, Ferdnand et al., eds. *The Four Gospels: Festschrift for Franz Neirynck*. BETL 100A. Leuven: University Press–Peeters, 1992.

Walker, D. "The Legal Terminology in the Epistle to the Galatians." In *The Gift of Tongues and Other Essays*. Edinburgh: T&T Clark, 1906, 81–175.

Wanamaker, Charles A. "Metaphor and Morality: Examples of Paul's Moral Thinking in 1 Corinthians 1–5." *Neot* 39 (2005): 409–33.

Watson, Duane F., ed. *Persuasive Artistry: Studies in New Testament Rhetoric in Honor of George A. Kennedy*. JSNTSup 50. Sheffield, UK: JSOT, 1991.

Wild, Robert A. "The Warrior and the Prisoner: Some Reflections on Ephesians 6:10-20." *CBQ* 46 (1984): 284–98.

Yaron, Reuven. *Gifts in Contemplation of Death in Jewish and Roman Law*. Oxford: Clarendon, 1960.

# Index of Scripture References

# Index of Classical, Jewish, and Patristic Sources

## Classical Literature

Aelian, *Nature of Animals*
17.11    23

Aeschylus, *Prometheus Bound*
926    212

Aeschylus, *Libation-Bearers*
249    18

Anaxandrides
53    104

Andocides, *Speeches*
1.85    86

Antiphanes
3.329    104

Antistitius, *Epigrams*
4.243    23

Appian, *Civil Wars*
4.117    63

Aristaenetus
2.1    200

Aristophanes, *Clouds*
81    102

Aristotle, *Art of Rhetoric*
1.15.2    167
1.15.14    167
3.2.6    4, 9
3.2.8    3
3.2.9    3, 225
3.2.10    4, 7
3.2.12    4, 7, 9, 10
3.2.13    3, 4, 5, 9, 130
3.3.1    8
3.3.4    167
3.4.1    8
3.4.3    8
3.10.7    3, 4
3.11.2-4    3
3.11.2-3    10
3.11.3    10
3.11.11    5, 8
3.11.13    5, 8
3.11.14-15    5
3.11.14    167
3.11.15-16    135

Aristotle, *Generation of Animals*
4.5.733    121

Aristotle, *Nichomachaean Ethics*
4.8.10    191
5.4.13    51

Aristotle, *Physiognomonics*
807    116

# Pseudepigrapha

# Index of Modern Authors

# Index of Topics